Routledge Revivals

Indigenization of African Economies

Originally published in 1981, this book examines the progress of a number of national efforts to move towards economic self-reliance. It consists of case studies from Egypt, Zambia, Ghana, Nigeria, Kenya, Tanzania, Ethiopia, Botswana, Lesotho and Swaziland and Senegal. The studies are set in a framework that outlines the historical background to African economic dependence, and they discuss the theoretical and practical implications of that dependence. It makes an important contribution to the study of indigenization, bringing together a group of African specialists writing from the inside, and articulating the continent's challenges with convincing authority.

Indigenization of African Economies

Edited by Adebayo Adedeji

Routledge
Taylor & Francis Group

First published in Great Britain in 1981 by Hutchinson & Co. (Publishers) Ltd

This edition first published in 2023 by Routledge
4 Park Square, Milton Park, Abingdon, Oxon, OX14 4RN
and by Routledge
605 Third Avenue, New York, NY 10158

Routledge is an imprint of the Taylor & Francis Group, an informa business

Publisher's Note
The publisher has gone to great lengths to ensure the quality of this reprint but points out that some imperfections in the original copies may be apparent.

ISBN 13: 978-1-032-58756-1 (hbk)
ISBN 13: 978-1-003-45136-5 (ebk)
ISBN 13: 978-1-032-58760-8 (pbk)
Book DOI 10.4324/9781003451365

Indigenization of African Economies

Edited by Adebayo Adedeji

Hutchinson University Library for Africa
London Melbourne Sydney Auckland Johannesburg
in association with the
African Association for Public Administration and Management

HUTCHINSON UNIVERSITY LIBRARY FOR AFRICA

Hutchinson & Co. (Publishers) Ltd

An imprint of the Hutchinson Publishing Group

24 Highbury Crescent, London N5 1RX

Hutchinson Group (Australia) Pty Ltd
30–32 Cremorne Street, Richmond South, Victoria 3121
PO Box 151, Broadway, New South Wales 2007

Hutchinson Group (NZ) Ltd
32–34 View Road, PO Box 40–086, Glenfield, Auckland 10

Hutchinson Group (SA) (Pty) Ltd
PO Box 337, Bergvlei 2012, South Africa

First published 1981

Set in Times

Printed in Great Britain by The Anchor Press Ltd
and bound by Wm Brendon & Son Ltd
both of Tiptree, Essex

British Library Cataloguing in Publication Data

Indigenization of African Economies
1. Africa – Economic conditions – Case studies
I. Adedeji, Adebayo
330.96′0328 HC502

ISBN 0 09 143730 X cased
0 09 143731 8 paper

Contents

Tables

Preface

The theme of the fourteenth Inter-African Public Administration and Management Seminar held in Maseru, Lesotho, from 27 October to 3 November 1975 was 'The prospects and problems of the indigenization of the private sector of African economies'. The seminar was of course sponsored and organized by the African Association for Public Administration and Management (AAPAM) and was hosted by the government of the kingdom of Lesotho.

The Inter-African Public Administration and Management Seminar, which has been held annually since 1962, has served as a forum where the most senior African government officials (ministers of state, top civil service administrators, university dons and senior executives of public enterprises), primarily from English-speaking countries, gather together to exchange views and offer suggestions and ideas to each other on some of the burning administrative and management issues of the day. A selection of some of the papers presented at the first twelve of these annual seminars (1962–73) has been published in a volume entitled *A Decade of Public Administration in Africa,* edited by Anthony Rweyemamu and Goran Hyden and published by the East African Literature Bureau in 1975.

But unlike the previous annual seminars, the Maseru seminar dealt with a much broader issue – an issue on which much of the future socio-development of Africa depends. And it was the first time ever that the problems of indigenization were examined at regional level. During the seminar the need for greater in-depth study of the indigenization process was generally accepted in order to ensure that African countries benefit from each other's experience, and the Executive Committee of AAPAM agreed to commission such a study. This volume is the result.

The countries that were selected for the study were Egypt, Ethiopia, Ghana, Kenya, Nigeria, Senegal, Tanzania, Zambia and the southern African countries of Botswana, Lesotho and Swaziland. These countries were selected in order to have a representative sample of Africa and of countries that differ significantly and sometimes fundamentally in their political systems as well as in their approaches to economic development in general and the indigenization policies and programmes in particular. The study has involved the collaborative effort of some fourteen scholars and administrators, drawn not only from different parts of Africa but from outside Africa as well. Because of the large number of people involved and the number of countries covered, this volume is being published a littler later than was originally scheduled.

But the subject of the study is as topical today as it was when the Maseru seminar was held in 1975, because today developing African countries have not yet achieved any break-through in their varied and various efforts not only to bring about the socioeconomic transformation of their countries but also to establish effective control over their economic destiny. Why this lack of success? What lessons can we learn from the experiences of the eleven countries covered in this volume? What prospects are there for a genuine indigenization of the African economy?

These are some of the questions that the various authors have tried to answer – not only in the general chapters (1, 2 and 13–15) but also in the country case studies (Chapters 3–12). If their efforts stimulate further policy-oriented work in this field, this research volume will have served a useful purpose.

I would like to express my sincere gratitude to all the contributors, one of whom – S. I. Edokpayi – I must single out. I am particularly indebted to him for his editorial assistance. I am also most grateful to the Ford Foundation, which, in addition to providing the financial support for the Maseru seminar, also generously supported this study and the publication of this volume.

Adebayo Adedeji

Part One

Introduction

1 General background to indigenization: the economic dependence of Africa

Adebayo Adedeji

Africa and the international economy

Although modern patterns of economic dependence in Africa are products of a profound global transformation that has occurred primarily within the last two centuries, African participation in an international economy has been significant for over a thousand years. From the ninth century to the end of the fifteenth century gold production from the West African forest zone and what is now Zimbabwe played a crucial role in underpinning the financial base of the Mediterranean and Indian Ocean economies. Control of this gold trade contributed to the rise of the western Sudanic empires and the city-states of the east African coast. It is true to say, however, that large areas of Africa were completely isolated from these developments.

During the fifteenth century innovations in marine technology made it possible for European ships to circumnavigate the African continent. The primary objective was the spice trade of the Far East, but every opportunity was taken to develop new trading opportunities on the African continent. Portugal retained a virtual monopoly of the African seaborne trade during the sixteenth century, but was subsequently ousted by Dutch, British and – in East Africa – Omani Arab competition.

The Americas eventually emerged as the central focus of European overseas expansion; mines, plantations, fisheries and forests provided new resources to stimulate Europe's economic development. The devastation of large sections of the indigenous population created a shortage of labour – particularly in the mining and plantation sectors – which was eventually solved by the importation of slave labour from Africa. If the Americas were the primary economic periphery of western European economic development, then Africa could be characterized as the 'periphery of the periphery'.[1]* From the early seventeenth century to the middle of the nineteenth century approximately 12–15 million Africans – the figures are still hotly disputed – were successfully

* Superior figures refer to the Notes and references which appear at the end of chapters.

removed across the Atlantic and, to a lesser extent, across the Sahara and the Indian Ocean. If one makes allowances for deaths in transit and as a result of raiding expeditions, we may be talking of a population loss to Africa of around 50 million people, although admittedly such a figure is very hypothetical.

What impact did this human haemorrhage have on the economic development of Africa? Was it positive or negative? Can it be argued that, in the absence of the slave trade, Africa would have been able to achieve a level of agricultural and industrial growth comparable to that occurring in Europe? While bearing in mind the dearth of available statistical data as well as the fact that the slave trade operated differentially over time and space (West and West-central Africa being most heavily involved), one might venture a few generalizations. The reduction of population in a situation where agriculture was the dominant economic activity, and where labour is generally acknowledged to have been scarce in relation to land, would almost certainly have resulted in reduced agricultural output. Industrial/craft production would have been less drastically affected: skilled craftsmen were rarely disposed of as slaves, and their products – protected by high demand, specialized consumer preference and high transportation costs – were not substantially affected by foreign competition until later in the nineteenth century. It is unlikely, however, that the slave trade made any positive contribution to an improvement in the productive capacities of African economies; there was little significant diffusion of technology into Africa from the rest of the world apart from the introduction of American crops like maize and cassava, and the nature of trade goods involved – cloth, firearms, liquor, baubles, some metals – did not greatly encourage further productive processes.

The question of whether the slave trade prevented Africa from achieving its own unique economic 'take-off' remains difficult, if not impossible, to assess. Besides the question of population loss, there are also factors of climate, soil, human and animal disease, transport and social organization that would have to be considered in combination before any persuasive counter-factual model could be constructed.[2] We know too little yet about how these factors operated in the past; indeed, to the detriment of development planning, we often know too little about how they operate at present.

As the depredations of the slave trade drew to a close, one is struck by the extent to which external demands and imports had not yet drastically damaged either the self-sufficiency of African economies or the African control over commercial and financial structures. This situation was to change during the nineteenth century as the Industrial Revolution defined a new set of relationships between Africa and the outside world.

As Europe, led by Britain, moved from rural agrarianism to urban industrial capitalism, it became increasingly dependent on the wider world for raw materials for its factories, food for its workers, and markets for its cheap, mass-produced goods. World trade increased rapidly; European capital flowed overseas to finance mining, railway construction and agricultural production; millions of European migrants spread to all corners of the globe. Africa moved from being an exporter of labour to being an exporter of raw materials – cotton from the Nile Valley, vegetable oils from West Africa, ivory from East and central Africa, and wool from the Cape Colony. Increasingly large areas were being involved in production for the world market. The last three decades between 1870 and 1900 saw the division of the whole African continent – Ethiopia and Liberia excepted – into twenty-three colonial possessions ruled by six European powers. This 'scramble' for territory took place in an atmosphere of industrial crisis in Europe (sometimes known as the 'Great Depression'); in a time of economic uncertainty individual European countries were encouraged to assume direct political control in Africa in order that their commercial position would be assured against other European (and African) competitors. New developments in tropical medicine, military technology and steam transport made it possible for the colonial powers to translate their paper claims into effective administrative control.

The foundations of the colonial economy

It has been recently asserted that:

> No period in the economic history of Subsaharan Africa has a stronger claim to being a watershed than the approximately two decades from the mid-1890s to 1914, when the infrastructural foundations of most contemporary national economies were laid down by colonial governments and commerce between Africa and the rest of the world grew at an historically unprecedented rate . . . the period saw a fairly dramatic strengthening of Africa's connexions with the international economy, and possibly the final, conclusive transformation of its economies into peripheries of the industrial capitalist centre of world exchange.[3]

An understanding of this period is therefore crucial for understanding the background to the essays in this book.

Colonial control was not established without years of bloody violence. This in itself had immediate economic repercussions – loss of life, confiscation of property and disruption of commercial networks – but, more important, it established the absolute authority of an alien government. Economic direction no longer had to await the impersonal call of market forces; it could now be hastened and articulated by administrative command. Since it was generally agreed in Europe that colonies should exist to bolster the economic development of the metropolitan economies, every effort was taken to expand the export-oriented capacity of the colonies and to suppress competing indigenous structures. Taxation was the universal lever that forced labour and produce on to the market; railroads provided the physical means by which vastly increased quantities of European imports could be shifted into the interior and new areas of production opened to exploitation. By 1914 a particular pattern of dependency had developed in most colonies (and sometimes on a regional basis): at the centre were the export enclaves – cocoa and groundnut farms in West Africa, mines in southern Africa and sisal plantations in East Africa; on the periphery were those areas that provided migrant labour to the export enclaves; intermediate were the areas that provided food and services to the export enclaves. Very few Africans could claim any longer that they operated in a traditional 'subsistence' economy that was untouched by demands of the international economy.

In at least two important respects indigenous self-reliance and self-sufficiency were being rapidly eroded. First, railroad expansion made it possible for the first time cheaply to distribute large quantities of imported goods; indigenous industries – particularly those involved in the manufacture of iron, cloth and salt – swiftly collapsed or were severely restricted in the face of this influx. Second, the quantity and variety of food production were adversely affected by the reallocation of land and labour towards export production. The loss of self-sufficiency in foodstuffs began before the First World War, became markedly noticeable in the interwar period, and today constitutes one of Africa's gravest economic problems.

The often haphazard partition of Africa led to a balkanization process where political boundaries cut across existing commercial networks and ethnic groupings. These were subsequently reinforced by tariffs, legal systems, currencies and the location of railroads. In this way the metropolitan countries forged vertical links with their respective colonies and discouraged horizontal communications between colonies in Africa. It became easier for British-ruled Nigeria to trade with London than with French-ruled Dahomey. The result is that, today, Africa has the largest number of minuscule states. Of the fifty independent African states, eight have populations of less than 1 million each, twenty have populations of between 1 million and 5 million; eleven with populations of between 5 and 10 million; and nine with populations of between 10 million and 30 million. Only two – the Federal Republic of Nigeria and the Arab Republic of Egypt – have populations of more than 30 million. Fifteen of the independent African states are landlocked, and eighteen of the thirty least developed countries of the world are to be found in Africa.

Depression and war: the years of instability

The other crucial period in consolidating Africa's economic dependence began with the Great Depression in 1929 and continued during the Second World War. It was a time when most regions were 'denied significant gains from trade by the severely disturbed state of the international economy but equally denied the opportunity to shift to a more autarchic path by official policies which favoured export production'.[4] Government direction of the economy increased enormously (particularly in marketing) in order to ensure that production was maintained, and even increased, in the face of a dramatic fall in commodity prices. African farmers, wage-labourers and merchants suffered a severe deterioration in their economic wellbeing. Two other groups – white settlers and 'big business' – found themselves in a relatively more fortunate position.

Contrary to popular belief, the European-controlled agricultural sector (concentrated in Algeria, South Africa, Kenya and Rhodesia but significant in other colonies) has had a remarkable history of ineptitude and inefficiency. Land was initially acquired from Africans by force – whether military or legal – and was often grossly under-utilized for years. After experimentation many of the smaller white settlers concentrated on growing African crops using African expertise and labour. In such circumstances they had to be protected from more experienced and efficient African producers. This was done by preferential access to transport, markets, extension services, tax resources and credit facilities; they were also aided by coercive labour laws and a prohibition on African cultivation of certain cash-crops.[5] A measure of the continuing inadequacy of European agricultural planning and technology can be seen in the post-Second World War example of the Groundnut Scheme in Tanganyika, where £38,870,000 was spent on an abortive project to grow groundnuts by mechanical cultivation in an area already rejected as unproductive by African producers.

It would be largely true to say that the same economic pressures and administrative measures that enmeshed peasant producers into an international economy also enabled European mercantile concerns progressively to extend their control over Africa's trade. Lebanese (in West Africa) and Indians (in East Africa) occupied an important intermediate position in commerce, while Africans were increasingly restricted to roles as petty retail traders. A process of amalgamation in the 1920s ensured that a restricted number of larger firms (like the United

Africa Company) came to dominate trade. The depression of the 1930s saw an extension of this oligopolistic influence as smaller firms were forced out of business and the larger firms reacted to insecurity by engaging in price-fixing and market-sharing. In such a situation of mercantile concentration and limited competitiveness it was the African merchant and producer who suffered most.

Since the end of the nineteenth century, mining had dominated the economies of southern Africa. It had attracted the bulk of private capital investment and provided the major value content of Africa's exports. Unlike agricultural production it was totally dominated by European technology, and unlike other European mercantile activities it was relatively unaffected by the economic uncertainties of the interwar period. Copper production boomed, and Northern Rhodesia experienced the highest growth rate of any African country in the 1930s. Gold prices rose and South African gold exports increased from £48.4 million in 1931 to £71.6 million in 1938. This expansion confirmed the dominance of the mining sector in southern Africa and – within South Africa itself – stimulated an extensive industrialization process.

Industrialization was feasible in South Africa because of unique political and economic circumstances, but in most parts of Africa it was actively discouraged by governments and European mercantile concerns – a strategy consistent with the view that Africa was to be a supplier of raw materials and a buyer of imported consumer goods.

Decolonization: an end to economic dependence?

The increasingly successful agitation for political independence in the post-1945 period has tended to disguise the fact that this was the period when European investment, European immigration and external trade between Africa and Europe reached unprecedented heights. Although the style of interaction was changing, the results were the same. Colonies were even more firmly locked into a dependent relationship with one metropolitan country. Their economies were increasingly geared to the export production of a very limited range of commodities and the importation of a wide range of consumer goods. The manufacturing sector was therefore severely restricted. Africans were restrained by virtue of racial discrimination, educational disabilities and financial circumstances from participating in effective decision-making processes, and – particularly where mining and European-managed agriculture dominated – were often barred from the most profitable areas of production and trade. It was difficult to escape the judgement that the function of the African economy was 'to produce for the world market under conditions which, because they impoverished it, deprived the members of any prospects of radical modernization'. It was not therefore 'in transition to "modernity"; as a dependent society it was complete, peripheral, and hence at a dead end'.[6]

African economies since political independence

The year 1960 was a great landmark in Africa's political history: sixteen countries achieved independence in that year alone. By 1980, with the exception of Namibia (South-West Africa), the whole of Africa had become politically independent.

Since the struggle for political independence had carried with it the promise of a better and more abundant life for all, of a just and egalitarian society, and of a bright future full of opportunities, the newly independent African governments embarked on planned development of varying degrees whose primary purpose was to accelerate the pace of socioeconomic development. Today, many African countries are now implementing their third or fourth five- or four-year development plan since independence. Although these plans have a variety of development objectives, the most common among them are: the achievement of a high rate of growth; the creation of employment opportunities to reduce the high rate of unemployment and under-employment in the economy; the production of high- and intermediate-level manpower to satisfy national needs; and improvement in the level and quality of services provided for the welfare of the people.

Unfortunately, Africa's overall economic performance since 1960 has been far from being satisfactory. Table 1 shows for sub-Saharan African economies the behaviour of the major economic indicators during the period 1960 to 1975. All the indicators except population show poor performance. Indeed, if the statistics are aggregated into three periods, namely 1960–5, 1966–70 and 1971–5, the deteriorating performance of sub-Saharan Africa is even more evident.

Of the many reasons that account for this deteriorating economic performance, the most decisive is the economic dependence of African countries and their excessive external orientation. Right from the start, the governments of the newly independent countries failed to bring about a complete break with colonial economic policy. Instead, they pursued this policy vigorously. Accordingly, most African governments, in their attempt to accelerate economic growth and diversify their economy, reinforced the colonial pattern of production–exploitation of primary commodities and the importation of factor inputs from abroad. Every effort was made to increase the production of export crops with which to earn foreign exchange essential for investment and payment for imports.

Table 1 *The African economies: selected economic indicators*

Africa south of Sahara	*1960–5 (%)*	*1966–71 (%)*	*1972 (%)*	*1973 (%)*	*1974 (%)*	*1975 (%)*
Total GNP (growth rate per annum)	4.0	5.5	4.5	4.8	5.2	2.9
Agricultural production (growth rate per annum)	2.5	2.6	-1.6	-3.7	6.3	2.9
Manufacturing production (growth rate per annum)	9.4	8.3	10.9	8.4	7.9	—
Population (growth rate per annum)	2.5	2.6	2.6	2.6	2.7	2.7
GNP *per capita* (growth rate per annum)	1.4	2.8	1.9	2.1	2.4	0.2
Gross investment (growth rate per annum)	6.6	7.4	-2.0	10.1	5.6	

The pursuit of this policy led to the first major crisis: instability in export prices and its resulting impact on planned economic growth. This destabilizing impact of fluctuating price levels of export commodities was intensified by the limited number of these commodities on which each country depended for financing imports. The insistence on a policy of export production of commodities for which there is relatively little domestic demand even when foreign demand falls significantly – cocoa and coffee are examples – has led to the continued benign neglect of food production. The cumulative effect of all this is that Africa, an overwhelmingly agricultural economy, has become increasingly dependent on food imports, food aid and food gifts to bail it out of its incessant food shortages. The failure to turn agriculture into a dynamic instrument for achieving internally generated, self-sustaining and self-reliant economic development is the one factor that has, more than anything else, impeded the economic advancement of Africa since independence.

The situation with regard to the manufacturing sector is not much better. Although the rate of growth of manufacturing output of about 8 per cent per annum has been impressive by historical standards, it should be remembered that the base is very thin and the coverage rather narrow. Africa's industrial development has been hampered by misdirected policies and by a lack of understanding as to how to stimulate and accelerate the process of self-sustaining growth. Thus independent African countries pursued an import-substituting industrialization policy and industrial growth has been overwhelmingly dependent on foreign investment and technical know-how, with governments competing among themselves to provide the most generous incentives to the foreign investor. And because of stiff tariff protection, the prices of locally manufactured products have generally been high and the quality low. Since the imported technical coefficient of these industrial establishments reflects the capital–labour ratio of the industrialized countries, they are invariably capital-intensive and have made no significant impact on the unemployment situation in the African countries. Besides employing limited labour, most of these establishments utilize little local raw material and therefore provide minimum linkage to other local industrial sectors.

African countries are in consequence today littered with heterogeneous collections of high-cost industries often of quite trival significance. African industrialization has not been planned with a view to developing local entrepreneurship, to helping solve the unemployment problem and to providing linkages to other types of local production, including agricultural production. Fortunately, a growing number of African governments are now coming to realize the fact that industry has an inner structural logic, that linkages within an industrial sector are as important for its vitality as linkages between industry and the other sectors. It is also being gradually understood that the importance of a sector depends not so much on its size as on its growth-promoting impact on other sectors.

However, the sector that has contributed most to the increase in GDP is mining. Its average annual growth rate between 1960 and 1970 was 12.4 per cent, as compared with 6.1 per cent for the manufacturing industry and only 2.2 per cent for agriculture.

The deepening of economic dependence

The analysis in the preceding section has shown that, after nearly two decades of political independence and economic planning, African economies are still heavily dependent on the economies of the industrialized countries. As a result the main characteristics and structure of their economies still bear a very close resemblance to what prevailed in the preceding colonial period, notwithstanding the increasing evidence of modernization and import-substituting industries that have been established during the period under review. In terms of quantitative indicators, as already demonstrated, overall performance has generally been disappointing, although in qualitative terms African peoples have come a long way towards improving the quality of life of the average man, woman and child during the past two decades.

Development planning, establishment of new industries, building of new roads, expansion in educational facilities as well as other development activities in the economic and social sectors have all contributed to the limited economic gains and social improvements and modifications designed to reduce economic dependence. Important decisions on development were now being taken locally rather than at the former metropolitan capitals. African governments now set national priorities, determine development strategies and allocate development resources. These notwithstanding, external political, economic and social factors – with new dimensions and characteristics – continue to influence African affairs, with the result that economic dependence has tended to deepen rather than decline. A vicious cycle of dependence would appear to be inescapable so long as Africa's development strategy maintained the old order of international economic relationships. This section is therefore concerned with illustrating Africa's growing economic dependence, a fact of life that is casting doubt as to whether Africa's declaration of a policy of self-reliance is a myth; and whether African states can mobilize the will and the resources needed to make a break-through in the restructuring of their national economies to make them self-reliant and internally self-generating and self-sustaining.

In order to demonstrate that economic development efforts in the African region over the past two decades have not significantly altered the dependence status of African economies, the position with regard to some major economic activities will now be reviewed.

Basic raw materials

Africa remains a major producer of raw materials for world markets in respect of commodities needed for the manufacturing industries of the developed economies. By the late 1950s world export of agricultural commodities from Africa as a percentage of world production amounted to 30–50 per cent for groundnuts, soybeans, cotton and palm oil; 50–90 per cent for copra, coffee, tea and cocoa, and 90–100 per cent for rubber and palm kernels.[7] In most of these commodities Africa held a leading or major position as producer, especially in respect of groundnuts, cotton, palm oil, palm kernels, coffee and cocoa. Two decades later, Africa has continued to be a major producer of raw materials for

Table 2 *Africa's share in world production of major raw materials, 1978*

Agricultural commodities	%	*Minerals*	%
Cocoa beans	62.0	Diamonds	66.0
Palm oil	34.2	Cobalt	45.3
Groundnuts in shell	27.8	Phosphate rock	22.9
Coffee (green)	26.1	Copper ore	17.5
Tea	11.0	Manganese ore	17.0
		Bauxite	15.7
		Uranium	15.2
		Crude petroleum	10.7
		Chrome ore	10.2

Sources: *African Target*, vol. 8, no. 1 (April 1979); ECA, *21 years of Service to Africa, 1958–1979* (Addis Ababa 1980).

the industries of the developed countries, as can be seen from Table 2. Its share of world production in many commodities has dropped appreciably, a reflection of increased competition with other Third World regions. This competition has generally been to the advantage of industrialized countries and to the detriment of producer countries.

Export-oriented economies

Economic development in Africa is predominantly export-oriented. This is due partly to the long tradition of association with the industrialized economies in which Africa's role was pre-determined as producer of raw materials in exchange for manufactured goods and economic services, and partly to the absence of any indigenous technological and manufacturing capacity for the local production of manufactured goods and technology that were needed for the modernization and transformation of the predominantly agricultural economies. To import more of the essential consumer goods and the capital goods that Africa needed to develop, more of its natural resources had to be exploited and exported abroad. An inherent problem resulting from this specialization as raw material producer and from competition with other producers in other regions for the markets of the industrialized countries has been the recurrent instability in the prices of its primary commodities. The latter phenomenon has also encouraged diversification to seek yet more outlets for new raw materials and the adoption of fiscal measures that attempt to cushion price fluctuations in the principal export commodities.

The concentration on a few major primary commodities has made

African trade highly vulnerable, with resulting wild fluctuations in prices, demand and supply that seriously disrupt national development plans. In 1970 eleven export commodities together accounted for 70 per cent of Africa's total export value. These were: crude petroleum (30.9 per cent), copper (11.6 per cent), coffee (6.5 per cent), cotton (6.0 per cent), cocoa beans (5.5 per cent), iron ore (2.6 per cent), wood and timber (2.0 per cent), diamonds (2.0 per cent), groundnuts and groundnut oil (1.8 per cent), and phosphate (1.3 per cent). By 1977 the leading ten commodities together accounted for 80 per cent of total export value.[8] The development effort in the natural resources and agricultural sectors in the 1970s has thus resulted in a greater entrenchment of the region's dependence on world markets for a few primary products.

It is also a sad truth that Africa's external trade is virtually all conducted with countries outside the African continent. Thus in 1970 only 5.3 per cent of the export and import trade in value terms was intra-African trade, and by 1977 this modest proportion had declined to 4.0 per cent.

Manufacturing and technological dependence

In order to counter the wild fluctuations in the prices, demand, supply and income of primary products, to reduce the risk of over-dependence on primary production and to modernize the economy and increase employment opportunities, African states have all adopted a policy of industrialization. Accordingly, local manufacture of goods previously imported has become a basic policy objective in national development strategy. Initially, this policy was pursued through the local manufacture of import substitutes, an effort that helped to conserve some foreign exchange. By the late 1960s a growing number of African states were expanding their diversification and manufacturing efforts to extend to the establishment of heavy capital goods industries, as can be seen from Table 3. The heavy manufacturing industries were chemicals, petroleum products, non-metallic mineral products, basic metals and metal products.

The intensification of the industrialization effort as pursued through industrial diversification, increasing import of capital goods, technology, and managerial and technical know-how, and the shift in manufacturing structure from light to heavy industries, have all combined to intensify Africa's growing dependence on the industrialized countries for machines, patents, licences and technology from abroad. The venture into heavy industries has made collaboration with transnationals, investment bankers and foreign investors inevitable, thus

Table 3 *Distribution of manufacturing value added between light and heavy industries*

Sub-region	*1970*		*1977*	
	Light (%)	*Heavy (%)*	*Light (%)*	*Heavy (%)*
North Africa	60.7	39.3	53.7	46.3
West Africa	71.3	28.7	65.4	34.6
East Africa	74.0	26.0	68.1	31.9
Central Africa	67.1	32.9	67.6	32.4
Developing Africa*	68.0	32.0	60.2	39.8

* excludes South Africa.

Source: Survey of Economic and Social Conditions in Africa, 1977–1978, part 1 (Document E/CN. 14/697), Table VI–5.

further deepening the economic dependence of the region. A case study by M. Germouni on engineering in Morocco, for example, clearly shows how the structure and technology of the industry is heavily dependent on the former metropolis.[9]

Foreign aid, loans and public debt

Africa's economic dependence on the industrialized countries have developed wider dimensions since the postwar years. The adoption of development plans from the late 1940s was particularly significant in the growth of new features in the financial and technical dependence of African countries. Planning economic and social development activities called for intensified efforts and massive mobilization of human and material resources for plan implementation. It also sanctioned development processes and patterns tailored after those of the developed countries. Even consumer habits, dress and living fashions had to be imported, and the goods and services to ensure these elements in the modernization of living habits in our urban centres had to be provided for in the development plans. Since African countries did not have all the funds and technical know-how for the realization of their development plans and the amenities promised to the people by politicians in their electioneering campaigns, they turned more and more to the industrialized countries for aid, technical assistance personnel and loans to carry out their development plans. It soon became normal for development planners to build 50 to 75 per cent external resources into national plan implementations. The dependence on foreign grants and foreign specialist personnel became intense;

foreign loans and foreign investors were sought with lavish incentives, and the dependence on these development resources widened.

In respect of public debt, for example, the total outstanding (disbursed) external debt of African countries rose from US$9.02 billion in 1970 to $18.88 billion in 1974 and $30.02 billion in 1976, while the total debt services rose to US$0.89 billion, $2.43 billion and $3.03 billion respectively. As the volume of external public debt increased substantially, the burden of servicing external public debt took an increasing share of earnings from the export of goods and services. By 1976 public debt service payments as a proportion of exports exceeded 10 per cent in Algeria, Egypt, Guinea, Zaire, Mauritania, Sierra Leone and Sudan, and reached nearly 10 per cent in Ivory Coast and Zambia.[10]

Notes and references

1 Samir Amin, 'Underdevelopment and dependence in black Africa – Origins and Contemporary Forms', *Journal of Modern African Studies*, vol. 10, no. 4 (1972), p. 11.

2 A stimulating discussion of these various factors is contained in Chapter 2 of A. G. Hopkins, *An Economic History of West Africa* (London: Longman 1973).

3 J. Forbes Munro, *Africa and the International Economy 1800–1960* (London: Dent 1976), p. 86.

4 ibid., p. 173.

5 An excellent survey of the protected white settler economy in Kenya in this period is Roger van Zwanenberg, *The Agricultural History of Kenya* (Nairobi: East African Publishing House 1972).

6 Amin, 'Underdevelopment', p. 520.

7 *Commodity Survey 1959* (New York: United Nations, 1960), p. 14.

8 *Survey of Economic and Social Conditions in Africa, 1977–1978*, Part 1 (document E/CN. 14/697/Part 1), p. 109.

9 M. Germouni, *Engineering, Structure, Superstructures et Dependance technologique;* ECONOMAP no. 22–23 (July/August 1978).

10 *Survey of Economic and Social Conditions in Africa, 1977–1978*, Part 1, tables IX–6 and IX–8.

2 Historical and theoretical background

1 The *raison d'être* of indigenization

Adebayo Adedeji

As we pointed out in Chapter 1, the economy of the typical African state by the time of independence consisted of three levels: Europeans at the top, commanding the large industries, major mercantile concerns and plantation farming; Asians and Lebanese in the middle, controlling medium-level industrial activities and wholesaling as well as the larger retail outfits; and Africans at the bottom, engaged in peasant farming, petty trading and labour services. Although these levels might occasionally overlap, there was definitely a hierarchical division of labour and economic rewards within colonial society.

The situation in the civil services was not much different at the time of independence. The administrative and professional posts were dominated by expatriates, with the Africans confined largely to clerical and messengerial posts. Admittedly, the situation was a little better in certain countries, even before independence had been won. In Nigeria and Ghana, Africanization of the civil services had gained momentum after the Second World War. But this was the exception rather than the rule. No such deliberate measures took place in former French, Belgian, Spanish or Portuguese colonies. Even in the British dependencies of eastern and southern Africa the situation was not much different; indeed, it was further complicated by the intermediate Asian presence in the civil service, police and armed forces. African education – so often left by default to missionary bodies – was restricted by financial considerations (particularly in the key 1929–45 period) and by a general educational philosophy that saw Africans as suited only for low-echelon posts in government and private service. This complacency changed after 1945, but – with the exceptions noted above – had yielded no significant results in trained manpower.

Yet immediately after independence, African governments relentlessly pursued the Africanization of their civil services. Literally overnight, Africans were catapulted from relatively junior posts to positions of high responsibility. They were rushed through crash training programmes provided by the hastily established institutes of public administration. As is to be expected, given the magnitude of the task involved – it is believed that the exercise involved training for some 100,000 to 200,000 expatriate-held posts which were Africanized between 1958 and 1968 – standards fell, and the level of performance and efficiency suffered. But today the majority of African administrations are entirely in the hands of their nationals. Indeed, it can be stated that, while the struggle for political independence was the dominant issue of the 1940s and 1950s, the Africanization of the civil service was the battle-cry of the 1960s. The sudden and rapid withdrawal of French civil servants and technicians from Guinea when it chose independence in 1958 showed most dramatically how dependent African states were on the expatriate personnel manning their civil services. The Africanization of the civil service, no matter what the costs in terms of loss of efficiency and effectiveness, became the only viable political alternative.

Given this experience, it is natural that African governments should as soon as it was deemed feasible turn their attention to the Africanization or indigenization of the key sectors of their national economies. The need to do this became more compelling as the people became disillusioned with their countries' poor economic performance since independence coupled with the deepening of the dependence of their economies on the industrialized countries. In order, therefore, to protect their political independence and control their economic destiny, many governments adopted nationalization as a strategy to effect local control of their national economies. Indeed, between 1960 and 1974 there were 340 cases of nationalizations and take-overs in sub-saharan Africa; the corresponding figure for the whole world during the same period was 875.[1] Thus Africa's share in total number of nationalizations during the period was 39 per cent. Most African countries took over at least one foreign enterprise. The only notable exceptions were the Ivory Coast, Liberia and Gabon. Some countries were motivated by a deliberately articulated socialist ideology; most were moved by a more general recognition that certain strategic sectors of the economy were best controlled by the state.

Nationalization in Africa has been concentrated in the large extractive industries – banking, insurance and petroleum distribution – and more rarely in manufacturing. The bulk of African nationalization was negotiated, and every effort was made to reassure private enterprise (whether foreign or domestic) that it had an important role to play in spite of such selective nationalization. However, in certain countries – Tanzania, Uganda, Angola, Mozambique and Ethiopia – socialist ideologies have determined a more wide-ranging nationalization, sometimes without effective compensation. In such countries public policy is against all private enterprise, whether foreign or indigenous.

However, not all African countries have seen nationalization as the only – or even principal – method of achieving economic autonomy. Many have opted for indigenization either as an alternative to nationalization or as a major complementary effort in achieving the goal of controlling the commanding heights of their economies. Whereas nationalization is the take-over of property by a government, indigenization is the process by which a government limits participation in a particular industry entirely or in part to citizens of the country, thus forcing alien owners either to sell to indigenous entrepreneurs or to withdraw from participation in certain economic activities. More often than not, the two terms – 'nationalization' and 'indigenization' – are used interchangeably, even though they are two different things.

Unlike nationalization, indigenization in fact encourages, develops and strengthens indigenous private enterprise at the expense of expatriate-controlled enterprise. Four types of indigenization can be identified. First, there is the indigenization of ownership, which aims at giving the indigenes of a country, either individually or collectively, ownership stake in the economic establishments in their country. Such indigenization of ownership can be accomplished through either public or private ownership or through a combination of both. There is, second, the indigenization of control, whose objective is to enable the indigenes of a country to exercise control – through the boards of directors – on the policies of the enterprises. While it is possible to have ownership indigenization without control indigenization, the reverse arrangement, namely control indigenization without ownership indigenization, can at best be weak or fragile. Third, there is manpower indigenization, otherwise known as Africanization. As already pointed out, this was the first form of indigenization policy applied to the civil service. The private sector, however, has also aimed at developing indigenous competence in modern industrial and commercial operations and management.

Finally, there is the indigenization of technology. This is in three phases, the first being the acquisition of technology from highly industrialized countries so as to enable developing countries to overstep many stages of development. The second stage is one of adaptive technology, a process of selection and adaptation in order to match imported techniques to African conditions. But both phases have a tendency to deepen the dependence of underdeveloped countries on industrialized countries, in tangible and intangible ways. In order to reduce such dependence, developing countries should have a major commitment to depend increasingly on technologies that they themselves have developed, which are suited to their needs and predicaments and their domestic natural resources and which, as Mrs Indira Ghandi, prime minister of India, remarked in an address to the 31st session of the Economic and Social Commission of Asia and the Pacific (ESCAP), 'will enable the building up of that national self-confidence in problem-solving, which is the essence of dependence'. This should be the ultimate aim of the policy of indigenizing technology.

It must be stated at the outset that indigenization is not unique in the history of Africa. Throughout the ages and in various countries the basic objective of indigenization has formed the cornerstone of economic policy, albeit in varying degrees. The expropriations of the thirteenth- and fourteenth-century English monarchs, some of the mercantile laws, the numerous laws regulating the activities of the colonies and some of the racial persecutions that have taken place in Europe in the nineteenth and early twentieth centuries were all aimed at the implementation of the indigenization policy as conceived in those times. The English mercantile laws, for example, were designed to strengthen the naval supremacy of England, to conserve foreign exchange, to monopolize the trade of the colonies, to reserve essential raw materials for English industries, and ultimately to ensure the potency of the English nation and economy.

To merely equate indigenization with Africanization is to trivialize it. The primary purpose of indigenization is economic decolonization, the reduction of economic dependence and the achievement of an increasing measure of self-reliance through internally located and self-sustaining growth. Once we define indigenization in this way, we have to relate our analysis of the problem to its political base.

2 The political context of indigenization

Claude Ake, *Dean, School of Social Science, University of Port Harcourt, Nigeria*

One of the major obstacles in the way of understanding the problem of economic dependence of Africa is the tendency to psychologise it. The problem is psychologized by resolving patterns and prospects of the quest for economic independence into the characteristics of African leaders. Thus Kenya's neocolonial status is explained in terms of the colonial mentality of Kenyatta and subsequent Kenyan leaders. Similarly, the failure of self-reliance in Tanzania is blamed on Nyerere's moderation and ambivalence towards socialism. In thus psychologizing the problem we forget men are largely products of their environment. We forget that men do not think, command and act in a vacuum; they do so always in response to the necessities of the situation in which they find themselves. If we do not refer to these necessities we cannot explain their behaviour.

Accordingly, I shall begin by looking at the necessities of the situation of those who ultimately are the policy-makers – the African ruling class. We want to understand their material base, their interests and the pressures they have to contend with. Since we are interested in delineating the structure of politics, we have to examine the African ruling class with reference to their most powerful competitors, for politics is the competition among groups to make public policy conducive to the realization of their interests and ideologies. Hence to define the politics of economic decolonization in Africa is to show the compatibilities and incompatibilities of the interests of the major groups (including the factions of the ruling class) in regard to the issues of economic decolonization, and subsequently to show what the ruling class may do and must do in the light of the prevailing configuration of interests and pressures. The overriding interest of the African ruling class is to maintain its hegemony; that is, to survive as a ruling class, to govern effectively, and as much as possible to win legitimacy for its authority. In Africa this may be said to have three major dimensions.

The role of international capitalism

The first of these dimensions is the very fact of economic dependence on the West or, what amounts to the same thing in this context, on international capitalism. The West constitutes the monopoly consumer of African primary products, and the monopoly supplier of technology, loans and grants to Africa. According to my calculations (based on GATT and UN trade statistics), the West's share of the total dollar value of Africa's exports was 78.19 per cent in 1965, 78.73 per cent in 1970 and 75.23 per cent in 1973. By contrast the share of the Communist bloc was 7.35 per cent in 1965, 7.02 per cent in 1970 and 8.45 per cent in 1973.[2] Africa's import statistics tell the same story. The West's share of total value of imports was 71.48 per cent in 1965, 70.41 per cent in 1970 and 72.54 per cent in 1973. That such dependence is a serious threat to the hegemony of the African ruling class is easy enough to see. First, it limits its competitive capacity in the international system and this in turn limits its domestic capabilities, such as the capacity to increase, and confiscate, the economic surplus. Second, it limits its overall control of its subjects and seriously undermines its legitimacy. A ruling class that came to power on the wave of the nationalist protest cannot afford to be seen to perpetuate colonialism.

That is simplifying a lot. It will be far more accurate to talk of the consequences of economic dependence for the factions of the ruling class rather than for the ruling class; for the consequences of dependence are not the same for all factions. For instance, as far as purely economic considerations are concerned, much depends on the role of the particular faction and the major source of its wealth, the factors that define the link with foreign capital. As far as the political liabilities of the popular perception of the bourgeoisie as collaborators with imperialism are concerned, they are far more serious for the hegemonic faction (the political rulers) of the bourgeoisie than for most of the other factions. Clearly, we must take account of analytic complexities such as these, although this cannot be done adequately here. Since we are interested in policy outputs in regard to decolonization, we are obliged to pay the most attention to the hegemonic faction of the ruling class. The generalizations regarding the liabilities of economic dependence would apply to this faction just because it is the hegemonic faction, and irrespective of its economic role or economic base.

The political dynamics of decolonization will not begin to emerge unless we try to see how dependence affects the interests of the two main competitors of the African ruling class, namely the African masses and international capitalism. First, the masses: it would seem that dependence is seriously detrimental to their objective interests. For one thing, dependence is the basis of the underdevelopment of which they are victims. As several theorists of underdevelopment, such as Samir Amin[3] and Tomas Szentes,[4] have shown, the dependence of Africa is the root of the disarticulation of African economics, the reduction of African economics to the monocultural export type, the relation of unequal exchange between the economies of Africa and the West, and the comprador character of the African bourgeoisie. In so far as dependence is reduced, these liabilities will be overcome and the prospects of development improved.

I have again simplified the picture quite considerably by dealing on a rather high level of abstraction, namely by thinking of objective interests and of the African masses as a class. The problems of doing so are serious and should not be glossed over. The multitudes who are lumped together as the 'African masses' are unfortunately not a class in any technical sense, though for some analytic purposes they might be treated as such. The difficulties of regarding the African masses as a class are related to the transitional nature of African economies. Although the capitalist mode of production dominates the bulk of African economies, there are still vestiges of other modes of production. Associated with the transitional character of African economies is the existence of substantial populations of peasants, workers, semi-proletarianized peasants, etc. There are substantial contradictions between these groups. Indeed, owing to forces such as tribalism, there are considerable contraditions *within* these groups. Finally, there are hardly any signs that these groups have the consciousness of being a class.

It is just as difficult to talk of the objective interests of the African masses as it is to designate them as a class. Not that such talk is not a permissible abstraction or even a useful analytic tool; but it can easily lead to mystification, encouraging us to substitute how people *ought* to act for how they actually act. The fact is that the African masses do not act in what appears to be their objective interests in the way that the African bourgeoisie, particularly the hegemonic faction, does. There are many instances of what one may call false consciousness, instances when the exploited, moved by factors such as tribalism, have co-operated to further the exploitative designs of the ruling class.

Still, we cannot think about the problems of the phenomenal world without simplifying. The notion of the African masses as constituting a class with objective interests is theoretically defensible and useful. The rather incoherent aggregation we regard as the African masses could be called an embryonic class. Whatever their differences, they share this crucial similarity: they have no control over the means of production. For all practical purposes they have nothing but their labour, which they realize largely at the mercy of the ruling class. The ruling class pumps out surplus value from them directly (as they barter the use value of their labour for its exchange value) or indirectly, by the use of state power. These factors that permit us to think of the African masses as an embryonic class also permit us to think of them as having objective interests. And because of the organic relation between capitalism in Africa, imperialism and underdevelopment, we must conclude that the objective interests include not only overturning existing exploitative relations of production, but also putting an end to dependence.

Turning now to the other group in competition with the African ruling class, generalizations are somewhat less hazardous. On balance, the interest of international capitalism lies in maintaining Africa's economic dependence, which is at once the effect and the means of its economic exploitation of Africa.

Given the nature of the interests of these three groups, it would appear that we would expect a pattern of political alignments that will pit the African ruling class and the African masses against international capitalism in a struggle for economic decolonization. For if, indeed, such an alliance were to emerge, the prospects of economic decolonization would be good. However, the possibility of this alliance is more apparent than real. To begin with, even though economic dependence quite seriously aggravates the problem of maintaining the hegemony of the African ruling class, it is unlikely to fight for economic independence to any serious extent. If the African ruling class does not maintain existing relations of production, it ceases to be a ruling class. And if it makes a serious effort to fight for economic independence while maintaining existing relations of production, it endangers its hegemony more than it would by putting up with the political and economic liabilities of economic dependence. These points will become clearer later.

There is another reason for discounting solidarity between the African ruling class and the African masses. Since the fight for economic independence is necessarily a battle against imperialism, it cannot be disassociated from the fight against capitalism. And to the extent that it becomes a battle against capitalism, it also becomes a battle against the African ruling class. Imperialist exploitation of Africa occurs precisely because of the existence of capitalism in Africa. For the most part, the African ruling class is the creation of Western imperialism and remains largely a tool of Western imperialism. To be sure, there are important contradictions between the interests of the African ruling class and international capitalism. However, their interests coincide on the fundamental issue of maintaining capitalist relations of production. The African ruling class survives in so far as capitalist relations of production are maintained. And international capitalism maximizes its exploitation of Africa by keeping African economies capitalist and dependent.

The problem of material base

The second aspect of the problem of maintaining the hegemony of the ruling class in Africa is its meagre material base. Even in the pre-colonial period the African bourgeoisie – whether rural, commercial or bureaucratic – was in a very embryonic state; the accumulation of wealth was hampered by the surplus of land to labour and various restrictions on the size of the market. Colonial economic policy, periodically combined with the vagaries of the international market, subsequently conspired to restrict even further African entrepreneurship. After 1945, however, conditions improved slightly. Restrictions were relaxed on the use of African land and labour, and the commodities boom of the late 1940s and early 1950s channelled more money into African-controlled agriculture and commerce. Although the African bourgeoisie was still weak by the early 1960s, it was expanding rapidly and was trying to use its newly won political power to build a more secure material base for itself. The incongruence between its political power and material base still remains a major threat to its hegemony, however.

The African ruling class cannot solve this problem by rapidly increasing the economic surplus for rather obvious reasons, the most important being that the very factors that maintain African economies in their present condition of underdevelopment preclude any significant increase of the economic surplus in the foreseeable future. That leaves the option of coping with the problem by manipulating the distribution of the already available surplus. However, by trying to increase its share of the economic surplus the African ruling class exacerbates the contradictions between it and its competitors, the African masses and international capitalism. But here again the contradictions between the ruling class and the masses is the more fundamental; for it exists in the sphere of production, while the contradiction between the ruling class and international capitalism exists in the sphere of the market. The appallingly small share of the economic surplus accruing to the masses is primarily an effect of their lack of control over the means of production. Therefore their struggle for the surplus must eventually amount to a struggle for revolutionizing the economic system. By contrast, the struggle for the surplus between the African ruling class and international capitalism is simply a struggle over distribution. It is mediated by the fact that these two competitors are in the final analysis factions of the same class and have a common interest in maintaining the existing economic system.

Revolutionary pressures

The third aspect of the problem of maintaining the hegemony of the African ruling class is the revolutionary pressures associated with the smallness of the economic surplus and of the political experience of the African masses, and the poverty of the African masses. We are all familiar with descriptions of desperate poverty in Africa, of the lack of the most elementary necessities and the inhuman toil to seek out a precarious existence. These conditions immensely threaten the hegemony of the African ruling class by making the struggle for the surplus particularly grim, and they bring the harshness of capitalist exploitation into clear relief. The revolutionary pressures created by this condition are reinforced by the political consciousness of the masses. The African masses were politicized by the nationalist movement in circumstances that entailed considerable radicalization. To win a following, the African nationalist leaders had to adopt a political ideology that focused on the oppressive character of colonialism. Against the colonizers' claim of a civilizing mission, the nationalist leaders asserted the right of self-determination and the equality of all men. This ideology radicalized the masses by teaching them to value equality and political participation and by sensitizing them to political and economic oppression. The demands arising from this radical consciousness are now directed at the

African ruling class, who are unable to meet them in any way compatible with the maintenance of existing relations of production. Since their stagnating economies give them little room for manoeuvring, they are increasingly resorting to violence to control the masses. However, their repression only deepens the contradictions between them and the masses. These revolutionary pressures not only deepen the contradictions between the masses and the African ruling class, but force the African ruling class to become more dependent on international capitalism, which also has a vested interest in containing these pressures.

We have to conclude that solidarity between the African ruling class and the African masses is unlikely, and that the more likely and more natural alliance will be between the African ruling class and international capitalism.

Politics and the course of indigenization

If the above conclusion is correct, then the prospects of indigenizing African economies are poor, for the favourable political condition for rapid and profound indigenization is solidarity between African leaders and the African masses. To understand why this is so, we have to be clear what profound indigenization entails. It entails a wholesale disengagement from the exploitative relations of Africa with other economies, particularly the capitalist West. In so far as Africans become implacable foes of imperialism and the whole syndrome of dependence associated with it, they have to do without most of the apparatus of international aid, imported capital, imported technology and imported consumer goods. Profound indigenization will have the effect of turning international capitalism into an implacable enemy of Africa. In short, the African country that undertakes profound indigenization will be generating stress and strain on such a scale as to make its total disintegration a real possibility. To be able to risk generating stress on such a scale, to be able to absorb such stress, the country will have to be very special. It must possess ideological clarity right from the leadership to the grass roots. It will have to have a lot of confidence in itself and its leaders. African countries hardly boast of these characteristics. For the most part they are class societies in which the ruling class has alienated and demoralized the masses, excluded them from effective political participation and brutalized them with violence. That is precisely why the bulk of African countries cannot indigenize their economies beyond a few symbolic measures.

It is now clear that the problem of indigenization of African economies is not really the purely economic problem that it initially appears to be. Nor is it initially a problem to be defined in terms of dealing with imperialism. It is most immediately, and most importantly, a political problem, the problem of getting rid of the comprador bourgeoisie.[5] The defeat of imperialism in Africa, which is inseparable from the process of indigenization of African economies, is nothing less than an act of revolution. But is is an act of revolution that presupposes a preceding act of revolution, namely the getting rid of Africa's comprador bourgeoisie. That is precisely why the problem of indigenization is so difficult, and why it cannot be solved immediately or in the short run.

Even though profound indigenization must presuppose the ousting of Africa's comprador ruling class, this class nevertheless has a substantial interest in carrying out some limited indigenization in order to strengthen its material base, to increase its political power at home and its competitive strength in the international system. It is the delicate balance between taking advantage of such opportunities and containing the pressure for radical economic decolonization that will frame indigenization policies in Africa.

Indigenization in Africa tends to take the form of Africanization and nationalization. Africanization is the process of giving Africans positions formerly held by expatriates. The significance of Africanization for furthering economic decolonization is at best marginal. As was suggested earlier, we cannot conclude anything about the relative economic independence of two countries by comparing the incidence of expatriate roles in those two countries. While Africanization does very little to further economic independence, it helps the African ruling class in some important ways. The replacement of foreigners gives them patronage and subsequently more power. It provides some leverage for putting pressures on their foreign competitors. While taking advantage of Africanization in this way, the African ruling class can represent it with some success as a serious effort at economic decolonization.

Nationalization appears to be the core of the strategy of the African ruling class for dealing with the issues of economic decolonization. Every African government has made or is making efforts to extend public control over the means of production and the economy in general Nationalization enables exploitation to be depersonalized. The surplus is not extracted directly by capitalists but by the state in the name of the people, and is subsequently appropriated by the ruling class. The nationalizations do little or nothing to further economic independence. Essentially they amount to a new partnership between the African ruling class and international capitalism to their mutual benefit and often reduce areas of conflict between them. By operating under the umbrella of the state, foreign capital reduces the visibility of its exploitation while enjoying new immunities. This appears to be just as true of radical, socialist states (like Tanzania) as of those with a capitalist orientation (like Nigeria).

Conclusions

The problem of indigenization of African economies arises on account of the integration of Africa into the world capitalist system by Western imperialism, and is to be understood in the light of this process and its consequences. As a result of this process, African economies became highly disarticulated, stagnant and incapable of overcoming stagnation; they became capitalist, ridden with class antagonism and dominated by an essentially comprador bourgeoisie. Because of the contradictions between the African bourgeoisie and the African masses – contradictions whose magnitude is reflected in the fearsome repression of most African states – the African bourgeoisie cannot risk the tremendous stress and strains that a radical attack on neocolonial dependence is bound to unleash. Because of the very neocolonial character of African economies and the essentially comprador character of the African bourgeoisie, the interests of the bourgeoisie coincide in fundamental ways with those of the imperialist, rendering it incapable of waging war against imperialism. In these circumstances it would appear that the indigenization of African economies hinges on the possibility of a political 'revolution' which will remove the comprador bourgeoisie from power. If that is so, then the struggle for indigenization is really an aspect of the class struggle in Africa – all the more so because of the organic relationship between underdevelopment, dependence and capitalism. Thus the structure of the politics of indigenization is the most basic type of politics: politics as class struggle.

Notes and references

1 L. L. Rood, 'Nationalization and indigenization in Africa', *Journal of Modern African Studies*, vol. 14, no. 3 (1976), p. 431.

2 My calculations are based on data from GATT *International Trade 1973/74* (Geneva 1974); *United Nations, Yearbook of International Trade Statistics* 1972/73 (New York 1974). For the purpose of these calculations, 'Africa' excludes South Africa; the 'West' refers to Western Europe, including EEC and EFTA countries, the United States and Canada; 'Communist bloc' includes Albania, Bulgaria, Czechoslovakia, German Democratic Republic, Hungary, Poland, Rumania, USSR, China, Mongolia, North Korea, North Vietnam.

3 Samir Amin, *Accumulation on a World Scale* (New York: Monthly Review Press 1974).
4 T. Szentes, *The Political Economy of Underdevelopment* (Budapest: Akademiai Kiado 1971), and *A Brief Survey of the Theories of International Trade* (Budapest: Institute of World Economics of the Hungarian Academy of Science 1979).
5 The *comprador* bourgeoisie are local middlemen who facilitate the access of foreign traders to the local market.

Part Two

Case studies

3 Introduction to the case studies

Adebayo Adedeji

The indigenization of the African economies as a development policy objective has gradually evolved, both in conceptual design and in practical application. As has already been noted in Chapter 2, indigenization has gone through different stages of evolution, and the scale of its operation has varied from country to country. It can at least be claimed that all independent African states are involved in indigenization measures with the aim of achieving ultimate economic independence. As a policy, however, one gets the impression that the approach to its development and application has been rather *ad hoc*, piece-meal and lacking in internal consistency. It has been a product of circumstances, and at times mainly of politicians reacting to unfavourable economic situations and the demands of small groups of indigenous businessmen who felt that the prevailing economic conditions put them in an unfair position *vis-à-vis* their foreign competitors. It was hardly the original work of development planners, although their involvement became inevitable after political decisions have been made.

Just as the articulation of a policy of indigenization came about in a piece-meal fashion, so the measure for its realization was equally *ad hoc* and unplanned. Writers, in appraising indigenization in retrospect, might tend to see clear interrelationships between legislative measures and institutional facilities for fostering indigenization objectives. In practice, administrative measures and institutional facilities (credit facilities, development banks, research and investment institutions, industrial estates and other investment promotion measures) were not always established and designed to fulfil indigenization policies. The former came about as a necessity in many cases and partly as a fashion in some others, while the articulation of full-scale indigenization policies came much later. However, there were specific economic sectors and sub-sectors where there was a policy of leaving operations, ownership and control in indigenous hands right from the early years of colonial administration.

Accordingly, the measures adopted and the approaches to indigenization have varied among African countries according to their economic and social circumstances as well as in response to the different colonial administrations that they inherited. Some countries have taken a pragmatic and cautious approach; others have taken deliberate and even revolutionary measures; a few have hesitatingly pursued indigenization measures without coming out with clear policy declarations; but none can be said to have been indifferent to the aim of getting the national economy ultimately into the hands of and for the benefit of their nationals.

Egypt might be singled out as the one African country that has, since the experience of the events leading to and succeeding the Suez Crisis and War, steadily pursued a policy of planned indigenization and nationalization, starting with the 1961 nationalization decrees. In that country a systematic approach has been made through a centralized planning mechanism and the operation of a regulated market economy to bring about public control of the economy at the expense of both indigenous and private enterprise.

In Nigeria and Ghana we find a determined effort in the approach to have the key sectors of their economies in local control and ownership. In their local context, 'key sectors' refer to areas where indigenous entrepreneurs have already demonstrated the capability and potential to exploit them to the fullest, with or without foreign participation, as well as to sectors that are strategic to national security and economic survival but in which the technological input requirements might be too sophisticated for indigenous entrepreneurs and where, therefore, state control, ownership or participation becomes desirable and inevitable. By contrast, Kenya, with a fast developing economy comparable to those of Nigeria and Egypt, has adopted an approach to indigenization that is rather cautious. The settler experience under colonial administration did not give indigenous entrepreneurs the appropriate environment to emerge and grow with self-confidence, unlike the position in most of West or North Africa. Indigenization policy was calculated and designed not to really hurt the settlers and foreign investors without adequate compensation or offer of alternative business opportunities. The effort was not to dispossess and replace alien entrepreneurs; rather, it was concentrated on increasing Kenyan participation in economic activities, convinced that continued economic expansion can better be assured with both foreign and indigenous investors participating to the fullest of their respective abilities, although indigenous entrepreneurs have to be specially encouraged and assisted.

Tanzania, Ethiopia, Uganda, Algeria, Mozambique and Angola belong to the same category by having adopted a revolutionary approach in nationalizing the key sectors and economic activities in their economies. In Uganda it was an officially declared economic war against alien, particularly Asian, economic domination. In those countries that fought bitter and protracted wars to win political independence, the indigenization of certain economic activities and wholesale nationalizations in broad economic sectors were seen as inseparable components of the total national effort in the fight against colonialism and neo-colonialism whose hold on their countries had political, economic, social and cultural dimensions in the design for the subjugation of the indigenous populations.

Swaziland, Botswana and Lesotho are a class by themselves. These are countries that, though politically independent for over a decade, still find their economies totally an enclave of the economy of the Republic of South Africa, in addition to having their share of the experience of the world-wide domination of the economies of developing countries by the markets, investments and technology of the industrialized countries. Faced with a rather helpless situation, they are making some modest beginnings to evolve what might be regarded as incipient indigenization of their economies. Compared with most other African countries, these South African enclave countries face unusual handicaps and have yet a long way to go in evolving meaningful policy measures for securing effective indigenization of their economies.

The intensity, complexity and scale of foreign economic domination, and the entrenchment of foreign investors in each African country, vary from country to country and from one sub-region of Africa to another; hence the differences in approach and in the measures adopted. The grip of foreign investments on each country's economy, and the direct and indirect influence that foreign investors and their associated agents exert on local politics and decision-making processes, have to some extent affected the will to take positive control measures, and, invariably, the actual measures taken and the operation of the machinery for implementing needed action.

Most African countries have adopted policies, measures, administrative machinery, legislative and institutional arrangements for fostering the indigenization of their economies. In this they have exhibited many features that are common to their efforts; operational details and the scope of the result to be achieved have often varied. The efforts in most cases have been piece-meal, and in all of them there is the characteristic absence of consistent and comprehensive long-term planning of indigenization measures within the framework of national overall long-term development planning.

The various case studies that follow offer detailed information on the experiences of different African countries in terms of the immediate circumstances that precipitated indigenization policies and measures; the approaches to evolving such policies and measures; the coverage and design of these measures; the legal instruments and administrative machinery for applying policies and measures; and the extent the desired objectives have been achieved or what distances still have to be covered in the effort to bring national economies under local control and management for the benefit of the countries involved.

4 Egypt

Mohammed N. Hanafi, *Institute of National Planning, Cairo*

The economic situation, pre- and post-independence

The area of Arab Republic of Egypt is about 386,299 square miles (1 million square kilometres). However, only 4 per cent can be said to be permanently settled and cultivated. The population is thronged in a narrow valley some two to twenty miles wide, cut across by the river Nile and Delta region. In addition, there is a new valley consisting of a series of depressions in the western desert and extending parallel to the Nile. The cultivatable land in these depressions is more than 3 million acres, but their agricultural development depends mainly on the availability of underground water.

The Arab Republic of Egypt has an almost uniform arid climate. The average annual rainfall is about five inches or less. That is why human existence in Egypt depends mainly on irrigation from the Nile. The total area under cultivation is approximately 6,119,000 feddans.[1] Much land is devoted to cash-crops, mainly cotton, in addition to the cultivation of subsistence crops.

Modern Egypt dates from the French expedition (1798–1801) and the subsequent reign of Mohammed Ali (1805–48). The former was too brief to leave any lasting mark on the country's economy; the latter, which lasted nearly half a century, was a period of great economic and financial innovation. Historically speaking, the reign of Mohammed Ali was an attempt to escape the fate to which the three previous centuries of Ottoman rule (1517–1805) had destined Egypt to a rising progressive, aggressive and exploitative new economic system, the capitalist system of Western Europe.

However, when the European powers successfully intervened, forced Ali to operate the 'Open Door Policy' and imposed the dismantling of state industrial and trade monopolies he had set up, not only did his whole economic system – new industries and all – collapse, but also, in the absence of a thriving and enterprising middle class, the door was laid open for swift infiltration, then invasion, then domination, by foreign capital.

Towards the end of Mohammed Ali's reign, the imposition by the European powers of the 'Open Door Policy' and the dismantling of state industrial commercial monopolies prepared the ground for foreign domination. There followed a succession of reigns characterized for the most part by the swift march of foreign capital, which advanced, from the financial point of view, along three successive routes: foreign public debt, foreign credit institutions, and foreign currency annexation. Such a swift advance, however, had not created for itself the institutional or superstructural base congenial to its activities.

After the British occupation of Egypt in 1882, the structural change of the Egyptian economy into a colonial economy followed the well-known pattern. In a few decades, the Egyptian economy had changed from a self-contained economy with only feudal external economic connections into a great cotton-growing farm supplying Lancashire factories with raw cotton.

One of the main tasks of the British occupation in Egypt (1882–1956) was to prevent the rise of an Egyptian bourgeoisie which would transform and modernize the economy. Yet the capitalist framework that foreign capital had had to establish, and the growth of a capitalist sector within the economy, even though this sector was dominated by foreigners and closely tied to the colonial type of exploitation, had inevitably led to the re-emergence of the Egyptian bourgeoisie after the eclipse it had had suffered during the early years of the occupation.

This bourgeoisie was at first associated with trade, but in the conditions of the First World War, which greatly restricted imports, it branched off into new directions, including manufacture, to supply the home market and the needs of the greatly expanded occupation army.

Great fortunes accumulated, not only from these new activities but also in agriculture from the sales of cotton by the landowners, which looked for new outlets for investments. It was in this climate, and in the climate of fear for the fate of the newly created and newly tasted activities and of the heightened struggle of the Egyptian people for national independence, that the first purely Egyptian bank, 'Bank Misr', was established in 1920, not only to enter the field of commercial credit, but also to sponsor the growth of Egyptian industry and other modern economic activities, such as insurance, maritime and later air transport. During this period, Egypt's most spectacular and most controversial entrepreneur was Ahmed Abboud, whose industrial empire was built up over a period of fifteen years.

By the early 1950s Egyptian industry had completed what might be called the primary stage of industrialization. During this stage the country replaced most of its more simple manufactured imports with domestically produced substitutes. However, food processing and textile industries were of overwhelming importance, while the manufacture of consumer durables, metallurgical products, inputs utilized by other industries and capital equipment were of little significance.

On the eve of the revolution (1952) the direct part played by the government in the economic life of the country still appeared relatively insignificant. Consumption and capital expenditure by the state represented about one-eighth of national outlay. The state's contribution to national output amounted to a mere 16 per cent of gross domestic product, most of which can be included under the heading of 'traditional public services', namely defence, justice, fiscal and social administration. Only 2 per cent of local production came from state enterprises (railways, postal services, the gas and electricity undertakings of the Cairo Municipality, and a petroleum refinery at Suez). As for employment, in 1947 just 8 per cent of the working force was engaged by public authorities, central and local.

Successive Egyptian governments from 1923 to 1952 displayed no strong disposition to force the pace of economic advance. Nevertheless, during that period all potential national wealth was exhausted to serve the interests of the feudal system, foreign powers and a number of foreign adventures. At the same time, the masses of the people lived in poverty, disease and ignorance, and during the past seventy years their standard of living has been sinking steadily because production has not kept pace with the increase of population.

Instability, corruption, rising economic problems and increasing dissatisfaction produced the conditions necessary for a revolution. In 1955, within a year after the revolution, all traces of British political influence were erased by the withdrawal of the British from Suez, the nationalization of the Suez Canal Company on 26 July 1856, and the sequestration on 1 January 1957 of nearly all British and French business interests following the abortive British–French–Israeli aggression in October 1956. Since the revolution, the state had appropriated more and more responsibility for economic development. To some extent the Egyptian government had appreciated the need to work with the private sector, and hence established mixed committees to draft economic plans. However, the failure of private investors to respond enthusiastically to exhortations and incentives from the government is one of the important factors behind the inadequate performance of the Egyptian economy during the years that followed the revolution.

When comprehensive planning opened in July 1960, the Egyptian government faced the problem of how to ensure compliance from the private sector with its plans for the economy. The nationalization and other decrees of July 1961 came more as the logical outcome of the extension of state control over the economy and as commitments of planning than as the fruit of an ideology-inspired social revolution. Decisions relating to investment and the allocation of key inputs were centralized and prices were not determined by the free play of market mechanism. In operation Egypt's productive organization stands between the command economies of Eastern Europe and the modified market systems of the West. Perhaps the term 'regulated market mechanizm economy' is roughly applicable to its unique amalgam of institutional forms and operational arrangement.

Egypt's economic problems are simple to understand but baffling to solve. Her principal resources are fertile agricultural land and an abundance of people; her critical dilemma is the pressure of population upon limited land resources. The statistics of income and consumption indicate no proper progress. From 1913 to 1950 real income per person not only showed no tendency to rise but fell sharply in the Great Depression of the 1930s and again during the Second World War. Egypt's economy is largely agricultural, with over 55 per cent of the population living in rural areas and driving their income from the land and with agricultural products, mainly cotton, constituting over 90 per cent of all exports. Although her economy is based upon agriculture, however, food must still be imported to keep the population at a bare subsistence level.

In comparison with most other agrarian economies, Egypt's agriculture is already highly developed. As a result of perennial irrigation and the extensive use of fertilizer, yields per acre of many crops are among the highest in the world; consequently the possibilities for increasing production through more intensive cultivation are quite limited. The productivity *per capita*, however, is relatively low, and it is continuing to decline at an increasing rate because of the increasing number of people on the land.

Social and political framework

A significant characteristic of the Egyptian society is the unbroken unity of the country throughout the millenniums of history. The Egyptian masses have a social and temperamental homogenity. Well over 90 per cent of the population are Muslims, and this fact is of some importance in explaining the orientation of Egyptians to their government. Islam does not separate religion from the state as some other religions do.

For over twenty-five centuries, Egypt was governed by foreigners, and there has been an almost unbroken tradition of centralized and authoritarian goverment. From the time of the pharaohs and continuing through the reigns of the Ptolemies, the Roman governors, the Turks and the British, administration of the entire country has been concentrated in the hands of a ruler and a small group of top-level deputies or ministers.

Although the number of foreigners in Egypt has always been small, their influence in political and economic affairs has been great. The principal alien residents of modern times have been mostly of Greek, Italian, French, Turkish and British nationality. With the exception of the Greeks, who often ran grocery stores even in the most remote villages of Egypt, most of the foreigners were city dwellers, who played a leading role in the early development of the country's commerce and industry. Although many of these one-time foreigners have become nationalized Egyptians, they are still considered as minorities, and many left the country after the 1956 Suez crisis.

Since the Second World War, the vexed issues of unity and Arab leadership have centred around Egypt. Alone among the Arab states, Egypt has consistently conducted herself as a regional 'great power', with interests and influence throughout the area and beyond. No one else in the region can begin to match her in numbers of bureaucrats, teachers, businessmen, bankers, military officers, engineers, lawyers, doctors, mechanics, journalists and so on. There are always surplus Egyptian personnel available for technical jobs in surrounding countries. The Egyptian Government is, therefore, in a position to undertake a wide variety of functions requiring suitably well-trained manpower.

However, Egyptians at mid-century were clearly a poor people, and in comparison with the industrially advanced countries of the world Egypt is still a poor country. The country's *per capita* income, at around $118, was approximately one-tenth of the average British income, and its distribution was very unequal.

Disease, sickness and early death characterized the existence of almost all who inhabited the Nile Valley, and life expectancy for the average Egyptian male at birth was only thirty-six years, while an American could expect to live up to sixty-nine years. Only about a quarter of the population over ten years of age could read and write compared with almost complete literacy among the world's wealthy societies.

In general, the village population has an extremely low economic status, with a low but improving literacy rate and a pressing need for improved social services. The burden of disease carried by the population is heavy. Nutritional deficiencies, epidemic and chronic eye disease, enteric fevers and dysenteries, tuberculosis, syphilis and bilharzia are all found at extremely high levels in Egyptian villages. No perceptible alteration occurred in the health of the population before 1945–9, when the death rate fell 4 points, to 23 per 1000, and this trend continued downwords during the 1950s.

Nevertheless, the economic and social status has risen for the masses since the 1952 revolution.

Concerning the fundamental guiding lines of the internal social transformation, the following remarks could be substantiated.

1 Apart from the small minority of very wealthy landowners affected by land reform and some minor amendments to the income tax, the new government made no direct attacks on property; in fact, very little distribution of wealth or income occurred during the early years of the revolution.
2 The government regulating was designed to influence the distribution of income by such measures as minimum wage legislation, controls upon rents, profits and prices.

Equally, it seems that the present system has created administrative possibilities for the redistribution of income through progressive taxation and social welfare expenditure. Besides, there was a continuous shift from agriculture to industry, construction and transport, which can be considered as an evidence of a rise in the standard of living.

3 The nationalization of the financial system in 1960–1 (together with the nationalization of large-scale modern enterprises) removed from positions of economic power and control the Egyptian commercial bourgeoisie, which after 1956 inherited many of the economic interests and potentialities previously held and exploited by foreigners. Besides, the nationalization process put into the hands of the state one of the most essential tools for planning the national economy.
4 The ambitious economic development progress of the Egyptian revolutionary regime, which has plunged into industrialization and social overhead investment on a massive scale simultaneously with large military expenditure, has provided a powerful incentive to develop political leverage.

The concept of indigenization in the Egyptian framework

An objective assessment of the indigenization process in modern Egypt must be based upon simple acceptance of the fact that the country has made commitments to pursue certain courses of action, and that the Egyptian people appear to accept these commitments without much reservation.

The first commitment is to national independence. In Egypt this is commonly referred to as 'positive neutralism'. The second commitment is to national security. The third is to internal agrarian reform and improvement in the social and economic welfare of the people, and the fourth is to industrialization. The final commitment is to restrict the number of expatriates who can be employed in business enterprises. The July 1961 laws of nationalization are the biggest triumph of the revolutionary drive in the social, political and economic fields. However, the people's control over all the tools of production does not necessitate the nationalization of all means of production; neither does it mean the abolition of private ownership or any infringement on the legitimate right of inheritance following therefrom. Such control can be achieved in two ways.

1 A capable public sector could lead progress in all domains, and bear the main responsibility of the development.
2 A private sector could, without exploitation, participate in the development within the framework of the overall plan, provided that the people's control is exercised over both sectors.

However, there are three concepts of indigenization:

1 indigenizing public administration and public services;
2 indigenizing cultural and educational systems and official language;
3 indigenizing foreign industrial enterprises and commercial business.

The third of these was the main concept of indigenization in the framework of the country. Therefore, during the foreign domination, as Sidney has remarked, 'to talk about England governing Egypt was a misuse of language. We do not govern Egypt – we only govern the governors of Egypt.'

Preparatory work undertaken

Egyptian development over the past century certainly seems *prima facie* to provide a good example of *laissez-faire*. For most of that time the rules established in Western Europe and the United States to temper and regulate capitalism have either not existed or have been enforced in a desultory manner. Besides, many of the larger production units, both in commerce and industry, were owned and managed by foreigners, who operated in the position of legal privilege granted to them under the Capitulations and until 1936 were not subject to Egyptian law. It seemed incongruous and unfair to impose rules upon Egyptian enterprises that were not applicable to their foreign rivals.

However, as early as 1922 a special council had been established to make proposals for the economic development of the country; and no doubt the transfer of power from British to native hands, together with the emergence of nationalism among certain sections of the Egyptian middle class, promoted more active participation by the state in economic affairs. After the First World War closer attention appears to have been paid to possible improvements to the infrastructure, and the government studied proposals for generating electricity from the Aswan Dam.

In 1935 a five-year plan of public expenditure on roads, railways and irrigation facilities received parliamentary approval. But war and the preparation not merely delayed the construction of new projects but also impaired the renovation and maintenance of existing social capital.

The free-enterprise phase of the Egyptian revolution (1952–6)

For the first time since Mohammed Ali, the Egyptian economy experienced the imprint of a firm government and the state moved farther along the spectrum away from *laissez-faire*. Even so, the years 1952–6 might appropriately be described as the free-enterprise phase of the Egyptian revolution, that is, the years when the revolutionary government attempted to achieve development by employing traditional methods and techniques, recommended by those who believed in the efficiency of private entrepreneurs in poor countries to respond to incentives and so set their economies along paths of sustained growth. Discussions began in October 1956 on a separate plan for manufacturing, and by the summer of 1957 officials of the newly formed Ministry of Industry had prepared a five-year plan which became operational the following year.

The government's commitment to plan industry not only led to the imposition of controls over the flow of investible funds but also predetermined that only manufacturing industrial projects approved by the state would be countenanced in future. On the other hand, the *sequestration of enemy property* represented a reaction to the Anglo-French attack of 1956, but the impetus grew into Egyptianizing the main arteries of the national economy. All foreign banks, insurance companies and commercial agencies were compelled to convert themselves into domestically owned joint-stock companies within five years. This policy was described by the government as a nationalist measure designed to rid the country of foreign influence over the investment policies of Egypt's financial institutions. Egyptianization had given back to the citizens the right to direct their own capital and manage their own funds, and foreign banks and insurance companies were simply transformed into Egyptian institutions. The Egyptianization laws placed the state in a perfect position to control the main channels of finance. In reality, there seems to have been no question of turning over financial institutions of such strategic importance to private entrepreneurs, a course that seemed implied by the term 'Egyptianization' as well as by a government statement explaining its policy.

Guided capitalism (1957–60)

In January 1957 the government placed nearly all industrial and commercial property possessed by the public under the management of a single institution, the Economic Organization, which, during its brief existence of four years, became the most important government agency for promoting industrial expansion. The influence of the Economic Organization upon industry between 1957 and 1961 is, however, difficult to gauge. Thirty-one industrial firms were affiliated to it in 1959. Some were old established public enterprises, such as petrol refineries; others had been founded more recently in association with private capital. A third group represented former British and French assets sequestrated during the Suez War. The Economic Organization embraced a complex of industrial property covering steel, minerals, chemicals and textiles. If we exclude small firms and concentrate upon the area of production encompassed by organized business, then the importance of the Economic Organization can be assessed in a more relevant way. Within this sector of industry the firms affiliated to the Economic Organization produced roughly a third of aggregate output and employed about 20 per cent of the labour force.

The Economic Organization was empowered to take over government interests in various joint-stock companies and also to acquire the capital of public enterprises. It was given the right to participate in and establish all kinds of companies, and it did in fact take over part of the share capital of a series of industrial concerns. The investments of the Organization in industrial companies already in 1957 amounted to £E38 million[2] and grew to £E49 million by 1960. Besides nationalizing the Misr Bank, the government obtained control over all the companies belonging to the Misr concern; a special Misr Organization was established in 1960 to run the bank and the many companies belonging to it.

Dr Kaissouny's Budget speech of 1957 recognized that 'the functions of government are no longer restricted to the classical ones of achieving security, justice, and defence, but have come to be varied and extended far and wide'. Through the Economic Organization and Misr group, the state compelled the organized sector of industry to retain more profits and invest only in an approved way, and the major companies virtually lost the power to initiate their own investment projects. Finally, the nationalization of foreign banks and insurance companies, together with the existing system of control over foreign exchange, gave the government sufficient powers to regulate and determine the allocation of finance through most of the economy. By 1958 the state had attained a position in which investment could be planned. Nevertheless, Dr Kaissouny assured businessmen that the government had established the Economic Organization not to compete with them, but merely to stimulate private investment.

It was not until 1957 that planning on a broad scale was introduced in Egypt. In that year two five-year plans, one for industry and the other for agriculture, were adopted and implementation started.

The nationalization and planning phase (1960–5)

The first comprehensive five-year plan for the period 1960/1961–1964/1965 can be considered in some ways as an extension of the two earlier ones. The introduction of a comprehensive five-year plan in 1960 pushed the Egyptian leaders into more specific statements about the kind of economic system they wished to create, and also revealed more sharply certain incompatibilities between central planning and private enterprise.

When all the qualifications have been offered for ambiguities in the definitions employed by the National Planning Committee for private and public sectors, it remains true that in 1959 the Egyptian government proposed to plan comprehensively an economy with a relatively small public sector and where at least two-thirds of national production took place outside its immediate control. Furthermore, politicians frequently and publicly emphasized their support for a mixed economy and close co-operation between public and private enterprise.

But in the whole, the private sector failed to achieve the targets established for it by the National Planning Committee. Thus by 1960 the nationalization of corporate property and the extension of further controls over agriculture and small-scale enterprises appeared a logical next step for a government committed to comprehensive planning and ambitious development targets.

By a series of presidential laws and decrees in July 1961, therefore, half the country's industry and the whole of its banking and insurance activities, together with the cotton trade and many construction, transport and trading companies, were nationalized. July 1961 may therefore be considered as the point at which the Egyptian economy was decisively changed in a socialist direction. This is not to say that no nationalization had taken place before 1961; on the contrary, the events of that year should be thought of not as a sudden break with earlier conditions and policies but rather as the end result, for the time being, of a development that began at the time of the nationalization of the Suez Canal.

Such being the case, the government had solved the problem of control by enlarging the public sector to include big industrial companies and all firms engaged in foreign trade, financial services, construction and transport. In order to introduce a much stronger measure of central control over farming, it had begun to transform agricultural institutions. In 1965 Egypt had emerged, in theory at least, as a 'socialist and co-operative society'.

Thus the years of the first five-year plan witnessed the demise of the old private enterprise system in Egypt.

Summaries of laws dealing with the various types of indigenization

Under law no. 138 of 1947, at least 51 per cent of the shares of a joint stock company had to be set aside for Egyptians, while the new law of July 1952 proclaimed that only 49 per cent had to be so reserved, and further stipulated that, if the required proportion was not taken up by native citizens within a month, then the share issues became open to public subscription regardless of nationality. Besides, Egypt had left the sterling area, and its government found it necessary, for the first time in the country's history, to establish independent exchange and commercial policies.

Sequestration

Sequestrations of funds and property, which had been imposed by presidential decree according to the provisions of the emergency law, were lifted by virtue of law no. 150 issued on 24 March 1953. This law stipulated that the ownership of funds and property referred to above should revert to the state and that the owner should receive a total compensation of £E30,000 unless their value was less than this amount, in which case the exact value should be paid in the form of marketable fifteen-year 4 per cent nominal bonds. The government might redeem these bonds wholly or partly after ten years at the nominal value. If sequestrated funds and property owned by a person or a member of his family included a commercial establishment that had not been sold by the sequestration, and its value did not exceed E£30,000, such establishment should be returned to them.

Nationalization

According to the decrees of July 1961, forty-four companies and establishments, apart from banks and insurance companies, were to be taken over completely by the state, while state partnership to the extent of not less than 50 per cent of the capital was imposed on eighty-two companies and establishments. In addition to this there were a large number of companies in which the government took over less than 50 per cent of the shares, and a good many of these were taken over completely in 1962. The following is a short review of the important nationalization laws promulgated during 1963, arranged in a chronological order.

1 In conformity with law no. 38 of 4 April, all cotton-exporting firms and ginning mills were nationalized with supervision thereof entrusted to the General Cotton Organization. Compensation would be effected by means of fifteen-year 4 per cent nominative, negotiable state bonds, which would be redeemable wholly or partly after ten years at par.
2 By virtue of law no. 51 of 28 April, all supply companies and establishments that were previously partly nationalized, in conformity with laws no. 118 and no. 119 of 1961, became fully owned by the state. Moreover, another seventeen establishments, mainly mills, were wholly nationalized. The administrative supervision thereof was entrusted to the General Organization for Flour and Rice Mills and Bakeries. On 13 June five chemical and pharmaceutical companies and establishments, previously partly nationalized, in addition to nine laboratories, became wholly state-owned, following the promulgation of law no. 65 of 1963.
3 Moreover, by virtue of the same law, the permits granted to fifty medical factories were terminated. The supervision of such establishments was entrusted to the General Organization for Medicines, Chemicals and Pharmaceuticals. Similarly, ten companies and establishments were wholly nationalized, and their supervision was entrusted to the General Organization for Internal Transport, in conformity with law no. 67 of 13 June.
4 By virtue of law no. 70 of 22 July, eleven contractors enterprises were partly nationalized with 50 per cent of the capital thereof taken up by the public sector.

Investment of Arab foreign funds and the Free Zones

The year 1974 witnessed major developments which were reflected in the various sectors of the economy. Thus measures were taken to consolidate and implement the 'Open Door' policy, and these were manifested in a number of economic and financial agreements which were concluded with Arab and foreign countries for the mutual protection of investments with the aim of promoting the flow of capital funds, providing adequate guarantees thereto and preparing the economy to be able to absorb the large investments projected during the five-year plan for 1976–80. The 'Open Door' policy aims at:

1 bringing about mutual benefits to the domestic economy as well as to Arab and foreign investors;
2 creating a climate conducive to the flow of Arab and foreign capital by transforming Egypt into a financial and monetary centre in line with the needs of the Arab world;
3 providing adequate safeguards against non-commercial risks and the necessary incentives for promoting foreing investment; and
4 giving priority to projects that will increase foreign currency receipt and attract advanced technological methods.

The promulgation of law no. 65 of 1971, in respect of the investment of Arab capital and the creation of Free Zones in Egypt, was one of the various steps taken within the framework of that policy. However, the practical implementation of the provision of this law revealed the need for its amendment in order to achieve the contemplated objectives in the mutual interest of both the national economy and the foreign investor. Consequently, this law was abrogated and replaced by law no. 43 of 19 June 1974, concerning the investment of Arab and foreign capital and Free Zones. It stipulated that projects already established prior to the enactment of the former law should continue to enjoy the privileges already granted, while projects established in accordance therewith should enjoy the rights and privileges to be determined in this connection.

The new law consists of four chapters, of which the first one embraces provisions related to the investment of Arab and foreign capital in Egypt, while the second chapter deals with joint ventures. Provisions concerning the general authority for Arab and foreign investment and Free Zones are covered by the third chapter, while the fourth is devoted to the provision pertaining to Free Zones.

Indigenization through the state versus private capitalism

As a result of the previous discussion, we can safely make the following generalizations with respect to the indigenization process through the state versus private capitalism.

During the 1820s and 1830s, Mohammed Ali proclaimed manufacturing a state monopoly and forbade any industrial production outside the public sector. In addition to monopolizing both the provision of raw materials to workers and the sale of their finished products, Mohammed

Ali attempted to expand industrial output by setting up mechanized factories for the manufacture of textile, glass, iron products, armament and ships. He usually imported the requisite machinery, engineering and managerial staff, while skilled labour from among urban artisans and small masters found themselves directed to work in government factories and unskilled peasants were likewise conscripted for the new industries.

Mohammed Ali's controls were dismantled by his successors, and the state entrepreneurs were freer to develop manufacturing and to utilize methods of production or raw materials in whatever directions they found profitable. With the exception of some sugar refineries, printing works, bakeries and clothing factories constructed by Ismail (which in any case, after a brief but unsuccessful experience as state enterprises, were sold to private capitalists), the government made no further efforts after Mohammed Ali to establish publicly operated industry. Nor was there evidence that the state attempted to foster private manufacturing; on the contrary, the complete absence of protection against foreign competition, together with the imposition of an excise duty of 8 per cent on local products, discouraged domestic enterprises.

Considerable impetus was afforded to the development of large-scale manufacturing firms by Bank Misr. The bank was founded by a group of Egyptian capitalists in 1919 to promote local industrial and commercial enterprise. The bank's good name and popularity, as a purely national institution, attracted private capital away from the more traditional channels of land, commerce and buildings. Bank Misr provided working capital, managerial and technical advice for all its affiliated companies. After the war, when Egyptian enterprises had again to face the full rigour of foreign competition, development slowed down, and between 1921 and 1930 the registered capital of industrial joint-stock companies increased by only 21 per cent. Much of this investment went into the so-called sheltered industries.

The decline after 1930 in the import of such foreign manufactures as shoes, cement, furniture, flour, cotton yarn and processed foods is very striking. By the eve of the Second World War the country was already self-sufficient in sugar, alcohol, cigarettes, salt and flour, and almost independent of foreign supplies for cotton yarn, shoes, cement, soap, furniture, matches, beer and vegetable oil – a situation in sharp contrast to 1913. In 1930, for the first time since Mohammed Ali, secured tariffs were levied and the government immediately revoked the country's traditional free trade policy and imposed duties of between 15 and 20 per cent *ad valorem* on a wide range of consumer goods likely to compete with domestic commodities.

Thus modern Egyptian industry found its birth in the second and third decades of the present century at the hands of financial capital, and moreover it acquired from the start a monopolistic nature. There is nothing very surprising in this: a native capitalism that starts late in economically underdeveloped countries is quick to learn and adopt the organizational forms and methods of internalizing exploitation that were reached by more advanced countries after decades of development.

Between the First World War and the revolution of July 1952 the Egyptian economy proceeded slowly to revert towards a centrally directed system. Impetus for this movement came from several directions, including two world wars and their attendant problems of control over production; the international depression of the 1920s and 1930s; the gradual transfer of political power from the British administration back to the hands of native Egyptians; and, finally, a growing but far from widespread appreciation among Egypt's rulers that the development of the economy and the protection of its citizens from some of the more deleterious consequences of uncontrolled private enterprises demanded action by the state.

Public investment by the new revolutionary regime appears designed, as indeed it had been since the time of Ismail, to create a more efficient infrastructure within which private enterprise could develop more rapidly and efficiently. However, from 1957 the state assumed more and more responsibility for the promotion of long-term development. Some changes in the attitude of Egyptian leaders towards private enterprise were, however, perceptible; and, as Professor Vatikiotis points out, to read President Nasser's speeches of 1958 and 1959 is to recognize the apparent shift in emphasis. Since then, however, an ideology of nationalization has grown out of events, and in government directives on the nationalization decrees of 1961, as well as in the drafting of the Charter of 1962. This ideology is quite articulate. The prevarication and ambiguity that had characterized the attitude of Egypt's mass media and leaders towards private business during the years of guided capitalism ceased after July 1961. From then on they justified the nationalization of corporate industrial and commercial property with slogans drawn from the familiar canons of socialism. As we have mentioned before, the years of the first five-year plan (1960–5) witnessed the demise of the old private enterprise system in Egypt.

Wholesale versus phased indigenization

Egypt's first large foreign industrial enterprises were founded by British, Dutch, French and American interests. Until 1936 the foreign firms were dominant throughout all industries. The Second World War gave the Egyptian-owned and managed industries their real impetus.

Hitherto foreign companies had dominated the beverage, tobacco and petroleum industries; afterwards, they were overshadowed by Egyptian enterprise, owing mainly to increased Egyptian investments in industry. Since July 1952 the natural forces of the market have been largely replaced by a conscious government policy as the prime mover of the structural transformation that has taken place. Later political development, such as the Egyptianization measures enacted after October 1956, accelerated this trend. From 1952 the state assumed more and more responsibility for the promotion of long-term development. The nationalization of the Suez Canal and the Suez War in 1956, followed by the taking over of British and French companies and other economic interests, were influenced by Egyptianization. President Nasser told the third Co-operative Congress at the end of 1957 that Egypt was now moving towards a 'socialist, democratic, and co-operative society', and the Egyptian press publicized this slogan most enthusiastically. An earlier law of 1957 providing for the full Egyptianization of Belgian companies and other economic interests from the winter of 1959–60 onwards further hardened the anti-capitalist atmosphere in Egypt. Its deficiencies, both as a social and as an economic system, received more and more publicity. In 1960 the government nationalized Bank Misr to ensure greater control over the private sector during the plan. Foreign trading firms passed into public ownership for much the same reason. The years 1960–1 were exciting and interesting for indigenizing the Egyptian economy. Introduction of a comprehensive five-year plan in 1960, as we have previously mentioned, pushed the Egyptian leaders into more specific statements about the kind of economic system they wished to create, and also revealed more sharply certain incompatibilities between central planning and private enterprise. Consequently, the Egyptian government faced the problem of how to ensure compliance from the private sector with its plans for the economy. The nationalization and the decrees of July 1961 came as the logical outcome of the extension of state control over the economy and of a commitment to planning.

In summary, the Egyptian government proceeded step by step to control and indigenize the economy within a short period of time. The system that replaced the old private enterprise economy is usually referred to as a planned socialist economy. Recently there has been much discussion of the economic 'Open Door' policy adopted by Egypt in order to accelerate the process of economic development for the purpose of raising living standards.

Type(s) of indigenization being pursued and the administrative, organizational and manpower (training) arrangements for initiating and fostering indigenization

As we have mentioned vefore, Egypt has a small, strategic, and in some respects quite modern, nucleus of indigenous industrial enterprises. If sufficient capital were forthcoming, the industrial sector might be readily expanded.

Various estimates give the increase of physical capital in industry as ranging from 169 per cent to 306 per cent between 1939 and 1960. The largest part of the increase took place between 1950 and 1960; part of the quite substantial industrial investment during the second hald of the 1940s was used to make up for the fall in the stock of capital during the war period. Concerning the capital output ratio, a 200 per cent increase in industrial production points to a fall in the capital–output ratio of about 10 per cent.

A comparison of the value of the stock of capital (estimate A in Table 4) and the value of industrial value added suggests a fall in the capital–output ratio from about 3.25 in 1939 to about 2.5 in 1960 (since the capital value figures are book values, the latter figure may have to be raised to about 3). In the study of the incremental capital–output ratio undertaken by Hansen and Marzouk, a figure of about 3 was found as an average for the period 1945 to 1962–3 for the economy as a whole.

However, Egyptian entrepreneurs had chosen to produce commodities where the amount of capital required per unit of output was relatively low, where productive techniques were less complicated, and where fuel and transport charges did not form a substantial proportion of the cost of the finished product.

Around 1950, Egyptian private enterprise provided employment for

Table 4 *Capital estimates for Egyptian industry, 1939–60*

	Estimate A				*Estimate B*			*Estimate C*
	*Current prices**	*1939 prices**	*Index at 1939*	*Alt. 1†*	*Alt. 2†*	*Alt. 3†*	*Alt. 4†*	*Index of h.p.‡*
1939	50	50	100	100	100	100	100	100
1950	200	53	106	180	164	149	132	130
1952	—	—	—	219	198	177	156	152
1960	700	152	304	406	354	301	269	295

Source: Hansen and Marzouk (1965), p. 129, Table 5.10

* E£ million.

† 1939 = 100. Alternative estimates made by the flow of capital goods method.

‡ Total of installed horsepower in industry.

92 per cent of the labour force, produced 84 per cent of the national output and was responsible for three-quarters of gross fixed capital formation. However, the ratio of dividends to paid-up capital for large firms remained high during the postwar period. In other words, shareholders continued to receive handsome returns on their money while industry experienced difficulty in attracting long-term capital, a situation that suggested that private investment may have been highly sensitive to distributed profit. The trend since 1956 has been that not all state directives are inimical to private enterprises, but that the attempts of the government to regulate, for example, private investment in houses or to restrain dividends may well have had a damping effect on incentives to save and to invest throughout the private sector.

However, law no. 7 of 1959 fixed the amount of dividends. Corporate enterprises were allowed to distribute not more than 10 per cent above their level for the previous year, and firms were compelled to invest in government bonds a proportion of their net profits equal to 5 per cent of the amount paid to shareholders. But protest from investors was so strong that the minister was persuaded to raise the maximum to 20 per cent. The government could not reasonably expect to restrain the distribution of profits and to attract an increased share of non-corporate savings into planned projects at one and the same time. Moreover, through possible effects on the confidence of potential investors, the policy of dividend limitation might well have reduced the overall volume of private savings. At the same time, the government was naturally anxious to remove any obvious obstacles to the flow of savings into industry. We have noticed that before 1952 Egypt was a private enterprise economy with foreign influence in many fields and with some direct, though limited, government interference. Through the land reforms, Egyptianization, sequestration and nationalization, and also through direct government investments, foreign influence was wiped out and the Egyptian economy became a mixed economy from both an ownership and a production point of view. The government owns or dominates practically all big and medium-sized industry, all big transport and finance companies, the main part of domestic wholesale and foreign trade, together with construction undertakings.

The companies affiliated to the Economic Organization were fairly important within the sphere of industry amenable to centralized authority; where the state owned 25 per cent or more of the shares of a company, the Organization possessed the power to appoint a majority of directors to its board and the managing director. Most companies affiliated to the Economic Organization came into this category. Even if the state's shareholding was less than 25 per cent, the Organization was still entitled to be represented on the board of directors, and policy decisions of all companies had to be reported. However, through the Economic Organization the state not only exercised closer control over all companies in which it possessed an interest, but also operated over a wide area of the economy, including trade, finance and light manufactures.

According to the July 1959 decrees forty-four companies and establishments, apart from banks and insurance companies, were to be taken over completely by the state, while state partnership to the extent of not less than 50 per cent of the capital was imposed on eighty-two companies and establishments.

In addition to this, there were a large number of companies in which the government took over less than 50 per cent of shares, and a good many of these were taken over completely in 1963. Furthermore, any person or organization was forbidden to own shares in certain specified companies exceeding a total market value of E£10,000. Excess shares were taken over by the state and compensation was to be paid to the previous shareholders in the form of negotiable government bonds, maturing after fifteen years and redeemable after ten years at a nominal interest of 4 per cent, to be paid by the companies. An individual could receive compensation only up to a maximum amount of E£15,000.

By a further decree the supervising authorities were set up. A Supreme Council for Public Organizations was created, consisting of all the members of the government (president and ministers). The individual companies and establishments, including both existing public enterprises and the newly nationalized private concerns, were attached to the various ministries according to the nature of their activity. The duties of the ministers were to 'undertake the responsibilities of extending advice and guidance, organization, control and supervision' and to 'implement the annual production schedules arranged for organization within his competence and approved by the Supreme Council for Public Organization according to plans'. Plans should stipulate the size and kind of resources, whether financial, material or manpower; they should also indicate the means of ensuring the availability of required potentialities. Plans should also regulate the use of these potentialities in production, investment, consumption, export and import, the means of financing the organization and of promoting the production efficiency of the workers, etc. In this way a series of special organizations were established. Attached to the Ministry of Industry were the General Egyptian Organization for Metallurgy, for the Foodstuffs Industry, for Weaving and Spinning, for Chemical Industries, for Building Materials and Ceramics and for Metallic Industry, for Engineering Industries, for Petroleum, and for Co-operative Organizations and Small Industries. Attached to the Ministry of War was an Organization for Military Factories, and to the appropriate ministties were attached organizations for agricultural enterprises, communications, trade, building, land reclamation, social insurance, etc.

In connection with the other nationalizations that took place in July 1961, the import trade was concentrated in a dozen state-owned agencies. At the same time all the leading cotton export companies were made public companies, and under the new cotton policy declared in August 1961, the Egyptian Cotton Commission was made the Central Agency for Marketing Egyptian Cotton.

Education and industry

It is worthwhile to remark that, before 1952, Egypt's educational system had but one aim – training for government service – and it has been relatively sucessful in this. It has trained engineers for the state railways and other government-operated industries; it has prepared statesmen for a plethora of ministries; it has turned out droves of functionaries to perform the routine tasks required for its far-flung bureaucracy; and it has produced thousands of teachers to man its government-operated schools and universities. The major educational objective of the New Regime for the next decade appeared to be the eradication of illiteracy. The elimination of illiteracy among the masses, however, is not likely to contribute much to the development of modern industries, which require a comparatively small but highly trained labour force.

Since 1952, the government has taken some measures to improve the training of industrial manpower. In 1955 it instituted long-overdue improvements in its poorly conceived and grossly inefficient system of vocational education. Instead of using the technical schools as a catch-basin for those unfit for an academic education, the new system provided for the selection of trade-school students on the basis of interest in, and aptitude for, industrial employment. It also established, for the first time, some machinery for vocational training in industries in the larger urban areas. These reforms call for a change in concept and an improvement in administration rather than for an increased investment of resources. The Productivity and Vocational Training Centres were established to encourage better utilization and development of skilled labour and of lower-level supervisory management.

There has been an obvious tendency to open new universities. There are indications, however, that the government is becoming concerned about the problem of developing the kind of high-level human resources that modern industries require. The seeds of organization planning, of management development and of broader emphasis on the human factors in industrial growth have been planted by the Institute of Personal Management and by some of the larger and more progressive concerns which use the services of foreign management consultancy firms to modernize their organizations. The Institute of Public Administration may set a pattern for advanced managerial and administrative training in government which could be applied in the industrial sector. Furthermore, the Institute of National Planning was established in 1961; this institute has done a great deal to provide the country and other Arabic nations with well qualified planning cadres.

Egypt has the basic institutions which, with some strategic changes and extensions, could effectively generate the highly trained manpower resources that modern technology demands. These same insitutions might even be utilized by other Arab states which have not yet developed their own.

Financing indigenization

Establishment and development of national banks

Shortly after the monetary reform of 1834 an attempt was made to create a credit institution. A number of foreign exchange dealers were already established in Alexandria and had a lucrative business speculating on the multiple currencies circulating in Egypt. The number of foreign traders residing in Alexandria and from Europe had increased from sixteen in 1822 to forty four in 1831. Mohammed Ali was already in the habit of borrowing from them and they of subscribing to his Treasury bills. The next logical step was the establishment of a bank; and a bank was actually established in 1842 – a mixed bank, with the government subscribing to four-sevenths of its capital and foreigners the rest. It was to be not only a commercial bank, but also the government bank, and it had the power to determine the value of various currencies. This bank, however, soon came to grief, ostensibly because of mismanagement, but more fundamentally because the basic requirements of modern credit institutions were lacking. It was left to foreign capital to force these requirements on Egypt, and in the process to annex the Egyptian economy to itself.

Finance for industrial needs was expensive and difficult to obtain. Capital costs depended upon the supply of investible funds to industry. Of course, the overall rate of saving and the willingness of persons and institutions to lend money to manufacturing establishments were factors largely beyond the competence of industrial managers.

The first steps towards the emancipation of the Egyptian financial system are closely connected with the rise of the modern Egyptian bourgeoisie and their share, after the First World War, in political power. That power, however, ultimately remained in the hands of the British and their allies until the revolution in 1952.

In 1919, Egyptian industrialists had promoted Bank Misr in order to channel investible funds towards manufacturing enterprises. Bank Misr was set up with Egyptian capital, thus paving the way for the establishment and development of national banking institutions, initiating an interest in economic development and encouraging Egyptians to divert their investments from agriculture to industry, trade and other fields. However, the foreign banks continued to predominate because of the absence of a supreme authority responsible for controlling monetary affairs. But in 1951 law no. 57 was enacted, granting the National Bank of Egypt some of the powers of a central bank in respect of control of the currency, credit and banking. This stage was also characterized by the setting up of several Egyptian banks such as Bank du Caire (1952) and Al Goumhouria Bank (1955), thus enhancing the position of Egyptian banks as a whole. Besides, industrial development came from necessity to be financed mainly from retained earnings, and small- and medium-scale enterprises continued to encounter such difficulties in obtaining funds that in 1949 the government founded the Industrial Bank to cater to their needs. Nevertheless, industrial corporations financed expansion very largely from internal sources.

Independence and planning of banking in Egypt

If we group together all financial institutions so as to include, in addition to commercial banks, specialized banks, insurance companies, savings offices and public social insurance schemes, we find that in 1956 foreign capital, principally British and French, controlled 60 per cent of the combined balance sheets of these institutions, while Egyptian private capital controlled 25 per cent (of which 90 per cent belonged to the Bank Misr) and savings offices and public social insurance schemes represented the remainder.

The decisive steps towards the Egyptianization of the credit system did not come until after 1956, the year of tripartite aggression that followed the Suez Canal crisis. Accordingly, law no. 22 of 1957 was promulgated, providing for the Egyptianization of all banks with the aim of ending foreign control of the banking system and directing investment policy in the interests of the country. Further legislation was enacted to provide for the public ownership of the banking system so that its policies would conform with the aims of economic development plans. The most important of these laws were those that provided for the nationalization of the National Bank of Egypt, Bank Misr and Banque

Belge et Internationale, the establishment of the Central Bank of Egypt by the relinquishment of the National Bank of Egypt of its central banking functions and its commencement of commercial banking operations in 1961. In July 1961, all banks and financial institutions were nationalized by virtue of the socialist decrees that were enacted, and this was followed in 1963 by several mergers, as a result of which the number of banking units was reduced to five commercial banks, three mortgage banks, an industrial bank and the Agricultural Co-operative Credit Organization. The purpose of this last step was to facilitate the co-ordination of monetary and financial policy between a limited number of banks, in addition to the belief that large banks were better able to finance large projects and that, because of their substantial resources, they would provide a more efficient service.

However, in July 1974 law no. 43 was promulgated regarding the investment of Arab and foreign capital and Free Zones, which aims at encouraging foreign investment under the 'Open Door' policy and consolidating economic development efforts. This was, heretofore, the preserve of the public sector.

Hard currency reserves, investment and the source of foreign finance

From 1947, when Egypt left the sterling area, to 1952 the government aimed to amass reserves sufficient to meet her external financial commitments. However, the reserves were exhausted, and by the end of 1957 Egypt began to resort to foreign long-term borrowing in order to finance her requirements of investment goods, which by this time began to represent an increasingly larger fraction of its foreign imports. In addition to suppliers' facilities, that is purchases on fully or partially deferred payments, agreements were made with various Western financial quarters relating to definite investment projects or purchases. The terms of payment extended on average from five to ten years of these agreements. The same period, however, saw the beginning of development loans from the Soviet Union, the German Democratic Republic, Czechoslovakia, Hungary, Poland and Yugoslavia. The loans were characterized by a low rate of interest, averaging 2.5 per cent and by stretching payments over a long period.

Domestic credit recorded a considerable expansion during the year, as it advanced vigorously from £2059.9 million at the end of 1973 to £2628.9 million at the end of 1974, thus realizing an increase of £569 million or about 28 per cent, as against £172.1 million or 9 per cent in 1973.

The economic impact of indigenization

Foreign technical assistance

First and foremost, the contradiction between the essential aim of technical assistance and its actual consequences should be stressed. Technical assistance is meant to explore and bring into operation local resources, in order to strengthen the economy to further its independence – that is, to render it gradually less dependent on foreign assistance.

The bulk of the technical assistance to Egypt was confined to those temporary and specific occupations in some industrial and infrastructural projects, such as the Iron and Steel Company, the High Dam project, etc. As technical assistance ended the critical skills and occupations involved were replaced by those of Egyptian personnel. The independence of aid from foreign political control has always been emphasized, and the decision-makers were always Egyptians.

Indigenous private investment and growth in entrepreneurial capabilities

In spite of the limited size of Egypt, its industrial sector is impressive. Many of the larger establishments have modern plants and equipment which compare favourably with even the newest factories in highly industrialized countries. Furthermore, in contrast to earlier days, when foreigners controlled most of the country's business enterprises, modern industry is predominantly Egyptian in ownership, management and employment.

We have already discussed the capital stock in Egyptian industry. Our main concern now is to provide an adequate cross-sectional view of entrepreneurship and management in the medium-sized and large industrial enterprises of modern Egypt.

The private companies were either in the joint-stock or limited corporation category. Each had an elected board of directors which delegated authority to the managing director, who was a member of the board and who was responsible to the board for administering and managing the corporation.

In the category of large independent enterprises, Egypt's most spectacular entrepreneur was Ahmed Abboud. His industrial empire was built up over a period of fifteen years. He hired his managers, engineers, chemists or administrators wherever he could find them. Some were from Western Europe, a few were former Egyptian government officials, some were Egyptian university graduates (but many more were not).

The largest manufacturing activity in Egypt is cotton spinning and weaving, and the dominant establishments were associated with the so-called Misr group. The Misr group also includes Egypt's main synthetic fiber plant and its largest rayon-spinning factories. All these establishment are controlled and partially owned by the Bank Misr, an all-Egyptian private institution which specializes in financing Egyptian industrial undertakings. These companies, which constitute the largest Egyptian-owned and operated industrial combine in the country, have done the most outstanding job of developing organizational and managerial talent in Egyptian industry.

The massive government investments (especially in the industrial, agricultural, energy and transport sectors) that have been allocated from the beginning of the 1960s to the present, together with measures taken to enhance the public sector's role, have resulted in the predominance of this sector in almost all spheres of economic activity. Thus, from the time comprehensive planning was adopted in 1960 until 1975, fixed public investment has totalled some E£6284 million. The public sector has seemed better equipped to train and develop professional and managerial resources. The government customarily sends members of the Egyptian top and middle management and professional groups abroad for training programmes, plant inspections and general educational development; and specialists from foreign countries are brought in to introduce new methods and to help train the local staff.

Productivity of labour and capital, 1937–60

Historically speaking, during the period 1937–60 as a whole the increase in average productivity of capital was less than the increase in average productivity of labour, and was even negative in the sub-period 1947–60. It is partly, as Hansen and Marzouk mentioned, an expression of the simple fact that an increased input of capital is the price to be paid for an increased productivity of labour. Sharply decreasing returns to factors in industry may produce the same result in spite of an increase in technical knowledge. A falling average productivity of capital alongside an increasing average productivity of labour is therefore not necessarily an indication of bad economic management; on the contrary, it may (though not necessarily, of course) be the outcome of an optimum use of capital.

The development of productivity during the years 1959/60–1975/6 is of special interest, because the period is characterized by heavy industrial investment, by nationalization in 1961, and by a large employment drive, including a shortening of the working week from forty-eight to forty-two hours in larger establishments from 1961–2. The rates of growth of labour productivity (value added per employee) were 2.8, 1.4,

6.8 per cent in agriculture, industry and electricity respectively during the period 1961/2–1964/5. However, the corresponding rates of growth of average real wages were 11.4, 4.7 and 5.4 per cent. In fact, the relations between the two rates seemed to be negative during that period, as the difference was very unfavourable. However, the rate of growth of productivity was less in some sectors during the period 1964/5–1969; e.g., it was about 5 per cent in agriculture, 0.2 per cent in industry and 6.9 per cent in electricity.

Overall restructuring of the economy and development

Between 1937 and 1960, Egypt had a clearly defined economic structure, the great part of the working population being engaged in agricultrue and related rural activities.

Throughout the nation as a whole in 1937, 69.5 per cent of all workers were engaged in the agricultural sector as against 61.8 per cent in 1947 and 56.3 per cent in 1960. This showed a gradual decline in the relative importance of labour absorption in the agricultural sector, a decline that was offset mainly by a growth in services activities, which employed 24.0 per cent of the active population in 1937, 29.2 per cent in 1947 and 33.9 per cent in 1960.

The relative distribution of employment in 1965 was 51.5, 16.3 and 32.2 per cent in the primary, secondary and tertiary sectors, while the rates for the value added were 28.0, 30.6 and 43.4 per cent respectively. The relative distribution of employment and value added in 1968–9 were 49.3, 15.5, 35.2, 27.8 and 44.4 per cent.

The number of workers employed in the various sectors of the economy in 1974 has been estimated at 9.186 million, thus recording a 2 per cent increase over the preceding year. The commodity sectors accounted for 64 per cent, the distribution sectors for 14 per cent and the services sectors for 22 per cent.

Table 5 *Percentage distribution of the value of the production of manufacturing industries in ARE, 1950–70*

Major groups	*1950 (%)*	*1959–60 (%)*	*1964–5 (%)*	*1969–70 (%)*
Consumer goods industries	74	65	49	49
Intermediate goods industries	24	29	43	44
Capital goods	2	6	8	7
Total	100	100	100	100

As regards wages, these went up by 9 per cent, so that total wage bill amounted to E£1723 million, with the commodity sectors accounting for 41 per cent, the distribution sectors for 16 per cent and the services sectors for 43 per cent.

Table 5 gives an illustration of the structure of the manufacturing sector in Egypt, and shows that the share of capital goods industry is rather puny – 2 per cent in 1950 and 7 per cent in 1969–70. In addition, the greater part of the intermediate goods are allocated to the requirement of consumer goods industry, which is not the optimum situation for development purposes.

Social and political implications of indigenization

Income distribution

Looking at the period since the 1930s as a whole, there were some changes that have had several different effects. One of these concerned the distribution of income, as between rich and poor as well as between Egyptians and foreigners. This is an area in which empirical data are extremely weak, and we must rely on fragments of information. The population censuses showed a decline in the number of foreigners in Egypt from 203,761 in 1947 to 143,312 in 1960; the numbers for 1937 were substantially higher. If average real income *per capita* in the whole economy had remained constant from 1937 to 1960 while 100,000 foreigners left the country, and assuming that average income *per capita* of foreigners was twenty times that of Egyptian nationals, the implication would be that average income *per capita* of Egyptians had risen by some 16 per cent over this period. The departure of foreigners does not necessarily and by itself result in higher income for Egyptians; it simply means that the statistical measure of average income *per capita* of all residents of the country can be a misleading indicator of the welfare of the citizens of the country.

A second aspect of income redistribution concerns the breakdown between rich and poor Egyptians. Here the primary development that comes to mind concerns the land reforms.

Concerning the distribution of the value added created in agriculture, the information available is very scanty. The National Planning Committee estimated that, for 1959–60, when the net value added amounted to a little less than E£400 million, about two-thirds was income from ownership, while one-third was wages and salaries. Here, however, income from ownership included returns imputed to owners working on their own land, while wages and salaries included wages imputed to such owners. This makes the estimate quite arbitrary, and at best gives us information only about the functional distribution of income between factors of production. But it is interesting because it points to a very low share of labour in agricultural value added.

For the year 1950 it is possible to obtain an estimate of the distribution of value added between absent owners, tillers owning the land that they till and tillers renting land. Value added was at that time E£60 per feddan, while the rent per feddan may have been about E£30. These figures can be applied to the distribution of holdings according to types of tenure, assuming the value added per feddan to be the same for all types of holdings. A similar calculation can be made for 1956, in which value added per feddan was again about E£60 and the average rent per feddan was as low as E£21. The land reforms implied a transfer of land from big owners to small owners. To some unknown extent, this meant a transfer from absent owners to owners tilling their own land, but some land must also have been transferred from big owners tilling their own land to small owners tilling their own land. With the distribution of holdings according to type of tenure as shown in Table 6, we can get an idea of the distribution between absent owners and tillers (owners and lessees) after the redistributions were completed. It has been estimated that in 1956 new holders still held about 200,000 feddans as lessees waiting for the ownership to be transferred to them from the Land Reform Committee, which temporarily took over all lands to be redistributed. If therefore, in Table 6 we move two million feddans from the tenancy group to the ownership group, we should have the approximate distribution according to tenure after the completion of the land reforms, and to this distribution we can apply the above-mentioned figures for rent and value added in 1956. On these assumptions, we find the distribution of value added 'before' and 'after' the land reforms of 1952.

Table 6 - *Distribution of agricultural value added*

Derived from	*'Before' land reforms of 1952**	*'After' land reforms of 1952**
Absent ownership	18	10
Active ownership	68	71
Tenancy	14	19
Total value added	100	100

* Percentages of total value added.

Needless to say, this calculation is crude and the margin of error large, but the figures do, we think, give an impression of the order of magnitude of one aspect of the distribution of income from agriculture and the change in distribution resulting from the Land Reforms of 1952. Taking into account that the value added accruing to active owners includes payments to the government (interest plus amortization) by the new owners, the net share of active owners has actually only increased from 68 to 71 per cent of the total value added. The interest payments to the government, however, are very modest, and the amortizations can be left out of the picture in this connection, since they are a kind of compulsory savings. The outstanding feature of the development is then a big drop, to almost one-half, of the absent owners' share in agricultural value added, and a rise by about one-third in the tenants' share. The main cause was undoubtedly the lowering of rents, which applied to all rented land. Two things have not been taken into account: illegal rent increases, and the effects of the new conditions for share-cropping. They pull in different directions, but we have not found it possible to estimate their impact on the distribution of income. Finally, it should be remembered that both active owners and tenants have to pay wages to workers, interest on loans, taxes, etc., out of their shares of the value added.

Although the main work on the farm is done by the tiller himself and his family, hired labour still plays a substantial role, especially on the bigger farms and in the seasonal peaks. Of the working population in agriculture, more than one-quarter may be employees. In connection with the land reforms, a maximum wage (of 18 piasters per day for men) was introduced, but it has never become effective.

Redistribution of the political power base and institutional factors

Before 1952 the economy was based on private enterprise, with very few restrictions, except for some feudal remnants still to be found in agriculture. Distribution of both income and wealth was extremely unequal, and absentee land ownership was a characteristic feature of the economy. Government policies, both monetary and fiscal, were on the whole passive, and mainly designed to promote the interests of the big landowners, merchants and industrialists, or the royal family itself. Development policies were not unknown. Improvements to the irrigation system have always been considered a government assignment; early industrialization, as we have seen, was conditioned by general protectionist tariff policies, and a more specific though very modest development programme was actually adopted by the old regime shortly before its fall. But all this was insufficient to cope with the growing population and the worsening conditions for the country's foreign trade, as is clearly shown by the stagnating *per capita* income; and social legislation was both inadequate and inefficient.

The revolution of 1952 had as its immediate purpose the carrying through of land reforms which both government and Parliament had repeatedly refused to support. Inevitably, therefore, the land reforms of 1952, which involved an expropriation and redistribution from big to small owners of about 10 per cent of the cultivated area (later reforms have increased this figure to about 15 per cent), came to dominate policies during the first years after the revolution. On the other matters, the policies of the new government, until the nationalization of the Suez Canal in 1956, were on the whole quite traditional, though there was a certain modernization of both monetary and budget arrangements, and some direct regulations were introduced, in particular in the field of foreign trade. But none of this went beyond the regulations applied by many Western European countries at that time. Development was an important part of the government's programme; public investments were expanded somewhat, and a special development budget was introduced. The main policy, however, was still of a general, indirect investment-promoting type; the tariff system was reorganized in 1954 in order to give increased protection for domestic industries and to promote capital goods imports, while company taxation included built-in investment incentives.

With the nationalization of the Suez Canal and the Suez War that followed at the end of 1956, policies changed rapidly. It is well known that the nationalization was decided upon as a way to finance the Aswan Dam after negotiations with the IBRD broke down. The Suez War carried with it further sequestrations and nationalizations of British and French property, which meant that the government suddenly found itself, more by chance than design, with the main part of the banking and insurance system in its hands, together with some other sectors of big business. The following year, 1957, saw the beginning of development investment. A five-year plan for industry and another for agriculture were adopted, and in 1960 these partial plans were amalgamated in a further comprehensive five-year plan for the period 1960–5. At the beginning of 1960 the big Misr concern, which had played a leading part in the early industrialization, was nationalized, partly because the investment plans of the concern did not conform with those of the government. Large-scale nationalizations followed in 1961, and these brought the bulk of big industry and wholesale trade under public ownership. A new round of land reforms was put through at the same time. The main economic motive for the nationalizations was to bring investment and company savings under the direct control of the government; but as a by-product, current production and trade also came to a large extent under government control.

Since 1961, then, the country has had a mixed economy with government and private sectors of about equal size.

Overall appraisal

The indigenization of the Egyptian economy was a complete success. There was no reduction in the level of productivity and production after the Egyptianization and nationalization measures.

However, the methods used in applying and managing the system of public ownership in Egypt have suffered from some drawbacks, and accordingly several of the projects implemented by the public sector have constrained economic development efforts. The public sector could have played a more positive role had it been well organized, but despite fifteen years of planned development the economy still faces severe problems in production and distribution, and these have taken the form of idle capacities, whether in plant or manpower, foreign currency bottlenecks, and a decline in the net return from economic development. In addition, bureaucracy has permeated many public sector bodies which were entrusted with work that should never have come their way because of their limited capacities. Accordingly, attempts have been made recently to rationalize the public sector and increase its effectiveness. For example, the National Council for Production and Economic Affairs recommended the formulation of a system of incentives to be related to production, quality of work and the reduction of operational waste; granting the necessary authority to company chairmen to decide on matters relating to the improvement of the efficiency of economic enterprises; granting the public sector freedom to deal with banks of their own choice; developing both the system of importation and pricing policy; and dealing with the deficiencies in the financial structures of public sector companies.[3]

Notes

1 One feddan = 1.038 acres.

2 E£ refers to the Egyptian pound = 100 piasters = 1000 milliemes. This was officially virtually at par with the pound sterling until May 1962, when the official selling rate was changed from E£1 = $2.838 to E£1 = $2.30.

3 I am greatly indebted to Professor Dr Ismail S. Abdalla, Director of the Institute of National Planning, Cairo, who generously gave his time to discuss considerable points in this essay and brought important ideas to my attention.

References

Among the many sources from which the information in this essay was drawn are the following:

Abdalla, Ismail S., 'Theoretical basis of organizing the public sector', Arabic Center of Political and Economic Studies, Al-Ahram Organization (1970).

Awad, Fouad H., 'Industrial policies in the ARE', *L'Egypte Contemporaine*, vol. 64, no. 351 (1973), pp. 5–54.

Central Bank of Egypt, *Economic Review*, Cairo: various series

El Darwish, M., 'The 1947 sterling balance negotiations', *L'Egypte Contemporaine*, vol. 57, no. 325 (1966).

El-Gritly, A., 'A development of the banking system', Cairo: Egyptian Society of Political Economy, Statistics and Legislation 1960 (in Arabic)

Girgis, M. *Industrialization and trade patterns in Egypt,* Tübingen: Mohr 1977

Hansen, B., and Marzouk, G. A., *Development and Economic Policy in the UAR Egypt*, Amsterdam: North-Holland 1965

Hanafi, M. N., 'Labour absorption in the Egyptian economy', unpublished Ph.D dissertation, 'Ain-Shams University, 1973

Harbison, F. H., and Fbralism, I. A., *Human Resources for Egyptian Enterprise*, New York: McGraw-Hill 1958.

Issawi, Charles, *Egypt at Mid Century*, London: Oxford University Press 1954

Khalaf, Hussein, *Innovations in the Modern Egyptian Economy*, Cairo 1962 (in Arabic)

Mabro, R., *The Egyptian Economy, 1952–1972*, Oxford: Clarendon Press 1974

Mabro, R., and Radwan, S. *The Industrialization of Egypt, 1939–1973*, Oxford: Clarendon Press 1976.

Mead, D. C., *Growth and Structural Change in the Egyptian Economy*, Yale University Press 1967.

Murad, M., and Moursi, F., *Foreign Currency Budget and Foreign Financing of Development with Special Reference to the UAR*, Cairo 1967.

O'Brien, P., *The Revolution in Egypt's Economic System*, London: Oxford University Press 1966.

Shafiri, M. Zaki, *Introduction to Money and Banking*, 3rd ed., Cairo 1956 (in Arabic).

5 Zambia

Jonathan H. Chileshe, *Chief, Trade and Financial Relations with the Third World Countries Section, UN Economic Commission for Africa**

Evolution of indigenization policy

To Zambia, the attainment of political independence from the British government on 24 October 1964 was just the beginning of a brave effort towards economic independence. Before British rule, the country (then called Northern Rhodesia) had been ruled by a variety of colonizing institutions. The most important one for the purposes of our present work comprised the British South African Company and its mining associates, which were primarily concerned with exploiting the country's mineral and commercial wealth.[1] The British government took over when the territory was turned into a British protectorate. The influence of British rule continued on the basis of shared responsibility with certain local expatriate vested interests. The British government's presence also continued during the period fo the now defunct Federation of Rhodesia and Nyasaland, as well as during the relatively short period of transition to political freedom (Kwacha) before the country became an independent and sovereign state.

At independence, the country's leadership awoke to realize how almost the entire economy was in the control of expatriates, mostly Europeans and Asians.[2] Copper and other mineral resources have given the country a reasonable chance to obtain sufficient foreign exchange for development, however. Zambia's Emergency Development Plan was designed to make a start on some of the many things left undone during the days of the Federation of Rhodesia and Nyasaland. This was followed by the K600 million First National Development Plan (FNDP), whose six principal targets had been defined as: the expansion of education linked to a Zambianization programme; expansion of health and social welfare; expansion of transport and communications; diversification of the economy; growth of incomes, employment and prices; and the narrowing of the existing gap between rural and urban sectors.

* The views expressed in this article are the author's, and do not necessarily represent those of his organization.

Pioneering indigenization in Zambia

Indigenous Zambians suffered profound racial discrimination before independence. For instance, it was against convention and the law of the land in colonial days for indigenous Zambians to be served on the same shop counters as expatriates, and there were many organized boycotts by indigenous Zambians aimed at breaking such discrimination in the expatriate-owned shops.

Notwithstanding the disadvantageous position in which racial discrimination placed Africans in the colonial period, an impressive list of indigenous Zambians showed an entrepreneurial zeal. Areas in which they excelled included transport, shops and groceries, hotels and retaurants, bars and, to a very limited extent, private law practice and freelance journalism. It is worth recalling that a number of indigenous Zambians were in fact quite active in the activities listed above long before the landmarks set in the Mulungushi and Matero economic reform programme – except, however, that the spread of their activities were rather too thin, and tended to be rather narrowly concentrated geographically.

The biggest area of economic and commercial concentration in the pre-independence era was the Luapula Province, with a thin spread into the Northern Province and later into some townships on the Copper Belt. The more notable indigenous Zambian pioneers in the commercial and transport sectors, whose activities covered the Luapula, Northern and Copperbelt provinces, were the Musango Brothers, Nsemukila, Kosta, the Mwenso Brothers, Luka Mumba, Kapesha, the Kalyafye Brothers, Kashimbaya and the Chisakula Brothers. Willie Harrington and Mubonda and sons were most active in the Western Province (formerly Barotse Province), while Dimba Brothers of Chikankata and Zalomuis of Choma concentrated their business activities in Southern Province; Thom Manda concentrated in the Central Province with his fleet of buses plying as far as Mumbwa; and Ziloli Mawere with a chain of stores and buses operated in the Eastern Province.

A majority of the pioneering Zambian business entrepreneurs who operated in the Luapula, the Northern and the Copperbelt provinces exhibited a somewhat common background. Almost all of those listed above had spent the early part of their lives in the Shaba Province of Zaire (formerly Katanga Province of Belgian Congo). It was there that they had observed and possibly participated in commercial activities. Indigenous Zaireans had impressed them by their ability to make strong headway by their business survival techniques despite the keen competition of expatriate Greek traders.

Investigations have revealed that Messrs Nsemukila, Kosta, Kapesha,

Luka Mumba, the Mwenso Brothers, Kalyafye Brothers, etc., had acquired their economic strength from trading in fish, which had proved to be very lucrative. Others among them branched out by trading in second-hand garments, which they bought from Zaire to sell in Zambia and Southern Rhodesia as hawkers using bicycles. It was only later that they were able to enter into more stable business operations like establishing home stores dealing in groceries and including the setting up of bars on the Zambian side of the Luapula river. The sale of 'Simba' beer was a very lucrative line of business. This beer was ferried across the Luapula River from Zaire for sale in the Zambian bars because Zambians living along the river could not easily obtain the Zambian local brew of castle or lager beer, and were in any case prevented by law from drinking European beer.[3]

Business centres were soon established at Lukwesa and Mwansabombwe villages and later spread to Mansa (formerly Fort Rosebery) and Samfya. With these developments came the emergence of bus transport services owned and operated by indigenous Zambians. The buses mostly plied between business centres within the Luapula Province and between those rural business centres and outlying places in the Northern and the Copperbelt provinces. Other bus transport services, provided by the other indigenous Zambians, began to emerge at about the same time in the Eastern, Central and Southern Provinces, though on a much smaller scale.

Pioneering by indigenous Zambian entrepreneurs was extended to even more sophisticated fields, including the establishment of hotels and restaurants. For instance, commercial entrepreneurship of the late Luka Mumba involved the owning and operating of a number of shops, and a boat service at Samfya; by that time he had gained so much confidence and experience that he decided to establish a modern hotel at Mansa. A number of hotels were soon established at Mwansabombwe and Lukwesa by the Chisakula Brothers on similar lines to those demonstrated by Luka Mumba in Mansa.

The contributions of pioneering Zambians to the policy of indigenization deserve due recognition. Modest as those efforts might have been, it still must be appreciated that those who attempted only managed to reach such heights against considerable odds. There were no government support facilities on which an indigenous entrepreneur could fall back. It was more than a question of survival of the fittest in an unaccommodating economic environment; with few exceptions, the existing institutional machinery had been so tailored as to make it inappropriate for indigenous Zambians wanting to break the monopoly of expatriate interests.

A common characteristic of the pioneering Zambian businessmen was their humble beginnings and the exclusive dealing forced upon them by the prevailing economic conditions of the time. In almost all cases, their business operations were without government financial assistance. It is great wonder that a few of these indigenous businesses were even able to survive beyond independence and to become part of the era of the state economic reform programme.

The late Luka Mumba was not the only Zambian pioneer to penetrate some of the reserved expatriate areas of control. For instance, Fitzpatrick Chuula, SC, opened the first private law practice on Cairo Road in Lusaka, which was later taken over by Edward J. Shamwana, SC. The latter started his law career as an assistant solicitor with a private expatriate law firm of Messrs Martin and Company. It took a lot of courage on the part of that firm to employ a Zambian lawyer. Mr Shamwana later moved into the legal department of the Lusaka City Council and became the first indigenous Zambian legal advisor. The public sector had accommodated the first indigenous lawyer in its operational structure. This action deserves to be highlighted as being of singular importance in dealing with the process of economic indigenization at the level of the local authorities. In April 1964, and before independence, Mr Shamwana established himself in private law practice in the premises that had earlier been occupied by his Zambian predecessor.

The Shamwana pioneering spirit has been quite diversified. For instance, he was the first indigenous Zambian to take over an expatriate manufacturing enterprise (Willy-Kit Limited). Experience provided by people like Mr Shamwana, SC, taken together with those of the other earlier indigenous pioneers in the field of commerce, became a source of strength among a number of other emerging indigenous Zambian businessmen. It is not unlikely that the leadership provided in pre-independence could have been used to a certain extent to draw some lessons for championing the course of indigenization of the Zambian economy in the post-independence era. In fact, in the struggle for independence United National Independence Party (UNIP) must have seen the plight of indigenous businessmen to want to correct the anomaly with independence.

Other pioneers among the indigenous Zambians include Titus B. Mukupo and Tanner Malinki, who established the first ever indigenous freelance journalistic bureau in Lusaka's Cairo Road. Thus, the country's process of indigenization must of necessity be reckoned as a sum total of the present and unsolicited contribution of past pioneering indigenous Zambians in many varied callings.

Political independence and indigenization

The preceding analysis has shown that some indigenous Zambians have always been quite enterprising. Notwithstanding the denial of opportunity during the days of the early pioneers, some were able to make appreciable headway.

The conquest of freedom on the political front exposed many weaknesses in the country's economy and also certain areas of strength for the new nation. One major weakness at independence was the lack of control of the country's economy by indigenous Zambians. Politically, this was a situation that the new leadership could not tolerate for long. Under the circumstances indigenization of the economic sector became the government's main aim. However, the machinery for such a course of action had not as yet been properly formulated, apart from a few scattered pronouncements and some weak inherited institutions.

The concern with which this matter was viewed in the early post-independence days was difficult to establish, mainly because there was no real national policy formulated for the sole purpose of fostering indigenization. Perhaps the seriousness with which independent Zambia desired to attain economic independence could be ascertained on the basis of what was repeated more than once at the famous Mulungushi Rock.[4] The Zambian head of state and government reiterated this seriousness of purpose at Mulungushi during the National Council of the ruling United National Independence Party (UNIP). He then stated that it was the determination of the party and government to see that the country's economy was put into the control of the indigenous population. However, the time and method of implementation had not been spelt out at the same time, except that the President reaffirmed that 'Political independence without matching economic independence [would be] meaningless. It is economic independence that brings in its wake social, cultural and scientific progess of man. . . .'[5]

In laying the foundation of a national policy on indigenization, the party (UNIP) and government had partly to base their efforts on pre-independence promises. It was also necessary to take account of the existing situation because of the interrelationships between the various sectors in the economy. The complexity of the question at hand called for a careful examination of which methodology could be applied to obtain the desired results.

A policy of indigenization during the colonial era (both by the then Northern Rhodesia Government and the ill-fated Central African Federation of Rhodesia and Nyasaland) does not seem to have been coherently formulated. If it ever existed, its objectives made a total mockery of Whitehall pronouncements. Experience has in fact shown it to have run counter to the aims of guiding a protectorate to eventual full political and economic independence: colonial policy in this field showed that Whitehall did everything in its power to ensure the political and economic entrenchment of the minority non-indigenous population.

Colonial policy showed itself more clearly through legislation, and through the discharge of powers conferred upon its colonial administrators, both of which operated against the economic interest of the indigenous population. Colonial administrators showed the greatest mistrust about the advisability of placing the economy under the control of the indigenous native population. Discrimination against the indigenous Africans of Zambia (then Northern Rhodesia) was not a declared policy as such, but one that was vigorously pursued in practice by many at official level – it was not practised only by the private expatriate interest alone.

Indigenous Zambians were able to develop their businesses only in African townships. These were areas where competition from expatriate businesss was not allowed. Even here, control was exercised by a white minority resident community which controlled the municipal and city councils. African Zambinas could not be issued with trading licences in areas reserved for either Indian or European traders. They were frowned upon if they dared seek licences to engage in areas or sectors pioneered by expatriates.

Control of economic affairs was considered a preserve of expatriates only. This was a view to which the colonial administration lent much credibility. The expatriate groups guarded this privilage, which they considered as a right, with absolute jealousy. Exceptions occured only when and where it became administratively impracticable to effect direct and immediate day-to-day control, as was the case in the remote rural areas of the so-called native reserves. But even in these few instances, the non-indigenous group could continue to influence affairs from their central vantage positions. For example, Paramount Chief Chitimukulu of the Bemba or Parmount Chief Lewanika of the Lozi, who had tried to restrict certain business activities of expatriates in their respective areas, found it very difficult to exercise the powers that they thought they had. Such powers as they could exercise were dependent upon the dictates of expatriate interests, whose influence could be brought to bear with great force.

The colonial administration can be indicted for its failure to lay a foundation for the indigenization of the economic sector. Agriculture, for example, continued to suffer from a mixture of piece-meal plans; it developed in such a way that it proved not quite conducive to indigenization at independence and immediately after. The colonial administration had made it possible for commercial agriculture to be dominated mostly by non-Africans, having bent backwards to assist white expatriate farmers to obtain the commanding heights of the agriculture sector.

For instance, it was a common practice for non-African farmers to receive generous assistance from the state in the form of financial credit to purchase needed farm implements, and loans with which to purchase seeds and fertilizer. In addition, necessary feeder roads were also constructed in order to make the expatriate farming areas more attractive and commercially viable. Examples of this were the Mkushi Block and in the Kabwe and Lusaka areas, where expatriate farmers engaged in the cultivation of cash-crops, tobacco and maize. Large tracts of land were often cleared at public expense as a subsidy to expatriate farmers and as an added inducement to the newly recruited inexperienced expatriate farmers. Expatriate cattle farmers engaging in ranching and/or dairy farming were also given comparable generous government inducements to enable them to become viable commercial farmers.

This kind of help was not extended to indigenous African farmers. Where there was a semblance of concern for them, the measures were always too weak and the policy not sufficiently well thought out. The high degree of indifference shown by the colonial administration to the plight of the indigenous farmers engaged in non-export cash-cropping agriculture confirms the view that the colonial administration had never conceived a national policy of indigenization for African entrepreneurs in the agricultural sector.

The abuse of privilege by non-African farmers was an everyday occurrence prior to Zambia's independence. Many an unscrupulous non-African farmer reverted to buying African agricultural produce at much lower prices for sale at higher prices through their privileged institution, the Grain Marketing Board (GMB). Non-African (expatriate) farmers were helped in this by existing legislation which made such practices possible.

For instance, the Grain Marketing Board, as established under section 3 of the Act, together with other buying agents and any buying consumer of African controlled products, were empowered under sections 3 and 4 of Chapter 246 of the African Grain Marketing (Deductions) Ordinance to make certain deductions from the final price paid for products purchased from an African producer. Provision of this ordinance stated that the Board, a buying agent or a direct consumer of such items could make any such deductions as he thought fit in respect of:

1 any levy imposed under the provisions of section 15 of the African Farming Improvement Funds Ordinance;
2 transport charges; and
3 handling charges.[6]

With independence, there was to be a re-formulation of legislation aimed at indigenizing the agricultural sector. At the same time, solutions had to be worked out on all fundamental problems of Zambian agriculture which went beyond those narrowly defined by the former colonial masters. The agricultural sector was to acquire some singular importance in diversifying the economy from its over-dependence on mining; legislation that had confirmed the above position was soon totally re-ordered.

Another area of great concern was that of mining and related activities. This one sector had dominated the Zambian economic scene ever since the discovery of copper on the Copperbelt and lead and zinc at Kabwe (formerly Broken Hill). No national policy on indigenization in the mining industry had been formulated, in spite of the fact that the sector was the most important in the country's economy. The colonial Northern Rhodesia government can be said to have fostered the creation and perpetuation of artificial restrictions on the advancement of the African mine workers, and on their ability to acquire higher-level skills. It was content with the *status quo*, and was more concerned with receiving revenue from the mining companies, assessed as taxes imposed on profits made by the companies on their various undertakings. Apart from this, the mining companies were assured of no central government interference and could go about their business leisurely, with no concern about integrating the indigenous population at higher levels in the mining undertakings.

The duality of the Zambian economy at independence was markedly clear. Both the agriculture and the mining sectors had exposed the dominance of the money economy. They showed very clearly that the economy revolved around the copper mining industry. This one sector supplied over 90 per cent of the country's total exports and not very much lower a percentage of the country's revenue. In addition, the sector generated and still generates the greatest direct and indirect income that the country needs for development.[7]

Income generated by developing and exploiting Zambian mineral resources has largely been used by the bulk of its recipients (mostly expatriates) to buy imported goods. The expatriate individuals and enterprises took advantage of the liberal Zambian tax concessions in repatriating cash out of the country. The most commonly used avenues consisted of personal remittances and dividends to shareholders of the mining companies. At one time also they included payments by the

Northern Rhodesian government to the British South Africa Company in the form of royalties for mining concessions held in the country. In the latter connection it should be recalled that the British South Africa Company had been established by royal charter in 1889; under the royal charter, the British South Africa Company was authorized to acquire and develop mineral concessions over an area that was not too well defined.

The new Zambian leadership took the nation into independence with quite an impressive achievement: it pulled off the first successful economic coup over expatriate vested interests in the mining sector. The Zambian government decided upon a show-down with the British South African Company (BSA) with regard to royalties. It called for the immediate abolition of the remaining life of payment of the mineral concessions before Independence Day. The would-be Zambian government offered and paid the BSA the sum of UK£2 million on a take-it-or-leave-it basis. The BSA and the British colonial government tried but with no success to raise the figure of UK£2 million offered to near the UK£18 million that was first demanded by the Company.

This was the first ever bold step taken by the new leadership to demonstrate that it could control the direction of certain sectors of the economy. The main concern of the government then had been to gain and retain control, but not at the expense of upsetting the apple cart. This dilemma has always faced the Zambian government, because it realized that one of the biggest shareholders of the BSA was the Anglo-American Corporation.

The new Zambian government had all along been quite aware of the considerable power wielded by the Anglo-American group in its own country's mining industry. The government was also aware that Anglo-American had the external means to use its power, if it so wished, to the detriment of Zambia's short-term future development because it operated in an area that more than constituted Zambia's lifeblood.

It was a very wise move on the part of the new government to take over the control of the remaining life of the concessions; otherwise it would have been held to ransom under the existing laws of Northern Rhodesia by an expatriate company. The laws of Northern Rhodesia, in fact, gave the rights to prospecting a clear and definite definition: prospecting, and any general development of the country by the government of the day, would have to depend first on safeguarding the interests of the BSA, whose claims to Zambian lands was quite extensive.

It must be recalled here that the rights and obligations of prospectors had been clearly defined under Chapter 91, sections 19 and 20, in the Laws of Northern Rhodesia. The law demanded that the prospector(s) should first obtain the permission of the property-owner before he could work near such items as buildings, ploughed land, growing crops, roads, dams and various other places.[8] It is possible that the concession owners would have found no difficulty at all under the law in inhibiting the proper functioning of the new government.

In a way, it was rather fortunate that the loss of face suffered by both the BSA and its principal shareholders (Anglo-American Corporation) over the royalties settlement did not result in any serious adverse economic effects for the new independent Zambian government. This was mainly because of the good negotiating tactics employed by the Zambian government. The settlement did not alienate a considerable number of outsiders. It was also fortunate in that it did not alienate the expatriate miners within the country itself, on whom the smooth functioning of the mines so heavily depended at the time.

During the pre-independence era, the United National Independence Party (UNIP) had declared itself committed to fighting for political independence as a stepping stone to the fight for economic independence. Once political freedom (Kwacha) had been attained, attention was to be turned to other fronts. It is therefore not surprising that the objectives of the UNIP's pre-independence constitution should have included, among other things,

1 the abolition of all forms of discrimination and segregation based on race, colour, tribe, clan and creed;
2 the need to secure the most equitable production and distribution of the wealth of the country in the best interests of the people of Northern Rhodesia;
3 the protection and promotion of trade, industry and agriculture in the interest of the people by legislation, and the protection of the interest of commercial traders and aid for them in their progressive businesses and schemes;
4 co-operation with industrial and other organizations and an acceptance of their affiliation, provided that such organizations complied with the policy and principles of the UNIP.

It has already been pointed out that, at independence, almost the entire Zambian economy was being controlled by expatriate Europeans and Asians. Expatriate interests not only controlled but also owned the country's largest business enterprises. Any of the would-be budding indigenous businessmen or enterprises in fields outside simple commerce, such as law or accountancy, were soon overshadowed by the incursion of aliens who opted to acquire immediate Zambian citizenship.

In the absence of any formulated national policy on indigenization, the expatriate and the newly enfranchized business interests found it relatively easy to continue to exploit Zambia's post-independence economic boom. Many of the expatriate business interests made excessive profits with no attempt to re-invest in the local economy or to help in its future development. Instead, they embarked upon a policy of impoverishing the economy by repatriating the profits to their countries of origin.

In 1968 President Kaunda found it necessary to point to the extent to which profiteering by the expatriate business enterprises had grown in spite of the fact that his country had been independent for only a short space of time. The Zambian President pointed out that he had observed that 'net profits, and I repeat, net profits, of some firms taken over amounted to between 25 and 30 per cent of turnover. . . . Dividends were often 100 per cent and 150 per cent of capital. Of course, there have been firms which have been making losses but closer examination of their affairs revealed that when the Zambian company was making a slight loss, the parent company was enjoying administration fees as high as 10 per cent'.[9] Under such a situation, one can appreciate the motivation that must have driven the UNIP, the government and the people of Zambia after a few years of independence to decide to put the economy under effective local control and ownership.

Indigenization and public corporations[10]

Pursuing a policy of indigenization is only part of the country's many efforts to foster development. The Zambian experience has shown more clearly that the process is one that is subject to a number of pressures, many of which can not easily be mobilized except at considerable cost to the economy. At one time or another I have offered certain general informed observations regarding indigenization. Writing for *Enterprise*, a Zambian magazine, I observed that there was merit in the state's being selective with regard to its participation. The article contained among other things advocacy that 'no State should attempt to undertake all levels of activities since that would be tantamount to accepting the lack of any enterpreneurship among its people whom it wished to direct. . . .'[11]

Zambia's economic reforms, as announced at Matero[12] in August 1969, were a mere continuation of the Mulungushi reform programme of April 1968. Both had the same objectives. The latter reform announcements reiterated in clearer terms all the principal objectives of the economic reform programme. Basically, they were aimed at the removal of foreign domination of Zambian economic life through the acquisition of control of most of the major means of production and services. At the same time, steps were put in hand for the development of genuine Zambian business enterprises.

An account of the achievements and progress made through the economic reform programme was presented by the government of Zambia in 1974 during the tenth independence anniversary celebrations. Research conducted by the author and discussions held with some UNIP members of the Central Committee, Cabinet ministers, executive heads of various parastatals and certain government and private sector officials, including the study of various public documents, reveal degrees of progress, areas of policy contradictions and continuing efforts to achieve targets. It would appear that the principal objective of all these structural changes was aimed at redressing the balance of economic power.

Through the 1968 economic reform programme, the Zambian government acquired over twenty-six major companies in the field of wholesaling and retailing, building materials and transportation. In addition, expatriate businesses were restricted to prescribed areas in the major urban centres. Companies were directed to plough back profits for re-investment in the country. The government placed limits on the amount of dividends and profits that could be remitted out of Zambia. Local borrowing by expatriate businesses was also restricted, since this then came within the ambit of the exchange control. The programme also tried to provide an opportunity for the indigenous population to acquire necessary finance for business undertakings and to operate over a wider area than was permissible before independence.

Zambia's aim of assuming control of the mining sector came closer to reality with an announcement that was made on 11 August 1969. In his famous Matero Speech, the Zambian President expressed public disappointment at the lack of any real development by the mining companies:

> First of all, I want to say to the mining companies that I am very disappointed at the virtual lack of mining development since independence. Apart from very small developments at Kalengwa and Mimbula Fitula and some further development at existing mines, we have seen nothing. The companies claim that the royalty system has been against new development. Nevertheless, I think they have not done enough towards further development of the country in which they make their great profits. Let me also say that I do not agree with the mining companies that royalties have been an obstacle to the development of the industry. I have been following their accounts and I know very well that they could have embarked upon further expansion if they chose to devote part of their profits for the purpose. Instead of reinvesting, they have been distributing over 80 per cent of their profits every year as dividends.[13]

In conclusion of this castigation of the shortcomings of the mining industries, the President then proceeded to invite the two mining companies, Roan Selection Trust and Anglo-American Corporation, to sell at least 51 per cent of their shares to the government.[14] The government had at last declared its intention to be an active owner with the private sector in exploiting its own mineral resources from then on.

As part of the economic reforms, the government had also acquired full and partial control over a number of new industries, banking and financial institutions. However, with regard to the banking sector it was considered prudent that the state create its own commercial bank (the Commercial Bank of Zambia) alongside those operated by Barclays, Standard and National and Grindlays Banks. The government also decided as part of its reform programme to take full control over all existing foreign-owned building societies and insurance companies.

The government's economic reform programme included prescribing areas and types of business in which expatriate business could continue to operate. The list of these prescribed commercial activities included retailing and wholesaling and was in addition to (1) builders' hardware and tools, (2) ammunition and arms, (3) bakery products, (4) furniture and householding fittings, (5) curios and antiques, (6) meat, fish and meat and fish products, (7) carpets and linoleum, (8) agricultural supplies and fertilizers, (9) jewellery and watches, (10) coal and coke. In order to implement this policy, it was decided to withhold the renewal of existing licences held by expatriates and not to issue new ones to them in the areas from which they had been excluded.

It was not as if the Zambian government was starting from scratch over everything. Thus, some attempt was made to use existing structures or machinery in implementing the new policy of indigenization. The Industrial Development Corporation (Indeco), an already existing government industrial and commercial body, was expanded to ensure the efficient and smooth running of the various industrial and commercial enterprises that had been taken over.

However, new mechanisms had to be created in areas where none existed, for the purpose of ensuring the implementation of the reforms. In case of the mining sector, the government set up the Mining Development Corporation (Mindeco) to look after the mining industry, viz. (1) Roan Consolidated Mines (RCM), (2) Nchanga Consolidated Copper Mines (NCCM) and (3) other existing and potential minerals and rights.

Operations covering transport and communications were to be supervised by the newly established National Transport Corporation (NTC). Under its umbrella were such subsidiaries as the Zambia Tanzania Road Services Ltd, Bulk Carriers of Zambia Ltd, United Bus Company of Zambia Ltd and Contract Haulage Ltd. In the course of time, the National Transport Corporation created a branch that operated a fleet of taxis (ZAMCAB) in response to a much needed commuter service in heavy populated urban areas.

The government had been experimenting in other directions in the course of these developments, basically with the hope of finding a most suitable form or forms for ensuring effective control. It had, for instance, set up the Ministry of State Participation with Andrew Sardanis as permanent secretary. Sardanis combined the post of permanent secretary of this new ministry with his old post of chairman of Indeco. A similar kind of managerial experiment was later repeated when Andrew E. Kashita was appointed Minister of Mines and Industry and still retained the post of executive chairman of Indeco.

The newest creation of public enterprises emerged in the field of finance. The government created the Financial Development Corporation (Findeco) to look after financial institutions like banks, insurance companies and building societies. The old Indeco institution and the newly created state machineries soon became subsidiaries of the Zambia Industrial and Mining Corporation (ZIMCO), which had earlier been constituted as the government holding company for Indeco and Mindeco.

Conclusion

The evolution of a Zambian policy of indigenization can be told in a variety of ways. This particular attempt cannot claim to have covered all aspects of the issue. A lot of other areas, especially such recent developments as the setting up of the Metal Marketing Corporation Limited (MEMACO), National Hotels Corporation Limited (HTC), National Import and Export Corporation Limited (NIEC), etc., have had to be temporarily excluded – not because they are not important, but rather to avoid over-dramatization of the issue. However, many of these will be referred to in the latter part of this chapter.

This analysis of evolution in policy and measures lays a basis for comparison with events in other parts of independent Africa. It also makes clear the fact that the intentions were noble and that the government had at least made some start in certain directions. But the process is not one that could be said to be based on any plan or policy resulting from evolutionary studies or discussions. It became a national policy in the light of Zambianization.

In this regard, this rather brief summary might as well draw on a message attributed in 1970 to the Zambian president, Dr K. D. Kaunda, in which he stressed the importance of state control in the face of development:

Development means much more than the statistics of growth. . . . It is still less than six years since independence and we have far to go. But already the reforms I announced at Mulungushi in 1968 and Matero in 1969 have done much to lay the foundations for a man-centred society. Some have called this nationalization. *It is, in fact, participation by Zambians in the control and ownership of the key sectors of their country. . . .*[15]

Legalizing the process of economic indigenization

A characteristic weakness of contemporary economic theory on indigenization is often the absence of any analysis of its principal legal aspects. Perhaps the difficulty arises from the fact that many economists have been too long exposed to a traditional approach, so that any other way of looking at the issue seems rather unorthodox and unacademic. It can only be regretted that this attitude has been permitted to continue over such a long period. In fact, legal aspects ought to be considered as complementary and necessary ingredients of planning for development.

A number of reasons will emerge as the analysis progresses to show the worthiness of this approach. Disregard of the legal aspects, or the lack of them in assessing and evaluating indigenization, would very much render incomplete the principal objective of this analysis. Economic and industrial development are an integral part of the process. Both must be nurtured within a given legal framework. My description thus far of early indigenous entrepreneurship and of the evolution of a Zambian policy on indigenization becomes more relevant when viewed against a clearly defined geographical legal boundary.

Merit exists, therefore, in calling for a much closer look at some of the legal aspects of the Zambian economic reform programme. Similarly, an examination of the Mulungushi and Matero economic reform programme would have to be on the basis of a certain relevant legal framework. In this connection, it will be useful to inquire into certain types of relationships, for instance, that which must exist between the timing and time lag of the announcements of the programme on one hand and the formulation of legal instruments to give effect to the pronouncements on the other. In a country like Zambia, where the rule of law continues to exist, it would not be possible to call for immediate action on certain activities unless due process of law has been complied with.

I do not intend to devote a considerable part of this study to analysing all the legal aspects of the Zambian national policy on indigenization, but I shall attempt to provide a summary of some of the more relevant regulations and laws.

Zambia's experience with the activities of a majority of expatriate business interests has not been a happy one. A majority of these interests can be accused of undermining the country's economic reforms. This was made possible because Zambia had inherited the old Northern Rhodesian legal system, which was ill-equipped to deal with the demanding situation arising at independence since it was not designed to provide for the indigenization of the economy.

In the short run, expatriate business interests were able to create a variety of economic undercurrents aimed at disrupting the economy after independence. For instance, many of them simply decided to run down their stocks. In this way, they managed to create shortages. Given the added advantage of their dominance of the economic sector, it is not surprising that such actions resulted in some serious temporary disruptions to the economy.

Similarly, local expatriate financial institutions were less accommodating in furthering the objectives of economic indigenization. The attitude of the expatriate lending institutions towards indigenous borrowers was one of considerable indifference. Through a carefully thought out pattern, they were able to adopt tactics of vacillation in dealing with applications from would-be indigenous borrowers. Applications from the latter were subjected to a finer degree of scrutiny, which delayed processing. This is because the banks continued to consider indigenous borrowers as a considerable financial risk.

There was no legal provision that could prevent or force either the local expatriate financial institutions or the other expatriate commercial interests to adopt a more favourable attitude towards indigenization of the Zambian economy. In fact, it would seem as if the programme on indigenization had been launched in total disregard of the undercurrents that expatriates were capable of creating in the economy – the Zambian government had relied too much on the 'carrot' in the form of appeals and less on the 'whip', which could have been provided only by its legal machinery.

The long-term adverse effects on the Zambian economy by expatriate interests are well known. The continuing dominance of expatriates in the various economic sectors of the country implied a need for prolonged remedial efforts. For instance, takeovers of certain expatriate business interests proved quite difficult. In many instances, management continued to be in the hands of former expatriate owners. There was very little that the legal system could do to ensure that the retained expatriates' managerial personnel conformed to furthering the objectives of indigenization.

Zambian experience has also shown that, although the state was the paymaster, this did give it the power to call the tune, except in a most general and rather remote way. Abrupt stoppage of expatriate operations initiated by state action was often followed by loss of foreign contacts and foreign supply. The Zambian legal system found itself unable to enforce a continuation of the supply line between the original foreign outside suppliers and the new local owners. Furthermore, offers of exemptions as an attempt to attract foreign investment carried certain risks. In the final analysis, they have tended to loosen the extent to which the state or the nation can exercise full control over certain sectors of the economy.

Putting the economic reform programme into effect took a relatively long time because of the time required to effect appropriate legislation. The Zambian legislative machinery exhibits most of the bureaucratic red tape of the British system. Thus, it is quite difficult for anyone or any institution to attempt to take arbitrary action or to bypass the various stages of the system. In other words, the system is not the kind that would assist an attempt to gain quick control of the economy.

A select list of certain laws of the Republic of Zambia presented in a summarized form may not be the best way to understand the country's policy of indiginizing the economy, but as a background, it can possibly help one to appreciate some of the issues and the framework in which the Zambian policy might have been developed. It could also be used to show the extent to which the government may have been able to use its legislative machinery in legalizing the policy. An illustrative list of the few selected laws of Zambia now follows:

1 Chapter 329 – Mines and Minerals Act;
2 Mines Acquisition (Special Provision) (Amendment) Act 1973;
3 Chapter 356 – National Agricultural Marketing Act;
4 Chapter 686 – The Companies Act;
5 Chapter 707 – The Trades Licensing Act.

Summaries of each of these Acts will be presented in a manner that preserves clarity and uniformity. They will include some degree of stress on certain sections which have some direct relevance to the policy of indigenization of the Zambian economy. Similarly, it will be necessary to include a legal interpretation of each of the Acts, and in certain other cases to refer to amendments which may have been made to the original Act pursuant to the economic reform programme.

We have already referred in some detail to the mining industry as an important economic sector. It was not surprising, therefore, that the government should have been faced with the problem of regularizing the supervisory authority over the mines. The government's decision to redeem in full the 51 per cent of the remaining equity shares still left a lot of room for expatriate company interests, because the indigenous Zambians in the mines and in the country were not yet in a position immediately to take over all the many facets of mining.

January 1970 saw the enactment by the Zambian Parliament of the Mines and Minerals Act (Chapter 329). This act was intended, above all else, to regulate the the law relating to mines and minerals, to provide for the granting, renewal and termination of mining rights; to establish a Mining Affairs Appeals Tribunal and define its jurisdiction; to define offences and provide for the making of regulations; and to provide for matters connected with or incidental to what was set out in the sections and sub-sections of the Act itself.

Provisions of the Act under sections 2 and 3 are of singular importance in respect of the indigenization of the economy and in particular the mining industry.

The legislative machinery is very often considered the most effective instrument, in several ways, for controlling a country's economic activities. Many actions are attributable to powers derived from legal provisions. For instance, sub-sections 1 and 2 of section 3 of Chapter 329 vests all rights to all minerals in the country in the president on behalf of the Republic. The vesting relates to ownership in mines and to searches for, and mining and disposition of, minerals. Provisions of sub-section 1 above take effect pursuant to sub-section 2 of section 3, Chapter 329; but, notwithstanding any ownership or otherwise that any person may possess in, and to the soil or under which minerals are found or situated. Thus, the action of vesting is not all that absolute, because others can lay counter-claims should it seem that they are about to be dispossessed.

Other provisions of the Act, together with the subsequent amendments to the Act, should have enabled the government to ensure control of the mining sector. One such amendment was the Mines Acquisition (Special Provision) (Amendment) Act 1973,[16] which was enacted in September 1973 in order to remove certain exchange control privileges previously enjoyed by the mining companies.

Existence of the Act with its subsequent amendments, as well as the creation of certain institutions, had demonstrated that the government had the means to effect and monitor affairs in the country's mining sector. However, legislation alone could not achieve the principal objectives. The legal system had to be supported by institutions capable of enforcing the new laws and regulations in order to be able effectively to control the mining sector. With this realization came the creation of Mindeco, a subsidiary of the Zambia Industrial and Mining Corporation (ZIMCO) chaired by the country's president.

A second piece of legislation of some direct relevance was the Trades Licensing Act – Chapter 707. This Act amended the law relating to licensing of certain businesses and provided for matters incidental to, or connected with, trade or commerce. The Zambian Ministry of Trade and Industry had put out what was called a 'Blueprint for Economic Reforms'.[17] The blueprint named January 1972 as the crucial date when existing systems of expatriate-owned businesses had to end.

The Act and the subsequent ministry blueprint attempted to explain the restriction message within the framework of the Mulungushi and Matero economic reform programme. It identified areas of restricted activities, types of individuals to be discriminated against, permissible partnerships, types of body corporates and goods that would be subject to control and restricted to indigenous Zambians, irrespective of how the latter constituted themselves. Thus, the licensing system was, for the first time in the country's short history since independence, being deployed to implement the above objectives.

Thus, sub-sections 1 and 2 of section 3 of the Act states that:

1 No person shall sell goods by way of business –
  (a) unless he is the holder of a licence; or
  (b) otherwise than in accordance with the terms of such licence.

2 Any person who contravenes the provisions of this Section shall be guilty of an offence.

Sub-section 1 of section 5 of the Act details various licences that may be issued under the Act;

(a) a Trading (Wholesale) Licence;
(b) a Trading (Retail) Licence;
(c) a Commercial Traveller's Licence;
(d) a Hawkers Licence;
(e) a Pedlar's Licence;
(f) a Pedlar's (Restricted) Licence;
(g) a Stall Licence;
(h) a Restricted Licence.

Section 9 of Chapter 707 of the Act specifies the country's licensing authorities. Sections 3, 5 and 17 of the Act set out the implied restrictions relating to trading. They also classify by types of licences and the restriction of certain licences to non-citizens and penalties for the avoidance of such licences.

In the terms of sub-section 10 of section 5 of the Act it was possible for a 'restricted licence' to be issued, but a non-indigenous trader had to fulfil other stipulations in the Act. Such a licence was to authorize the sale of tobacco, cigarettes, breadstuffs, pastry, confectionery and non-alcoholic beverages by any person named therein:

(a) on any railway station or airport specified therein if such person has no store or place of business on such railway station or airport; or

(b) at premises situated in any area specified therein other than a municipal or township.

Section 17 of the Act was amended by Statutory Instrument no. 41 of 1969 pursuant to decisions taken both at Mulungushi and Matero restricting the issuance of certain licences to non-citizens and the avoidance of such licences. Section 28 of the Act gave powers of prescribing (1) areas, (2) goods, (3) wholesale areas and (4) reserved licences other than the commercial traveller's licences.

Sub-section 1 of section 17 of the Act as amended demanded the issue by licensing authorities of certain restricted licences to non-Zambian citizens and avoidance of such licences:

Save with the consent in writing of the Minister, no licensing authority [could] issue a reserved licence to an applicant who is not a citizen of Zambia unless:

(a) in the case of application for a reserved licence other than a trading wholesale licence:
 (i) A. the area in which the applicant intends to sell goods is wholly within a prescribed area, and
 B. at the time the application is made, the applicant is the holder of a licence authorising him to sell such goods in such area in the same manner of business as the licence applied for would, if issued, authorise: or
 (ii) the goods in respect of which the application is made are prescribed goods;

(b) in the case of an application for trading (wholesale) licence:
 (i) A. the area in which the applicant intends to carry on business as a wholesaler is wholly within a prescribed (wholesale) area, and
 B. at the time the application is made, the applicant is the holder of trading (wholesale) licence authorising him to carry on business as a wholesaler in such area;
 (ii) the goods in respect of which the application is made are prescribed goods.

Sub-section 2 of section 17 of the Act requires the licensing authorities to observe certain criteria in respect of the issuance of reserved licences to a body corporate or to a partnership of which a partner was a body corporate. In this connexion, it was stated that:

the Licensing Authority shall, unless such reserved licence is issued with the consent of the Minister, submit the case to the Minister for his consideration, and if the Minister is satisfied, after such inquiry as he may make or cause to be made with respect to such first mentioned body corporate or partnership, that such first-mentioned body corporate or partnership is not a citizen of Zambia, he may by statutory order, revoke such reserved licence.

Another area of concern to any Zambian policy of indigenization is agriculture. Over three-quarters of the Zambian population is estimated to live in the rural areas and derive their livelihood from agriculture. The difficulty of mobilizing effective self-generating effort in the Zambian rural sector may in part have been due to a mistaken concept of development. Agriculture is the mainstay of the Zambian rural sector, yet there has been a considerable lack of policy co-ordination at the level of production and marketing. Several agricultural products in the rural areas cannot find ready markets. Agricultural co-operatives have been mooted all over the country, but with little success. For instance, over half the 900 co-operatives established in the country up to 1968 turned out to be total failures, with the others merely struggling to exist. The legislation and laws under which agriculture has been developed and the established agricultural institutions have in many cases worked at cross-purpose to the principal objectives. Apart from poor management of some of the institutions, the same legislation seems to have contributed to the lack of proper and efficient marketing facilities.

Hitherto, we have had occasion to refer to Chapter 246 of the Laws of Northern Rhodesia and Federal Act no. 23 of 1957 relating to some marketing facilities for the country's agricultural produce. With independence and the new government's declared intention (at least at Mulungushi and Matero) to control the economy, it was only to be expected that some action would be taken in that direction.

In consequence, the government enacted Chapter 356 – the National Agricultural Marketing Act (no. 30 of 1969). The old Grain Marketing Board of Zambia and the Agricultural Rural Marketing Board were dissolved and ceased to exist by section 42 of the Act. The new Act created a National Agricultural Marketing Board (Namboard) and committees thereof: 'to prescribe the powers, functions and duties of such Board and Committees; to regulate and control the prices and marketing of certain agricultural products and agricultural requisites; and to provide for matters incidental to the Sections and sub-Sections of the Act'.

Thus the legal machinery was called into play, extending or making modifications to regulations relating to the agricultural sector. The Act was used to strengthen the hand of the government in its aim of breaking the backbone of foreign domination. In the words of the country's President, 'To the Zambian individuals it is important for me to say that . . . we have carried out all the political, economic, social, fiscal and legislative measures in order to make life easier and cheaper for all. The results of our actions may not be felt now. . . .'[18] Through its legal machinery, and by providing certain incentives, the state was attempting to bring the indigenous Zambians to the new frontiers of economic freedom and independence.

Experience in Zambia, in as far as indigenization through the legal machinery is concerned, has shown that the feat of promulgating and/or making amendments to existing laws alone is not enough. Such actions represent a mere nibbling at the edge of the real problem confronting Zambia's pursuit of economic independence. Control must not only be acquired, but it must be seen to have been acquired by the attainment of developmental as well as definitive directional results.

Directional results envisaged from changes in the legislative machinery have not been achieved as originally envisaged by the country's leadership. A number of expatriate enterprises have found many loopholes in the policy and the legislation itself. Both old and new laws and regulations have tended to give the leadership a false sense of satisfaction and security.

A typical example is the Companies Act – Chapter 686 of the laws of Zambia.[19] This piece of legislation was lifted from the old British Companies Act enacted in the 1920s and partially revised in the 1940s. There is no denying that this particular Act was nurtured under British commercial conditions. Transplanting the Act into Zambia and expecting it to apply to Zambian conditions without suitable changes was not only unrealistic but rather unfortunate. It should have been brought into alignment with the country's reform programme. Hence the Act has been found wanting as an effective instrument in implementing a national policy of indigenization of the economy.

According to the provisions of the Act, every company operating in the country must register with the Registrar of Companies and Patents. A minimum registration duty has been established at K10, at the rate of 25 *ngwee* for every K200 or part of declared authorized capital of the company. Working backwards, it is possible to establish certain other factors about this registration duty of K10. It implies that a minimum of K8000 must be declared as authorized capital for initial registration. The fact that an applicant declares a minimum of K8000 or raises the authorized capital to K100,000 or more cannot be taken to mean that the company will plough an equal sum of money into its operations. One other glaring shortcoming of the Act is shown by the lack of provision to compel companies registered to invest their respective authorized capital within the country or in operations associated with their companies over a specified period.

There is nothing in the Companies Act that prevents a company, after satisfying the legal requirements, to devalue its capital. Shares can be privately sold for anything below K1 per share. Thus, a declared authorized capital of K8000 could in practice represent only K2000 or less if and when sold at about 25 *ngwee* per share. The Act confers no powers of inspection or enforcement of its provisions on the Registrar of

Companies, who is the executing agent of the state. Such inadequacies tend to negate policy on indigenization of certain sectors of the economy. The Act should have been amended accordingly and made complementary with other Acts which may have been purposely promulgated to assist with the country's policy of indigenization. So far, there seems to be very little correlation between the Companies Act on one hand and, say, the Mines and Minerals Act (Chapter 329) and the Trades Licensing Act (Chapter 707) on the other.

Thus, figures obtained from the Registrar of Companies and Patents relating to the actual numbers of companies registered and the authorized capital declared in the country over any given period can be no indicator of the country's economic buoyancy. The register is of only limited use, both as a barometer of the country's rate of development and in the furtherance of indigenization. The Act makes possible the existence of a directory of company activity in terms of intention rather than actual operation. It is useful in establishing the names of directors, as demanded by certain sections of the Trades Licensing Act (section 17, Chapter 707), but even here, it is doubtful whether some of the names given on the register are in fact not a mere front.

The inadequacy of the Companies Act has now been recognized as requiring certain amendments, but rectification of some of its deficiencies has been rather slow. At the time of this research, I learned that the Law Development Commission of Zambia had put out a notice in the local press announcing its intentions of wanting to reform the Act. This revision exercise should be conducted together with that of the Pioneers (Industrial) Act, since both have much in common. In fact, the latter has proved beyond all doubt to be the most dis-investment legislation that was ever enacted by the Zambian Parliament. Monopoly power conferred upon certain Zambian enterprises in respect of pottery and transformer manufacturing has had the most long-term dis-investment and dis-indigenization effect in the Zambian economy. It is now an established fact that next to no appreciable tonnage of Zambian clay has been used in the manufacture of pottery. No transformers have ever been produced in the country to justify the action taken in granting of monopoly status pursuant to the Pioneer (Industry) Act.

In pursuit of Mulungushi and Matero economic reforms

A number of major economic developments have taken place from about 1969 as a result of the Mulungushi and Matero economic reform announcements. It is not possible to cover all of them in this rather limited space. Nevertheless, it is important not to view them simply as a matter of state versus private sector interests. Part of this conflict arose because, by the time the programme was actually announced, the economic situation had drifted to a stage where the private sector had everything to lose if it did not co-operate with the state in implementing the principal objectives of the country's economic reform programme.

To all intents and purposes, both the Mulungushi and Matero announcements could be listed among some of the country's great landmarks in the struggle for economic and industrial independence. The speed with which legislation was rushed through by the government in order to give those announcements a sense of legality could leave no one in any doubt about the serious commitment of the Zambian government to its policy. The government had used the platform provided by the Assembly at Mulungushi in 1968 and at Matero in 1969 to make clear some of its intentions as regards the future of the country.

It would seem as if the government had tried to clear its conscience. This is borne out by the government's declaration which stated that its hands had been forced by a visible lack of change of mind on the part of both small and big expatriate business interests. The government felt quite justified in accusing the latter of reluctance to share voluntary economic and industrial responsibility with the indigenous population. President Kaunda's 1970 speech showed very clearly that the state had been courting expatriate companies ever since independence, hoping all along that the latter would, without coercion, offer the state a meaningful partnership in the control of their business undertakings.

It is, however, a matter of conjecture whether the Zambian government would have been content with the existence of independent private expatriate business enterprises, assuming that they were not subject to greater local (Zambian) control. There was no evidence prior to the measures taken by the government that the private expatriate companies would soon invite the state into partnership, or that they were showing any real signs of change of attitude towards indigenization of the economy. The state was placed in a rather embarrassing situation of having to wait indefinitely. In the end therefore it was compelled to act: the state had either to set up its own industrial or commercial enterprises in direct competition with existing expatriate companies, or to force its entry by acquiring some or all of the expatriate-dominated companies.

Unfortunately, the bulk of the expatriate business interests failed to appreciate fully the seriousness of the issue at hand. In fact, they seemed taken aback by the president's announcement made in 1968 at Mulungushi. Hence, it was not until November 1970 that they were awakened to the fact that Zambia's destination was not going to be totally capitalistic or orthodox socialistic. Even then, it was not at all clear what meaning the Zambian leadership attached to its rejection of capitalism.

The Zambian president took the trouble, during the National Council of the United National Independence Party on 10 November 1970, to elaborate on how the state envisaged its assumption of control of the national economy. The president stated that the state had decided to participate in all the key areas of economy and industrial activity. The fact that there was no mention of nationalization meant among other things the retention in some *mild* form of capitalism. Regrettably, the head of state and government did not at the same time offer an explanation of the concept of state participation, except by inference of rejection of the principle of 'exploitation of man by man'. From the Zambian point of view, on the other hand, 'non-orthodox' socialism was above all else aimed at putting control in the hands of Zambians. It was not a matter of pursuing an ideology like nationalization for the sake of nationalization.

The government also spelled out what it considered to be the various options of state participation in the economy. There was no intention of a total elimination of non-indigenous business enterprises from the Zambian economy; all the same, it was made abundantly clear that the reins of control were to be taken over from the foreign companies who had played such a dominant role in the past.

This can be deduced from the ensuing laws and regulations formulated in pursuance of the Mulungushi and Matero economic reform announcements. It had been hoped by the government that, from both the Mulungushi and the Matero 'Declarations of Intent', the dominant expatriate companies would try to meet the government half-way. The expatriate companies had still very many options. One would have been for them rapidly to increase the participation of the indigenous Zambians in their businesses within the country, for example by initiating a system of localizing the personnel of their companies.

There was also a serious gap in effective control of the economy at the executive level in the expatriate companies, in terms of the share or lack of share of directorships held by indigenous Zambians before the Mulungushi and Matero economic reforms. The number of indigenous Zambians serving as board members in expatriate mining, industrial and commercial companies such as Anglo-American Corporation, RST Group, Barclays Insurance Companies, the Lonhro complex[20] and British-American Tobacco (BAT) were then insignificant and quite limited. It is only much later that Zambians began to join such boards. (Notable in this regard was the appointment of an indigenous Zambian, Mr Elias M. Chipimo, as chairman of Standard Bank of Zambia Ltd.) It was not so much a lack of indigenous talent upon which to draw, although admittedly most of the then available indigenous talent was employed by the Zambian government as civil servants. But the basic reasons for the non-participation of indigenous Zambians were the high degree of vested interests associated with dominant corporate groups in Southern Rhodesia and South Africa. It should be noted that many of these companies were still administered from Southern Rhodesia and South Africa; thus local companies did not, in fact, decide any policies, but simply carried out policies from their respective headquarters.

The importance of the mining industries to the Zambian economy was stressed above. Thus, this would seem a likely area in which to begin the examination of state participation.

The central government should have legislated to make it incumbent upon the expatriate mining companies to initiate appropriate training programmes aimed at enabling the indigenous Zambians to take over certain operations within a specific time. Admittedly, the mining companies had tried some semblance of training programmes. For instance, in the 'Copperbelt of Zambia Mining Industry Year Book for 1966' there appear words to the effect that the mining companies had not relaxed their policy of training and education within the industry:

> The mining companies not only maintained their long standing scheme of industrial training, increased the emphasis on a number of them, but in many aspects broke new ground in 1966 by launching additional training and educational facilities. Further to the 1965 programme of training for promotion and Zambianization these additional schemes meant that prospects for local employees were appreciably enhanced. The number of employees given formal education or training during the year was in the region of 15,000 at a cost to the industry of some three to three-and-a-half million pounds.[21]

The mining company in explaining how the money was spend, laid emphasis on what can be called areas of concentration within the field of training and education:

1 training for promotion;
2 learnership in occupations as wide-ranging as surveying, assaying, accounting, etc.;
3 selection and placement, which was being undertaken with the assistance of the government's Educational and Occupational Assessment Unit;
4 adult education, including scholarships and other forms of assistance given to enable selected individuals to attend courses of vocational training at colleges and universities both in Zambia and abroad;
5 induction training of new workers.[22]

The extent to which this much talked about training in the mining industry had taken root could only be judged against later results. Also of considerable significance to the training programme adopted by the mining companies were the Dagleish and Brown Commission Reports. In this regard, it might be useful to compare the 1966 position to that reflected in the Zambian Mining Year Book of 1973.[23]

Both the Anglo-American Corporation and the RST Group had by 1966 established for each of their mining operations an elaborate system of management consisting of a chairman, directors and administration for the separate groups, but with a lot of interlinkages created at directorate level. Some directors of one group also held directorships in the other group. The only group to have had an indigenous Zambian director on two out of six of its boards of directors was RST.[24] In contrast to RST, there was a total absence of an indigenous Zambian director or any of the boards of the Anglo-American Corporation, at least up to 1966. There were no indigenous Zambians in senior posts of administration in any of the groups.

However, in 1973 there were beginning to be some visible signs of change, particularly in the predominance of indigenous Zambians as directors. This was mainly a result of the Zambian government's having acquired 51 per cent equity participation,[25] rather than a voluntary act on the part of the expatriate mining companies. Possible areas for the mining companies to have played a significant role could have been in the localization of certain administrative posts. It is possible that the mining companies' training and investment cited in respect of 1966 could have begun to show certain signs of speeding up Zambianization. But even here, the trend was not at all general. It tended to confine itself to the Roan Consolidated Mines Limited (RCM), where the first indigenous Zambians were appointed as assistant managers of administration at the mines. Anglo-American Corporation had even found it impossible to place some three indigenous Zambians whom it had trained abroad.

By 1973, on the other hand, the post of company secretary in both the Nchanga Consolidated Copper Mines Limited (NCCM) and the Roan Consolidated Mines Limited had been turned over to indigenous Zambians – again, presumably because of government control and influence.

The Zambian government had already declared its intention to acquire majority ownership in the mining companies. There was no room for turning back the current. This decision did not go unchallenged in open debate, expressed mostly through the local and overseas press. For instance, a local newspaper carried a story on 29 November 1969 in which it alleged that a group of Zambian civil servants and businessmen had thought that the government had been outwitted in the negotiations leading to the acquisition of a 51 per cent equity participation against 49 per cent left to the mining companies, when the takeover agreement was concluded. The acquisition of the 51 per cent of RST and Anglo-American Corporation shares was obtained by the Zambian government at the cash price of K209 million, payable over a period of eight and twelve years respectively to the two companies, and the payment was subject to a fixed interest rate.

Subscribers to the above view were also disturbed by the fact that the Zambian government was continuing to pay management fees to the two companies, based partly on a percentage of sales, with the likely possibility of placing the government in the unfortunate position of paying millions of Kwacha a year to the mine management even though the industry might not be making a profit. Doubts were also voiced about just how effectively the government would exercise its control over the mining industry itself.

The mining takeover agreement concluded between the government and the two expatriate companies had a fixed expiry period. The agreement limited the possibilities and extent to which the Zambian government could make unilateral changes to certain of the fundamental contractual terms. Such action was possible only if the government was prepared to be called upon to redeem in full, and for that matter in United States dollars, the outstanding ZIMCO bonds (1978) and loan stocks (1982), payable for the government's 51 per cent shareholding in RCM and NCCM respectively. Above all else, the contract agreement had conferred a wide range of veto rights upon the 'B' directors in regard to financial policy of both NCCM and RCM. As it turned out, these particular provisions had been worked into the contract primarily to protect the interests of the minority shareholders.[26]

It is aspects of this kind, when taken together with other provisions in the agreement, that tended to subtract from the government the supposed reins of control resulting from the total takeovers of the mining industry. In addition to the management and consultancy contract, the minority shareholders comprising the Roan Selection Trust (RST) and Anglo-American Corporation (AAC) did also acquire a sales and marketing contract. In the course of this analysis, I have had personal discussions with several of the principal official negotiators. It has been stated that the above agreement had been reached as a compromise solution after protracted negotiations. Some still hold the view that it was both necessary and unavoidable at the time because of the complexity of the matter itself.

It has been argued all along by the protagonists that such a course of action was necessary in order to ensure a continuity of management and also to retain available technical know-how which the Zambian government could not provide from within or by the deployment of indigenous Zambians at the time of the takeovers. Perhaps George K. Simwinga must be credited for saying what many a Zambian must have thought about the deal at the time. Earlier we had occasion to refer to a newspaper story of 29 November 1969 which in fact cast the first doubts about the results of the negotiations. It is therefore logical to presume that Simwinga was not very much off the mark when he said that 'The cost of this continuity has been an absence of meaningful government control'.[27]

Comments on the terms of acquisition have not been lacking the world over. The issue has been a subject of considerable discussions in a number of learned academic books[28] and journals. It is an undeniable fact that the terms of acquisition were not a total victory for the Zambian government. This is because they conferred more than commensurate benefits on the 49 per cent minority shareholders over a period pending the redeeming in full of the bonds. To counter some of these weaknesses, the government resorted to creating certain institutional machineries. For instance, the Mining Development Corporation (Mindeco) was created and charged with handling the government's mining business interests on a commercial basis.

It was against the above background, and perhaps also to avoid unacceptable criticism as well as what was likely to be continuing internal adverse popularity, that the government took certain measures to overcome the disadvantages inherent in the contract. On 31 August 1973 the Zambian president announced certain measures that the government had decided to take in order to ensure effective control of the mining industry, notably to redeem the outstanding bonds in full in August 1973. Effects resulting from this action partly led to the Zambian economic crisis of 1975–6.

The Zambian government had kept its part of the bargain and had played the game according to the rules. The government was therefore able to introduce its own way of running the affairs of the mining industry. The first such act was to install the Minister of Mines and Industry as chairman of the two mining companies.[29] A board of directors was established, each to run the affairs of RCM and NCCM. Each board consisted of two classes of directors. Six 'A' directors represented the majority shareholders (the Zambian government). The government nominated indigenous Zambians for all its posts of 'A' directors.[30] The second category was designated 'B' directors, and five posts were allocated to represent the minority shareholders.

Another major step taken by the government was to counter the sales contract entered into with the mining companies. The government decided to establish a local metal marketing company. In the words of the Zambian Information Service, 'Through these measures Zambia [was] now in full control of the mining industry and [was] free to influence the management of the mining companies, since the managing directors of both RCM and NCCM are Government appointed, and to use the profits for the expansion of the industry and economy as a whole.'[31] The establishment of a local marketing corporation seems to have made some appreciable progress in the desired direction. The state had taken steps to ensure its control of that one sector. But such control to be meaningful had to be measured against the fulfilment of the main objectives that the government had first set itself.

It would be interesting to trace some of the effects that these moves created on the other sectors in the economy. One rather noticeable impact was the rapid rate of localization in a number of expatriate companies, partly out of fear of certain likely unpleasantness and partly out of a genuine desire to assist the government in carrying out its declared policy.

Available evidence would seem to point to the fact that the state was quite determined to check expatriate domination of the country's industrial sector. State participation in the mining sector did not in fact set the pace. Rather, it followed examples pursued in the other sectors of the economy, for example through activities carried out by the Industrial Development Corporation (Indeco). Indeco's organizational structure as a parastatal organ has had to undergo certain changes as a result of this general development. One such change was to make Indeco a subsidiary of a new parent company, the Zambia Industrial and Mining Corporation (ZIMCO), under the chairmanship of the country's president.

Indeco was already a well established public enterprise before the Mulungushi and Matero announcements. The state therefore had the advantage of an institutional structure which could, with certain improvements, be turned to good use, particularly if the government wanted quickly to implement a national policy on indigenization of the economy. Consequently, Indeco was empowered to negotiate values and terms of payment for fair value represented by book value of companies in which the state was to participate. The Zambian president had instructed the refusal of payment for such things as 'business goodwill or for future profits' for any of the expatriate companies acquired by Indeco on behalf of the state.[32]

The state has used the institutional structure provided by Indeco in its attempt to indigenize the country's industrial, commercial and financial sectors. The rather rapid and considerable growth of Indeco's activities in the last few years is a clear indication of this. This trend was particularly noticeable after the Mulungushi economic reform announcements. During the period 1969–71, Indeco grouped together over eighty subsidiary and associated companies. As an industrial and commercial enterprise, it represented quite a sizeable stake in the Zambian economy, approximately £70 million. Indeco's profits during the same period were estimated to represent about 21.8 per cent of shareholder's equity and about 7.7 per cent of group net assets. Indeco's profits before taxation in 1974 were about K31,619,000, or about K4,573,000 over those recorded in 1973, and represented a total turnover of about K332,394,999 as against about K286,002,000 in 1973.[33]

Industrial, commercial and financial activities of Indeco in the period 1969–73 were quite wide and far-ranging. They extended to breweries and textiles; to cement and an oil refinery, fertilizers, transport, property and hotels; to wholesale and retail trading and to finance, and also included rural enterprises. Prior to this period, government activity through Indeco had been confined to new business enterprises of special types, particularly those hardest to develop.

On the basis of available statistics, it has been possible to detail some of the activities embraced by Indeco in the recent past: one insurance banking company, in which it holds a 51 per cent share; two oil marketing companies, with shareholdings of 50 and 51 per cent respectively; 12 transport companies, in which the shareholding is between 51 and 67 per cent; 7 manufacturing companies where the shareholding is between 51 and 100 per cent; 4 companies in the field of consumer trading at 51 per cent shareholding; 8 companies dealing in building supplies in which the shareholding is between 51 and 100 per cent; 6 rural enterprise companies in which the shareholding is between 51 and 100 per cent; 4 property companies where the shareholding is between 80 and 100 per cent; and several associated companied in which Indeco holds shares of up to 50 per cent; and a wholly owned travel agency company.

Through Indeco, the state was able to obtain increased indigenous participation in the country's economy. Because of Indeco's shareholding, the privately controlled companies were obliged to accept a certain degree of localization of expatriate personnel of their companies. It was no longer a question of confining Zambians to posts of personnel officers. Indigenous Zambians were being appointed as general managers and directors to a number of company boards in which Indeco was a business partner. In this way, the government was beginning to exert a certain substantial degree of influence on the various sectors of the economy.

It can also be said that, through Indeco or its representatives, the government had created a channel for co-ordinating the policies of the public sector with those of the private sector. In the past there had been a clear absence of direct contact between the public and the private sectors in respect of co-ordination and harmonization of economic policy. The only way to ensure that this would occur was through the use of certain government institutions (ministries) to formulate legislation for observance by the private sector. The latter could make certain representations but was never consulted at the initial stages or during the preparatory stages of the legislation itself.

The composition of Indeco subsidiary companies as well as its field of activities have been subjected to change during its lifetime. Some of the changes were taken at the insistence of the government; others were introduced as a result of either internal or external pressures. One such external factor was Rhodesia's Unilateral Declaration of Independence and the insistence by the United Nations on all countries to apply economic sanctions against the Smith regime.

The indigenization policy of the private sector, proved to be quite a difficult task to implement. There is no denying that without direct state intervention very little would have taken place. There were still very many forces acting against the trend of events. Not least of these was the fact that some of the foreign private business interests were devising ways of undermining the credibility of the national indigenization policy. As mentioned earlier, financial assistance required by the indigenous Zambians to acquire certain specific operations was not forthcoming from the locally controlled expatriate financial institutions. Experience proved that the availability of finance in institutions not under direct state control could not be relied upon to further the objective of economic indigenization.[34] The would-be Zambian entrepreneur wishing to participate in the government's policy of indigenizing the economy was thus seriously constrained by the difficulty of obtaining necessary capital. In an attempt to overcome this constraint, the government decided to operate various loan schemes itself to assist its indigenous enterpreneurs.

It will now be useful to turn to some of the schemes that were operated through Indeco. One such scheme was established to cater for experienced existing and potential Zambian entrepreneurs. Loans under this scheme were offered at comparatively favourable rates of interest. Applicants were obliged to put up certain forms of security, like third-party guarantees or land or property title deeds.

Another scheme of a comparatively small nature in terms of size, individual amounts granted and the total fund allocated to it was established for the less experienced indigenous business community. The small loans scheme, as it was called, was intended for those indigenous Zambians who needed the helping hand of the government to stay in business. The government had already recognized the fact that without state support many Zambians had no hope of continuing to exist as business entities. The existing expatriate commercial financial institutions had already shown that they were not to be relied upon. The few Zambians who got approval for credit and loans were often notified too late for the recipients to take any advantage of the offered assistance. In most cases the approval was also given with a chain of conditions which the indigenous borrower often could not meet.

The small loans scheme was administered by Indeco and was based on decisions reached by a Small Loans Committee chaired by the then minister of state in the Ministry of Commerce, Industry and Foreign Trade. Loans approved by the Committee were used mostly to finance business purchases rather than for new real investment. The scheme seemed to suffer from the outset from the fact that the amounts allocated were not quite sufficient to enable the Committee to cover all the projects assessed that had been considered as meriting assistance. The limit imposed on the maximum amount that could be approved in one way or another proved a blessing in disguise for the continuation of expatriate domination. Similarly, it postponed the day of penetration by the indigenous entrepreneurs into a number of other areas still under foreign control.

Indigenous Zambian recipients of loans from financial institutions established by the state, particularly those made available through Indeco schemes, were required to make the bulk of their purchases from or through the Zambia National Wholesale Corporation (ZNWC) except when this was impracticable. This condition had the effect of partially reducing the dominance of some expatriate supply companies. Through this action the state was able to introduce a form of discrimination against the foreign-controlled commercial sector in favour of public sector institutions. At the same time, the state had also created competition in a field in which certain sections of the private sector had been enjoying what can be called an unimpeded freedom of commercial activity.

There is, however, one major project that was financed by the small loans committee which must be cited despite the limitation referred to above. This one major project has turned out to be in line with what the policy should have aimed at. A loan of some considerable amount (in terms of the average loans given by the Committee) was approved to enable the completion of the Kasama Kwacha Relax Hotel.[35] This was a significant act, for the completion of the hotel in Kasama added not only to that town's, but also to the country's rural commercial and hotel infrastructure. Furthermore, at a time when all hotels in the country were owned or leased by expatriate interests,[36] the funds made available were for a project that was to be solely owned and run by an indigenous Zambian. The state institution had shown through this action that it is capable of taking a calculated risk. It had also shown that the state could initiate competition not only with the private sector but also with enterprises in which the government itself had a commercial interest. Thus, the Kwacha Relax Hotel was going to be a direct competitor with the government's only guest house in Kasama and its neighbourhood, which up to that time was the only place providing quasi-hotel facilities.

Indeco was increasingly being actively involved in developing industrial and commercial activities in the rural areas under government guidance. This was in conformity with one of the government's objectives, which wanted the money economy to serve the development of its subsistence economy in the rural areas. Indeco's policy of indigenization must surely include activities undertaken by Rucom Holdings (also known as the Rural Enterprise Group). Underneath Rucom Holdings there were various operating companies, most of which were owned jointly with foreign investors. The most important of them consisted of maize milling, fishing, timber milling (Zambesi Sawmill), country hotels and Rucom Industries Limited (a company with several different activities).

It is quite possible that some of the activities carried out in the rural areas by Rucom Industries Limited could be used to show the extent to which the public sector had tried to indigenize the Zambian economy. Areas for activities by the Rucom Industries Limited were well defined. The company did not set out to undertake or do everything conceivable in the rural areas. Criteria used for activities chosen for each particular area varied only slightly. In most cases, selection was generally based on the sufficiency of the market for the product in question. The other criteria that were applied seemed to aim at providing for balanced provincial development, as well as simply to put the control of the economy in the hands of the indigenous population. This possibly serves as an explanation for the rapid construction of bakeries, which on completion were turned over to local indigenous entrepreneurs.

Experience not only in Zambia but also in other independent African countries has shown that expatriate and external agencies can not be relied upon to assist African entrepreneurial development. The few that came forward were suspected of trying to thwart local efforts. On the other hand, some of them gave only very little assistance. It is because Indeco had tried to fill some of these gaps in the economy that it earned itself the praise of being one of the country's three (Indeco, Findeco and Mindeco) prongs of economic independence.[37] Therefore, Indeco assumed the role of acting as the government's tool for industrialization under the supervision of the then Ministry of Commerce, Industry and Foreign Trade.

A number of senior officials in the then Ministry of Commerce, Industry and Foreign Trade had long acknowledged certain serious shortcomings in the national policy of indigenization, even with the money made available for various Indeco activities. It so happened that a lot of indigenous Zambians who received business loans were, in fact, turning out to be appendages or outlets for expatriate suppliers and distributors. The then Ministry of Commerce, Industry and Foreign Trade gave a lot of thought to some of the possible ways of overcoming such anomalies.[38]

One such device was the establishment of a state-owned wholesale agency known as the Zambian National Wholesale Corporation (ZNWC). It had been hoped that the newly created corporation would help in breaking the Asian traders' monopoly in the area of wholesaling. Provincial branches of the ZNWC were planned and have since come into operation. By establishing the ZNWC at provincial headquarters, Indeco and the then Ministry of Commerce, Industry and Foreign Trade (or the government) had hoped to reduce transport and other overhead costs incurred by many of the indigenous businessmen. Another reason for establishing the corporation, although not publicly admitted, can be explained within the general context of enabling the state to control the economy through a central price mechanism. It was the government's desired objective to use the mechanism of ZNWC to remove the price disparity between the urban and rural areas in respect of similar merchandise.

At about the same time, the government had established a Price Control Unit within the then Ministry of Commerce, Industry and Foreign Trade. It had been hoped to effect the control of prices at both wholesale and retail levels. The government had assumed that, by establishing the ZNWC, it would be possible to create the necessary impact in the general price trends in the country. But both the Price Control Unit and ZNWC as new control mechanisms suffered from similar constraints. Both had very small staffs, and yet they were expected to operate over a rather wide area. Second, the frequency of changes in the administrative structure tended to render their operations a little less effective and denied them the merit that goes with continuity. Third, no mechanism seems to have been provided for the two operational machineries to co-ordinate their respective operations despite the fact that both were under the direct supervision of the same government ministry.

At this point attention needs to be focused on the decision taken during the third round of the Mulungushi economic reforms which forecast the intentions of the state or the public sector to enter into partnership with the private financial organizations. It had become apparent at the conclusion of that meeting that the method to be adopted or applied was not to be very much different from the one that had been applied in respect of Mindeco and Indeco.

Thus, the emergence of the State Finance and Development Corporation (Findeco) came as no total surprise. From the point of view of the Zambian government, the step in this direction represented a completion of the state participation trinity (i.e. Indeco, Mindeco and Findeco). Findeco was conceived at Mulungushi in November 1970 as the government's organ with overall responsibility for supervising and co-ordinating existing and future corporate financial interests. Unfortunately, Findeco came into being not long after the dismal failure of the Credit Organization of Zambia (COZ), which had cost the state a lot of financial and material resources through mismanagement, too much political pressure on disbursement of loans and an inability to collect debts from indigenous Zambian debtors. Many of the indigenous borrowers considered loans obtained from COZ, especially if obtained because of political pressure, as an independence struggle bonus and therefore felt no obligation to repay.

It is therefore possible to understand some of the causes of the initial disenchantment expressed in certain quarters. A considerable number of outsiders had already accepted (not that they could do otherwise) the fact that independent countries, particularly in Africa, should be free to go on minding their own business. But this did not imply that they could be prevented from pointing to certain glaring shortcomings. This is apparently what happened in case of the criticism that was voiced about the objectives and structure of new Findeco. From the point of view of certain informed sources, the 'establishment of the new Findeco failed to strike the note of logic, neatness and consistency that previous moves in the field of state participation had done'.[39]

The Finance Development Corporation (Findeco) as a group consists of the following institutions:

1 the State Finance and Development Corporation Limited, which is wholly state-owned; basically, this functions as a holding company with overall supervision of the activities of its subsidiary institutions and also protects the interests of its shareholders in them;
2 the Zambia State Insurance Corporation Limited, which was created in its present form in 1968 and is wholly state-owned, with overall supervision of its two subsidiaries – the Zambia National Insurance Brokers Limited and City Radio, in which it owns 70 and 50 per cent respectively of equity shares;

3 the Zambia National Building Society, owned as a corporate body by the individual depositors although administered by the government through its sole ownership of the 800 A shares;
4 the National Commercial Bank Limited, a 98 per cent state-owned bank established in October 1969; basically, it undertakes normal commercial banking transactions and has also tried to emphasize assistance in promoting agriculture and the development of agro-industries in the country;
5 the Industrial Finance Company Limited, which is wholly state-owned, and which was incorporated in 1969 mainly to rationalize lending activities previously carried out by the Industrial Development Corporation (Indeco).

State participation in the economy within the general context of industrial, commercial and economic indigenization following the Mulungushi economic reforms was a mixture of a number of considerations, as was described above. There can be no denying the fact that the entry of the public sector created among other things competition for the private sector in a number of areas. However, some of the pressures for the ensuing competition that the private sector encountered was a result of Rhodesia's Unilateral Declaration of Independence (UDI). Ripples created by that one action on the Zambian economy had considerable consequences, even though the act took place outside the Zambian border. Rhodesia's UDI came barely a year after Zambia became independent. And because of the rather close association developed through history between Zambia and its southern neighbours, it became very necessary not only to change certain priorities but also to place stronger emphasis on speeding up the indigenization of the Zambian economy.

During a major part of the colonial régime and also during the time of the Federation of Rhodesia and Nyasaland, the Zambian economy was treated as an outside economic structure. Zambia's economy had been purposely made into a periphery activity of the economic activities of Southern Rhodesia. It was therefore not surprising that the Zambian president decided on 10 November 1970 to use some of the powers conferred upon him under the Zambian Constitution in section 24 of Chapter 707 of the laws of the Republic of Zambia to evoke trading licences in respect of the following Rhodesian subsidiary companies: Avida Trading Company Ltd; Morris Wineries Ltd; Coombe and Dewer Ltd; Wholesale Radio Supplies Ltd; Evergló Electric Ltd; Harrison and Hughson Ltd; Central African Bag Company Ltd; Miller Motors Ltd; Sager Motors Ltd; Truck and Car Spares Ltd.

The Zambian government was thus able to demonstrate that it had moved into active participation and was no longer content to remain a spectator of the country's economic activities. Thus, state participation was upheld and promoted by the activities of Indeco, Mindeco and Findeco as subsidiaries of ZIMCO. However, despite such an active degree of participation, the state did not seem to have been in total control of the economy. This analysis has been borne out by certain events that have happened since those actions were taken.

For instance, the state found itself powerless to prevent certain temporary disruptions to the economy caused by the running down of stocks by foreign-controlled companies. Experience had also exposed the fact that measures preventing the expatriation of foreign currency by expatriate businesses were not quite effective. The newly acquired power of control was not capable of accelerating the ability of the indigenous Zambians to take over all facets of the economy. Similarly, control enjoyed by the state within Zambia could not used to force ex-territorial suppliers to continue supplying to the new indigenous business enterprises in order to keep the Zambian economy running while the government devised permanent solutions.

Economic development through indigenization[40]

To a certain extent, the preceding analysis must have shown how indigenization can be turned into a tool for or against a country's goals of economic development. Perhaps another way of showing the correlation between the two alternatives could have been employed, or the subject could have been tackled on the basis of providing answers to specific questions. Nevertheless, sufficient background material has been provided to enable the interested reader to reach not too wild a conclusion about the way Zambia has been proceeding in developing her economy.

Conclusions to the Zambian experience and experiments could therefore be examined on the basis of answers to specific questions related, among other things, to:

1 the extent to which the current Zambian economy is a result of the country's indigenization policy;
2 whether the legal machinery has been properly exploited to the full;
3 how certain historical landmarks, including the Mulungushi and Matero economic reform programmes and also the country's Leadership Code, may have either speeded up or retarded the process;
4 possible shortcomings or short-sightedness associated with institution-creation as well as some of their structural changes demanded by changed circumstances or on-the-spot experience;

5 what may have influenced the government to act differently towards certain sectors of the economy; and
6 the relation and effect of the Party's (UNIP) supremacy.

Indigenization within the Zambian context does not seem to have been nationally formulated to cover all sectors over the same period. For instance, its beginning, the rate of implementation and targets achieved by each sector exhibited considerable variations. One only needs to compare how it has been pursued at state, public, parastatal and the private sector levels in order to arrive at the conclusion that there must never have been a national policy on the issue.

Evidence gathered from discussions with a wide range of some of my most knowledgeable Zambian colleagues shows that there was no pressure on the part of the Zambian government to indigenize either the public or the private sector in the early days of independence. The policy of indigenization of the Zambian economy has not evolved from any evolutionary studies or discussions; it became a national policy, i.e. 'Zambianization', with independence, but no policy statement as such on how it was to proceed was ever issued.

The process of indigenizing top civil service posts had not been as rapid as one would have expected. For instance, the post of permanent secretary in the Ministry of Finance was still held by a white expatriate as late as 1967. The second most senior posts, those of under-secretaries in many Zambian ministries, particularly the then Ministry of Commerce, Industry and Foreign Trade, and the Ministry of Transport, Power and Communications, were still held by white expatriates up to as late as 1969. This state of affairs was most incompatible with a policy of indigenizing the economy.

Indigenization of other public sectors, and especially those of strategic economic importance, apart from the top civil service posts referred to above, proved rather difficult. The public sectors of local authorities in the urban areas were considerably slow in appointing indigenous Zambians to posts of senior or chief executive, in spite of the fact that the post of mayor had for some time been occupied by indigenous Zambians in many line-of-railway cities and towns. It was the City Council of Ndola that led the way by indigenizing the post of chief executive with the appointment of Mr Julius B. Sakala as first town clerk.

In the period immediately following independence just as after the announcement of the economic reforms between 1968 and 1970, there appeared to be no immediate concern for indigenization at the parastatals level. Rather, the government seemed more concerned with consolidating its gains of the control of the parastatals. This could be attributed in part to a definite lack of any guidelines provided by the government. Thus, even the private sector did not consider itself under an obligation to indigenize its various economic activities. If anything, the reaction of the private sector in pursuing mild forms of indigenization could be stated to have been a mixture of considerations and not from fear of government coercion. Possibly one most compelling reason seemed to have been their anticipation of the government's reaction to Rhodesia Unilateral Declaration of Independence (UDI) and all those associated with Southern Rhodesia.

The Zambia's reaction to Rhodesia's UDI was unmistakably clear. Not least of all was the enactment by the Zambian Government for security reasons of the Immigration and Deportation Act (Chapter 122 of the Laws of Zambia). The Act was intended to regulate immigrants' and visitors' entry into and remaining within Zambia; to provide for the removal from Zambia of criminals and other specified persons; and to make provision for matters incidental to the Act itself.

The significance of the above Act requires no further explaining. It is an already acknowledged fact that at the time of the UDI decision on 11 November 1965, the Zambian economy was very much part and parcel of the Rhodesian and South African economies. A great majority of expatriate companies in Zambia were only subsidiaries of Rhodesian and South African companies. Thus, all their central management and policy control were either in Salisbury, Bulawayo, Johannesburg, Pretoria, Durban or Cape Town. Chief executives of Zambian local companies came and went on the Zambian scene as they pleased.

The Zambian government was compelled by circumstances to ensure that such an economic relationship should not be exploited by non-indigenous business interests against the overall Zambian interest. Thus, Sections 9, 10, 11, 12 and 13 of the Act demanded, respectively, that:

1 entrants must appear before immigration officers;
2 entrants and others must be examined in order to ascertain: their identity; their objects for entry into Zambia; the nature of their claim to remain in Zambia; and whether they might be prohibited immigrants;
3 certain visitors must reappear before immigration officers;
4 security could be required from entrants; and
5 persons leaving Zambia must be examined.

It is not unreasonable to suppose that the indigenization measures undertaken by some of the foreign-controlled businesses was influenced partly by what was laid down in the above Act. It is also possible that such action may have been taken by foreign-controlled businesses in order to avoid the likelihood of local harassment, as well as out of genuine economic considerations. For instance, the expatriate businessmen must have begun to realize that they stood to make considerable gains with an increase in the use of local human resources. Circumstances had changed in Zambia; the top political and civil service posts were held by the indigenous people, and expatriates were quick to realize that indigenizing certain sectors of their business operations could facilitate their contacts with the government.

The importance of the Immigration and Deportation Act lies in the fact that it was instrumental in shepherding the private sector into adopting measures of indigenization of some of their economic activities. The extent to which this action has enabled the private sector to contribute to development is a matter that is subject to various interpretations.

The private sector would like everyone to believe that it was not government policy that forced it to indigenize some of its operations. This could well be correct, since there was no government machinery that demanded this kind of action, apart from some early labour reports. For instance, during the National Convention on the Four-Year Development Plan in 1967, Committee 'G', chaired by the then Hon. J. M. Chimba, MP, recommended among other things legislation to speed up Zambianization.[41] He sought a law to compel employers to submit the educational and professional qualifications of their expatriate labour force. It was hoped that in this way it might be possible to check on any unnecessary delay in promoting Zambians. In fact, the government had already accepted the recommendations of the Brown Commission, which recommended, *inter alia*, that progress in Zambianization ought to be reported at regular intervals.

Control by the state of the private and certain public sectors became possible because of an increase in the tempo of creating parastatal organizations. The action proved to contain not only the strength for development but also certain serious contradictions. The strength of Zambian parastatals in fostering economic development is a subject already dealt with above; it is more the weaknesses that we need to turn our attention to in the last part of this section.

A number of weaknesses have been identified. A major one relates to the fact that certain public enterprises had been established with very little preparation in respect of the concept and mode of their envisaged operation. This would seem to have been the cause of the failure of a number of them. Closer examination has also shown that consideration of the aspect of economic development had not been given sufficient weight to influence or temper the final decisions. Similarly, the control by the state of the economy, which had been hoped for with the creation of the machinery, could not in the end be realized.

Another weakness of the system was the great reluctance on the part of the decision-makers to accept certain results as unavoidable. For instance, it was completely unrealistic to expect parastatals to wear two hats at one and the same time. Some parastatals have failed to make any economic headway, not only because of managerial inefficiency of their structures, but also because they could not balance the objective of being viable commercial enterprises with their other role of providing a social service.

We would not wish to issue a general condemnation of all agricultural parastatals. But when seen in the light of the activities of the defunct Credit Organization of Zambia, then one begins to have some doubts about their usefulness.

The Credit Organization of Zambia (COZ) can be taken to illustrate how a well-meant institution can fail to achieve its objectives. COZ was created by an Act of Parliament in 1967 and incorporated under Chapter 353 of the Laws of Zambia. It was to promote and provide financial assistance for agricultural, fishing and commercial purposes as well as to provide for matters incidental to the provisions of the Act. Broad areas established for purposes of consideration for loans by the Credit Organization of Zambia included:

1 farmers for all or any of the purposes mentioned in section 29 of the Act;
2 co-operative societies;
3 farmers' associations;
4 the establishment, purchase or improvement of commercial and other business projects, etc.

Some of the evidence gathered in respect of COZ and its contribution to Zambia's development makes sad reading. The general conclusion is that COZ failed to achieve most of its principal objectives. The Organization had been launched with a very substantial amount of money, some of which came from abroad, but years later closed its operations with a reported deficit in the neighbourhood of £13 million. COZ not only failed to run its own affairs but almost dragged down with itself the viable Land Bank of Zambia when the latter was forced to merge with the former.

There is no doubting the fact that COZ would have been viable if only its protagonists had allowed for thorough preparations of its envisaged operations. There should have been a careful selection of its managerial staff, of projects financed and of borrowers. In terms of staff, the Organization should not have been used as an outlet for political appointees who had not been absorbed into political posts. In terms of borrowers, on the other hand, political pressure should not have been exerted to the extent that the Organization was forced to give loans even to obviously doubtful cases.

A parallel lending institution, the Industrial Finance Company (IFC), was later established in 1969 with objectives similar to those that had motivated the creation of COZ. The IFC, between 1969 (the year it was created) and 1972 had been able to lend about K1.4 million to indigenous Zambians. About K0.5 million of this amount had been lent in the rural areas and the remainder, amounting to K900,000, in the long-established urban-industrial areas. A much bigger proportion of the Company's funds should have been lent in the rural areas had rationalization been strictly adhered to. Already the Industrial Finance Company admits that it had been compelled to write off K2 million as irrecoverable bad debts.

Indigenization through parastatals has been a mixed blessing for the Zambian economy. Economic reforms spelt out in the Mulungushi and Matero economic reform programme have indeed helped with transferring of economic control to the government in a very big way, as can be seen by the present fields under ZIMCO and other institutions outside ZIMCO like the Development Bank of Zambia, Dairy Produce Board, Cold Storage Board, Zambia Railways, Zambia–Tanzania Railway, etc. However, they have not given as much to the indigenous population as one would have expected.

Reforms introduced in order to increase Zambian participation in the remaining activities of the private sector included restricting local borrowing by expatriates from banks and also the exclusion of expatriates from many retail selling outlets, and trading licences in general, both wholesale and retail. But these measures were aborted by the mere fact that some of the ZIMCO subsidiaries have tended to acquire wider trading activities, leaving very little for the private or individual indigenous Zambian entrepreneur.

This whole issue can also be reviewed against the country's philosophy of humanism. There can be no denying the fact that the reform programme has 'created a form of State capitalism where tremendous power is thus concentrated in the hands of a small managerial group who have their hands on the important switches and whose elitist attitudes set social patterns far beyond their immediate realms of command'.[42] Thus, it can be observed that there is practically no shared responsibilities between the government and the indigenous population in economic control. There are practically no examples where the government is in partnership with individual nationals.

There has emerged in recent times, however, a noticeable number of

Zambians who have entered into medium- to large-scale businesses. For a majority of them this has been possible through the acquisition of expatriate-owned companies. A few others have managed to start new enterprises in a variety of commercial fields.

There is no documentary evidence to show that Zambia has ever had a consistent policy on indigenization. Available evidence is rather isolated and can be obtained only by studying a range of activities that the state has taken with the aim of encouraging indigenous Zambians to participate in the economy. Common forms of assistance have consisted of the provision of trust funds or some sort of financial lending institutions. However, there is also an unmistaken apprehension by the state of activities of its own nationals outside the government or public sector. It is as if Zambian nationals who work in private companies or on their own are not considered to be contributing to indigenization of the Zambian economy. But indigenization cannot ever succeed if it restricts itself to the contribution of the government or the public sector. For a long time, most of Zambia's available indigenous manpower with technical and professional skills was absorbed by the government or public sector areas. As pointed out also by Mr E. A. Kashita, it is only over the last few years that the rapid turnover of personnel from the government and the public bodies has enabled the private companies to start meaningful indigenization programmes.

State control can have many advantages, but it can also have certain disadvantages. The Zambian experience of state control has a number of telling lessons. What therefore may be some of the country's glaring shortcomings? One such shortcoming arises from an absence of co-ordination of policy among the various sectors in which it operates. Another of these observable shortcomings is the lack of sufficient numbers of trained and experienced local personnel with managerial capacity and a clear sense of dedication and urgency. The state has at times pre-empted its own control owing to frequent changes or, rather, rush replacement of technical skills, as well as to its inability to define precisely the roles of some of the institutions.

For instance, there is little evidence to show that the National Import and Export Corporation (NIEC) keeps itself well informed about local production. Many Indeco subsidiaries are engaged in the production of products that NIEC still continues to import and distribute in the country. It is not known to what extent import programming of NIEC takes account of local production. Imports by NIEC of similar products as those produced by some Indeco subsidiaries ought to be encouraged only on the understanding that competition could improve efficiency and quality in the local industries. But such imports should only be purchased against well ordered and co-ordinated targets as established between NIEC and its sister production units within the country.

There are certain structural changes to the working of parastatals which require a further careful re-examination, mainly to establish their consistency with a policy of indigenization and control of the economy by the Zambian government. The decision taken of making certain Cabinet ministers chairmen of boards of directors of certain parastatals is one that requires further re-examination – not to challenge Cabinet decisions, or to call for reversal; but rather, to determine the advantages or otherwise of such a move. The decision had been made in the first place in order to provide a bridge between Cabinet and the country's public economic and commercial sector. From the government's point of view, this particular structural change was intended to keep Cabinet well informed of economic activities in the public sector. Furthermore, it was thought that it could make easier the passage through Cabinet of certain policy matters since the Cabinet ministers who were chairmen could be expected to brief their Cabinet colleagues of the background to the decisions of their respective boards of directors. Similarly, it was hoped that the various boards of directors could in turn be kept informed about the current thinking of Cabinet on several issues. In this way, it was thought that parastatals might be facilitated in the programming of some of their activities.

Admittedly, parastatals must provide a social service to the nation. But the extent to which they can do this is limited by considerations of commercial viability. Experience has shown this structural change to be full of contradictions. The first is manifest in the fact that each board of directors on which a minister is chairman could no longer deliberate freely. An invisible guillotine to an honest exchange of views by equals is removed. The tendency has been for board decisions tending to give greater weight to political rather than economic considerations, since in the end such decisions require a Cabinet endorsement.

The chief executives of the parastatals have become increasingly fearful of taking certain necessary commercial decisions. Many have naturally been fearful of possible unfavourable reaction from their respective chairmen rather than from the board of directors. Another point that must be acknowledged is that nearly all the various boards of directors are rendered less effective by this arrangement. No board can any longer claim to be the *de facto* authority that it had previously been. It can no longer exercise or speak its mind on the affairs of the corporation in the presence of a Cabinet minister, especially if the minister is the kind who will not entertain opposite views from his own. The biggest sufferers of this structural change have been the corporations themselves and the country's rate of economic development.

This apart, experience within Zambia has shown that indigenization through parastatals has tended to gravitate towards the growth of monopoly power. To a certain extent, this monopoly power has brought some hardship to the nation. It would, however, be naive to blame all shortages in the Zambian economy on state policy or control. Rather, they should be blamed on the operation of the monopolistic powers conferred upon certain parastatals. A number of these parastatals have tended to over-concentrate upon a single import source, so that, if there is a disruption in supply from that one single source, the country inevitably suffers from a prolonged period of shortages of the item(s) in question.

Thus, the monopoly power conferred upon parastatals has not only shielded them from competition, but has also prolonged inefficiencies among some of them. Some parastatals have tried to hide their inefficiency by extending their coverage to viable private enterprises; but no sooner are those enterprises acquired than they are rendered unproductive. Examples of this were provided by the end results in the operations of certain fishing enterprises on Lake Tankanyika and the United Bus Company of Zambia (former Central African Road Services), which have since been acquired as part of the bigger monopoly state enterprises.

It was stated, in the leaflet on 'Zambia's Economic Revolution', that:

> Zambia, on Independence, took over the reins of government but the economic sector remained entirely in the hands of non-citizens. . . . This was the direct result of the colonial policy of denying economic opportunities to local citizens. . . . So much so that exclusion from economic activity and opportunity for Zambian entrepreneurship was absolute. . . . Obviously, no responsible government would allow a situation like this to continue. . . . It has therefore been imperative that . . . the Government on behalf of the people must participate in the major sectors of the economy and at the same time induce an atmosphere in which Zambians must individually and corporately share in the commercial and industrial life of the country.[43]

This background statement proceeded to castigate expatriate 'business and industry' in Zambia, most of which

> would not be prepared to face a national crisis with Zambians. Accordingly, they therefore work on extreme liquidity, maximize profits on minimum capital investment, always planning to return home when conditions [in Zambia] became, in their opinion, intolerable or when they had sent enough money abroad to enable them to retire in comfort. . . . Unfortunately, Zambians for reasons of prolonged economic discrimination have neither capital nor the skill to participate in the economic life other than as employees or consumers. In the circumstances, therefore, it is only the Government . . . that can participate . . . and ensure that the nation has control of the vital resources in the country, and

also provide avenues for the acquisition of skills pertaining to economic development and participation. . . .[44]

President Kaunda has already given the lead in fearlessly exposing Zambia's own weaknesses and difficulties in human relations, especially politically. The above forthright remarks of His Excellency the President of Zambia were contained in his introductory address on Zambia's Economic Revolution delivered at the National Council of UNIP at Mulungushi on 19 April 1968.

It is perhaps against this background that the I have gathered the courage to examine implications and likely possible contradictions of certain recent policy pronouncements. I can therefore be forgiven when I point to a certain degree of contradiction in some of the policies being pursued in the country. Reference has already been made to difficulties created for paraststals as a result of superimposing ministers as chairmen of boards of directors.

The concept of indigenization in regard to ownership, capital and dividends, control management, manpower and technology is very much *adhoc*, and it is difficult to draw any trend from acts or practices of the government except in regard to local borrowing, where a Zambian-controlled company (that is, one in which shares held by Zambians or government corporations are more than 50 per cent) is on a one-for-one basis. Equally, in the remission of dividends abroad, the ratio is 15 per cent of paid-up capital or 50 per cent of after-tax profits, whichever is less, but if there are no intentions to remit these funds then there are no limits to the ratio of profits to capital.[45]

Experience has shown that the government does acknowledge the fact that certain institutions cannot be controlled by decree, especially as there were not sufficient indigenous Zambians with the requisite skills and experience. Measures have, however, been taken to put Zambian executives at the top of the two biggest corporations in the mining sector: Nchanga Consolidated Copper Mines (NCCM) and Roan Consolidated Mines (RCM). However, it will be many many years before any meaningful presence of Zambians will be detected in the lower ranks of some of the very complex technical and professional fields.

In any case, as I was constantly reminded, it is not known whether it is the Zambian government policy to totally indigenize the management of the two above mining corporations. It would appear at the moment as if the government intends to permit the continued shareholding of 49 per cent by outsiders. Underlying the considerations must surely be the acceptance of the fact that the country does not want to isolate itself from available sources of foreign investment.

From the above analysis, it is clear that indigenization for development has been successful only to a limited extent. Over and above, the analysis of the indigenization process in Zambia has exposed the fact that the desired goal of control of the economy through indigenization cannot be achieved without careful planning and co-ordination of all sectors and activities. Careful planning and decision-making at the highest level in the country, however, is not sufficient; there must also be the full co-operation of the Zambian people.

Zambia's experience, like that of other developing countries, has shown these aspects to be only two of the quantifiable dimensions of administration. And both require, if they are to be followed by good organization, control and supervision. The country's leadership and the people themselves are both basically agreed on the need to continue and further the aims and objectives of economic reforms as a basis for consolidating what has so far been achieved.

Notes

1 Francis L. Coleman, *The Northern Rhodesia Copperbelt 1899–1962* (Manchester University Press 1971); Richard L. Sklar, *Corporate Power in an African State* (Berkeley: University of California Press 1975).
2 William Tordoff (ed.), *Politics in Zambia* (Manchester University Press 1974), pp. 15–19.
3 Based on oral interview with Mr Michael C. Sata.
4 Mulungushi Rock lies about halfway between Kabwe (formerly Broken Hill) and Kapiri Mposhi on the Great North Road. This is the place where the all-out strategy for political struggle was hatched by UNIP.
5 President Dr K. D. Kaunda's speech at the National Council of the United National Independence Party, Mulungushi, 19 April 1968.
6 *Laws of Northern Rhodesia*, vol. 7, ch. 246, sections 3 and 4, pp. 2 and 3; and *Federal Act No. 23 of 1957* as established as the Grain Marketing Act in 1957 by the federal legislature.
7 Robert E. Baldwin, 'Wage Policy in a Dual Economy – The Case of Northern Rhodesia', *Race*, vol. 4, no. 1 (November 1962), pp. 73–87.
8 *Laws of Northern Rhodesia*, ch. 91, sections 19 and 20 (Lusaka: Government Printer).
9 Dr K. D. Kaunda, 'A Plea for Understanding', Address to the Overseas Development Institute, London, 18 July 1968.
10 I wish to acknowledge my gratitude to all those persons who contributed selflessly to the final product of this chapter during my

research for information in Zambia between 12 and 21 May 1977. In particular, I wish to thank Hon. R. C. Kamanga, MCC; Hon. A. K. Shapi, MCC; Hon J. M. Mwanakatwe, MP and Minister of Finance; Mr E. A. Kashita, for going through parts of the script and suggesting amendments in addition to providing written comments to a questionnaire; Mr V. S. Musakanya; Mr C. H. Mutale, for going through parts of the draft, Mr Michael C. Sata; Mr E. J. Shamwana, SC; Mr L. R. Edwards, chief executive, Zambia Industrial and Commercial Association; Mr Joseph Chileshe and the officials of the Ministry of Commerce and Foreign Trade, especially Mr E. J. Chanda, for facilitating contracts with a cross-section of the Zambian community.

11 J. H. Chileshe, 'Indigenization', *Enterprise*, no. 2 (1975), p. 43.

12 Matero is a township to the West of Lusaka. It has risen into fame because, like Mulungushi Rock, it was the place where the Zambian president decreed some of the country's major economic decisions relating to indigenization.

13 Dr K. D. Kaunda, 'Towards Complete Independence', *The Matero Speech*, (Lusaka: Zambia Information Services, 1969), p. 28.

14 George K. Simwinga of the University of Zambia has discussed 'The copper mining industry of Zambia' as a case study of nationalization and control in *What Government Does*, ed. Matthew Holden, Jr and Dennis L. Dresang (London: Sage, 1975), vol. 1, pp. 84–93.

15 Dr K. D. Kaunda, 'Strength for the Challenges Ahead', *Financial Times*, 13 August 1970, p. 15 (italics added).

16 *Mines Acquisition (Special Provision (Amendment) Act 1973*, Act no. 45 of 1973, (Lusaka: Government Printer, 1973).

17 Ministry of Trade and Industry, 'Blueprint for Economic Reforms', (Lusaka: Government Printer, 1971), 4m N899 7/71, pp. 1–6.

18 Kenneth Kaunda, *This Completes Economic Reforms: Now Zambia is Ours*, (Lusaka: Zambia Information Services, 1970) p. 12.

19 The Laws of the Republic of Zambia, ch. 686 – Companies Act, (Lusaka: Government Printer).

20 Alderman Tom Mtine was one of the first indigenous civic leaders to be mayor of Ndola, a prosperous city on Zambia's copperbelt. He joined the board of Lonrho's Zambian subsidiary and has since become its chairman. He has served as board member for several companies, like Rothmans, etc., apart from at one time being chairman of Zambian Airways.

21 *Copperbelt of Zambia Mining Industry Year Book 1966* (Kitwe: Copper Industry Service Bureau Ltd), pp. 24–5.

22 ibid, pp. 24–5.

23 *Zambia Mining Year Book 1973* (Kitwe: Copper Industry Bureau).

24 At the time, Alderman Safeli H. Chileshe, MP, was the only indigenous Zambian to be appointed as director by the RST Group on the board of the Mufulira Copper Mines Limited and the Roan Selection Trust Limited. Mr Chileshe, like his counterpart, Alderman Mtine, was the first indigenous mayor of the City of Lusaka and held directorships with the British-American Tobacco (BAT), Barclays Bank, Tanganyika Investment, etc.

25 In addition were the requirement of work permits and strictures from political platforms about localization or Zambianization.

26 It has, however, been pointed out that there was not a single instance of this veto power of 'B' directors having been used. Furthermore, there was no lack of power on the part of the 'A' directors to reject *any* item on the agenda to be considered by a board.

27 Simwinga, 'Copper mining industry', p. 87.

28 Mark Bostock and Charles Harvey (eds), *Economic Independence and Zambian Copper: A Case Study of Foreign Investment* (New York: Praeger, 1972), pp. 169–73.

29 The Hon. H. Mulemba, MP, as Minister of Mines and Mining Development was the first Zambian to become chairman, although the negotiations following on 30 April 1973 announced were not completed. The second chairman was Hon. Elias A. Kashita, MP, Minister of Mines and Industry.

30 The only exception was P. H. A. Brownrigg, formerly of Anglo-American Corporation who was nominated as an 'A' director on the board of Nchanga Consolidated Copper Mines Ltd along with L. M. Lishomwa, L. J. Mwananshiku, W. M. Chakulya and F. C. Sumbwe.

31 'About Zambia', no. 13 (Lusaka: Zambia Information Services), p. 6.

32 Dr K. D. Kaunda, *Zambia's Economic Revolution* (Lusaka: Zambia Information Services, 1968), p. 46.

33 Indeco Limited, *Annual Report and Accounts*, for the year ending 31 March 1974.

34 Chileshe, 'Indigenization', p. 43.

35 At the time of approval of the loan, Mr Timothy Chinunda, the proprietor of the Kwacha Relax Hotel, an indigenous Zambian, was also a building contractor.

36 The only other rural hotel operated by an indigenous Zambian was that owned by the late Mr Luka Mumba of Mansa (formerly Fort Rosebery) in the Luapula Province. But this project owed nothing to state assistance and was in fact established before Zambia became an independent sovereign state.

37 President Kaunda, *This Completes Economic Reforms: Now Zambia is Ours*, p. 11.

38 Mr Goodwin H. Mutale, the then permanent secretary in the Ministry of Commerce, Industry and Foreign Trade, had been instrumental in getting me to organize and run the first-ever country-wide residential training seminar for indigenous Zambian enrepreneurs. It was held in 1967 at the Evelyn Hone College of Further Education (Lusaka) on local commercial business. It included sessions in basic simple bookkeeping, etc. Lecturers were drawn on a voluntary basis from the local business community and included Mr Edward J. Shamwana SC, who lectured on some aspects of the Zambian legal systems relating to Zambian business. Participants paid for their cost of attendance at the seminar. Some applicants had to be turned away owing to lack of space. This one course demonstrated that the indigenous Zambian businessman was able to take advantage of opportunities if only they could be offered. One major omission of the Zambian policy, which up to 1974 had not been rectified, was the lack of any training opportunities for the indigenous Zambian businessmen.

39 Anthony Martin, *Minding their own Business* (London: Hutchinson, 1972) p. 251.

40 For the purpose of exploring more deeply a wide range policy issues relating to the question of indigenization and development of the Zambian economy, I held discussions with Messrs E. A. Kashita, V. S. Musakanya, J. W. Shaw and P. J. Chisanga. Mr Kashita has served as permanent secretary in various government ministries, executive chairman of Indeco, Cabinet minister for Mines and Industry and chairman for both NCCM and RCM before going into the private sector. Mr Musakanya has served as secretary to the Cabinet, minister of state and governor of the Bank of Zambia before going into the private sector. Mr Shaw has been in the private sector but has served the public interest in various capacities both as a consultant or as director on various state boards and was for some time chairman of Zambia Airways. Mr Chisanga has served as permanent secretary in various government ministries, secretary to the Cabinet and as administrative secretary to the country's Party Central Committee, and could well drift into the private sector at a later stage.

41 Republic of Zambia, *National Convention on the Four-Year Development Plan*, (Kitwe, 11–15 January 1967), p. 55.

42 Kenneth Kaunda, *Humanism in Zambia, Part II* (Lusaka: Zambian Information Services, 1974).

43 Zambia Information Services, *Zambia's Economic Revolution*

(Lusaka: Zambian Information Services, 1968), pp. iii and v.

44 ibid., p. vi.

45 E. A. Kashita; part of a written reply to my questionnaire on 'types of indigenization being pursued in relation to: ownership, capital and dividends, control/management/manpower and technology'.

References

Beveridge, A. A., 'Economic independence, indigenization and the African businessman: some effects of Zambia's economic reforms', *African Studies Review*, vol. 17, no. 3 (1974), pp. 477–92

Beveridge, A. A., and Oberschall, A. R., *African Businessmen and Development in Zambia*, Metuchen: Scarecrow 1979

Bostock, M., and Harvey, C., *Economic Independence and Zambian Copper: A Case Study of Foreign Investment*, New York: Praeger 1972

Curry, Jnr, R. L., 'Global market forces and the nationalization of foreign-based export companies', *Journal of Modern African Studies*, vol. 14, no. 1 (1976), pp. 137–43

Daniel, P., *Africanisation, Nationalisation and Inequality: Mining Labour and the Copperbelt in Zambian Development*, Cambridge University Press 1979

Martin, A., *Minding their Own Business: Zambia's Struggle against Western Control*, Harmondsworth: Penguin 1975

Sklar, Richard L., *Corporate Power in an African State: the Political Impact of Multinational Mining Companies in Zambia*, University of California Press 1975

6 Ghana

K. A. Owusu-Ansah, *Deputy Director, Ghana Institute of Management and Public Administration, Ghana*

In recent years, national governments in independent Africa have been promulgating public policies that seek not only to reduce the dependence of their economies on external forces but also to help them gain control of their own economies. The commonest options that have been open to them include (1) outright nationalization, whereby the state, by legislation, either confiscates, seizes, or compulsorily controls certain foreign enterprises; (2) establishment of state economic organizations to complement and/or compete with or oust alien enterprises; (3) discriminatory administrative practices, such as import control through import licensing, immigration control through a quota system, exchange control through allocation of foreign exchange, and credit control; and (4) the direct transfer of ownership to citizens as well as the local equity participation in alien enterprises. All these methods are in operation in Africa. But the strategy that has in the last eight years caught the headlines and fired the imagination of the articulate public in Ghana is the twin one of citizen ownership of, and local equity participation in, a number of enterprises hitherto the preserve of aliens. This process is called *indigenization*[1] in this essay.

When a state moves to adopt a policy of indigenization it is usually for a number of reasons: (1) to prevent foreigners from owning the production or distribution of commodities of strategic importance, and thereby to reduce the vulnerability of the security of the state; (2) to have a say in the policy and management of such enterprises and to reduce the returns that may be repatriated at the expense of the country; (3) to break alien monopoly of certain trades and industries and thus carve a niche for the employment of local personnel in such enterprises; and (4) in the case of a country just out of colonial domination, to raise the socio-psychological status of the citizens *vis-à-vis* the aliens through the promotion of local persons to positions hitherto virtually reserved for foreigners. All these no doubt contributed in a way to the shaping of legislation on indigenization in Ghana. But it would appear that the Ghana government was forced to adopt a policy of indigenization for the first time in 1968 more for economic *survival* than by any calculated move either to achieve economic independence or to assume command of the economy.

The purpose of this essay is to examine the overall policy and implementation of indigenization in trade and industry in Ghana by tracing the evolution of public policy on the involvement of the indigenes in industry and commerce since the attainment of the country's political independence, by examining the problems of implementation of each significant policy, and by giving an idea of the possible challenge that the existing policy poses for Ghanaians in the light of its development and execution so far.

The economic environment

The major exports of Ghana are cocoa, gold, timber, manganese and diamonds; among the minor exports are palm kernels, butter, bauxite, copra and kola nuts. The country is essentially a producer of raw materials; indeed, the single crop, cocoa – accounting for from 55 to 75 per cent of Ghana's total exports – provides the backbone of its economy. In contrast, the imports are mostly manufactured goods. Sale of locally grown foodstuffs largely makes up Ghana's internal trade.

The colonial period

The economy bequeathed to Ghana on its attainment of political independence in March 1957 had a definite profile. On the one hand, the foreign exchange position of the country was reasonably sound, thanks to the savings made in Britain by the Gold Coast Cocoa Marketing Board. On the other hand, the economic structure was fragile. As a producer and exporter of raw materials essentially, many of the major economic decisions affecting the country were still taken outside it. Ghana depended, as it does even now, on a one-crop economy. Investment capital was scarce, and the little that trickled in was used mainly in laying the social and economic infrastructure that British capital needed to do its business in the colony. The pattern of commodity use was highly import-oriented. Migrant workers – mainly from neighbouring West African countries – formed an important part of the labour force in administrative jobs, mining and the cocoa industry. And there was commercial *growth without development*, in the sense that very few indigenes participated in the development of the commercial sector of the economy.

The economy under the CPP (1957–65)

With the coming to power of the Convention People's Party (CPP) in 1951, the tempo of economic development was dramatically stepped up. A ten-year development plan, drawn up by the colonial officials, was slightly expanded, and by and large was executed within five years. The focus remained on investment in infrastructure. Many new schools, communication networks, health facilities, water and electricity supplies, and government buildings appeared. Another five-year development plan (covering 1957–61) had the same infrastructure bias – to provide the basis for both agricultural and industrial development. A few industrial concerns were initiated during this period. The implementation of this policy was appropriate at the time because the country's foreign exchange position was far from being shaky. But the political inability of the government to distinguish between foreign and domestic savings led to over-extensive withdrawals of foreign exchange when, with careful fiscal policies, the government could have drawn more on internal resources for financing the developments. The most ambitious of the development plans – the seven-year development plan for 1964–70 – was financed from both the domestic banking system and external sources. A significant effect of these plans, especially the last one, was a steep rise in government expenditure, which necessitated a continuous deterioration of the budgetary and balance of payments positions. When, ultimately, the government was overthrown in February 1966 for reasons mainly of economic mismanagement and drastic economic measures, the economy was characterized by acute shortages of foreign exchange, an unbearable external debt, declining domestic savings, substantial unutilized industrial capacity, a stagnant agricultural sector, soaring unemployment, and a markedly increased social mobility and influence of alien migrants from neighbouring West African countries. Practically no change in the *structure* of the economy had occurred.

The economy and the National Liberation Council (NLC)

The NLC, which came to power as a result of the coup of 1966, adopted a policy of 'stabilization and consolidation' until July 1968. To reduce the pressure on domestic resources and on the price level, government investment expenditure was substantially cut and thousands of workers in public corporations and agencies were systematically laid off. And in an attempt to restore equilibrium in the balance of payments, imports were reduced, partly by tightening up fiscal controls and partly by holding down the level of investment and employment. But despite these corrective measures, the balance of payments position did not show any significant improvement.[2] In a further attempt to tackle the balance of payments problem, the NLC decided in July 1967 to reduce the external value of the Ghanaian currency by 30 per cent. This also failed to improve matters.

The NLC did, however, succeed in bringing the fire of inflation under control. The balance of payments position also showed considerable improvements, particularly in 1968. These results were achieved at heavy costs in terms of stagnation and unemployment.

In an attempt to solve these problems, the government in July 1968 launched a two-year development plan for the years 1968–70 which aimed at resuming economic growth at the annual rate of 5 per cent and at reducing unemployment. Because of the nature of the economy then, imports were liberalized.

The Progress Party government

The civilian government of Dr Busia which assumed office in September 1969 considered the army of unemployed inhumanly large and the rate of recovery of the economy dangerously low and slow, and therefore decided to embark on a programme of accelerated growth. To this end, imports were further liberalized. The import bill rose just about the time the world cocoa market suffered a decisive relapse. Sweeping and drastic fiscal measures were announced in July 1971 to seek to solve these problems. In the meantime, the balance of payments position continued to deteriorate. There were also the external debt repayment obligations to be met soon. In desperation, the Busia government gave in to IMF insistence and devalued the *cedi* by as much 44 per cent soon after Christmas in 1971. Two weeks or so afterwards, the government was dismissed by another military junta.

The National Redemption Council

The junta, which called itself the National Redemption Council, was later re-constituted in October 1975 into a Supreme Military Council to make it possible for military service commanders to be in the government by virtue of their position. It took two major decisions immediately upon taking over the reins of government. One was the upward adjustment of the exchange rate, which had the effect of raising the value of the cedi from 55 cents to 78 cents. The other was to undertake a thorough and rigorous review of the terms and conditions of external debts and to reject all obligations arising from suppliers' credits found tainted with fraud and corruption.

Realizing that Ghana's economy was suffering from the basic

weaknesses of over-dependence on one crop (cocoa) for the bulk of its foreign exchange earnings and from the import orientation of the economy, the government has taken a number of economic measures aimed at resolving these problems ultimately. It has adopted a policy of economic self-reliance, by which food crop agriculture is actively encouraged in a bid to meet local consumption; in association with other producer countries, it is seeking the acceptance of the principal consumers of cocoa of a commodity price agreement; it has launched a programme of 'Operation Feed Your Industries' to cut down on imported raw materials for local industries; and it has resorted to selective import control and has stepped up economic activities in the public sector in an attempt both to cut down recession in the economy and to reduce unemployment. How far these measures bear fruit will depend on real hard work.

Socio-political framework

The colonial era

The economy of the country at the end of colonial rule consisted of three levels: Europeans and Levantines at the top, holding the large commercial enterprises and industries (mainly mining); Asians (and Middle Easterners) in the middle, doing much of the wholesale and retail trading; and Africans at the bottom, continuing in farming, market trading and rudimentary services. Most of the principal consumer marketing activities were in the hands of foreign companies – primarily Europeans and Asians. Even the area of smaller consumer activities had not been spared foreign penetration. In the urban areas, Asians – notably Lebanese and Indians – assisted largely by loans granted by foreign banks operating in the country during its pre-independence era, had carved out a sizeable share of the petty consumer trading. Some of the Asians had established virtual monopoly over the taxi and general transport services, spare parts and other merchandise. With their West African alien counterparts, they dominated retailing in shops in fierce competition with a few Ghanaian nationals in the local consumer 'markets' in the urban areas. These aliens – Asians as well as Africans – between them dominated the craft and service occupations as well as the mining labour force in the country.

The first organized economic pressure groups in Ghana were formed by Europeans with mining and merchant interests. The Gold Coast Chamber of Mines was inaugurated in 1928, followed soon afterwards by the Association of West African Merchants (AWAM). It was not until 1957 that the Federation of Ghana Industries (which in 1962 was re-christened the Ghana Manufacturers' Association) emerged, ostensibly to champion the cause of indigenous business. In the field of commerce three Chambers of Commerce were created by expatriates to represent their interests. If a Ghanaian Chamber of Commerce existed at this time, it was dormant. Indeed, until the Chambers of Commerce were reconstituted into the Ghana National Chamber of Commerce – with both European and African membership – by a legislative instrument in 1968,[3] there was a total expatriate domination of the group.

The business elite in Ghanaian politics, 1957–66

As far as indigenous private enterprise is concerned, the CPP era can be conveniently divided into two periods: the 1957–60 period, when indigenous private enterprise benefited in a modest way from the government; and the 1961–6 period, when expansion of the state sector was pushed at the expense of private enterprise.[4]

The 1957–60 strategy

Many of the local entrepreneurs had assisted the government party financially and in other ways to successfully contest the crucial elections conducted on the eve of the country's attainment of independence. As compensation for the assistance rendered, they expected the newly installed CPP government:

1. To give them preference in the award of construction and supply contracts and in the allocation of the services provided by state-run public utilities;
2. to expand the business opportunities available to Ghanaians by offering state enterprises for sale and by forcing foreign firms to surrender their leases of prime timber-bearing lands; and
3. to prohibit foreign enterprises from engaging in retail trade.[5]

The response to these demands was very modest indeed. Esseks sums it up in the following words:

> Building contractors did receive preferential treatment in the awarding of smaller public works contracts. Ghanaian timbermen were given a significant increase in the scarce shipping space available on the government-owned railway. On the other hand, only one small state enterprise was sold to Ghanaians. No foreign-held timber leases were cancelled by the Government; and neither legal action nor significant administrative pressure was applied to force expatriates out of retail trading, or to limit their roles in other fields of commerce, except for cocoa purchasing. . . .[6]

(where all private entrepreneurs – both European and African – were eliminated). All this occurred during a period when the government was financially capable of assisting the local entrepreneurs and when the indigenous business community had adequate access to decision-makers in the government.[7] The importance of the community could perhaps be traced to three main political disadvantages: the absence of a tradition of business partnership and managerial know-how; the low esteem in which members of the indigenous business community were collectively held, socially and politically, by the public; and an inability to pay the 'kick-backs' to the government party to the tune easily afforded by some of the established non-African firms.[8]

The 1961–6 strategy

In July 1960, there was clear change of economic direction. In a rather dramatic reshuffle, the minister responsible for trade lost his portfolio; some of the other pro-business ministers also suffered setbacks; and the Report on Aid to Ghanaian Businessmen was shelved. In October the same year, Nkrumah announced that his government would give no further assistance to local private business;[9] only small-scale enterprises not incompatible with a socialist society would be assisted.

The government party had amassed sufficient power to rig or dispense with elections. The financial support of indigenous businessmen was no longer essential for the retention of the party in power. Nkrumah could afford politically to drop the pretence of sympathy with their aspirations. The general policy now was to discriminate against private enterprise – both domestic and foreign – in order to expand the state sector of the economy.

In the face of stiff competition offered by the much favoured state enterprises set up by the government, many of the indigenous private enterprises withdrew or contracted. Into some of the fields vacated by local entrepreneurs in the urban areas moved a few Asians with medium technology who could afford the bribes demanded. 'Expatriate capitalists [also] were informal allies in his [Nkrumah's] efforts to contain the growth of indigenous capitalism', according to Esseks, because 'he had been content to allow Lebanese, Indian and European firms to outsell their Ghanaian private competitors until state enterprises were strong enough to edge them all out'.[10] In the villages too the immigrants were no less firmly established. A phenomenal increase in the tempo of socioeconomic development, as well as the government's open invitation to foreigners to enter the country in the name of African unity in the early 1960s, had combined dramatically to step up African alien population in the country. Through membership of the government party, most of these aliens acquired considerable power and affluence in their localities. It was not uncommon to find one group of West African aliens operating as money lenders, occasionally even without licences, fully controlling trading activities and granting loans to Ghanaian petty traders and peasant farmers at cut-throat rates of interest. Many farms became mortgaged or pawned to immigrants as securities for some of these loans. Another group of African aliens seized control of the corn/maize, yam and meat trades. Around Ashanti and Brong-Ahafo especially it became a tradition that only members of this group distributed yams and maize. Some of these immigrants went to the extent of buying the whole of a farm's proceeds well in advance of the harvest season, to be retailed to Ghanaian sub-agents.

So at the end of the CPP rule, the economic stratification of the industrial and commercial community remained intact except that, in the field of commerce, in quite a number of the rural areas, a further differentiation of the African group in the bottom scale had virtually occurred with the African aliens now occupying the upper stratum.

The National Liberation Council of 1966–9 and the promotion of Ghanaian business

The National Liberation Council – the junta that forcibly removed the CPP from office – published its policy statement on the promotion of Ghanaian business enterprises in 1968.[11] The government statement left no doubt in the minds of the Ghanaian business community, and the public at large, about its intention to give positive encouragement to Ghanaian enterprises. The step was, to all intents and purposes, wholeheartedly welcomed by the Ghanaian business community.[12]

The declaration of intent was followed a few months later by the promulgation of the Ghanaian Enterprises Decree, which gave legal effect to the policy. The lobbying capacity of the Ghanaian businessmen at this time was improved compared with their performance in the period of the previous regime, in spite of their organizational shortcomings. This appreciation in their position and bargaining strength was enhanced by the reappearance of privately owned daily newspapers and the development of new Ghanaian business interest groups. The greatest single contributory factor was the change in government attitude towards indigenous businessmen, with the accompanying government hypersensitivity.[13]

The Progress Party government of 1969–72

The Progress Party government, which came to power on the return of the country to civilian rule in September 1969, issued an order within seven days of taking office, which provided for the deportation of all aliens lacking valid residence permits in fulfilment of an election pledge to provide extensive aid to Ghanaian private enterprise and to exclude aliens from certain branches of commerce. Some 150,000 people are believed to have been affected. But the effect of the order was partially vitiated by the practice of the minister responsible for the interior to grant Ghanaian citizenship or residence permits to a considerable number of the affected aliens.[14]

The order was a precursor to the Ghanaian Business (Promotion) Act of June 1970, which expanded upon, and strengthened, the 1968 Ghanaianization Decree. In introducing the Bill, the minister responsible for finance underlined the fact that the proposed measure sought to take the Ghanaian Enterprises Decree of 1968 a step further by (1) accelerating the pace of transfer of the economy into Ghanaian hands; (2) extending and clarifying the scope of Ghanaianization; and (3) strengthening the machinery for the positive promotion of Ghanaian business.[15] The June 1970 Act brought forward the deadline prescribed by the earlier decree, for aliens to leave wholesale and retail trade, from the original July 1973 to August 1970.[16] Even though the Act of 1970 sought to achieve a certain measure of comprehensiveness, it did not go all the way to meet the desires of certain sections of the population.[17]

The National Redemption Council

The charge in government in 1972 did not fundamentally alter the policy that sought gradual and incremental transfer of control over the economy into Ghanaian hands. For instead of taking the more radical step of confiscating alien businesses, the new government seems, in its Investment Policy Decree, 1975, not to steer too far from the gradualist traditions set by the two previous governments.[18] It is its other legislation – the Ghanaian Enterprises Development Decree, also of the same year – that seems to have slight ideological undertones in some parts.[19]

Thus all the post-1966 governments appear, by and large, to have been convinced of the advantages of the gradualist approach over outright nationalization in that the former approach entails less risk of damage to the economy without compromising the ability of the government to extend indigenization in future; encourages employers of the enterprise concerned to offer their management and other professional skills to the government in the hope that they will retain their pensions and other entitlements; and emphasizes the willingness and desire of the government to co-operate with foreign enterprise.

Early attempts at increased Ghanaian participation

The Ghanaian Enterprises Decree, 1968

Faced with such a grim economic situation, the government in 1968 promulgated the maiden policy for promoting Ghanaian business. A decree – the Ghanaian Enterprises Decree, 1968 (NLCD 323) – was published, giving legal effect to that policy. The main aim was to create opportunities for indigenous businessmen, to raise the level of intermediate capital goods production by forcing out aliens from simple operations which required neither huge capital nor sophisticated technical skills, and to optimize local retention of profits and thus minimize the drain on foreign exchange.

The decree prescribed the appointment of a committee called the Ghanaian Enterprises Committee, made up of sixteen members (ten *ex officio* members and six local businessmen), to:

1 Advise the government on appropriate policies for promoting Ghanaian enterprises;
2 ensure the efficient implementation of any such policies;
3 examine any questions concerning commerce or industry that the government may refer to the committee and to report to the government on questions referred;
4 receive and examine complaints and petitions arising from the implementation of government policies on the promotion of Ghanaian enterprises and to recommend to the government such action as the committee considers necessary.[20]

The major fields of enterprise reserved by the legislation for local ownership were: selling in 'markets' engaging in petty trading, hawking or selling from kiosks; retail trade with an annual sales volume of C500,000 or less; wholesale trade with an annual sales volume of C1 million or less; any taxi service; any business for the sale under hire-purchase contract of vehicles for taxi service; any 'small-scale enterprise' which requires simple production or operation techniques or a capital of C100,000 or less; and any enterprise concerned with the representation in Ghana of overseas manufacturers.[21]

A number of prohibitions were also laid down. Ghanaians used by aliens as a front would be imprisoned without the option of a fine. An alien offender was to have his immigration quota withdrawn. Every alien who operated any reserved enterprise was required, not later than *three* months after the date of the publication of the decree, to institute a training scheme for Ghanaians which was designed to equip them with all the skills needed for the operation of the reserved enterprise concerned; and no taxi or vehicle could change hands at a price higher than that assessed by authorized persons in the State Transport Corporation.[22]

The Ghanaian Business (Promotion) Act, 1970

Representations were made by the Ghana Chamber of Commerce and other organized sections of the Ghanaian business community for certain amendments to be made to the legislation to bring it more in line with the demands and pressures of the time. It was as a result of the recommendations of official committees appointed to look into the representations that the Ghanaian Business (Promotion) Act, 1970, came into force replacing the Ghanaian Enterprises Decree, 1968.

As readers may recall, the Ghanaian Enterprises Committee set up under the superceded decree was responsible for the actual implementation of the government policies for the promotion of Ghanaian enterprises, and generally for administering that decree. That Committee was now converted by the Act into an *advisory* body only, to assist the minister responsible for economic planning who was charged with the responsibility of administering and implementing the provisions of the Act. The size of the committee was reduced from sixteen to six, with representatives of businessmen removed, ostensibly to permit speedy consultation and action.

There were other significant departures. For example, as from 30 June 1971 a new category of enterprises not mentioned in the original decree was also to be reserved for Ghanaian ownership. These were: commercial transportation by land, bakery, printing other than printing of textiles, beauty culture, produce brokerage, advertising and publicity, and manufacture of cement blocks for sale.[23] The provision in the decree for alien employers to introduce training schemes for the enhancement of skills of Ghanaian employees was repeated but without the imposition of a time limit for employers to institute the schemes.[24] The minister for economic affairs was for the first time empowered to appoint 'business inspectors' to carry out such functions as would give effect to the Act.[25] And the minister could, with the prior approval of the Cabinet, by executive instrument permit alien manufacturers to do retail and wholesale trading in items manufactured by them in their own premises.[26]

The most important feature of the Act was of course the reservation of more economic activities to Ghanaians only. The principles that governed the selection of those areas of economic activity were:

1 that their operations should fall within the technical competence of the Ghanaian labour force;

2 that the size of investment and labour required should fall within the competence of Ghanaian managerial talents;
3 that there should be an adequate supply of Ghanaian businessmen with the know-how and experience to enter the selected fields; and
4 that the take-over of these fields by Ghanaians should create no major gaps or cause major disruptions in the economy.[27]

To implement the Act, a number of structures and financial arrangements were made. Within the Ministry of Economic Planning, for instance, a division was set up as the main technical organization for servicing the Ghanaian Enterprises Advisory Committee and for co-ordinating the activities of various agencies concerned with the government's programme for the promotion of Ghanaian business enterprises. This division was in December 1970 hived off from the ministry to become the Office of Business Promotion with an independent non-civil servant executive in charge with powers to recruit and operate outside the confines of the civil service. The functions of the Office of Business Promotion include:

1 provision of small Ghanaian businesses with technical assistance and advisory services in key functional areas of business organization and management;
2 supervision of the administration of a special financial assistance scheme for small-scale indigenous businesses (i.e. the Small Business Credit Scheme);
3 assistance to Ghanaian entrepreneurs in the identification, preparation and execution of small-scale projects; and
4 regulation of the expansion of alien enterprises in the non-reserved fields of economic activity.[28]

The Management Development and Productivity Institute opened a number of Advisory Bureaus in the country to offer professional advice to local entrepreneurs in such subjects as office management, simple accounting, data processing and allied fields. The Ghana Institute of Management and Public Administration was also expanded by the addition of an Administrative Staff College.

The financial institutions also had a function to perform. The Bank of Ghana introduced a Credit Insurance Guarantee Scheme to encourage local banks to give loans to small-scale enterprises. The Ghana Commercial Bank and the Standard Bank of West Africa set up Development Financing Units to cater for the medium-term needs of Ghanaian businessmen; the services offered by these units included small loans and technical assistance to businessmen in sales organization, purchasing techniques, stock control and accounting.

Quite apart from the provision of loans and other financial facilities to agricultural and industrial entrepreneurs, the National Investment Bank, through its technical department – the Development Service Unit – provided consultancy services such as feasibility studies for Ghanaians seeking to enter business or operate in new areas of undertakings. Its Post-Finance Department was also responsible for the setting up of accounting records for customers who could not afford to employ full-time accountants. The Act did not specifically cover the main areas of operation of the Agricultural Development Bank, but that Bank proposed to finance Ghanaian businesses engaged in distribution and marketing of farm produce and to provide advisory services for such enterprises.

The government also directly made some dramatic overtures to indigenous business. In the 1971–2 Budget, it offered to guarantee to commercial banks up to C100,000 to support any transaction for the acquisition of non-Ghanaian business by an approved client. It also established a Small Business Credit Scheme with an individual ceiling of C5000 to finance businesses within reserved areas. The Small Business Credit Scheme had two main objects: to increase access of local entrepreneurs taking over from aliens or operating in the priority sectors of the economy to organize credit on reasonable terms to supplement the resources that were available through the normal banking systems;[29] and to arrange for money to be made available in a small way to enterprising citizens who lacked capital resources for initiating viable businesses. By the end of December 1974, the government had invested about C10 million in loans under the Small Business Credit Scheme to about 6500 Ghanaian entrepreneurs. The Post Office Savings Bank (now National Savings and Credit Bank) immediately raised its interest on deposits from 2½ to 5 per cent in compliance to government orders, and the liquidity ratio for commercial banks was also reduced from 50 to 45 per cent.

Problems encountered

Several problems were encountered in the implementation of the legislation, some short-term, others long-term.

Short-term difficulties These included inadequate domestic financial resources, temporary disruption of economic activities, unemployment, unavailability of offers, lack of foreign exchange and racketeering in currency. Available information indicated that in retail and wholesale trading alone, the problem involved about 600 alien enterprises with an estimated investment of C15 million and a labour force of some 4000.[30]

No banker would compromise on basic principles of lending, and it was difficult to imagine that the banks would, within a matter of a few weeks only, accommodate Ghanaian businessmen, a large number of whom might not hitherto have been operating bank accounts, to the tune of C15 million for the purchase of the retail and wholesale businesses alone. Applications for loans submitted by many Ghanaian companies to the banks for the acquisition of the enterprises of departing aliens were therefore either turned down for various reasons or were approved too late to be of meaningful assistance to the applicants. Many aliens who had not received offers from Ghanaians for the purchase of their businesses by the zero-hour closed down these shops and stores in accordance with the law. Stocks of essential commodities which should have been in circulation remained locked up. Where ownership of alien enterprises had changed into Ghanaian hands, the aliens had not replenished their stocks in anticipation of shut-down and the new Ghanaian entrepreneurs had insufficient time within which to place orders. The result was the incidence of artificial shortages.

The change of ownership of the enterprises involved a displacement of some of the 4000 employees. Given sufficient time, the displaced persons could have been absorbed into the system: instead, they became unemployed. The national problem of unemployment might not have been affected if these persons were replaced by registered unemployed persons, but this did not happen, as Ghanaians preferred to employ their wives and relations who might not have registered as unemployed.

It was not possible that the prevailing balance of payments position of the country would permit the economy to bear the additional strain. When remittances were not authorized officially, those affected resorted to illegal currency dealings, smuggling and black marketing. Because the Act did not stipulate the manner in which business were to be transferred, a great number of bargains were made through private treaties which were often shrouded in secrecy. In some cases, exhorbitant good-will payment was demanded of Ghanaians; on other occasions, the vendors either got the proceeds from the sale of their enterprises transferred out of the country through the black market, or got the prospective Ghanaian buyer, most likely to be a member of the new rich of the previous governments, who had large amounts of money stored in foreign banks, to pay for the business in foreign exchange while the owner put the equivalent in cedis in the local bank for eventual transfer abroad.[31] And yet some of the finance is believed to have come from nominal credit systems under which vendors, to give a semblance of acquiescence, transferred their businesses to their nominees who would pay eventually from dividends accruing to them. Such a nominal transfer still left many aliens in effective control. In many of the cases,

Ghanaians would appear to have been used as fronts – a thing punishable under the Act. Such strategies were compounded by the lack of co-operation, and other activities of fronts where that offence was officially suspected.[32]

Before the transfer of ownership of any business could be effected, it was necessary to agree on the price, and the price could be ascertained through valuation by professionally qualified valuers. Considering the number of enterprises affected and the availability of expert valuers – architects, accountants, commercial bankers, transport engineers, etc. – it was not possible in practice to complete the valuation before the deadline of 1 August 1970 set for indigenization of one category of alien enterprises. Some of the businesses were therefore purchased without proper valuation.

As if these problems were not enough to confound the fledgling Ghanaian business neophyte, the central government introduced a temporary surcharge in the 1970–1 financial year on many imported goods in the country, which had the effect of abnormally raising local prices while, by reason of association with the European Economic Community, neighbouring francophone countries enjoyed cheaper tariffs and customs duties. The result was that many aliens who left the retail trade sector in Ghana were known to be operating on the country's borders, dealing in the same trades and dumping cheaper goods from the neighbouring territories on Ghana through smuggling.

Long-term problems These were concerned mainly with managerial ability, lack of foreign contacts, exemptions of aliens in specified fields, and the administration of the Act.

Because the Act did not set any deadline for the training of Ghanaians to assume managerial and other key positions in the reserved enterprises, many of the alien enterprises in the unscheduled fields did not make an effort to train Ghanaians.

Under an import control system, market information has not been imported in certain commodities because sellers' markets had existed in them. But some Ghanaian businessmen experienced difficulty in obtaining credit facilities abroad from manufacturers and suppliers because, with the removal of alien overseas business representation, certain overseas banks appeared unwilling to grant the normal 180-day credit facilities to them.

Exemption permitted under section 31 of the Act made it possible for an affected alien retailer or wholesaler to pose as a manufacturer because alien manufacturers were permitted to enter the wholesale and retail trade, so long as the items were manufactured by themselves in Ghana. It wás feared in many circles that some of these firms sold imported goods alongside what they manufactured locally because the enforcement agencies had 'difficulty in identifying the make of goods in the outlets of manufacturers licensed to sell their own goods in the retail outlets'.[33]

In the administration of the Act problems were also rife. As neither the Ghana Chamber of Commerce nor any other organized business community for that matter was represented on the Ghanaian Enterprises Advisory Committee, the views of the indigenous business community were inadequately felt in the corridors of power. Another drawback was that central and regional loans committees set up to administer the small business loans delayed approval of loans to suitable Ghanaian businessmen; and often politics was the overriding consideration. Furthermore, to ensure a more effective supervision of the business operations of aliens, the 'business inspectors' should have been full-time officials with a knowledge and experience in business management or commerce; and yet, the regional chief executives who were entrusted with the duty of business inspection had neither the time nor the expertise to ensure effective implementation of the Act.

The latest policy on investment and indigenization

It is not strange therefore that in the Investment Policy Decree, 1975, and the Ghanaian Enterprises Development Decree, 1975, which were simultaneously published in April that year, the government sought to plug the loopholes that bedevilled the Ghana Business (Promotion) Act which the decrees superseded with effect from 1 January 1977.[34]

Remedying legislative defects

The principal measures proposed for removing the laxities in the legislation may be summarized as follows.

1 A government committee – the Investment Policy Implementation Committee – is to be set up, under the Investment Policy Decree, to act as an intermediary or investment broker in transactions between vendors and purchasers of alien businesses falling under the decree and to be responsible for determining prices at which the assets should change hands.[35] The purpose of this measure is to eliminate secret private treaties, with all the cheating of indigenes that usually took place under the Business Promotion Act.

2 The committee is empowered to find ways of disposing of the unbought shares or the whole of the alien enterprise if, for any reason,

there are not enough Ghanaians to buy the property or shares thereof.[36]

3 The committee has power to set aside dubious transactions entered into before or after the commencement of the decree.[37]

4 Any affected alien who adopts Ghanaian citizenship after his capital has become vested in the committee would not be allowed to operate as a Ghanaian citizen unless be joins forces with the state or individual citizens.[38]

5 A time limit is imposed on alien enterprises to institute training schemes aimed at equipping their Ghanaian employees for supervisory and managerial positions in the enterprises. The firms are also obliged to submit annual progress reports on these training schemes.[39]

6 The Office of Business Promotion yields place to a full-fledged commission financed not only from moneys provided by the government and its agencies but also from interest on loans granted under the Small Business Credit Scheme and its own investments.[40] The membership of the commission includes local businessmen.

7 As a means of fostering African solidarity, nationals of member-countries of the Organization of African Unity who still operate some of the scheduled businesses in Ghana are exempted from the provisions of these decrees, if similar privileges are accorded Ghanaian businessmen in their own countries.

Notwithstanding the improvements in legislative provisions, a mention of possible problem areas would appear to be germane if officials are to avoid some of the administrative problems that have cropped up under the existing Act. Two areas are isolated for comment. One is that the structural relationship between the Investment Policy Committee and the Ghanaian Enterprises Development Commission is unspecified and unclear, even though the functions (especially the power to appoint business inspectors and to oversee the transfer of businesses) as well as membership of the two structures overlapped in several respects. The other is that effective policing of the decrees depends very much on the qualification, experience and background of persons chosen for the post of business inspector.

Socioeconomic factors

Apart from correcting technical defects of the existing legislation on indigenization, the two new decrees seek to achieve at least two main objectives, affecting what may be referred to as the external and the internal economies respectively of the country. They are:

1 external factor: widening the scope of fields of economic activities reserved for local (i.e. state and indigenous individual) participation and thus reducing the economic dependence of the country on foreigners;
2 internal factors: (i) control by the state of the economy (*vis-à-vis* private entrepreneurship); and (ii) redress of income inequalities.

Scope of economic activities reserved for individual Ghanaians

The new policy extends the scope of areas reserved for indigenous businessmen and makes participation of Ghanaians obligatory in a number of enterprises in which aliens were previously allowed to operate without Ghanaian participation. Apart from the existing prohibition of aliens from trade of less than C500,000 capital, from selling in markets and from engagement in petty trading and hawking, the decree extends the list of enterprises wholly reserved for Ghanaians by the addition of such commercial projects as sale under hire-purchase contract of motor vehicles, produce brokerage, pool betting business and lotteries, estate agency and travel agency businesses, and of such industrial enterprises as ordinary manufacture/tailoring of garments, textile screen hand printing (including tie and dye), tyre retreading, and manufacture of suitcases, briefcases, etc. Also, no alien company will be allowed to operate in certain fields without Ghanaian participation. These fields include eight commercial projects, some of which are the distribution and servicing of motor vehicles, tractors and spare parts, wholesale distribution and distribution of petroleum products, etc., as well as some thirty-six industrial projects (including butcheries, breweries, motor workshops, sawmilling, and manufacture of candles, chalk, writing ink and rubber products). In the agricultural sector, poultry farming as well as fish and shrimp trawling are affected in the same way.[41]

The survival of enterprises providing such basic necessities as sugar, salt, soap, detergents, fertilizers, petroleum products, lubricants; hatchets, hoes and other manually operated agricultural implements; animal feed, milk, baby food; textiles; beer, cement, rubber tyres and tubes, and flour, is subject to at least 50 per cent participation by Ghanaians. These are sensitive economic areas where shortage of products has often in the past caused the government much embarrassment and political headaches.

Moreover, foreign enterpreneurs of large enterprises are forbidden from operating in the fields of banking, timber and mining as from the expiry date if at least 40 per cent of the capital is not owned by Ghanaians.[42] Where the timber or mineral industry or the enterprise providing basic necessities of life employs higher capital than C500,000 or higher turnover than C1,000,000, the state should own not less than 55 per cent of the capital; the rates are, however, drastically reduced to as low a figure as 20–30 per cent in the case of aluminium and oil industries, for obvious reasons.

Thus. although their impact on the national economy could be only marginal, the decrees have the merit of promoting and accelerating the transfer of ownership and control of specified alien industries crucial to the economic survival of the country to an indigenous private sector and to the state within the given period.

Financing indigenization

Quantitative data

There is no gainsaying the fact that the success or otherwise of the twin legislations will depend not only on the availability of, and the demand for, securities, but also on the investment climate created by the central government. Preliminary data collected by the Capital Life Investment Board indicated that the total value of the shares affected by the Investment Policy Decree would be between C55 million and C75 million.

Registration

As at 31 December 1976 – the deadline for the coming into force of the decree – some 290 companies had been considered by the Ghanaian Enterprises Development Commission, out of which three had been granted exemption from the provisions of the decree by the government; of the remaining 287 companies, 204, including 12 that went public, complied with the legislation. The rest were yet either to file evidence of compliance or to submit the names of the proposed participants for approval as directed by the Commission. And there was evidence of evasion by some companies.[43]

Public offers

Altogether twelve enterprises, including the widely known commercial houses, published prospectuses to invite Ghanaians at large to purchase their shares. The state, acting though the Ministry of Finance, acquired shares in four such companies. Most, if not all, of these public offers were over-subscribed and the Committee had, in accordance with the decree, to impose guidelines for the allotment to ensure that the small investor was as far as practicable satisfied. Some C33 million worth of shares were made available to the state and Ghanaians through these public offers.[44]

State participation

In addition to the four public offers in which the state acquired shares, the 'reserved capital' in the two foreign-owned banks and 20 per cent of the equity of five foreign insurance companies were taken up by the state. The rest of the enterprises in which the state acquired shares are a flour mill and four other companies in which state participation was raised to meet the requirements of the decree. Altogether, the state acquired some C14 million shares at a cost of C20.26 million.[45]

Sources of finance

The price of indigenization is being met largely out of individual savings of Ghanaians. According to statistics, the total demand liabilities of the commercial banks as at 31 January 1976 amounted to some C930 million, including savings account balances of C264 million. If the savings figure is abated by 30 per cent to take account of amounts held by non-Ghanaians, the major portion of the balance of C184 million could be made available for use by Ghanaians to acquire shares in alien businesses. Savings balances held by the banks for the Ghanaian public are therefore a ready source for investment in equity shares. If education on investment in company securities is accelerated, it should be possible to assure Ghanaian investors that ownership of these securities is a serious alternative investment to ownership of popular real assets like residential buildings.

There is a snag, however, with this source of financing. Financial institutions also provide a source of finance to industry. Short-term loans for working capital and long-term loans for expansion are provided to industry by the banks. These same banks are going to be called upon to provide finance for the acquisition of mere shares. Again, share purchase is going to compete with industrial expansion for the use of scarce capital. If savers whose deposits provide the banks with the funds for loans withdraw these deposits for share purchases, they may reduce the banks' ability to lend. Industrial expansion might be adversely affected as a result. The situation could be eased tremendously if the foreign banks and multinationals who have millions of unremitted profits would be willing to re-invest in the country. There is no evidence that they are prepared to do this, however, and already, according to the governor of the Bank, some C28.2 million of such funds had been repatriated by the end of February 1977.

A mutual fund company – the National Trust Holding Company Ltd – has been formed since December 1976 to mobilize funds for investment in the productive sectors of the economy and to broaden the equity base of industrial and commercial enterprises in the country. There is for instance the underwriting activities of the company, designed to assist in raising capital for the establishment of new or the expansion of existing public companies. There is also the brokerage service, designed to provide expert advice and counsel to Ghanaians seeking investment openings in the country. Also, the company has a scheme for lending to individuals and organized groups to enable them to acquire shares in alien companies and for investment in enterprises wholly reserved for Ghanaians. Finally, it will provide a ready market for the purchase and sale of shares. Two development banks and two insurance corporations have together contributed C3.25 million towards the initial capital of the company.[46]

Yet another source of funds is the Small Loans Scheme, initiated under the Business Promotion Act of 1970, which is being continued under the Ghanaian Enterprises Development Decree of 1975. A large number of Ghanaian businessmen operating in the reserved areas of commerce and industry have been assisted financially. By the end of December 1975, some C16 million had gone into loans, either to help them purchase businesses from aliens or to enable them to undertake new viable business activities.

Investment climate

A 55 per cent investment tax that had, before the implementation of the Investment Policy Decree, been imposed on individuals for some years has been abolished, making dividend payments attractive to would-be investors. Apart from granting this tax exemption, the government consciously seeks to create a business environment that is conducive to pronounced participation of the private sector in the future economic development of Ghana. The facilities offered through the banks and other financial institutions for potential businessmen to acquire capital have been expanded. Another positive measure is the provision for the granting of attractive concessions, including tax holidays, for a specified period to certain export-oriented and agro-based industries. Also, the country is now better organized for stricter import controls, better prices for exportable commodities and a more meaningful export drive. Moreover, subject to its external payments position, no restrictions will be imposed on the transfer out of Ghana of imported capital or profits and dividends on local investments.[47] This should dispel any fear of the government expropriating foreign investments in the future.

Evaluation of economic impact of indigenization

On foreign private investment

Alien investors who are already established in the country have over the years built up a fund of dividends which they have not been able to repatriate because of the country's unfavourable foreign exchange position. These funds properly belong to the overseas shareholders of these companies, being the reward for their investments; for as long as the foreign shareholders remained the owners of the entire equity of these companies, they were prepared to allow the use of these accumulated dividends as a source of working capital or of finance for expansion. Now that they are being compelled to dispose of part of the ownership, some of them are reluctant to place these monies at the disposal of the new joint ventures. They would prefer to keep these sums apart and, if permitted, to invest in short-term bonds so that they can earn some interest to counter the effects of inflation. Government restraints and controls are seen by such companies, especially the multinational corporations, and the international business community in general as costs.

On the other hand, it is easy to exaggerate the probable adverse effect of such measures on future inflows of foreign investment. First, because foreign corporations have a general preference for wholly owned subsidiaries, public statements of representatives of any such corporation may give an impression of a harder line than would actually be taken by the company, with part of the public posturing aimed subtly at deterring encroachment on its property rights.

Second, the idea of indigenous participation is not new to any modern investor with any foresight. Most international companies have come to terms with it and prefer teaming up with either governments or nationals of their host countries rather than going it alone, since there are very few countries indeed that leave foreign-owned firms uncontrolled completely. As has happened with the prosecution of the 1970 Act in Ghana, the initial fears of alien companies were removed with firm assurances that Ghanaians are prepared to pay a fair price for the facility and that both 'alien' capital and expertise would be needed in the development of the country for a long time to come. As far as the 1970 Act is concerned, there is not much evidence so far, according to the Office of the Ghanaian Enterprises Commission, that the implementation of the Act has had a perceptibly adverse impact on foreign private investment.

Foreign technical assistance

To the extent that the indigenization policy acts as a deterrent to foreign investment, it should affect only direct private foreign investment; it should not significantly affect aid flows and technical assistance from the international agencies, or, in many cases, governmental aid flows.

This is so because a large part of foreign assistance supports the establishment or expansion of public enterprises which operate either separately or jointly with foreign private enterprises. In considering requests for foreign aid, the question of whether or not the recipient operating agency is to be a public enterprise is as important as other review criteria, such as economic feasibility, contribution to economic growth, technical soundness and market demand.

Since the indigenization exercise encourages the establishment of joint public–private foreign investment, it is probably likely that foreign technical assistance to these areas might have even increased.

Indigenous private investment and growth in entrepreneurial capabilities

Enterprises listed under the First Schedule to the Decree are to be wholly acquired by Ghanaians. The alien owners are required to sell out to indigenes. This change in ownership may hamper expansion – the new Ghanaian owners may lack expertise and may have to spend time to acquire the requisite knowledge; expansion programmes planned by the alien owners may have to be shelved – on the other hand, foreign companies have, by joining and strengthening Ghanaian businessmen's organizations and by accepting Ghanaian equity investments, helped a great deal in promoting Ghanaian entrepreneurship.

Productivity

There is no evidence that labour productivity has declined or increased as a result of the indigenization programme. No special study has yet been conducted into this aspect of the exercise.

Initially, productivity of investment must have decreased since some of those who took over affected foreign businesses did not have the managerial experience to plan, allocate or record their use of equipment, supplies or labour. The Office of the Ghanaian Enterprises Development Commission estimates that some 80 per cent of small-scale Ghanaian entrepreneurs keep inadequate records of their business transactions.[48] The shortage of 'middle management personnel' must have accentuated the problems Ghanaian entrepreneurs had to face in the initial stages.

Overall restructuring of the economy and development

Although the economy of Ghana would still be subject to the vagaries of the global economic situation, its structure is likely to change in due course from a framework with colonial and dependent orientation to one with the ownership and control of the bulk of the country's enterprises in the hands of Ghanaians or the state. This process may be speeded up if, in the absence of a law prohibiting non-voting shares, the number of foreign preference shares, if any, would not be made to frustrate the desire to see that ordinary shareholders of Ghana reap the fullest benefits of their investment. In times of inflation, hoarding and the multiplicity of middlemen in the retail trade could be contained through effective agricultural and fiscal policy measures, intensified law enforcement and adequate co-operative distribution systems respectively; and provided there is no alienation of major foreign investors who may continue to operate in the unscheduled areas of the economy. It would, however, appear to be too early to estimate meaningfully the effect of the indigenization programme on the structure of the economy.

Social and political implications of indigenization

Apart from commitment of the government to the principle of national development through self-reliance, the Ghanaian Enterprises Development Decree, 1975 (NRCD 330) sets itself two other tasks: to enable the state to gain control of the economy; and to ensure the equitable distribution of the resources of the land and the wealth accruing therefrom.

State control of the economy

It is in line with the basic position of the outline of the country's present five-year plan that it is the public sector, not the indigenous private sector, that should assume control of the economy. Government, through its functionaries, is better placed to evaluate and monitor the performance trends of the businesses involved than are several thousand Ghanaian shareholders scattered throughout the country, with their atomistic participation. The massive intervention of government's in the acquisition of the share capital of enterprises in schedule II should help achieve effective indigenous involvement in the control, if not the management of these enterprises. But has the government the required financial resources for such acquisitions? Against the background of the balance of payments position and the policy of national self-reliance, this question will be decided in large part by the capability and willingness of the populace to bear increased taxation and the willingness of the affected foreign firms to re-invest their accumulated profits.

Socialization of the benefits of indigenization

As already mentioned, one of the proclaimed aims of the Ghanaian Enterprises Development Decree is to redress income inequalities in Ghana. But two main forces – one centrifugal, the other centripetal – are likely to be at work in the redistribution of income in the country with the coming into force of the indigenization decree.

On the one hand, the indigenization policy will tend to concentrate a large amoung of Ghana's resources in the hands of very few highly placed persons, mostly in the urban areas, who have the means and influence to gain access to the major sources of funds. The severity of this problem may, however, be toned down by a provision in the decree that permits the Commission to establish financial assistance schemes for the promotion of small-scale Ghanaian businesses.[49] Also, most of the enterprises listed in schedule 1 and 2 of the indigenization decree are situated in the urban areas, where the conditions for the maximization of profits are reasonably satisfactory. As most of the rural areas in Ghana are economically depressed, the effect of the policy on indigenization, favouring as it does the economic opportunities in the urban areas, will be to worsen the already deplorable conditions in the rural areas unless the government, true to its declared intentions of intensifying rural agriculture and infrastructural development as well as providing cottage industries, takes positive steps to reduce the imbalance.

On the other hand, there is provision for the government to buy businesses, or to dispose of them publicly, where these remain unsold after the expiry date. Also, in respect of the scheduled enterprises, Ghanaian workers are obliged to hold such percentage of the capital of the enterprise concerned as the Enterprises Development Commission may, with the approval of the Commissioner for Economic Planning, prescribe.[50] Already, the Ghana Trades Union Congress has bought shares in such companies. Also, any capital owned by Ghanaian workers would, where the workers of the enterprise exceed nine in number, be held in trust for such workers by a registered co-operative society formed by the workers; and any financial assistance required for the acquisition of shares would be granted to the workers through such society.[51] All these measures are meant to reduce the atomistic nature of shares held and to enable the small investor to exercise real control over the businesses rather than accept the position of a powerless sleeping partner.

However, this should not lead to automatic participation in management. In order not to subject such workers to unnecessary stresses, care should be taken not to allow them to participate at the level beyond that at which they feel competent. Even this should be done only after a thorough study of the workers involved to find out whether they want to get involved in decisions affecting them and to what extent, and also after creating an awareness among them that they share at least some goals with the organization.

Overall appraisal

Most of the local equity participation of foreign concerns in Ghana falls into three main categories: government participation in selected large extractive industries owned by multinational corporations; government participation in small branch enterprises of multinational corporations like banking, insurance and petroleum distribution; and comprehensive citizen participation in small and medium-sized enterprises owned by alien residents.

With regard to the first category, the government has already taken the required minimum shares of each of the large enterprises of over C0.5 million capital or C1 million turnover, mineral enterprises and large timber operations. Large enterprises producing basic necessities like sugar, fertilizers and rubber products have been similarly affected. Petroleum refining is now wholly in the hands of the state. But the 30 and 20 per cent participation in aluminium industry (VALCO) and petroleum production respectively, authorized to be taken by government, has not been implemented to date, despite the 1975 decrees on indigenization. The government's required minimum involvement in the ownership of the foreign banks has proceeded smoothly. As regards the small- and medium-sized enterprises, all enterprises in twelve categories of simple industry (e.g. surface transportation, bakeries and real estate) are now in Ghanaian hands, while foreigners still dominate large retail and wholesale enterprises as well as thirteen or so categories of industry (e.g. petroleum distribution, auto assembly, pharmaceuticals and plastics). The process of indigenization has been generally evolutionary and gradual, and not directed at any particular country.

With indigenization of foreign enterprises, access to international capital markets, experience and facilities may be limited. The pace of investment in the country may be adversely affected even though it is a bit too early to say whether or not indigenization has deterred foreign investment in the country, whether foreign investors are relectant to invest readily in the country. And because of insufficiency of training and experience, some of the Ghanaian replacements for expatriate staff in the large firms may initially not be able to maintain the managerial standards set by some of the departing expatriates.

On the positive side, the indigenization programme has revealed the great investment capability of the Ghanaian public. Involvement of workers in the programme is contributing to increased industrial peace and harmony. And socialization of the benefits is progressing in such a way as to reduce concentration of wealth in the hands of a few individuals only. On the economic plane, because the large firms have not been nationalized outright, key personnel with management and technological skill and ability are generally not inclined to leave the enterprises since they have no doubts about their future in the industry or country. An even more obvious advantage is that earnings from industry – particularly the extractive – are higher under local ownership, and Ghanaians are receiving experience in managing businesses and industries now.

As explained earlier, indigenization under the 1970 Act was poorly executed administratively: aliens sought evasion through ownership fronts, exceptions to the rules and citizenship changes; local citizens often got cheated in the transfer process; and implementation was generally harsh and inadequately planned. There is now every indication that the responsible organizations have learnt their lesson. This is seen in the painstaking attempts to plug all loopholes in the legislation and to carry out the 1975–6 programme with considerable attention to legal forms and social justification.

But there are still a few crucial problems to be overcome. These include the persuasion of the foreign owners of firms to agree to reinvest substantial portions of their unremitted profits in local industrial and commercial expansion. The practice of some Ghanaians to act as fronts for alien businessmen continues to thwart the indigenization effort. There is also the set of problems that illiteracy imposes on citizen ownership of small-scale concerns – problems of supervision, accounting, making contracts; in short, the problem of achieving a degree of business rationality without functional literacy. In the larger enterprises, also, the appropriate Ghanaians not only need to admit limitations in management but also need to take full advantage of the facilities existing through agencies that can assist them to improve on their businesses. A further obstacle to future progress is the weak sense of obligation on the part of some Ghanaians to repay money borrowed from the government. In many ways, the important period in the provision of financial assistance to Ghanaian entrepreneurs comes after the loan has been made. Yet, hampered by lack of adequate operating funds and qualified staff, the Office of the Ghanaian Enterprises Commission has generally been unable to carry on effective follow-up activities. Particularly in the case of newly established businesses, the large number of failures could have been significantly reduced had there been loan extensions and had review officers been available to visit each enterprise regularly, inspect the premises, examine the books, check the inventory, discuss problems and prospects with the entrepreneur, and advise him where to obtain the technical assistance he might need.

Conclusion

The basic framework for indigenization on industry and commerce has surely been laid. What Ghanaians make of this opportunity would depend, *inter alia*, not only on their collective commitment to the philosophy of national economic self-reliance, but also on their efforts to resist the temptation to be used as fronts against the interests of the nation; on the adequacy of the training given to the small-scale local entrepreneur; on the ability of those who come to occupy high positions in the large undertakings to acquire relevant managerial and professional or technical expertise in good time; on the effective resuscitation, rehabilitation and revitalization of co-operative operations on a national scale; on the preparedness of the alien entrepreneur to re-invest a portion of his dividends for expansion; and on the degree of goodwill that attends the change-over or exchange transactions between Ghanaians and alien businessmen. This is the challenge.

Notes

1 The term 'indigenization' is used very broadly in this context to include (1) local equity participation, whereby the government takes up a certain proportion of the capital or economic activity of a specific enterprise; (2) citizen ownership, whereby the government reserves certain sectors or industries for itself, or reserves the ownership of certain categories of industry and trade exclusively for possession by its own citizen; and (3) localization or Africanization, which entails the replacement of foreign workers by local employees or citizens of the country.

2 Naseem Ahmad, 'From "liberation" to "redemption": economic policy in Ghana between the coups, 1966–72', *Universitas*, vol. 3, no. 1 (n.s., 1973), pp. 51–2.

3 The Ghana National Chamber of Commerce Inc. Instrument, 1968 (L.I.611).

4 J. Esseks, 'Government and indigenous private enterprise in Ghana', *Journal of Modern African Studies*, vol. 9, no. 1 (1971), pp. 11–29.

5 ibid. See also Sir Leslie M'Carthy, *Report of the Chairman of the*

Committee on Aid to Ghanaian Businessmen (Accra, 1960 mimeo).
6 Esseks.
7 ibid.
8 Apaloo Commission Report, especially the evidence of Krobo Edusei, one-time minister of state for protocol in the CPP government; of Augustus Kofi Oduro, then president of the Ghana National Contractors' Association; also *Daily Graphic* (18, 28 and 31 March 1966).
9 *Ghanaian Times* (10 October 1960), as quoted by Esseks.
10 Esseks, p. 25.
11 Ghana Government, *Government Policy on the Promotion of Business Enterprises* (Accra, 1968), p. 1.
12 Read the statement by the then president of the Association of Ghanaian Businessmen in the *Daily Graphic* (28 March 1968), p. 3; the expressions of support by some prominent members of Ghanaian businessmen in the *Daily Graphic* (10 July 1968; 17 March 1968), p. 16; the editorials of *Daily Graphic* (9 July 1968) and of the *Legon Observer*, iii, 15 (19 July 1968).
13 Esseks, pp. 26–7.
14 It was revealed at the JNK Taylor Assets Commission, which probed the assets of members of the Progress Party Government, that the then minister of interior issued over 5500 residence permits and nationalization certificates to affected aliens for handsome 'fees', contrary to the spirit of the law.
15 Ghana Parliamentary Debates, 23 June 1970, Accra, col. 1068.
16 The Ghana Business (Promotion) Act, 1970.
17 Ghana Parliamentary Debates, 23 June 1970, Accra, col. 1075.
18 The Investment Policy Decree, 1975 (NRCD 329), *passim*.
19 The Ghanaian Enterprises Development Decree, 1975 (NRCD 330), *passim*.
20 NLCD 323, section 3.
21 NLCD 323, section 11.
22 NLCD 323, sections 19–20, 14, 27.
23 NLCD 323, sections 11, 12 and 13.
24 NLCD 323, section 16.
25 NCLD 323, section 18.
26 NLCD 323, section 31.
27 One-Year Development Plan, July 1970–June 1971, pp. 151–2.
28 Report on the Role and Activities of the Office of Business Promotion, August 1970–June 1974 (Accra-Tema: Ghana Publishing Corporation, 1974).
29 The economic priorities of the government since 1971 have been: export promotion; import substitution and small manufacturing

industries; transportation of foodstuffs for local consumption.
30 Ghana Parliamentary Debates, 23 June 1970, Accra.
31 Editorial, *Daily Graphic* (26 November 1970); editorial, *The Pioneer* (26 November 1970).
32 Report on the Role and Activities of the Office of Business Promotion, p. 18.
33 ibid.
34 The original deadline of 31 December 1975 was later extended by a year to December 1976.
35 Section 19 of the Investment Policy Decree, 1975.
36 Section 19(4) of the Investment Policy Decree, 1975.
37 Section 26(1) of the Investment Policy Decree, 1975.
38 Section 23 of the Investment Policy Decree, 1975.
39 Section 18 of the Investment Policy Decree, 1975.
40 Section 10 of the Ghanaian Enterprises Development Decree, 1975.
41 First and Second Schedules of Investment Policy Decree, 1975; Part I, sections 1–4 of the Decree.
42 Part II (i.e. sections 5–10) of the Investment Policy Decree, 1975.
43 Report (CIB/INVEST/1) submitted by the executive secretary of the Investment Policy Implementation Committee to the senior principal secretary, Ministry of Finance on 5 January 1977, p. 3.
44 ibid, p. 3.
45 ibid, p. 4.
46 Speeches by the governor of the Bank of Ghana and the National Investment Bank at the formal opening of the offices of the National Trust Holding Co. on 3 December 1976.
47 Section 37 of the Investment Policy Decree, 1975 (NRCD 329).
48 Information obtained through correspondence with that Office.
49 Section 12 (1) of Ghanaian Enterprises Development Decree, 1975.
50 Section 13 (1) of the Ghanaian Enterprises Development Decree, 1975.
51 Section 13 (3) of the Ghanaian Enterprises Development Decree, 1975.

References

Grayson, Leslie E., 'A conglomerate in Africa: public-sector manufacturing enterprises in Ghana, 1962–1971', *African Studies Review*, vol. 16, no. 3, December 1973, pp. 315–45

Hart, Keith, 'Small-scale enterpreneurs in Ghana and development planning', *Journal of Development Studies*, vol. 6, no. 4 (July 1970), pp. 104–20

Kennedy, Paul, 'African businessmen and foreign capital: collaboration or conflict', *African Affairs*, vol. 73, no. 303 (1977), pp. 177–94
Kennedy, Paul, 'Indigenous capitalism in Ghana', *Review of African Political Economy* (London), no. 8 (January-April 1977), pp. 21–38

7 Nigeria

Emeka Ezeife, *Federal Ministry of Economic Development and Reconstruction, Lagos*

The economic situation pre- and post-independence

The 'modern' sector of the Nigerian economy was heavily dominated by foreign business from the pre-independence times to the first decade and half after independence. This sector includes industry, banking, insurance, transportation, haulage and distributive trades. The predominance of the foreign businesses is largely explained by a number of factors, among which was the patronage and strong backing of their parent companies in the industrialized countries. This in essence meant access to superior techniques, personnel and the immense financial resources of their parent bodies.

In contrast, the indigenous businesses had neither the necessary capital of their own nor easy access to the financial market. They were, and still are, new to the idea of resource-pooling for large-scale operations, and lacked the managerial skills, experience and knowledge of modern business methods required for operating large trading and manufacturing units. Hence the low level of participation by Nigerians in the ownership, control and management of businesses. Even with an increasing participation by Nigerians in the operation of businesses after independence in 1960, there was still a heavy, and in many sectors almost exclusive, concentration of shareholding and management positions in alien hands. Most of the Nigerians who held any equity interests at all were really token shareholders in the expatriate businesses.

The results of a study conducted on some aspects of the ownership and control structure of 1320 businesses, representing about 80 per cent of all companies registered in Nigeria by 1970, are quite relevant in this connection (see Table 7). It shows, for example, that Nigerians account for slightly less than 40 per cent of shareholdings in the companies covered by the survey; the balance of 60 per cent was in expatriate hands. If the study had been restricted to industrial enterprises, the percentage of Nigerian holdings would have been much lower, but this provided enough information to show that after a decade of political indepen-

Table 7 *Ownership and control structure of business enterprise in Nigeria*

Shareholders value of shares (₦)	*Numbers* Nigerian	Expatriate	Total	*Percentages* Nigerian	Expatriate	Total
2	146	113	259	56.4	43.6	100.0
2–2000	267	418	685	39.0	61.1	100.0
2001–10,000	182	193	375	48.5	51.5	100.0
10,001–20,000	62	124	186	33.3	66.7	100.0
20,001–40,000	46	82	128	35.9	64.1	100.0
40,001–100,000	47	128	175	27.7	73.2	100.0
100,001–200,000	28	80	108	25.9	74.1	100.0
above 200,000	43	120	163	26.4	73.6	100.0
Total	821	1258	279	39.5	60.4	100.0

Source: O. Teriba, E. C. Edozien and M. O. Kayode, 'Some aspects of ownership and control structure of business enterprise in a developing economy: the Nigerian case', *Nigerian Journal of Economic and Social Studies*, vol. 14, no. 1 (March 1972).

Hence the bulk of the Nigerian modern sector businesses were still owned and directed by foreigners.

Before the attainment of independence in 1960, no appreciable efforts were made at encouraging indigenous participation in economic activities, since the country was being governed as a colony of the British Empire. However, with the attainment of independence status, attempts were made by the Nigerian government to encourage active indigenous participation in commercial and industrial activities. These attempts, which included the provisions of financial and managerial support to aspiring indigenous businessmen, took mostly the form of moral persuasion. The early measures achieved some success in distributive trade and produce marketing and resulted in the emergence of a few indigenous businessmen, but the areas of large-scale distribution and industry were largely unaffected.

By 1966, the dominance by foreign businesses had become a concern not only to the government, but also to most Nigerians. Government efforts at encouraging indigenes to develop their potential were interrupted by the political difficulties of the second half of the decade of 1960s. However, by 1970, with crises over, the issue of indigenization became prominent once more. The first attempt at evolving a policy was made with the launching of the Second National Development Plan 1970–4, which indicated the direction of policy in this area. The policy was subsequently elaborated in the Nigerian Enterprises Promotion Decree which was promulgated in 1972.

The concept of indigenization

Indigenization within the Nigerian context is the process of increasing local involvement in the ownership, control and management of economic activities in the country. It is a gradual process of promoting indigenous participation in all aspects of the economy, especially in those areas that have hitherto been dominated by foreign business.

The policy of indigenization is seen as complementing political independence, which is in line with the strong belief that political independence would be meaningless without a good measure of economic independence. The policy is designed along lines similar to those of other nations which prevent foreign capital from stultifying their social, economic and political independence.

However, indigenization in the above context was not designed to bring about any outright nationalization or complete takeover of foreign businesses. Rather, it was designed to change the existing structure of foreign domination and to ensure adequate opportunities for indigenous participation. The approach to indigenization has therefore been designed not to discourage foreign investment in Nigeria; in fact, the various legislations on the scheme have been formulated to assure a place for continued foreign investment in the country. The scheme is also designed to ensure that Nigerian entrepreneurs are enabled to develop their own expertise and management skill, and to ensure active participation of Nigerians in these areas of economic activity that are still under foreign control. The policy is therefore seen as a preventive action against the danger that could result from any sudden withdrawal of foreign investment owing to factors other than economic considerations. It is also intended to guard against the difficulty of controlling foreign businesses which are answerable, first and foremost, to their foreign owners whose interests may not at all times tally with the aspirations of the nation. The scheme is designed to minimize the factor incomes that foreign businesses remit abroad by way of dividends.

Approaches to indigenization

Evolution of national policy on indigenization

For nearly three decades, Nigerians have clamoured for increased participation and increased involvement in the operations of economic activities in the country. As a response to this, the Nigerian government evolved a national policy on indigenization which was spelt out in Nigeria's Second National Development Plan 1970–4. The main objective of the policy was 'to raise the proportion of indigenous ownership of industrial investment in the country'.

This was to be achieved through effective government public sector control of at least 55 per cent of the equities of the iron and steel basic complex, petro-chemical industries, fertilizer production and petroleum production, especially for local distribution. Furthermore, such large and medium industries as food, forest products, building materials and construction industries, and plantation production of traditional cash-crops and basic raw materials for processing industry, were to be run as mixed ventures with government and private participation at a minimum of 35 per cent of their equities.

As a matter of general policy, the government was to encourage nation-wide equity participation in all manufacturing industries. The government role was to acquire shares and encourage Nigerian nationals wishing and willing to participate in industrial development to do so.

However, government policy on indigenization changed drastically with the promulgation of the Nigerian Enterprises Promotion Decree, 1972. Even though the objective of the legislation was to encourage and protect Nigerian participation in those areas of the economy in which Nigerians are competent, the scheme was designed to achieve the following:

1 to create opportunities for Nigerian indigenous businessmen;
2 to maximize local retention of profit;
3 to raise the level of intermediate goods production;
4 to raise the proportion of indigenous ownership of industrial investment; and
5 to increase Nigerian participation in decision-making in the larger commercial and industrial establishments.

The focus on private indigenous participation, which is an important characteristic of the decree, was a major and radical departure from the initial policy and the basic philosophy of public sector leadership as contained in Nigeria's Second National Development Plan.

The Nigerian Enterprises Promotion Decree of 1972 was amended three times, in 1973, in 1974 and finally in 1977, to reflect changes in policy resulting from experiences with the implementation of the indigenization programme. The most radical changes were contained in the Decree of 1977, which was a follow-up of the report of the Industrial Enterprises Panel established to assess the progress in the implementation of the programme and to make recommendations on necessary amendments to ensure an increase in the level of indigenous participation in affected enterprises. The new changes in the policy included the granting of more powers to the re-constituted Nigerian Enterprises Promotion Board to seal up all defaulting enterprises and dispose of them by selling to willing Nigerian buyers in accordance with the Nigerian Enterprises Promotion Decree of 1972.

Indigenization pressure groups

The pressure groups that were pushing the indigenization policy include such organizations as the Nigerian Chamber of Commerce and Industry, and individuals and associations of indigenous businessmen. For instance, after the promulgation of the Decree of 1972, indigenous businessmen mounted considerable pressure to expand the range of enterprises reserved exclusively for Nigerians to include advertising, public relations, estate agencies, pharmaceutical trades and the purchasing and marketing of export produce. The Chamber of Commerce and Industry for its part deplored the idea of government or public sector agencies participating and competing with indigenous private citizens in the acquisition of foreign enterprises.

Preparatory work undertaken

In 1976, the federal government set up the Industrial Enterprises Panel to evaluate the implementation of the Nigerian Enterprises Promotion Decree and assess the extent to which the aims and objectives of the federal government in establishing the scheme had been achieved. The Panel was further required to recommend amendments to the decree with a view to increasing the enterprises affected by it as well as the level of indigenous participation in such enterprises. It was also to examine such ancillary matters as the mechanics of meaningful indigenization, the development and use of indigenous capacity and the managerial structure of businesses affected by the scheme.

The basic conclusion of the Industrial Enterprises Panel was that the 1972 indigenization scheme succeeded only in a limited way, that is in the narrower and short-term objectives of the decree. Having identified this reasons for the limited success of the first phase, the Panel went on to make suggestions as to how to remedy the anomalies of that period. Some of the highlights of their findings were as follows.

1 A good foundation has been laid and valuable lessons learnt, and the opportunity offered by the review should be utilized to tie up all loose ends and correct the basic short-comings of the decree.
2 Though the indigenization effort was fundamentally directed to give Nigerians participation and control of the economy, some Nigerians

were found to have actively been in collusion with foreigners to frustrate some of the intentions of the government. Consequently, the government decided that the period between the submission of the report and the end of 1977 should be regarded as a mopping-up period within which the first phase of the indigenization programme should be completed.

The basic recommendations of the panel were incorporated into the Nigerian Enterprises Promotion Decree of 1977.

Summaries of laws dealing with the various types of indigenization measures

Nigerian Enterprises Promotion Decree no. 4 of 1972

This was the legislation by which the objectives of indigenization were put into effect. It classified enterprises into Schedules I and II. The enterprises classified under Schedule I were reserved exclusively for Nigerians. Those businesses that were a little more complicated and were therefore required to have 40 per cent indigenous ownerships were placed in Schedule II. Even here, foreigners were not allowed to participate unless the paid-up capital was up to ₦400,000 or the turnover was up to ₦1 million. The remaining enterprises involving activities requiring high technical skills were not classified and were open to both indigenous and foreign participation.

All enterprises affected by the decree were expected to comply with its provisions on or before 31 March 1974. The Nigerian Enterprises Promotion Board was set up simultaneously to implement the provisions of the decree.

The Decree no. 4 of 1972 was amended subsequently as follows.

Nigerian Enterprises Promotion Decree no. 28 of 23 June 1973 This made it possible for application for exemption under the parent decree to be made earlier than four months to the appointed day, that is, 31 March 1974. Under the original provision such applications could not be entertained. This decree also made it possible for state officials to be designated as inspectors of enterprises; prior to the amendment, only federal civil servants could be appointed as inspectors.

Nigerian Enterprises Promotion Decree no. 7 of February 1974 This amendment transferred the haulage of petroleum products from Schedule I to Schedule II of the original decree. The reason for the amendment was to avert possible shortage of petroleum products in some remote parts of the country which lacked well organized and properly managed indigenous transportation system.

This amendment brought stevedoring and shore-handling under Schedule I and clearing and forwarding agencies business from Schedule I to Schedule II.

Phase II of the indigenization programme

Consequent upon the acceptance of the report of the Industrial Enterprises Panel, the federal military government decided to advance the indigenization policy further by expanding the scope of the original Decree no. 4 of 1972. The objectives of this new phase of indigenization were clearly summed up in the broadcast of the head of the federal military government on the decision to embark on the second phase of indigenization.

> In embarking on indigenization, Government has been influenced by the need to place control of the Nigerian economy squarely in the hands of Nigerians and to ensure that Nigerians are the main beneficiaries from the resources of their country.

The Nigerian Enterprises Promotion Decree 1977 The most significant aspect of the indigenization decree is the inclusion of all alien enterprises within the scope of the indigenization scheme. All enterprises operating in Nigeria were reclassified into three categories, namely Schedules I, II and III. As before, Schedule I covered those enterprises that were to be wholly owned by Nigerians. The new Schedule II comprised mostly enterprises that were more complex and more capital-intensive. In view of the fact that they are critical to the process of technological transfer, the Nigerian equity participation in businesses under this category was raised to 60 per cent. The newly created Schedule III encompassed all other enterprises not specifically listed in Schedules I and II. This minimum Nigerian equity participation was fixed at 40 per cent.

Appropriate penalties were prescribed for any contravention of the decree. All defaulting enterprises were to be sealed up and taken over by government and disposed of to willing Nigerian buyers in accordance with the Nigerian Enterprises Promotion Decree 1972. The reconstituted Nigerian Enterprises Promotion Board was empowered not only to seal but also to prosecute defaulters. The decree further directed that prospective buyers of businesses sealed up for contravening the decree should retain the workers employed in such businesses. That means that the businesses must be sold as 'going concerns'. Such buyers must also undertake to continue to give the services that the former alien proprietors of the business were providing. The decree further directed that all acquisitions in respect of which satisfactory proof of purchase could not be produced by the purchasers should be revoked.

Indigenization through state versus private capitalism

Three models of indigenization are distinguishable for economies that have undergone or are undergoing the process of indigenization:

1 public sector-led model;
2 private sector-led model;
3 mixed economy model.

Under (1) above, the public sector provides the policy instrument and plays a leading role in the indigenization process. The public sector lead might have resulted from the weaker position of indigenous private enterprise, with the public sector having the financial and administrative machinery for the implementation of the indigenization programme. The responsibility in such a case devolves on the government for the finance, control and management of businesses affected by the indigenization programme.

The private sector-led model envisages major responsibility for private enterprise in the indigenization programme, with the public sector limiting itself to formulating policies and providing the necessary administrative machinery for the implementation of the programme.

The mixed economy model, however, envisages the direct and effective involvement of both the private and public sector in the indigenization process.

The experience with indigenization in Nigeria comes under the third classification, even though the Second National Development Plan envisaged a more dynamic role for the public sector. The promulgation of the Nigerian Enterprises Promotion Decree of 1972 was designed to assure an active involvement of both the public and private sectors of the economy in the indigenization process. Under the present arrangement, the public sector is responsible for the formulation of the indigenization policy and for providing the necessary instruments and administrative machinery for the implementation of the scheme. In addition, the government has increased its participation in the management and control of the economy by acquiring a majority shareholding in such strategic sectors of the economy as insurance, banking and the oil industry. These sectors had experienced a long-standing monopoly of alien enterpreneurship. The public sector has therefore provided the necessary support and has also offered an opportunity for the development of private sector entrepreneurial capacities and capabilities. The private sector was given a wider area of operation in the indigenization process. These areas come under Schedules I and II of the Indigenization Decree of 1972 and under Schedules I, II and III of the Decree of 1977.

Wholesale versus phased indigenization

The Nigerian government has adopted a phased rather than a wholesale approach to indigenization in order to forestall the attendant problems that would have arisen from the adoption of a wholesale approach.

Indigenization itself is a process of protracted negotiations involving the transfer of physical assets as well as the management and control of alien businesses to indigenous businessmen. However, with an acute shortage of qualified Nigerians, any wholesale transfer of businesses of the size and complexity as those being transferred would no doubt overstretch the management capabilities of the few young Nigerian businessmen who had not been exposed to managing such businesses. Phasing the programme not only ensures a smooth transfer without adverse effects on the economy, but also ensures continuity in the operations and management of the affected businesses. It further ensures that the repatriation of the proceeds from the sale of such businesses is spread over a reasonably long period of time to avert any possible adverse effects on the economy.

The major disadvantage of phasing the indigenization scheme is the generation of a lack of business confidence among foreign businesses who are faced with the choice of either selling up their businesses or continuing their business operations within the limits imposed by the indigenization policy. Alien businessmen who choose to continue operating in Nigeria are therefore faced with the uncertainty of the future of their businesses.

Types of indigenization being pursued

The types of indigenization being pursued vary with the types of businesses affected by the decree. In some cases it involves outright transfer, and in other cases a partial transfer, of the ownership, control and management of the enterprise and its accompanying technology. For instance, according to the classifications in the Nigerian Enterprises Promotion Decree of 1972, all businesses falling under Schedule I are to be transferred to Nigerians: the ownership, control and management are therefore required to pass to Nigerians.

However, the Nigerian participatory interest in those businesses that fall under Schedule II of the decrees of 1972 and 1977 was fixed at 40 and

60 per cent respectively. The new Schedule III under the decree of 1977 envisages a minimum of 40 per cent participatory share in the ownership and control of all enterprises falling under it.

All businesses affected by the decree are required by law to mount comprehensive training programmes for the Nigerian personnel to ensure an effective transfer of the control and management of such business. The ultimate goal is to Nigerianize all top posts hitherto occupied by foreign personnel. However, adequate provision has been made to allow expatriate personnel to be employed in positions to which qualified Nigerians could not be secured.

The reasoning behind the adoption of this transfer process was to ensure the development of indigenous expertise at appropriate levels of participation. It was based on the strong conviction that Nigerians were capable of owning and managing all the businesses classified under Schedule I and, ultimately, all the other businesses under Schedules II and III, which were considered to be currently beyond the effective control and management of Nigerians. The policy objective was, therefore, to share the ownership, control and management of enterprises with aliens, and thereby to acquire the necessary skills to take over effectively in due course.

Administrative, organizational and manpower (training) arrangements for initiating and fostering an indigenization institutional framework

The *Nigerian Enterprises Promotion Board* was established by the Nigerian Enterprises Promotion Decree of 1972 and empowered 'to advance and develop the promotion of enterprises in which citizens of Nigeria shall participate fully and play a dominant role'. The Board, which is responsible to the government through the Federal Commissioner for Industries, is the principal body charged with the responsibility for the effective implementation of the decree. The secretariat of the Board was established in April 1972 as the central co-ordinating organ. It comprises three divisions – the Administrative, Inspectorate and Valuation Units. The Administrative Division is responsible for the day-to-day functioning of the Board. The Inspectorate Division is responsible for inspecting buildings and premises or businesses in order to ensure that affected businesses complied with the provisions of the Indigenization Decree. This unit constitutes the direct enforcement agent of the Board. The Valuation Unit, consisting of experts in various disciplines in engineering, accounting, law, architecture and management, is responsible for valuing businesses undergoing the transfer process. However, owing to acute shortage of qualified personnel, the Board resorted to the use of the services of the Industrial Inspectorate

Division of the Federal Ministry of Industries in rendering valuation services to prospective Nigerian buyers of affected enterprises.

The *Nigerian Enterprises Promotion Committees* were set up in each of the states of the federation as state arms of the Board. Their principal function was to assist and advise the Board on the implementation of the indigenization scheme and to ensure that its provisions were complied with by aliens resident or carrying on business in the states.

Technical and management support The Nigerian Council for Management and Training was reconstituted and commissioned by the Nigerian Enterprises Promotion Board to formulate policies on management education, training and development and to design suitable training programmes for Nigerian businessmen in furtherance of the Nigerian Enterprises Promotion Decree of 1972. It was also made responsible for co-ordinating the activities of institutional programmes and using the Centre for Management Development to implement its training programmes. The centre had commenced courses in conjunction with the University of Lagos Continuing Education Centre for Nigerian businessmen and managers on how to acquire businesses under the scheme. The centre has also established a Business and Advisory Unit to provide direct and meaningful assistance in the management needs arising from the implementation of the indigenization schemes.

A number of existing institutions have also been involved in the provision of support in the implementation of the indigenization programme. Among them is the Industrial Training Fund, which is responsible for promoting and encouraging the acquisition of skills in industry and commerce with a view to generating a pool of trained indigenous manpower sufficient to meet the needs of the economy. The Nigerian universities and polytechnics also organize seminars and conferences for Nigerian businessmen and managers.

The indigenization decree also empowered the Capital Issues Commission to determine the prices at which all alien enterprises or their shares were to be sold or transferred. The Commission was empowered to determine the timing of such sale or transfer and to lay down the terms and other conditions, including the manner of the selection of the buyers or transferees or the manner of the allotment of the shares among the buyers or transferees.

Financing indigenization

Sources of funds

The Nigerian Bank for Commerce and Industry was established by Decree no. 22 of 5 May 1973 with an authorized share capital of ₦50 million (with the loan capital subject to negotiation) to assist Nigerian entrepreneurs in the provision of necessary funds for the purchase of the affected foreign businesses. The bank was also empowered to purchase stocks of shares that could not be taken up by the Nigerian public in furtherance of the indigenization exercise. As at 31 December 1975, the bank had given approval to sixty enterprises with a loan capital of ₦54.9 million and equity subscription of ₦4.8 million.

The commercial banks were given specific directives by the central bank to allocate a higher percentage of their credit to businesses in which Nigerians held a majority of the shares. Consequently, the federal government acquired 40 per cent of the equity of three major foreign commercial banks so that it could effectively influence their policy towards a more liberal attitude to indigenous businessmen. It is estimated that during the period of the transfer exercise, the banks supported the purchase of shares amounting to about ₦20 million.

Other sources of finance to Nigerian entrepreneurs include the Nigerian Industrial Development Bank, the government-owned insurance companies, and some other government-owned specialized financial institutions. These financial houses served as important instruments of indigenization measures. The operations of the Nigerian Industrial Development Bank were expanded to enable it to assist prospective buyers of businesses. Hitherto, the bank had been providing full investment facilities including appraisal studies and medium- and long-term finance to viable businesses. The federal government-owned Nigerian Insurance Company of Nigeria (NICON) was expected to provide all classes of insurance and re-insurance as well as to provide long-term financing of viable projects. Its activities were to be complemented by state-owned as well as private insurance companies.

Other specialized institutions designed specifically for the financing of small- and medium-scale businesses were established in the states. The purely agricultural projects were to be financed by the agricultural credit banks and the state agricultural credit/investment banks. In the area of housing and real estate development, the Nigerian Building Society and State Housing and Property Development Corporation were expected to provide funds to indigenes.

External financing did not play any role in the purchase of alien businesses. One would expect that, possibly, funds from external sources would have been utilized in paying for alien businesses that had undergone the transfer process. However, the role of external funds became passive in view of the remarkable performance of Nigerian businessmen and other purchasers of alien businesses in adequately meeting the financial requirement of the exercise.

Quantitative data

The analysis of the data received from the affected enterprises shows that about ₦88 million would be required to achieve total takeover of all the businesses under Schedule I and the acquisition of 40 per cent equity of businesses under Schedule II. However, between 1972 and 1975, when 209 out of 357 enterprises under Schedule I and 529 out of 593 enterprises under Schedule II had complied with the provisions of the decree, the total value of enterprises taken over under Schedule I was estimated at ₦13 million and the value of shares acquired under Schedule II was approximately ₦109 million. Total investment by Nigerians in the purchase of alien businesses therefore stood at ₦122 million. It is, however, thought possible that the above figures are underestimates, since no reliable records are available, especially on enterprises that were sold privately and were therefore not reported to the Nigerian Enterprises Promotion Board. Also, the difference between the estimated figure and the actual market value is explained by the usual upward movement of the market value of shares that have changed hands, resulting mainly from speculations in the transfer process.

In the 1970–4 development plan, net factor payments abroad for the four years of the plan were projected at ₦1520 million or an average of ₦380 million a year. This represents 10 per cent of the gross domestic product at market prices. Net factor payments abroad were raised to ₦3590.4 million for the five years of the Third National Development Plan, 1975–80, or an average of ₦718 million per year. The performance in this regard up to the 1975/6 financial year is shown in Table 8.

The explanation for the trend shown in Table 8 is not far-fetched. The remarkable increase in the net factor payments abroad during the 1972/3–1973/4 is largely explained by the repatriation abroad of the proceeds from those businesses that were disposed of to Nigerians over the period. Even though the sale of businesses continued after 1973/4,

Table 8 *Net factor payments abroad, 1971–2 to 1976–7*

Period	*Net factor payments (₦ millions)*	*Percentage of GDP at market prices*
1971/2	323.8	4.5
1972/3	599.3	7.8
1973/4	606.3	6.8
1974/5	375.8	2.5
1975/6	173.7	1.1
1976/7	402.5	2.0

there was a downward trend in the net factor payments abroad. This trend is explained largely by the buoyancy of the economy and the confidence that foreign businesses had in the economy.

Private institutions – types and sectors serviced

It is estimated that, during the period of the transfer exercise, the commercial banks supported the purchase of shares amounting to about ₦20 million. Private savings and funds from pensions and provident funds provided another ₦14 million. A greater proportion of funds came from the private savings of individuals, associations and a number of corporate bodies. A breakdown of the sectors serviced is not available. There was, however, no discrimination among sectors as to how funds from the private sector were utilized.

Overall evaluation of the effectiveness of financial arrangement for indigenization

One of the problems earlier identified as constituting a bottleneck to a successful implementation of the indigenization scheme was lack of adequate funds to acquire the alien businesses affected by the indigenization decree. However, after two years of indigenization, this worry was no longer justified because of the heavy and unprecedented oversubscription that attended all the offers of shares to the Nigerian public.

However, the method of share transfer gave rise to a lack of effective utilization of the facilities that the Lagos Stock Exchange and the Capital Issues Commission provided. In the case of the Lagos Stock Exchange, only thirteen additional companies had quotation rights by September 1974. As at 1 January 1972, twenty-two companies were quoted on the Stock Exchange. Also, purchasers were generally under considerable disability both as to price and marketability because private companies were excluded from the jurisdiction of the Capital Issues Commission. It was observed that, in fixing the value of shares by the Commission, its valuations have always differed from those shown in the prospectus of the companies. This difference is accounted for by the fact that the Commission's valuation is based on an average actual profit for a number of years while the company's rates have been based on the expected profit for the accruing year ending immediately following the issue of the prospectus. The result has been that most businesses preferred to dispose of the businesses by private treaty, rather than go through the Capital Issues Commission. This explains why more businesses changed hands privately, instead of by quotation on the Stock Exchange.

Evaluation of the economic impact of indigenization

Foreign private investment

One of the fears generated by the Indigenization Decree was that it would scare away foreign investment. The behaviour of direct investment since the introduction of the indigenization scheme confirmed this trend. Direct investment reached a peak of ₦327.8 million in 1972 but fell to ₦243.5 million in 1973, and stood at ₦281.7 million in 1974. The provisional figures, however, showed an increase in 1975 when direct foreign investment increased to ₦359.6 million.

Other private long-term capital movement showed the same trend as direct foreign investment. It fell from ₦10.8 million in 1971 to ₦6.0 million in 1972 and further to ₦1.8 million in 1973, picking up to ₦20.1 million in 1974. There was, however, an increase in other private short-term capital over the period: it rose from ₦640.6 million in 1971 to ₦765.8 million in 1972 and ₦999.6 million in 1973, but fell to ₦753.5 million in 1974.

The above trends could be explained by two distinctive factors: the effect of the indigenization scheme, and the buoyancy of the economy. Other short-term capital movements could be explained as the response to the boost that the economy enjoyed from oil production. However, the behaviour in direct investment is explained by a combination of the two factors earlier identified. Table 9 explains the pattern of foreign investment in Nigeria between 1971 and 1975. Foreign investment in oil production has fluctuated during the whole period, while non-oil investment dropped in 1973 and dropped further in 1974 until it picked up in 1975.

The above investment behaviour raises the question of the impact of the indigenization scheme on capital inflow for such an economy as Nigeria. Because of fears nurtured by some foreign businessmen as to what the ultimate goal of the Nigerian indigenization policy is, this has produced the effect of reducing the value of foreign investment in the country (see Table 10).

Table 9 *Direct foreign investment in Nigeria, 1971–5 (₦ million)*

Year	*Oil*	*Non-oil*	*Total*
1971	14.0	148.8	162.8
1972	195.8	132.0	327.8
1973	115.5	128.0	243.5
1974	186.2	95.1	281.7
1975	210.5	149.1	359.6

Table 10 *Other capital movements (₦ million)*

Year	*Short-term*	*Long-term*
1971	640.6	10.8
1972	765.8	6.0
1973	999.6	1.8
1974	753.3	20.1
1975	?	7.4

The place of foreign capital cannot be underestimated in the economic development process of a developing country like Nigeria. Foreign capital comes in a package along with appropriate management and technology, but it carries with it both benefits and costs. The question, therefore, is whether the overall benefits outweigh the overall costs from the standpoint of the economy.

While direct foreign investment has a positive impact on domestic savings, foreign exchange supply, real wages, external economics and the overall national productivity, there are varying viewpoints as to how significant this impact would be in any given case. With regard to the impact on national income, for example, reaction has been diverse and contradictory, varying from an overstatement of the contribution of foreign investment to a denial that the contribution could be significant. The intensity of the controversy surrounding foreign investment need not be surprising, given its extended political and social consequences, quite apart from the economic ones. Indigenization, *per se*, has its own far-reaching implications for a developing economy like Nigeria. The critical point, therefore, is the amount of trade-off between the two. If Nigeria has to indigenize, it has to pay a price for it. If it decides to approach its objective gradually, it has to live with a little bit of a scare of foreign investment.

Foreign technical assistance

It is hard to judge at this stage the impact of indigenization on the inflow of foreign technical assistance because most of the bilateral and multilateral technical assistance agreements entered into with Nigeria have been long-standing agreements and long negotiated. However, foreign technical assistance to Nigeria has reduced considerably over the past few years. The reduction can be explained by factors other than the introduction of the indigenization programme, although it is true that this programme would tend to reduce the inflow of foreign technical assistance into the country. Just as Nigerian businessmen constitute a very strong pressure group in the indigenization process, so are the foreign businessmen a strong pressure group in their home countries, and would mount pressures on their home governments to provide less technical assistance in Nigera. In fact, the reduction in technical assistance to Nigeria is largely explained by Nigeria's being a member of the Organization of Petroleum Exporting Countries (OPEC), since several donor countries decided to reduce aid to oil-producing developing countries.

Indigenous private investment and growth in entrepreneurial capabilities

Indigenous private investment has increased considerably as a result of the introduction of the indigenization scheme. The transfer of 58 per cent of all the enterprises classified under Schedule I and previously owned by alien businessmen, and 529 out of 593 businesses under Schedule II, has resulted in an investment of ₦122 million by indigenous private investors. This transfer has been accompanied by a substantial growth in the capabilities of indigenous entrepreneurs. Nigerian businessmen and managers have been made to accept challenging positions in the businesses that were hitherto owned and managed by alien businessmen. They have, in the process of learning by doing, acquired the expertise and entrepreneurial ability that had hitherto been the preserve of alien businessmen. This achievement is considered remarkable, especially among Nigerian investors, who have not yet developed much of a shareholding and investment habit in larger enterprises and have not been exposed to managing the complex business enterprises that have been transferred to them.

Even though the achievements with the first phase of the indigenization programme have been remarkable and encouraging, the challenges posed by Phase II of the programme, even though requiring greater efforts on the part of Nigerians, are expected to increase further the indigenous private investment and the growth in the entrepreneurial capabilities of Nigerians. This second phase of indigenization involves more indigenous funds and an increased participatory role for Nigerians.

Labour productivity and productivity of investment

No current study has been done in this area to find out the effect of indigenization on the productivity of labour and capital. However, the economic indicators have shown that over the period between 1972, when the scheme was launched, and 1974 there was a slow-down in industrial growth resulting largely from the implementation of the indigenization programme. However, there was a recovery from this slow-down as from 1975. For instance, the rate of growth in industrial output, which stood at 6 per cent in 1974, increased to about 19 and 20 per cent in 1975 and 1976 respectively.

The significant changes that occurred as a result of the introduction of the indigenization programme was a reversal of the experience prior to the introduction of the programme. Labour, for instance, played a more important role than capital in its contribution to growth in productivity before the introduction of the programme. However, the indicators have shown that, generally speaking, capital contributed more to the growth in productivity after the launching of the indigenization scheme.

There was a slight decline in labour productivity after the launching of the scheme. This is attributed to such factors as the labour unrests that were experienced around the period, and the transfer of the operations and management of more enterprises to Nigerians who were still understudying the processes. The productivity of investment showed an upward trend in spite of the indigenization programme. The reason for this trend is largely explained by the buoyancy of the economy, especially the oil sector.

Overall restructuring of the economy and development

There has not been any remarkable changes in the structure of the economy as a result of the indigenization scheme. The operation of the economy has continued in the same pattern as the pre-indigenization period. However, the control and management of businesses is gradually being transferred to Nigerians in line with the provisions of the Indigenization Decree. Aliens continue to manage a number of businesses, especially those that are too complex for Nigerians to take over yet.

Social and political implications of indigenization

Income distribution (personal)

When the Nigerian Enterprises Promotion Decree was promulgated by the federal military government in 1972, the intent of the government was to ensure that Nigerian citizens and associations had the opportunity of participating justly in the ownership of business enterprises in the country. However, none of its provisions expressly or implicitly concerned itself with the avowed egalitarian objectives of the government. Through the two methods of acquiring shares – by private placing of shares or by sale through the Stock Exchange – the pattern of share acquisition has led to the emergence of a few Nigerian capitalists and business tycoons at the expense of the masses. Those who acquired shares were, by and large, the élite who were already in business as proprietors and business executives, as well as civil servants, university staff, members of the armed forces and other professionals who had adequate personal savings or effective access to money from institutional lenders. The teeming millions consisting of poor urban workers and the peasants in the rural areas were not able to participate in this acquisition process.

As a result, there was an unintended concentration of shareholding in the hands of the higher-income group, thereby perpetuating the already skewed income distribution (hitherto in the favour of alien businessmen). The fact that a substantial proportion of the capital with which these shares were purchased had come from sources that are, by and large, public – e.g. the Nigerian Bank for Commerce and Industry, the major commercial banks in which the government has substantial or controlling shares – aids the perpetuation of the élite class and runs contrary to the egalitarian objectives of the nation. One of the major weaknesses of the scheme has been the creation (though unintended) of opportunities for a handful of Nigerians who have enriched themselves at the expense of the masses. This is considered a social as well as economic problem requiring immediate correction. Egalitarianism as an objective should have been pursued in the process of indigenization.

Regional imbalances

The mere concentration of most businesses in urban centres, and more especially in the federal capital of Lagos and the state capitals, means a disparity in the balance of businesses between the rural and the urban centres. Most businesses are therefore concentrated among the urban population. Another dimension is the skewness in the distribution in favour of the southern part of the country at the expense of the northern part. This confirms the fears expressed in certain quarters that the southern part of the country was more prepared for the transfer process than the northern part. This regional disparity therefore shows that the indigenization programme never took account of government commitment to the policy of even development throughout the country.

Redistribution of the political power base

It is difficult at this stage to trace any changes in political power base that can be related to the indigenization programme. The farthest any generalizations can go is that the programme has given rise to the emergence of a few Nigerian capitalists and a concentration of economic power in the hands of these Nigerians. Within the Nigerian context, and at this stage of our economic and political development, economic power cannot be regarded as being synonymous with political power.

Overall appraisal

Substantial progress has been recorded between April 1972, when the indigenization scheme was launched, and 30 June 1975. For instance, 738 out of about 950 enterprises affected by the Indigenization Decree have complied with the letters of the decree. Of this number, 209 out of 357 enterprises under Schedule I have been wholly transferred to Nigerian businessmen. Also, out of the 593 enterprises under Schedule II of which Nigerian indigenous participation is 40 per cent, 529 representing 89 per cent have complied. The total value of enterprises acquired by Nigerians under Schedule I amounted to ₦13 million, while the value of shares acquired under Schedule II was approximately ₦109 million.

It is, however, risky, apart from being too early, to use the success of the indigenization scheme to measure the degree of dependence of the economy on the rest of the world. This is mainly because Nigeria would continue to depend on the outside world, *inter alia*, for her raw materials, industrial inputs, machinery and equipment for her industries and for finished products to meet the needs of the growing population.

Furthermore, it would also be too early to use the success of the indigenization scheme to determine the elements of dependence that have increased as a result of the indigenization programme. All that can be said at this stage is that the Nigerian economy is no longer as dependent on foreign interest as it was in the first decade after Nigerian independence. It could also be said that the indigenization programme has not produced any serious adverse effects on the performance of the economy.

On the performance of the economy, the indigenization scheme has resulted in an increase of the gross national product as a proportion of the gross domestic product to 97.4 and 98.9 per cent for 1974/5 and 1975/6 respectively, instead of the forecast figures of 93.8 and 95.5 per cent projected under the Third National Development Plan and as compared with 93.2 per cent in the 1973/4 financial year. This ratio stood at 98 per cent in 1966, 95.5 per cent in 1971/2 and 92.7 per cent in 1972/3. This high ratio of gross national product to gross domestic product as from 1974/5 can be explained partly by the participation of the government through the Nigerian National Oil Corporation in the equity of oil companies and partly by the progressive implementation of the indigenization programme; the combined effect was a reduction in the share of factor payments abroad in the gross domestic product.

Obstacles to future progress of indigenization

A number of obstacles have been identified in the process of implementing the indigenization scheme. Appropriate measures have been taken to remove these obstacles. However, the following are still to be completely removed.

1 There remains a lack of adequate technical know-how to appraise the business that Nigerians are acquiring. One of the criticisms of the first phase of the indigenization scheme was that some of the Nigerians who acquired businesses in fact purchased mere shells without substance. This stemmed from their lack of sufficient technical and financial knowledge of the businesses they were acquiring, with the consequence that they either took over worthless businesses or else paid prices far in excess of the market values of such businesses.

2 There is a negative effect on the future trend of foreign investment. Already some foreign businessmen have been speculating that the ultimate goal of the scheme was full nationalization. This is more so with the introduction of the second phase of the scheme, which further reduces the areas as well as the extent of foreign involvement in economic activities in the country. This therefore raises the big problem as to what the future will be for the continued foreign investment that is still required for the sustenance and growth of the economy.

3 There is inadequately trained and inexperienced manpower to manage the indigenized businesses as efficiently as the displaced aliens. Even though this problem has been minimized by the comprehensive training programme mounted by the Centre for Management Development and the Nigerian Institute of Management, the challenges posed by the introduction of the second phase may further escalate this problem. All told, the evidence from available indicators points to the fact that the first stage of the indigenization process has not witnessed serious management problems. However, with the increase in the scale of indigenization under Phase II, this problem is bound to assume greater proportions than was experienced in the first stage. The managerial ability of Nigerian enterpreneurs may therefore be more heavily taxed.

4 Some Nigerians have been used as fronts in the indigenization process. The common practice during the implementation of the first phase was the device by a number of alien businessmen to use Nigerians as cover for the continued operations of their businesses. Only the business names were changed to reflect the new direction in

the ownership, and management of such businesses still remain in the hands of the aliens. Appropriate penalties have, however, been prescribed for those who contravene the provisions of the decree.

Prospects and unresolved problems

The prospects for a smooth transfer of alien businesses into indigenous hands are bright. The experience so far with the implementation of the indigenization programme has shown that, given the opportunity, Nigerians are capable of running their economy. With the introduction of Phase II of the scheme, more avenues are open for the participation by Nigerians in the ownership, control and management of their economy. The programme therefore affords Nigerians the opportunity of handling a substantial proportion of the economic activities that have hitherto been in the hands of foreigners. It also afords greater job opportunities for Nigerians and an increase in their responsibility, especially among Nigerian managers. The scheme further has the effect of exposing Nigerians to the new management techniques and the development of indigenous financial institutions.

The major problem still to be resolved, however, is the restricted spread of share ownership that characterized the purchase of stocks and shares under Phase I of the indigenization scheme. The decree had left the option of selling shares privately to the public to the discretion of the business affected by the decree without addressing policy towards a wider share ownership. The consequence was that there was a concentration of share ownership in a few hands. This fact runs contrary to the government-declared objective of egalitarianism. Appropriate measures are therefore called for to increase the level of public awareness of investment opportunities in the country to ensure a wider spread of share ownership in the country.

References

Collins, Paul, 'The political economy of indigenization: the case of the Nigerian Enterprises promotion decree', *African Review*, vol. 4, no. 4 (1974), pp. 491–508

Collins, Paul, 'Public policy and the development of indigenous capitalism: the Nigerian experience', *Journal of Commonwealth and Comparative Politics*, vol. 15, no. 2 (1977); reprinted in Paul Collins (ed.), *Administration for Development in Nigeria*, Lagos: African Education Press 1980

Hoogvelt, Ankie, 'Indigenisation and foreign capital: industrialisation in Nigeria', *Review of African Political Economy*, vol. 14 (1979)

Nigerian Economic Society, *Public enterprises in Nigeria*, Ibadan 1974

Odufalu, J. O. 'Indigenous enterprise in Nigerian manufacturing', *Journal of Modern African Studies*, vol. 9, no. 4, (December 1971), pp. 593–607

Olakunri, O., 'Capital mobilization for small and intermediate enterprises', *Management in Nigeria* (Journal of the Nigerian Institute of Management Lagos), vol. 8, no. 5 (March–April 1973), pp. 196–200

Onwuchokwa, G. M., 'Bankruptcy law and the Nigerian enterprises promotion decree', *Management in Nigeria*, vol. 11, no. 6 (1975), p. 32

Turner, Terisa, 'Two refineries: a comparative study of technology transfer to the Nigerian refining industry', *World Development*, vol. 5, no. 3 (March 1977), pp. 235–56

Udo-Aka, U., *et al* (eds.), *Management Development in Nigeria: The Challenge of Indigenization*, Oxford University Press for the Centre for Management Development 1978

Usoro, Eno J., 'Government policies, politics and industrial development strategy in Nigeria', *Nigerian Journal of Economic and Social Studies*, vol. 16, no. 2 (July 1974), pp. 243–53

8 Kenya

Claude Ake, *Dean, School of Social Sciences, University of Port Harcourt, Nigeria*

What is the Kenya government's conception of indigenization? The government sees indigenization essentially as Kenyanization of personnel and ownership. The 1963 manifesto of the Kenya African National Union, the party in power, sets the moderate tone of the indigenization policy of Kenya. The manifesto called for the training of Kenyans and the correction of 'racial disbalance in the Civil Service, commerce and the professions'. What this manifesto offered was a minimal programme of indigenization, namely the indigenization of personnel. The same type of indigenization policy was proclaimed in the celebrated policy statement (Sessional Paper No. 10), *African Socialism and its Applications to Planning in Kenya.* The policy was again reiterated in another policy entitled, *Kenyanization of Personnel in the Private Sector* (1967). However, the latter paper contained indications of a broader concern than the mere replacement of expatriates with Kenyan employees in government and the private sector. The paper asserted that a 'truly Kenya national prospecity cannot be built if the management of key commercial and industrial concerns remain in the hands of non-citizens. Kenyans must participate and be involved in the policy making and its execution in all sectors'. In the Development Plan 1970–74, a policy of indigenizing ownership began to emerge clearly. Without abandoning its attention to the 'Kenyanization of Personnel Programme', the Plan began to stress economic independence. It stated that 'the attainment of economic independence requires that Kenya citizens predominate in all walks of economic life. For this reason, the Plan contains proposals – and financial allocations – for funds to be lent to citizens to enter commerce, industry, transport or to expand their activities if they are already started'. The Development Plan 1974–78 continued and reinforced this trend.

Thus the government of Kenya conceives indigenization in roughly the same way as most African governments. As in most African countries, official documents of Kenya tend to blur the distinction between the indigenization of ownership and personnel and the indigenization of control; extension of indigenous ownership of productive assets is claimed as an achievement of economic independence and the localization of the control of the economy. Kenya's desire to increase Kenya participation in the economy and to 'transfer productive assets to Kenyans' is matched by an equally great concern to refrain from alienating foreign capital and reducing foreign investment and technical assistance. This in turn is associated with what must be the most unique feature of indigenization in Kenya, namely a preference for increasing indigenous economic participation in *new* economic expansion to the displacement of aliens in existing enterprises. This thrust in indigenization policy is particularly true of the industrial and commercial sectors. It is much less true of agriculture, because the supply of the basic factor of this sector – land – is fixed.

Indigenization of the agriculture sector

Kenya was a settler colony. And this was the source of some of the most fundamental contradictions in its colonial history. The white farmer, a capitalist farmer, needed land in large quantities. In 1934, the white farmers were given a monopoly of the high-potential land in Kenya, the so-called White Highlands. This white preserve was about 16,700 square miles, of which about 12,000 square miles or roughly 7.5 million acres was actually alienated. By monopolizing this land, the white settlers created 'the land problem' or 'the land question'. In addition to land, the white farmers needed labour to work their land and protection from competition from peasant agriculture. Thus pressures mounted for monetizing the peasant economy and proletarianizing the peasant. At the same time, measures were taken to protect the white farmer against competition from peasants. For instance, the Coffee Plantations Registration Ordinance of 1918 prevented Africans from growing coffee, while the Native Produce Ordinance of 1935 limited marketing, particularly wholesale trade, to Europeans and Asians. Taxes were introduced to force peasants into the money economy as wage-earners, and compulsory recruitment of labour was tolerated. Measures such as the Resident Natives Ordinance turned expropriated peasants into cheap labour; and other measures, such as the Registration Ordinance and the Masters and Servants Ordinance, increased the power of white farmers to keep Africans as wage labourers. The alienation of African land and the measures associated with it nurtured and focused the African struggle against colonialism in Kenya. As the nationalist movement gathered momentum, it became increasingly clear that the resolution of the struggle between nationalism and colonialism would hinge on the land question. Finding the nationalist movement unstoppable, the colonizers decided to come to terms with it and de-radicalize it by finding a compromise on the land question. This was how it came about that the colonial government and the white settlers of Kenya themselves initiated a programme of indigenization of agriculture. The programme was facilitated by the growing commercial and economic strength of Europeans in commerce and industry. Already by 1955 the product of European agriculture was equalled by the value of manufactured goods.

The compromise that emerged was the decision to transfer some of the mixed farms in the White Highlands to Africans. Only 2.1 million out of the 3.7 million acres of mixed farms was to be settled. It was argued that the retention of the remaining 1.6 million acres by white farmers was necessary in the interest of the economy. The 2.7 million acres of ranches in the White Highlands was also to remain in white hands, ostensibly because it was too important for the economy and not suitable for subdivision. The 1.5 million acres of plantations was also to remain in white hands because it was too expensive to be bought out, unsuitable for subdivision and crucial for export earnings. The idea was accepted, and the Million Acre Settlement Scheme was subsequently launched in 1961. It settled 35,000 families on 470,000 hectares of land at a cost of approximately K£30 million. The average size of the farms was about 12 hectares.

The ideas of the land transfer and land settlement schemes took root, and as it turned out the Million Acre Settlement Scheme became only one of a series of such schemes. It was followed by the Harambee Settlement Programme, which settled about 400 families on 6500 hectares of land. There was also the Ol Kalou Settlement Scheme, which was started in 1964 to settle 2000 families on 56,000 hectares of land. In 1965 came the Squatter Settlement Scheme, later called the Haraka Settlement Scheme, apparently the least successful of the schemes – it settled an estimated 14,000 families on about 105,000 hectares of land. In 1971 the Shirika Settlement Schemes were launched. The programme was designed to settle landless people, and was scheduled to be carried out in two phases. The first phase, scheduled for completion in 1973, was to settle 5300 families on 53,000 hectares of land. The second phase, scheduled for completion in 1978, was to settle 14,000 families on 139,000 hectares of land. There are plans for more settlement schemes, but the emphasis has changed from transfer of land from European to African farmers to reclaiming marginally useful land such as the arid zones, which constitute over 60 per cent of the country. It is hoped that the development of these areas will increase agricultural outputs as well as deal with the problems of unemployment and land hunger.

The settlement schemes encountered many problems. They proved very expensive. The Million Acre Scheme alone cost approximately K£30 million. The Kenya government contributed only about K£3 million and had to borrow the rest, mainly from the United Kingdom. The high cost of the settlement imposed a great financial burden, not only on the government but also on the African beneficiaries of the scheme, who eventually had to repay the money that the government had borrowed to enable them to acquire European land. The average cost of establishing each of the smaller-scale farms under the Million Acre Scheme was over K£700. The debt burden of the African farmers is easily illustrated. Of the K£1.7 million that had been billed to farmers by the end of 1966, 55.7 per cent were in arrears. Of the K£3.9 million billed to settlers by the end of 1968, 43.7 per cent were in arrears and 23.7 per cent had been outstanding for at least a year. The Van Arkadie Mission of 1966, which looked into the debt problem of the settlement schemes, pointed out that the new settlers were invariably in the position of having to put 70 per cent or more of their farm income into debt repayment.

The financial problems were by no means the only problems of the settlement schemes. They also put great stress on extension services. Administering them proved to be a very complex process which made heavy demands on the government's resources; and their administrative complexity caused long delays with the result that the programme fell well behind schedule. However, it would appear that the financial problems weighed heavily with the Kenya government and its decision to de-emphasize and decelerate land transfers. For the financial year 1963/4 the government had devoted about 75 per cent of development expenditure for agriculture to land transfer programme. For the year 1968/9 the proportion was less than 50 per cent and the Development Plan 1970–4 promised even more drastic reduction – to less than 22 per cent. The Development Plan 1974–8 devotes only K£12.74 million to land transfer and settlement out of a total development expenditure in agriculture of K£90.21 million, that is, a share of only 14.21 per cent of development expenditure for the plan period.

The reasons for the deceleration of the land transfer programme are interesting. They are stated in the Development Plan 1970–4. According to that document, 'Kenya has been using a very high proportion of her available agricultural development funds for the land transfer programme. However, the economical benefits from doing this are marginal at best.' The document goes on to argue that the most that can be expected from the land transfer is a modest increase in productivity and perhaps a little increase in employment. Unimpressed by these advantages, it goes on to say that 'the financial transactions involved in transfering land in this way have a substantially adverse effect on the balance of payments', and that 'there are better ways in which available funds can be used to promote agricultural development'. This is perhaps somewhat more pessimistic than the facts would warrant. For one thing, despite its many problems, the land transfer scheme did not have an adverse effect on productivity. Surveys carried out by the Kenya government and based on large samples showed that the average value of product per hectare rose from KSh. 160 in 1964/5 to KSh. 247 in 1965/6 and still higher to KSh. 299 in 1966/7. The proportion of the output that was being sold instead of being retained on the farm rose from 30 per cent in 1964/5 to 40 per cent in 1966/7. It is hard to escape the suspicion that the decision to de-emphasize land transfer was influenced by ideological factors. The decision is also more in harmony with the general thrust of Kenya's development strategy as well as with Kenya's indigenization policy in commerce and industry.

Indigenization in commerce and industry

Kenya's indigenization policy in commerce and industry is quite uniqiue in that it is far less interested in taking over foreign-owned enterprises than in increasing African participation in new economic expansion. The government of Kenya is very clear on the reason why it has opted for this approach. It argues that money paid for compensation to aliens for nationalized assets 'would most likely leave the country, increasing our foreign exchange problems'. The government argues further that 'if the nation's limited domestic capital is used to buy existing land, livestock, building, machinery and equipment, the nation has no more productive assets than before, only their ownership has changed'; rather, it loses the 'new resources that could have been purchased instead' and the added output that would have come from the new resources.

The process of indigenization by industrial and commercial expansion is carried out principally by the following institutions: the Industrial and Commercial Development Corporation (ICDC); the Development Finance Corporation of Kenya (DFCK); the Industrial Development Bank (IDB); the Kenya Industrial Estate Programme (KIE); and the Rural Industrial Development Centres (RIDC).

Industrial and Commercial Development Corporation

The Industrial and Commercial Development Corporation (ICDC) was established in 1954. It was originally called the Industrial Development Corporation. Its purpose was to further 'industrial and economic development of Kenya through initiation, assistance, or expansion of the industrial, commercial, or other undertakings or enterprises in

Kenya or elsewhere'. The Industrial Development Act of 1967 changed the Corporation's name to its present one. But what was involved was more than a change of name. While the Corporation was still primarily concerned with the original task of promoting economic development, especially industrial development, it was now to give serious attention to the task of indigenizing the Kenya economy. The ICDC tries to attract foreign capital and to encourage them to go into partnership not only with the Corporation but also with Kenyans. It hopes that such partnerships will give Kenyans not only business opportunities but also the benefit of the managerial, administrative and technical skills that foreign investors will bring with them. The Corporation aids indigenization by providing Africans with the means to take over alien businesses or set up new ones. It has a scheme for helping entrepreneurs to establish new small- and medium-size businesses; a borrower can get up to KSh. 750,000 to buy equipment or to construct or buy a building to set up an industry. These loans are usually repayable over a period of five to ten years. In 1975 the IDC set up a scheme by which Africans who have savings are encouraged to register with the Corporation. The Corporation advises them on investment opportunities as they arise and ensures that the money is properly invested. It prepares feasibility studies on potential projects, disseminates this information to Kenyans as well as to foreign investors, and assists in meeting the long-time loan requirements of such projects. The Corporation also promotes joint ventures with foreign investors, with the expectation that in due course its own shares in such ventures will be transferred to individual Kenyans when they have enough capital. Through this scheme some Kenyans were able to acquire shares in East African Industries Ltd, Block Hotels Ltd, Union Carbide (Kenya) Ltd, and Raymond Woollen Mills (Kenya) Ltd.

The ICDC has helped indigenization by providing, through its loan scheme, credit to Kenyans taking over the business of non-citizen Asians who are barred by immigration and trade licensing laws. From 1965 to 1971 the Corporation loaned about K£2.5 million to Kenyans; the vast majority of these loans went to the acquisition of non-citizen Asian businesses. The ICDC also aids indigenization through some of its subsidiary and associated companies. For instance, the Kenya National Properties Ltd, which was established in 1968, helps Kenyan businessmen to procure suitable business premises by giving them loans and helping to guarantee loans for such purpose. This company has not been doing very well, owing mainly to lack of funds. Indeed, in February 1975 property loans were suspended and the company has remained virtually inactive since, its only source of income being rents from the Mackinnon and Mutos buildings. Another subsidiary of ICDC that is supposed to play a particularly active role in indigenization is the Kenya National Trading Corporation. Established in 1965, the objective of the company is to promote Kenyanization of wholesale and retail trade and the export trade, especially in primary products. It promotes indigenization by its influence over licensing and the regulation of the import and export trade. The Company has been highly successful in the indigenization of retain trade. The Kenya National Trading Corporation was established mainly to assist in the transfer of commerce to citizens and also to engage in state trading activities. The Corporation undertakes warehousing, wholesaling, authorization of imports by its agents, and the distribution of locally manufactured goods.

Finally, the ICDC aided indigenization through its Small Loans Schemes, which it administered on behalf of the Kenya government. These schemes are designed to give financial assistance on reasonable terms to small-scale entrepreneurs. The names of the various loan schemes indicate the types of entrepreneurial activities that they are meant to aid: Small Industrial Revolving Fund, Small Commercial Revolving Fund, Small Property Revolving Fund, Machinery Loans Fund. Although these loans are meant principally to aid economic development and the growth of employment, they have also helped Kenyans to acquire small businesses owned by non-Kenyans such as wood-working, clothing, leather processing and shoe-making. The scale of operation of these schemes is rather limited, however, owing to a shortage of funds. For instance, for the year 1974/5 a total of KSh. 54 million was disbursed to 1087 clients on these schemes; approvals in the same year came to only KSh. 49 million for 810 clients. The schemes are also threatened by repayment problems, and it would appear that the government's commitment to the scheme is wavering. In the financial year 1975/6 the funds all together approved loans for only 610 applicants to a total value of KSh. 34 million. This compares rather unfavourably to 810 approvals to the value of KSh. 49 million in 1974/5. The level of disbursement for 1975/6 barely matched the level for 1971/2. The administration of loan schemes is now done by the Kenya Industrial Estates.

Development Finance Company of Kenya

The Development Finance Company of Kenya (DFCK), the most important associated company of ICDC, plays an important role in indigenization. The Company was incorporated in September 1963 with an authorized share capital of K£4 million, of which K£3 million was to be subscribed equally by the ICDC, the German Development Corporation, the Commonwealth Development Corporation and the

Netherlands Overseas Finance Company. The DFCK supplements the efforts of the government in promoting economic development. It gives special attention to the establishment and the expansion of 'manufacturing and processing industry based on Kenya's agricultural and forest products'; as well as the tourist industry. It helps with feasibility studies, consultancy services and medium- and long-term loans. Its investments in projects range from K£20,000 to K£300,000. In carrying out these functions the Company has given special attention to maximizing Kenyan participation in its projects. It has helped to increase the participation of Kenyans in the economy, particularly in the hotel industry, textiles, motor vehicle components, agricultural processing, sugar production, wood processing and paper and pulp.

The Industrial Development Bank

The Industrial Development Bank (IDB) was incorporated in January, 1973 with an authorized capital of KSh. 40 million. But it was soon necessary to increase the authorized capital by KSh. 80 million in order to strengthen the Bank's borrowing base.

The Bank was created to supplement the ICDC. It invests in and promotes medium- and large-scale industrial enterprises. Its assistance usually goes only to projects requiring investment of more than one million shillings. Up to September 1975, IDB had approved investments of about KSh. 119 million in twenty-four projects. It promotes indigenization by encouraging Kenyan participation in its projects and by affording investment opportunities to Kenyans. As of June 1976, the total investment of IDB was KSh. 125.4 million in loans and KSh. 36.9 million equity in some twenty-seven projects.

Kenya Industrial Estates Ltd

Kenya Industrial Estates Ltd was originally a subsidiary of ICDC created specifically to further indigenization. According to the Development Plan 1970–4, the main purpose of the industrial estates scheme is to provide an opportunity for Kenyans to take part in the industrial expansion. The programme entails the construction of factory buildings which are rented to Kenyan entrepreneurs at reasonable rents. The estates have administrative and technical service blocks attached to them. The entrepreneurs themselves have to provide their own working capital. But they get technical and management services in the running of their enterprises. They may have machinery and equipment on a loan basis and the loans may be up to 100 per cent of the cost of these assets. Entrepreneurs wanting to increase the scale of their operations or to diversify may also obtain premises within the estate to do so. There are estates in Nairobi, Nakuru, Kisumu and Mombassa, and more are planned for Nyeri, Eldoret and Kakamega. For the plan period, 1974–8, the projected operating cost of the Industrial Estate Programme was K£750,000.

Rural Industrial Development Programme

Something akin to the Industrial Estate Programme on a small scale exists for the rural sector. This is the Rural Industrial Development Programme. This programme was initiated in 1971 in order to further the development of rural small-scale industries. It aids indigenization by helping the 'development of Kenyan entrepreneurship and technical skills', but this is not its sole objective, and perhaps not the most important one. Its other objectives include job creation in rural areas, the promotion of industries using local raw materials, and the promotion of rural economic development. This programme entails the establishment of centres at district headquarters in the country. The centres, which are supposed to cost about K£90,000, contain such facilities as administrative blocks, classrooms for courses and repair workshops. The programme also has a revolving loan fund to help participating entrepreneurs purchase tools, equipment and machinery. Up to the end of 1977, the Kenya Industrial Estates was an arm of ICDC. As of January 1978 it became an independent government body. It has taken over some of the roles of the ICDC and the Investment Development Bank, particularly the financing of small and medium scale enterprises. The reorganized company has a loan of KSh. 800 million from the World Bank. Some of this money is to be used for the financing of 190 workshops in different parts of the country and also for the continuation of the Industrial Estates Programme in Eldoret.

Other indigenization mechanisms

Apart from those just discussed there are other institutions and mechanisms dealing with indigenization in Kenya. One is trade licensing, which has been very effective in breaking the monopoly of Asians in the retail trade and putting it largely into the hands of Kenyan Africans. By the Trade Licensing Act of 1967, non-citizens were excluded from trade in rural areas and from the periphery of the urban centres. These restrictions were extended eventually to include most commodities. The National Construction Company has also played an important role in the indigenization of Kenya. The Corporation, which was founded in 1968, has aided Kenyan entry into the construction industry by giving loans, performance bonds and guarantees for Kenyan contractors. It also helps them by subcontracting to them, and by extending services such as accounting, estimating, planning and purchasing.

Kenyanization has also benefited from the use of the immigration control, work permits, the Trade Licensing Act, and the Import, Export and Essential Supplies Act. It has also benefited from the efforts of the Kenyanization Bureau. This Bureau keeps a manpower register of citizens available for all kinds of jobs, and advises the government of the manpower what can be imported into the country and for how long. This Bureau has made an invaluable contribution to the indigenization of the public service.

Progress of the indigenization process

How effective have Kenya's indigenization policies and institutions been in promoting indigenization? This is unfortunately not an easy question to answer, because of the thrust of Kenya's approach to indigenization, which is concerned not so much with displacing aliens in established positions or enterprises but rather in increasing their participation in economic expansion.

First of all, it is necessary to begin by taking note of the fact that, for the Kenya government, the overriding goal of economic policy has been the increase of economic development. On this score Kenya has achieved a respectable record in comparison to the performance of most African countries – an average growth rate of 6.2 per cent for the decade 1964–74. Kenyans are clearly participating in this economic expansion

Table 11 *Kenyanization of high- and midde-level occupations, 1972*

Occupational group	*Total* (no.)	(%)	*Citizens* (no.)	(%)	*Non-citizens* (no.)	(%)
Managerial occupations	15,708	100	9,936	63	5772	37
Professional occupations	5,747	100	1,973	34	3774	66
Semi-professional or technical occupations	31,310	100	23,339	75	7971	25
Skilled office and clerical occupations	25,625	100	21,179	83	4446	17
Skilled manual occupations	21,431	100	17,834	83	3597	17
Total	99,821	100	74,261	74	25,560	26

Source: Development Plan 1974–1978, Part 1 (Nairobi Government Printer 1974), p. 94.

Table 12 *Occupational and racial distribution of public and private employment in Kenya, 1964*

Occupational group	*Proportion of jobs held by Africans*		
	Public sector (%)	*Private sector* (%)	*Ratio of public to private*
Professional and technical	40.6	10.7	3.79:1
Administrative, execitive and managerial	53.4	21.9	2.44:1
Teachers	95.9	31.5	3.04:1
Clerical	70.6	33.7	2.09:1
Sales	38.0	44.7	0.85:1

Source: Kenyanization of Personnel in the Private Sector (Nairobi: Ministry of Labour 1967), p. 2.

Table 13 *Existing supply and projected additional demand for managers in Kenya, 1972–8*

Occupational group	*Number of managers (1972)*	*Number of non-citizens (1972)*	*Additional number of citizens required (1972–8)*
General managers	1214	894	1,800
Production managers	177	116	300
Specialized managers	254	150	450
Farm managers and supervisors	4273	490	1,400
Managers n.e.c. and working proprietors	9590	4122	10,000
Clerical and other administrative supv.	2306	588	1,900
Production supervisors and general foremen	3152	744	3,200
Total	20,966	7104	19,050

Source: Development Plan, 1974–1978, Part 1 (Nairobi: Government Printer 1974), p. 106.

of the country, as is evident by their inroads into the construction industry, the tourist industry, agriculture, tourism and retail trade. What is not so clear is how far indigenization is taking place – that is, how far personnel, ownership and control have been indigenized in the course of these increased opportunities for Kenyan participation in the process of economic development.

To begin with personnel, the evidence is quite clear here. Considerable progress has been made as Tables 11 and 12 indicate. Progress is

Table 14 *Racial distribution of private companies in Kenya, 1965 and 1973*

	Registered capital K£1–499	*% of firms*	*£500–10,000*	*% of firms*	*£10,000+*	*% of firms*	*Total*
1965							
African	33	94	2	6	0		35
Asian	45	56	12	15	24	29	81
European	42	75	4	7	10	18	56
Mixed	17	81	2	9.5	2	9.5	21
Total	137		20		36		193
1973							
African	34	28	70	58	17	14	121
Asian	25	12	97	49	76	38	198
European	23	23	34	34	42	42	99
Mixed	10	15	31	46	26	39	67
Total	92		232		161		485

Source: Nicola Swainson, 'The rise of a national bourgeoisie in Kenya', *Review of African Political Economy (1977)*, p. 45.

evident but it is modest. The government is very unlikely to achieve its goal of complete Kenyanization of personnel by 1982. This is all the more so because of the government's anxiety over alienating foreign investors and also on account of the rather limited effort that is going into management training. Table 13 indicates the manpower shortages.

The picture in regard to the indigenization of ownership appears to be essentially the same as the picture in the indigenization of personnel – evident but modest progress. Table 14 gives a rough idea. It is based on a sample of 485 private companies taken from the Company Register. The table is a very crude indicator of indigenization and should be interpreted with caution. The category 'African' does not coincide with 'Kenyan', and the categories 'Asian' and 'European' do not quite coincide with 'alien'. There are many Asians and Europeans who are Kenyans. But it should also be said that some of them are paper citizens, so to speak, having taken up citizenship as a temporary convenience under the pressure of indigenization. The table understates the degree of indigenization because it does not include companies that are by definition predominantly Kenyan. The distortion caused by this is to some extent neutralized by the category 'mixed company', which is likely to be more alien than indigenous if analysed in detail. As is to be expected, Africans own more small companies while the big companies still remain in the hands of Europeans and Asians. As far as indigenization of control is concerned, it would appear that very little progress has been made in this respect. But more of this later.

Some problems of indigenization in Kenya

Note has already been taken of some of the problems of indigenization in Kenya, particularly the problem of finance. Related to this is the problem of the limited scope of some of the indigenization schemes, for instance the relatively small number of people who have been able to benefit from the activities of the loan schemes and institutions such as the Kenya Industrial Estates and the Kenya National Properties Limited. Mention has also been made of the complex administrative problems of land settlement and land transfer, types of problems that do not arise for most African countries. It would appear that the Kenyans who have advanced as businessmen or managers or administrators in the course of indigenization have performed well, as shown, for instance, in the rising productivity of the transferred European farms and the generally excellent performance of the public companies. What appears to be deficient is the supply of high-level manpower, especially in the managerial areas. It would appear that there is need to increase the training institutions and facilities available for high-level management training, and also to expand the facilities of existing training institutions, namely the Kenya Institute of Administration, the Management Training Advisory Centre, the National Industrial Vocational Training Centres, the Kenya Industrial Estates and the Kenya Institute of Management. The need for expansion of the facilities and higher output is illustrated by the following statistics. The Management Training and Advisory Centre is estimated to have given the benefit of its programme to only 6000 people between 1966, when it was established, and 1974, according to the Development Plan 1974–8. The Centre was expected to train only 1000 people a year for the plan period. On a rough estimate, all the companies in Kenya spend only KSh. 3 million to send their employees for management training in 1978.

Finally, it should be mentioned that the Kenya government is perhaps too cautious in its indigenization policies. For instance, it could put stronger pressures on foreign firms to indigenize personnel instead of relying so much on exhortation and mild incentives. It is indicative of the government's caution that it rejected the suggestion of the ILO mission to introduce a tax on the employment of expatriates. The Central Organization of Trade Unions has complained bitterly about the Kenya government's excessive restraint in the pursuit of indigenization of personnel both in the private and the public sectors, and has compiled evidence to back its indictment.

Broader problems

It remains to consider two broader problems of indigenization in Kenya.

The first is the tendency of indigenization policies to contribute to inequality and even to class formation. The land settlement schemes, particularly the Million Acre Settlement Scheme, appear to have had this effect by giving sizeable and generally profitable farms to Kenyan Africans who were usually already rather well off. This happened partly because the government was worried about the economic consequences of subdividing the land too much, and also because of the obvious attraction of giving land purchase loans to people who could provide good collateral as well as some evidence of entrepreneurial success. Similar considerations affected the distribution of agricultural development loans as well as the extension service. The loans and the services went to the big farmers because the government was worried about the decline of the efficiency of large farms and a subsequent decline in foreign exchange earnings. For instance, according to the Development Plan 1974–8, the Agricultural Finance Corporation had in 1972 a total loan portfolio of K£14.2 million: K£12.0 million was lent to about 2500 large-scale farmers and only K£2.5 million to 14,500 small-scale farmers.

The indigenization of commerce and industry displays the same tendencies toward economic stratification. The bulk of the money spent to encourage Kenyan participation in commerce and industry went largely to those institutions, programmes and projects that benefited already successful Kenyans. For instance, the ICDC would not give loans of less then £500, and its loans tend on the average to be about £3000. These loans were given on sound business principles. There are very few Kenyans who were in a position to give the collateral to earn loans of such magnitude. The Industrial Development Bank does not normally aid projects of less than £50,000. Only Kenyans who are already fairly successful could operate on this scale. Furthermore, it was the already wealthy Kenyans who were co-opted as partners by alien businesses under pressure of the popular demand for indigenization; they were also the ones who had the savings to benefit from the shares acquired by public corporations and passed on to Kenyans. The other side of the coin is that those programmes and institutions that have greater potential for diffusing the benefits of indigenization more widely have very limited capital, so that their impact is quite limited. To illustrate, all the Small Loans Schemes approved a total of only 632 applications in 1975/6 for a total value of KSh. 42,861,080. The number of loan recipients was 1343 in 1971/2.

The second problem is that the indigenization policies of Kenya do not appear to be making any significant contribution to the indigenization of control and the reduction of economic dependence. To begin with, if the government is to reshape the economy in favour of making it more independent and more indigenized, its role in economic expansion has to be substantial. But it would seem that this is not the case. To illustrate, the government projected a total investment outlay of K£100 million for the plan period 1970–4. But it was only willing or able to contribute K£922,000 for the period. It rationalized this by arguing that 'the total amount is less important than the fact that government is ready to participate on a joint basis with private investors and by so doing, indicate its confidence in particular projects and thereby get them under way more quickly than might otherwise be the case'. The fact of the matter is that this level of government contribution could not give it much scope to restructure the economy. This point applies to the major institutions by which the Kenya government hopes to restructure the economy and indigenize it, namely, ICDC, DFCK, the Investment Development Bank and the Industrial Estates Ltd. These institutions are not very strong financially, and they are dominated by alien capital. Because of this, they are not able to reduce the domination of alien capital over the economy. To start with DFCK, the government only owns 25 per cent of the capital, the rest belonging in equal shares to the German Development Corporation, the Netherlands Overseas Finance

Company and the Commonwealth Development Corporation. The company depends primarily on foreign capital to finance its projects. Indeed, its major function is the attraction of foreign investment.

The Industrial Estates Ltd is also heavily dependent on foreign capital. As noted earlier, it has just been reorganized and given increased responsibility. It starts its new life as an independent corporation with the help of an KSh. 800 million loan from the World Bank. It is also negotiating a further loan of KSh. 20 million to finance its projects. Its development budget for the first year is KSh. 20 million. Even if all of this development expenditure came from the Kenyan government, the corporation is hardly saved from domination by foreign capital. The case of the Industrial Development Bank is not dissimilar. Since the Bank was launched in 1973 with a share capital of KSh. 40 million, virtually all its credit has come from foreign sources: the first line of credit was a KSh. 35 million loan from the World Bank. This was followed by a second line of KSh. 71 million, also from the same source in 1975. Other sources of credit have been the KSh. 16.8 million from the Export Credit Guarantee Department of Morgan Grenfell in the United Kingdom and a KSh. 11.0 million from the German Development Company. New lines of credit are being sought from the World Bank, the Arab Bank for Economic Development in Africa and the European Investment Bank.

As for the ICDC, according to the Development Plan 1970–4, it was scheduled to hold only 16 per cent of the total equity in all ICDC projected investment. This would hardly put it in a position to restructure the economy and indigenize ownership and control significantly. One of the better-known efforts at indigenization by ICDC was a well advertized programme of buying shares in profitable companies and subsequently selling them to Kenyans. A student of Kenya, Colin Leys (*Underdevelopment in Kenya*), found that by 1970 59 per cent of the shares had been bought by some 1900 Africans with an average shareholding of £50 to a grand total of £100,000, or only 0.02 per cent of the net assets of the thirty-six companies listed in the Nairobi Stock Exchange in 1970. The ILO Mission, which looked into indigenous participation in investment, found that during the period 1960–70 indigenous participation in foreign-owned enterprises was 42.8 per cent, 39 per cent in Indian investment and, on average, less than 25 per cent in all other investments. The Mission found that 'foreign-owned' enterprises, which accounted for 57 per cent of gross national product in 1967, might have increased their share of the gross national product to as much as 65 per cent by 1970. It may well be that indigenization is merely concealing dependence instead of reducing it. What is reasonably clear is that its contribution to the localization of control, and indeed of ownership, is marginal at best.

References

Kaplinsky, Raphael, *Readings on the multinational corporation in Kenya*, New York: Oxford University Press 1978

Kitching, Gavin, 'Modes of production and Kenyan dependency', *Review of African Political Economy*, no. 8 (January–February 1977), pp. 56–74

Leys, C., *Underdevelopment in Kenya: The Political Economy of Neo-Colonialism*, London: Heinemann 1975

National Christian Council of Kenya, *Who Controls Industry in Kenya?*, Nairobi: East African Publishing House 1968

Swainson, N., 'The rise of a national bourgeoisie in Kenya', *Review of African Political Economy*, no. 8 (1977), pp. 39–55

9 Tanzania

S. S. Mushi, *Head, Political Science Department, University of Dar es Salaam*

Every country at one stage or the other has to tackle the problem of controlling its national economy. This is one of the fundamental problems that countries emerging from colonialism, as was Tanzania, have to face as soon as they attain political independence. Thus it was recognized that 'economic nationalism' was a logical follow-up of, and natural sequel to, the 'political nationalism' that led to independence. The nationalization measures taken by the Tanzanian government after the Arusha Declaration[1] were defended as a logical expression of economic nationalism.

> Such an economic expression of nationalism is nothing new in the world; although the manner of the action may have been particularly Tanzanian, its motivation is common enough. Every country – whether it is capitalist, communist, socialist or facist – wants to control its own economy. . . . Ideological differences between countries affect method, not necessarily the fact, of securing national control.[2]

Tanzania is one of the few African countries that have formulated a relatively coherent ideology which attempted within the context of local conditions to solve the crucial issues relating to (1) the control of the national economy so as to minimize external and internal exploitation, (2) the expansion of national wealth, and (3) the distribution of this wealth among individuals, groups and regions within the country. The Arusha Declaration and subsequent policy statements[3] provided the foundation for the indigenization process of the Tanzanian economy. The purpose of this essay, therefore, is to outline this process briefly, pointing out the problems and prospects it has revealed and the lessons that the experience has provided.

The manifestation of economic nationalism in several African countries since their attainment of indepecence has generally taken the form of two main models of indigenization of the economy, corresponding fairly broadly to the two alternative patterns of development. The first model seeks to localize or 'Africanize' the economy without 'socializing' it; thus the major means of production and distribution are gradually placed under the control of the indigenous people. Its main preoccupation is to 'Africanize' capitalism. The second model seeks to localize the economy and to abolish capitalism and all forms of exploitation, whether by foreign investors or by African themselves. Tanzania, in *The Arusha Declaration and TANU's Policy on Socialism and Self-Reliance* of February 1967, adopted the second model of indigenization through socialization.

Accordingly, Tanzania embarked on the process of indigenization with a clear ideology and political commitment, and consequently with a higher level of political resources. This partly accounts for the results thus far achieved, as will be shown in later sections of this essay.

In addition to mobilizing political resource for the fulfilment of its economic nationalism, Tanzania as a poor ex-colonial country had to contend with three other basic resources, all of which became necessary in the indigenization process: (1) material resources, both financial and natural; (2) human resources for full participation in the production effort; and (3) technical resources in the form of technical and scientific knowledge and skills in a variety of fields – economic, administrative and managerial – as well as institutionalized technical capability in research centres and training institutions. These were the resources that Tanzania had to mobilize for the achievement of its indigenization goals.

It follows, then, that the indigenization of the economy would require a radical change in the structure of the inherited colonial economy and in the pattern of investment so as to ensure a steady growth of the four resources needed for the indigenization effort: political, material, human and technical. The remaining sections of the essay, therefore, are intended to show: (1) how the Tanzanian leadership has attempted to expand these resources which formed the pillars of its indigenization policy; and (2) how the financial and administrative infrastructure has been working in relation to the three vital questions, namely (1) how to control the economy; (2) how to expand the national wealth; and (3) how to distribute that wealth to a wider population.

Mechanisms for controlling the economy

Tanzania has devised a number of mechanisms for controlling its economy since 1967. In this essay, however, we shall focus on the four main ones: (1) control through nationalization; (2) control through the central bank; (3) control through the parastatal system and (4) control through the co-operative movement.

Control through nationalization

By 1966, Tanzania had seen the inadequacy of the inherited economic and financial structure. The enunciation of the ideology of the so-called 'African socialism' in the early 1960s was not accompanied by the requisite institutional changes;[4] and in practice it meant a mixed economy with heavy reliance on external sources of investment capital and skilled manpower. Moreover, between 1963 and 1966, efforts to attract foreign investment and manpower to implement the First Five-Year Development Plan (July 1964–June 1969) were generally unsuccessful; instead, there was a flight of capital from the country through foreign planters, traders and industrialists.[5] Thus, nationalization was accepted in principle as the only alternative in the effort to control the economy and to direct the country's future development.

Among other things, therefore, the Arusha Declaration of February 1967 laid down the guidelines for the nationalization of the economy. The policy was to place the major means of production and distribution under the control and ownership of the people of Tanzania through the state machinery. In terms of the Declaration, the major means of production and distribution are the following: land, forests, mineral resources, water, oil and electricity; communications, transport, banks, insurance, import and export trade; wholesale business; the steel, machine-tool, arms, motorcar, cement and fertilizer factories; the textile industry; and any other big industry on which a large section of the population depend for their living, or which supplies essential components for other industries; and large plantations, especially those that produce essential raw materials.[6]

Despite these sweeping nationalization measures, the economy would still remain 'mixed'. Thus, three main sectors of the economy were defined: wholly state-owned enterprises, state-controlled enterprises, and an open sector. These were expanded to four industrial sectors in the Second Five-Year Plan, launched in July 1969, specified as follows:[7]

1 *Wholly government-controlled industries* These include a limited number of strategic industries in which the government or parastatal organization will own 100 per cent of the equity. The main ones are banking, insurance, petroleum exploitation and armaments.
2 *Government-controlled industries* These include the basic industries in which the government (or its appointed agent) usually acquires more than 50 per cent of the voting and participating shares of sufficient concerns to account for the major share of that industrial branch in order to exercise effective policy control.
3 *Partnership joint ventures* This group includes industries upon which a large section of the population depend for their living, or which provide

essential components for other industries. In these industries the government or its appointed agents (including co-operatives, workers' organizations and local government bodies) would play an active role, although not necessarily holding a controlling interest.

4 *Open industries* These include all other industries not falling under sectors (1)–(3) above. They are open to all sectors, including government, local and foreign private investors, etc. Within this group, there are a number of industries that involve small and medium-scale operations, most of which can be handled by co-operatives and village collectives.

It should be emphasized that nationalization in Tanzania was conceived as a mechanism for the control of the surplus as well as a means for promoting socialist development. Thus an argument is marshalled in the Second Five-Year Plan that:

> Considerable benefits will accrue in the long run from the expansion of public ownership because: (a) it will be possible to create a genuine Tanzanian industrial know-how faster than under conditions of unrestricted private enterprise; (b) it will be possible to pursue a more effective industrial strategy than is possible under private enterprise; (c) the profits made in industry will be reinvested in Tanzania.[8]

A few comments need to be made with regard to the above benefits of nationalization so as to avoid the confusion between nationalization and such concepts (or goals) as socialism, development and self-reliance. First, nationalization must not be equated with socialism, although it is a necessary aspect of it in a country where the economy is externally controlled. Nationalization merely resolves the contradiction between foreign and local control of the economy in favour of the latter; this can be done by a simple act of legislation. Socialism goes beyond these legal relations of production, and involves the resolution of contradictions in the social relations of production which are by far more complex. For, as Peter Meyns has summed up the case:

> State ownership of the means of production is not in itself a guarantee that planning will be directed towards the construction of socialism. In fact, we know for instance that in industrialized capitalist countries an increasingly important sector of the economy is under state control. However, planning in those countries functions exclusively because and to the extent that it maintains and consolidates the principles of capitalism.[9]

Second, nationalization in itself is not a sufficient guarantee for a self-reliant development. This is because, as we have pointed out earlier, indigenization of the economy must entail growth in the level of material and technical resources controlled locally. Tanzania's experience has shown that, at low resource level, the goal of self-reliant development requires a more radical restructuring of the economic structure than the simple act of nationalization.[10]

Third, nationalization, *per se*, does not necessarily lead to an 'indigenized' economy. Indigenization of the economy requires, among other things, a complete reorganization of the country's financial infrastructure so as to prevent the surplus from flowing out of the country, and an investment policy that is deliberately geared to the removal of the historically transmitted roots of underdevelopment. Tanzania's efforts in this direction are examined in the sections below.

Control through the central bank

Until mid-1966, the East African Currency Board (EACB) played the role of a central bank for the three East African countries (Kenya, Uganda and Tanzania). Its functions, however, were geared to benefit Britain, for it was designed in such a way that surplus funds were kept in British banks and invested in lucrative ventures outside East Africa. Efforts to establish an East African central bank between 1963 and 1965 were frustrated by the failure to create an East African federation. Thus each East African state went ahead to establish its own central bank.

In December 1965, the National Assembly passed an Act to provide for the establishment of a Tanzanian central bank (i.e. the Bank of Tanzania), which started functioning in June 1966.[11] This proved to be an important financial infrastructure when, eight months later, the Arusha Declaration led to the nationalization of foreign banks and industries; for one of the central bank's functions was to regulate and oversee the entire banking and credit policy in the country. It would have been much more difficult to regulate the financial activities of the new National Bank of Commerce and the National Insurance Corporation if the Bank of Tanzania had not been established before nationalization of the key financial institutions.

The functions of the Bank of Tanzania include the following: to issue currency, to manage the country's gold and foreign exchange reserves, and to advise the government on economic and related fiscal matters. By controlling foreign exchange and regulating credit, the Bank would strive to foster monetary stability, which had depended on the stability of sterling in the past. Thus, the Act stipulated: 'Within the context of the economic policy of the Government the activities of the Bank shall be directed to the promotion of credit and exchange conditions conducive to the rapid growth of the national economy of Tanzania, due regard being had to the desirability of fostering monetary stability.[12]

With regard to the function of controlling and administering the country's foreign reserves and assets, the Bank adopted a policy of diversification of its foreign exchange holdings, especially after the devaluation of sterling in 1967. This was in line with the objective of monetary stabilization. Furthermore, in August 1971, following the instability in the international monetary system, the shilling was for the first time pegged to the American dollar. Kenya and Uganda followed suit to avoid a loss in their transactions with Tanzania within the ailing Common Market.

Another important aspect of foreign reserves management concerns the level of foreign reserves that the country should maintain at any given time. The Bank of Tanzania Act 1965 stipulated that the Bank should at all times endeavour to maintain foreign exchange reserves equal to an aggregate amount of not less than the value of four months' imports as averages for the last three preceding calendar years. The stipulation is in sharp contrast to the days of the East African Currency Board, when funds were hoarded in London banks irrespective of the development needs of the East African countries. Commenting on this policy ten years after its establishment, the central bank authorities have argued as follows:

> Since foreign reserves are savings, it is then true that if these savings rise excessively some worthwhile development projects may, as a result, fail to secure the necessary funds for execution. Hence it is desirable to maintain only a reasonable balance to ensure that the country appears viable and able to meet its commitments promptly, but at the same time avoid the possibility of appearing as though it is hoarding.[13]

What level of foreign reserves a country should maintain at any given time is, of course, a matter of judgement for each country in the light of its development policies, objectives and priorities. However, given the unpredictable nature of the weather, fluctuating world market prices and Tanzania's own experience in the past decade (e.g. drought and famine of 1973–5), the four months' import figure appears a reasonable target. In this connection, it is to the credit of the Bank's sound foreign reserves management policies that the famine of 1973–5 did not claim many lives in Tanzania as it did in a number of other much wealthier African countries – it was possible in Tanzania to stop the importation of luxury goods in favour of mass consumption goods.

The Bank plays an important role also in controlling foreign credits or loans. For example, it provides advisory service to the government in respect of international payments agreements entered into between Tanzania and foreign governments or instutitions. These include purchase agreements under supplier's credit, commodity credits, direct cash loans and other credits. In particular, the Bank advises the government on the foreign exchange implications of the payment terms of such agreements, on the ability of Tanzania to repay the credits in foreign exchange upon maturity, and on the overall usefulness of the country's membership in an international financial or monetary institution. This function is of immense significance to the national goal of reducing dependency on foreign sources of development finance as far as possible. Usually, after a credit agreement has been concluded between Tanzania and a foreign government, a separate agreement is worked out and concluded between the Bank of Tanzania and the central bank of the other country to ensure smooth payments under the credit agreement.

The Bank's strong Exchange Control Department is undoubtedly one of the most important means for economic management in Tanzania. As the bank authorities have put it; 'it is one of the major instruments which enable the Government to secure and safeguard the economic independence of this country, as well as facilitate the declared national goal of self-reliance.'[14] Although the exchange control function is vested in the minister of finance (Treasury), the minister delegates its administration to the Bank. The Exchange Control Ordinance requires the Bank to control all transactions in foreign currency (or gold). All transactions with international or foreign exchange implications are prohibited unless permitted directly by the Bank of Tanzania or indirectly through the authorized dealers (mainly the National Bank of Commerce and the People's Bank of Zanzibar). The following five broad categories of transaction must be directly or indirectly permitted by the central bank before they are entered into:[15]

1 Purchase, sale, borrowing or lending of foreign currency or gold and the maintenance of balance in foreign countries;
2 payment to non-residents or into their accounts in Tanzania's financial institutions;
3 import or export of any financial instrument or bill of exchange, e.g. cheques, currencies, drafts, travellers cheques, securities and gold;
4 transfer of securities between non-residents and residents, and acquisition and holding of foreign securities; and
5 under section 23 (1) of the Exchange Control Ordinance, the exportation of goods of any type to any place outside Tanzania.

To those accustomed to the so-called 'free enterprise' economic arrangements, the above restrictions may appear unduly restrictive or even 'inward-looking'. In practice, however, there are built-in mechanisms which ensure flexibility and efficiency without sacrificing the primary function of financial control. First, there is the mechanism of delegation. For example, while the Bank demands that all exporters register with it, the powers to control exportation of goods have in fact been delegated to the Commissioner of Customs, who ensures that such exportation is in the national interest.

Second, the Bank's exchange control and imports departments are assisted by an independent company, namely the General Superintendence Company Limited (established in 1972), in ensuring that the goods authorized for importation actually come into the country and that the price, quality and quantity are acceptable. The company checks and makes comparison as to price (to avoid 'over-invoicing'), quality and quantity of any goods with value exceeding Shs.20,000 that are to be imported into the country.

Third, non-luxury personal remittances, such as payments in respect of business travel, education, health, emigration and even pilgrimage for the religious, are usually permitted by the Bank. Finally, the Bank of Tanzania keeps the other financial institutions and all importers and exporters, as well as the general public, well informed about new regulations by means of regular circulars and bulletins. Thus, strictly speaking, the control function of the central bank had not led to 'over-insulation' of the economy, as it may appear on the surface.

In brief, the whole purpose of the Exchange Control Ordinance is to conserve and ensure proper use of the country's foreign exchange; and to ensure that the nation's foreign reserves are used on goods and services that will promote social and economic wellbeing of the majority rather than simply catering for the tastes of the few 'Westernized' élites in the urban areas, as it was before the Arusha Declaration.

Following the Arusha Declaration and the nationalization measures of 1967, there were instances of capital flight from the country, particularly through members of the Asian commercial bourgeoisie. This trend increased after the nationalization of buildings in early 1971.[16] Furthermore, between 1967 and 1971 there was conspicuous contradiction between the ideology of socialism and self-reliance and the continued importation of luxury goods – such as glamorous personal cars – from abroad by the urban political, commercial and bureaucratic élites. A number of measures were taken from 1971 onwards to curb these tendencies.

First, the government banned the importation of private luxury cars and other luxury goods, giving priority to large vehicles for transport purposes and capital goods directly related to development, including farm and industrial machinery, construction equipment, etc. Thus, in November 1971 an Import Licencing Department of the Bank of Tanzania was established to control imports; and an Exports Department was created in April 1975 to provide a focal point from which the country's export drive was to be co-ordinated.

Second, there was a sustained political campaign to educate both the leaders and the led on the importance of conserving the nation's foreign reserves and attacking all forms of economic sabotage. For example, Clause 32 of the Party Guidelines issued in February 1971 stipulated:

> In our external trade, we must avoid using our foreign reserves in buying items which do not help our economy. The Government and its corporations must be an example. Our importing agencies must be given guidelines appropriate to our policy of Socialism and Self-Reliance, and the guidelines must be adhered to. It is the duty of every Tanzanian, and particularly a leader to remember that shortage of foreign exchange weakens our economy and endangers our national independence.[17]

Third, to ensure that the financial institutions act as watchdogs for the economy and government policy, localization of manpower employed in these institutions was accelerated. Thus by mid-1976 the financial institutions (banks, insurance, etc.) were more 'localized' than all the other institutions. For example, by June 1976, of the whole establishment of 445 in the Bank of Tanzania there were only two expatriates (an economic and a banking adviser). The National Bank of Commerce (NBC) has a comprehensive training programme for its own personnel as well as for the other financial institutions. Most of its courses are given at the Institute of Financial Management, which has the capacity to train financial managers and accountants to the highest level possible. It is expected that by 1977, ten years after the Arusha Declaration, all financial institutions in the country will have been almost wholly manned by Tanzanians themselves.[18]

Finally, the government has recently found it necessary to strengthen the legal apparatus to make it more effective in guarding the economy against sabotage and illegal expatriation of surplus. The measure taken between 1974 and 1976 include: (1) the creation of an 'Anti-Corruption Squad'; (2) the creation of a special inspectorate unit within the Treasury to check and supervise the financial and investment policies of the various parastatal bodies; and (3) the prescription of more severe sentences to all cases entailing economic sabotage or smuggling, which has risen rapidly in the past five years. Indeed, despite the above control measures, there still exist avenues of economic drain, especially these relating to the management of the parastatal system. These will be discussed in the following section.

Control through the parastatal system

The Arusha Declaration started a new era of corporations, companies, boards and authorities. These constituted the parastatal system. By mid-1976, virtually all important economic activities of the nation – mining, industry, commerce, construction, agriculture – were controlled (or regulated) either by parastatal bodies or by co-operative societies. There is a special Standing Committee for Parastatal Organizations (SCOPO), which is responsible for defining and enforcing the terms of service in parastatal organizations.

The extent of nationalization of the economy is revealed by the following figures. Between 1964/5 and 1974/5 government spending multiplied five times to become 38 per cent of the GNP by 1975. Whereas the private sector contributed 72 per cent of total investment in 1964/5, it contributed only 36 per cent by 1975; and the nationalized sector contributed 64 per cent (and 73 per cent of total monetary investment). Thus the success of the Tanzanian economy depends to a very large degree on performance in the public sector. In other words, economic success will depend on the extent to which the parastatal organizations are able to: (1) increase productivity per unit of factor input, and (2) block the avenues of foreign exploitation.

As we mentioned earlier, the Tanzanian economy is not a fully planned economy; it is still a market economy to a very large extent – for three main reasons. First, although the private sector has shrunk, it still accounts for about a third of total investment. Second, the government has to bargain with its foreign (private or public) partners in the case of the joint industries. Third, even in the case of wholly state-owned industries, the government cannot have a completely free hand, depending as it does on foreign expertise, consultancy, capital and technology. These factors make it difficult to have a comprehensively planned economy even after nationalizing the major means of production and distribution. Consequently, not all the avenues of foreign exploitation have been blocked – at least not in the initial period.

Unlike other revolutionary regimes, Tanzania paid full (or fair) compensation for the nationalized industries. This fact restored the confidence of foreign investors, as has been witnessed by their readiness immediately to undertake joint ventures with the government. Foreign companies have co-operated with the parastatals in two other ways, namely in undertaking management contracts and in providing consultancy services. In other words, apart from capital investments in joint ventures, *technique* has become the new and very lucrative form of private foreign investment in Tanzania's parastatals. In fact, during the initial years, 1967–71, foreign companies took the initiative in formulating new projects and selling them to the corporations. This was so because the local managers were the former senior bureaucrats in the civil service, with neither industrial experience nor 'marketing intelligence', and who had only a limited number of planning personnel.

A number of criticisms have been made against the working of the parastatal organizations, especially during the first four years following the Arusha Declaration. Although most of these criticisms have been directed to the National Development Corporation (NDC), which is the body directly concerned with the industrial development of the nation, they apply to the other organizations as well.

First, the parastatals have been criticized for following capitalist investment criteria, by (1) concentrating on import substitution industries; (2) producing luxury goods such as beer and cigarettes; and thereby (3) ignoring mass consumption goods and services. Second, a related criticism is that these organizations had no long-term strategy based on social benefit criteria, and that consequently investments were based in major cities, thereby ignoring small towns and villages. This is linked with the third criticism, namely that the parastatals such as the NDC tended to prefer investments in capital-intensive projects to labour-intensive projects, a contradiction in view of the fact that the country had a labour surplus. Fourth, the co-operation with foreign firms was introducing new forms of dependency (financial, technological and psychological), and new forms of exploitation (through joint ventures, over-invoicing, high fees for management and consultancy services). Fifth, to crown it all, only a few parastatals achieved satisfactory productivity levels or made significant profits during the first five years.

Since the above criticisms have been well documented elsewhere,[19] we require no further elaboration here. It suffices to note that the parastatals have not been able to block all the avenues of foreign exploitation. This is due largely to Tanzania's technological dependency: dependency on foreign consultants, expertise in various industrial fields, patents, machinery, etc. The hope is that technology will eventually be 'transferred'. Yet, unless there is care, such transfer may be delayed – for several reasons.

First, Tanzania's non-alignment policy has led to importation of technology from both the socialist and the capitalist camps, as well as from the relatively more technologically advanced Third World countries (e.g. India). The difference in models and levels of sophistication have often led to confusion and a lack of consistency in importing the requisite skills to the local technocrats. Moreover, this fact tends to compound the problem of spare parts.

Second, the capitalist technical assistance agencies are for obvious reasons often unwilling to transfer sophisticated technologies to underdeveloped countries. This would lead to the closure of their markets. This unwillingness is even greater where it involves a public sector; for the capitalists believe that the productive and commercial sectors of the economy should be left to private investors (local or foreign).

Third, attempts to imitate or to master a particular machinery or model have often been frustrated by frequent changes of models and rapid technological progress in the metropolitan centres. Moreover, as Peter Neerso has correctly pointed out, there are also practical problems in the transfer of technology without direct co-operation with a private firm, especially in industries using sophisticated technologies:

In industries using sophisticated technologies the pertinent know-how is most often not vested in a single person, but in a group of persons. In these industries, transfer of technology can only take place through a team of persons whose skills are complementary and who can work well together. It is very difficult for a development assistance agency to recruit an entire such team at the same time; and even if it is possible, such a team is handicapped by not being able to obtain technical advice from a parent company in a developed country.[20]

Fourth, in so far as the so-called transfer of technology entails domestication or 'internalization' of innovation, it cannot be achieved without a conscious industrial strategy. Industrialization strategy and choice of technique go hand in hand because 'the actual range of available techniques is largely dictated by the source of existing capital equipment', and as long as capital goods continue to be imported from the industrially advanced countries, 'machinery embodying techniques that correspond to the factor proportions of the periphery will be difficult to realize'.[21] The lessons from the above weaknesses and criticisms have been learnt by the Tanzanian policy-makers. This is reflected in the policy changes and further controls imposed over the parastatal organizations during the past five years. We shall outline these changes briefly.

The new strategy and forms of control, 1969–76

There has been a re-thinking since 1969 with regard to a new strategy for industrialization, indigenization of technology and control of the parastatal organizations. In political rhetoric, as well as in the Second Five-Year Development Plan introduced in July 1969, emphasis has been on an industrial strategy emphasizing small-scale (cottage) industries; labour-intensive, technical training starting with locally available (traditional) techniques; enlargement of the internal market by improving transport facilities, communications and distribution of goods and services; improvement of the human resources by giving priority to rural health, education, water and better housing. This new industrial strategy was expected to dominate the Third Plan, which was to be launched in July 1975 but was postponed owing to unfavourable economic conditions.[22]

There has also been a re-thinking about the best way to deal with the foreign management contracts and consultancy services. It is admitted that these must continue till the country achieves its goal of self-sufficiency in skilled manpower – estimated to be 1980 in the First Plan (1964–9) but now considered to be later. In the meantime, the contracts would be subjected to a more rigorous scrutiny by the government. Thus in 1971 a revision of the existing contracts was undertaken, and from then on all new contracts were to be approved by the Economic Committee of the Cabinet. In each case, the government would insist on the inclusion of a specific provision for training local staff and another stipulating that the management fee would depend on profitability of the company. This was expected to induce efficiency of the managing agents. A third provision would demand that investment should take into consideration the need for the industry to increase social benefits to the larger population.

Each of these provisions has created practical problems at the level of implementation. First, for reasons discussed above, the foreign managers and consultants have not been enthusiastic about training local manpower. Very often, it is the least capable who are apprenticed to prove their uselessness while the capable are frustrated and discredited to perpetuate dependency. Second, calculation of the management fee is also problematic. The fee may be a lump sum, a part of the turnover of the project, a part of the profits of the project, or a combination of these factors. The lump-sum approach places the country at a disadvantage, for it does not encourage higher productivity. The turnover approach would tempt the managing agents to increase turnover irrespective of the costs. A fee based on profitability of the company or project may be the best for Tanzania, but it is certainly not the most attractive to the managing agents. This is because other government demands, such as its being labour-intensive, paying higher minimum wages, etc., tend to lower the level of profits. In practice, then, a compromise solution is found in a combination of the above factors, a lump sum plus a part of the profits being the commonest formula.[23]

Third, the social benefit criteria is seen by the foreign managing agent as contradicting the goal of higher productivity and profitability. On the one hand, he sees the profitability criteria as favouring capital-intensive methods, which are unacceptable to the government. On the other hand, he sees the social benefit criteria as favouring labour-intensive methods, which he considers unprofitable and political charged. No lasting solution has been found.

The parastatal sector underwent a major re-organization in 1969. The changes affected the NDC in particular, which had grown too large and was split to give rise to separate companies and subsidiaries such as the

Tanzania Tourist Corporation (TTC) and the National Agricultural and Food Corporation (NAFCO). Five years later, the State Trading Corporation (STC) was also reorganized, leading to the creation of twenty regional trading companies (RTCs) working under the umbrella of a Board of Internal Trade (BIT). This reorganization exercise was geared to higher efficiency and greater control by the government. Thus, in 1969 all parastatal holding corporations were put under the pertinent 'parent' ministries. For example, the NDC was put under the Ministry of Commerce and Industries, NAFCO under the Ministry of Agriculture, TTC under the Ministry of Natural Resources, etc. Furthermore, all the parastatals were later brought under the direct control of the Treasury and the Ministry of Planning and Economic Affairs, for these ministries were charged with the responsibility to scrutinize and approve all parastatal projects. In this way, the government is able to ensure that parastatal investments are consistent with national development goals.

The other institutions that have exercised control over the parastatals include the General Superintendence Company, which, as we pointed out earlier, inspects shipment of goods into Tanzania in order to check their quality, quantity and prices. This company was established in 1972 in co-operation with a Swiss company to counter the practice of illegal export of capital through over-invoicing of imports. By managing the import licencing system, the Bank of Tanzania has also exercised control over parastatals' use of foreign exchange; so has the National Bank of Commerce, which provides short-term loans to parastatal companies. Similarly, the Tanzania Investment Bank (TIB), which is an important source of long-term finance for new parastatal projects, is well placed to influence parastatal investment policies. For example, the TIB has different interest rates for different categories of projects, with lower interest being charged on projects geared to the satisfaction of the immediate social needs of the populace. This is one of the ways the government hopes to solve the profitability-versus-social benefit dilemma posed earlier.

Further legal means of control have been resorted to lately. By the Specified Companies Act of 1972, the government sought to restrict remittances of profits of the foreign companies operating privately or in partnership with parastatals. The Act gave full powers to the Minister for Finance to regulate the levels of dividends and the use of cash flows of such companies and corporations. How this move affects the profit motives of those concerned is not yet clear.

Finally, political forms of control have also been used. In 1969 it was decided to establish party branches in all government and parastatal offices (and 'factories') with fifty or more party members. In 1970 the Workers Participation Management Programme was introduced; and between 1975 and 1976 a total of twenty-five political commissars who were graduated from the Party Ideological College at Kivukoni were posted to key organizations. These are supposed to be the guardians of government and party policies at the key centres of production, and are expected to encourage worker exertion and to protect the industry concerned against economic sabotage. In some cases, the workers' participation programme has been able to generate the expected 'class struggles', successfully exposing the reactionary elements in the management (both local and foreign); in other cases, however, it has led to workers' frustration and apathy.[24] It is rather too early to comment on the effectiveness of the other 'populist' roles.

Indigenization by co-operativization

The co-operative movement has also played an important role in the indigenization process in Tanzania. The first co-operative societies emerged in the 1930s at the initiative of the peasants themselves. These provided the peasants with a protective mechanism against the exploitation of the Asian middlemen. This initiative occurred mainly in the cash-crop areas, especially in those areas growing coffee and cotton.[25]

The co-operative movement received substantial government support after independence, leading to the creation of the largest indigenous co-operative movement in the continent. The government campaigned for the establishment of co-operatives all over the country. Four types of co-operative emerged: marketing, consumer, transport, and savings and credit co-operatives. The Co-operative Union of Tanganyika was formed in 1961 as the apex organization of the co-operative movement, and a Co-operative and Development Bank was created. The government considered the co-operative movement as an instrument for self-reliant development and indigenization of the economy, especially for the marketing of various commodities within the country. Thus the existing Co-operative Societies Ordinance was changed so that the Registrar of Co-operatives could no longer refuse to register a co-operative society.

With this emphasis and increased credit facilities, co-operative societies, which had increased slowly from a mere 62 in 1948 to 857 in 1961, increased to 1533 by 1966 and 1737 by 1969. By 1964, co-operative societies were already handling a flow of goods and services worth more than £25 million a year, and about one-third of the country's foreign exchange earnings came from them. The aim was that by the early 1970s all produce that lends itself to co-operative marketing should be in the hands of the co-operatives, with the assistance of marketing boards.

Some of the co-operative societies and unions ventured into

processing industries. For example, the Nyanza Co-operative Union formed a subsidiary company, the Nyanza Industrial Company. By 1968 this company had taken over many privately owned ginneries and mills – seventeen ginneries, thirteen oil mills, seven rice mills and two sisal factories. Co-operative involvement in processing industries and commercial ventures increased rapidly after the Arusha Declaration. Very often, however, they ended up in financial disaster.

Despite its participative role in the indigenization process, the co-operative movement had a number of weaknesses. First, most of the co-operatives formed after independence became ineffective largely because they had been imposed from above. Some bureaucrats have correctly termed them 'political co-operatives', organized from the top 'without genuine local demand or even understanding'.[26]

Second, local politicians used the co-operative movement as a means of transferring scarce resources from the central government to their constituencies irrespective of whether or not these co-operatives had viable development plans. By 1964, the Minister concerned was becoming disturbed by the growth of petty co-operatives which he saw 'not only toiling in the fields, but also in the shops, the banks, the work-shops and garages', with no sense of direction; and the Minister was inclined to discourage them:

> Flattered as I am by the constant references both inside and outside this House to the desirability of establishing new co-operatives of every sort and kind, and vastly expanding at great speed the activities of the existing societies, I must make it quite clear that as the Minister responsible I am here to encourage the establishment of successful co-operatives only, and not just a mushroom of hay-wire prestige co-operatives.[27]

Third, training of personnel did not keep pace with the rate of growth of the co-operative movement, and thus many co-operative societies went bankrupt or failed to pay their debts. Moreover, the absence of proper accounting procedures led to corruption and a misuse of funds. A presidential committee summed up the weaknesses of the co-operative movement as follows: The proliferation of societies and marketing boards was a new form of 'middleman'; progressive farmers were benefiting at the expense of the smaller farmers; the movement was becoming undemocratic, and the peasants were losing faith in their leaders.[28]

There was a re-thinking about the role of the co-operatives and marketing boards after the Arusha Declaration. They were now considered a transitional phenomenon which would be supplanted by the Ujamaa Villages programme. The ultimate aim was that Ujamaa Villages would become multi-purpose co-operatives, making the existing societies and unions redundant. The co-operative movement was abolished in mid-1976 following a decision of the National Executive Committee of the Party. With the new powers bestowed on villages by the Villages and Ujamaa Villages Act, 1975, it is hoped that the villagers themselves will exercise more control over their produce than it was possible under the old co-operative movement.

The post-Arusha development strategy

Tanzania's development strategy after the Arusha Declaration has been based on the ideology of socialism and self-reliance. The leadership has consistently argued that Tanzania's development and indigenization policy will succeed or fail depending on the extent to which the government adheres to the norms of self-reliance enunciated in the Arusha Declaration.[29] Self-reliance is conceived at two levels: the national level and the village community level. We shall focus our attention mainly on what this concept has meant in practice at the national level, particularly in relation to the efforts to mobilize development resources locally and externally. Before we examine this record, however, two issues relating to this policy require clarification.

First, the two concepts of *socialism* and *self-reliance* are seen as being organically interlinked. As President Nyerere has put it: 'The truth is that it is not possible to accept socialist without self-reliance, or vice versa.'[30] This position is in line with the argument that under the existing conditions 'periphery capitalism' cannot result in an indigenized, self-reliant economy; whereas self-reliance in development is an application of the lesson that 'only Tanzanians are sufficiently interested to develop Tanzania in the interest of Tanzanians . . . socialism is an application to economic and social life of the doctrine of human equality'.[31] Both the ethical and instrumental aspects of the policy are thus given a developmental justification, with socialism (*Ujamaa*) defining a socioeconomic organization which is consonant with the maximum development of the human resources and self-reliance defining the methods and development inputs to be used, namely local materials and efforts of the people.

Second, in both theory and practice, however, the emphasis on self-reliance is not supposed to mean autarchy. As the Declaration puts it, self-reliance is a recognition that 'the development of a country is brought about by people, not by money', and that 'money, and the wealth it represents, is the result and not the basis of development'.[32] The policy is clear on the conditions under which foreign assistance is to be accepted or rejected: 'Gifts and loans . . . which start off or stimulate our own efforts are useful. . . . But [those] which weaken our own efforts should not be accepted without asking ourselves a number of questions.'[33] Comments on Tanzania's performance since the Arusha Declaration, therefore, must keep these policy objectives in mind.

Mobilization of internal resources

The most important lesson learnt from the first five-year development plan (1964–9) was the need to intensify the mobilization of internal resources, both financial and human, rather than continuing with the expectations of massive foreign assistance. As we pointed out earlier, the plan had envisaged external sources accounting for about 78 per cent of the total central government investment, but it accounted for only 35 per cent, the remaining 65 per cent being contributed locally.[34] Failure of foreign investment, therefore, contributed to the policy of self-reliance.

Mobilization of internal resources has taken four main forms: (1) direct and indirect taxation; (2) creation of savings and financial institutions (3) governmental loans and parastatal re-financing; and (4) village-based self-help activities. We shall examine these initiatives briefly.

Direct and indirect taxation

Savings through direct and indirect taxes and levies have been one of the most important sources of development finance in Tanzania since the mid-1960s, and taxes have increased in amounts and variety with the passage of time. In response to the failure of foreign finance, the government introduced a special development levy in 1965 with the specific purpose of increasing forced saving. This was imposed on personal incomes and agricultural crops. In 1966, the levy on most agricultural crops was replaced by additional export taxes and increased export duties.

Following the Arusha Declaration, the need for a more socialist tax system was felt. Thus in June 1967, the Minister for Finance announced in his Budget speech significant changes in the tax system, making taxation more equitable and the collection of taxes more efficient. Among other things, the development levy was integrated with the personal income tax which was made more progressive for those in the upper incomes, and the corporate profit tax was also increased. Another important change was introduced in 1969, when the government instructed the district councils to stop collecting local rates and produce cess as of 1 January 1970. This meant that only the central government would collect direct taxes.[35] This also meant exempting the poorer sections of the peasantry from paying taxes.

Further changes were introduced in 1970, the main one being the introduction of an indirect sales tax on a variety of imported and locally manufactured articles. In so far as the tax was heavier on imported luxury goods, it had the effect of discouraging the 'conspicuous consumption' habits of the local bourgeoisie, thereby resulting in national savings. Again, the fact that imported goods were more heavily taxed than locally made goods encouraged the consumption of home-made products, thereby boosting sales for the Tanzanian infant industries.[36]

It should be emphasized that the tax structure in Tanzania has socialist as well as development objectives. Thus the level of taxation and total tax collection as a percentage of GNP is presently significantly higher in Tanzania than in most other Third World countries. This is particularly true since the introduction of the new Income Tax Act in 1973 and the further upward revision of taxes in June 1976. With all those changes in the tax structure, it has been possible within a space of fifteen years to reduce the earning differential between the highest and lowest earners from about 79:1 in 1961 to about 6:1 in 1976.

In quantitative terms, direct taxes rose four-fold from Shs.264 million in 1967/8 to Shs.1007 million in 1974/5. Similarly, indirect taxes rose four-fold from Shs. 589 million to Shs.2423 million during the same period. Table 15 (page 225) shows the growth of these taxes from 1967/8 to 1974/5.

Savings and financing institutions

To mobilize local resources for capital formation and investment in social and economic infrastructure, the government has encouraged the formation of savings and credit societies as well as creating a number of financial institutions. This effort predates the Arusha Declaration. Savings and credit societies started as self-help co-operative financial organizations which encouraged thrift among their members by saving on a planned basis. They gained encouragement from the Credit Union of Saskatchewan, Canada, and the Credit Union League of Michigan, USA, which sponsored the so-called Tanganyika Project.[37]

Recognizing the role of such societies in the development process, the government made provisions for them in the first five-year plan, leading to the formation of the Savings and Credit Union League of Tanganyika in 1964. A Savings and Credit Society Section was created within the Co-operative Division of the Ministry of Agriculture and Co-operatives, with the goal of establishing 400 societies by 1969. However, by 1970 there were only about 270 registered savings and credit societies with over 50,000 members, and with share savings totalling Shs.6.5 million. Most of these funds were outstanding in the form of loans to members.

Some of these societies have entered into special arrangements with the National Insurance Corporation to insure their members so as to provide an inducement to save. The societies provide loans to their members for various social and development projects, thus enhancing the spirit of self-reliance.[38]

Apart from the financial aspects, savings and credit societies and unions have also contributed to the development process through their educational programme on the meaning of thrift and on planned saving, and also through the democratic elections of their leaders and discussions of issues of common interest. The societies have encouraged their members to have confidence in their own ability to improve their lives and to help themselves through mutual help and support. As Binhammer has commented, in connection with some of the progressive societies, 'The evidence to date indicates that those with hardly any schooling are learning to manage their own financial affairs as a result of the educational programmes and practical experiences provided by the societies.'[39]

Apart from savings and credit societies, the government has mounted a strong campaign since 1967 for peasants and workers to save through the National Bank of Commerce and other financial institutions. Thus by 1976 there were either NBC branches or sub-branches in most district headquarters and some of the larger townships up-country. It is expected that in future banking facilities will be extended to the Ujamaa villages as well.[40] The people are also encouraged to save by purchasing Treasury bonds and other government securities, by purchasing national lottery tickets, and by taking life insurance with the National Insurance Corporation. Other forms of saving include accumulation of surpluses by co-operatives, marketing boards and parastatal institutions, and compulsory contributions to the National Provident Fund (NPF) and the National Union of Tanganyika Workers (NUTA).

Government loans and parastatal re-financing

The government finances the parastatal organizations from locally mobilized funds and/or external loans and grants with the hope that they will be able to take off quickly and become financially self-reliant. The parastatals are also expected to generate sufficient finance to support their subsidiary companies and leave a significant surplus for other national projects. Thus profitability is emphasized. For example, the legislation establishing the National Development Corporation (NDC) stipulated that:

in carrying on its business the Corporation shall have regard to the economic and commercial merits of any undertaking it promotes, finances, develops, manages or assists and shall use its best endeavours to secure that its business as a whole is carried on at a net profit, taking one year with another.[41]

As we have noted, however, some parastatals have been criticized for failing to strike an acceptable balance between the 'profitability' principle and the 'social criteria' principle emphasized after the Arusha Declaration. Very few have actually made a significant profit, not only because of 'political interference', as it is often claimed, but largely because of inexperience, corruption, inefficiency and financial swindling by external consultants.

Even such a key parastatal like the NDC has not yet become a self-financing institution. Up to the end of 1968 its main sources of finance were Treasury grants and intergovernmental credits, income from investments in and loans to subsidiary and associate companies, loans from the government and international institutions, equity participation by other parastatal bodies, and the re-financing of its own equity holdings. Between 1965 and 1969, its major source of income was dividends and interest payments from its subsidiary and associate companies. Apart from the mining concerns, however, most of the other subsidiary and associate companies were making losses rather than profits during that period. Thus of the thirty-four such companies, only sixteen paid dividends or interest to NDC in 1969, most of the total payments coming from the well established (but nearly exhausted) William Diamonds Limited.[42]

By 1969, other parastatal bodies were beginning to face serious liquidity problems as well. The NDC attempted to resolve liquidity shortages among its group companies through mutual financing. Such internal financing, however, would soon lead to loss of government control over parastatal investment plans. Thus to relate the financing operations closely with overall financial and economic planning, the government issued a regulation in 1971 to the effect that inter-company lending would become subject to price authorization. Liquidity problems had the effect of pushing the parastatals further away from the principle of self-reliance (their main *raison d'être*), leading to greater dependence on external sources of funding. It is therefore not surprising that, although internally mobilized funds rose rapidly between 1967 and 1976, foreign aid increased even more dramatically, as we shall se below.[43]

From about 1969 onwards, the government development expenditure depended more and more on internal and external borrowing because a large proportion of the tax revenue had to be used to meet the rising recurrent budget. As can be seen in Table 16, internal loans and grants

Table 15 *Tanzanian government recurrent revenue, 1967–8 to 1974–5 (Shs. million)*

Source	*1967–8*	*1968–9*	*1969–70*	*1970–1*	*1971–2*	*1972–3*	*1973–4*	*1974–5*
Direct taxes	264	339	352	448	532	602	697	1007
Indirect taxes	589	661	827	917	899	1324	1911	2423
Other	277	270	398	318	428	439	415	560
Total	1130	1270	1577	1683	1859	2357	3023	3990

Source: The Treasury; figures have been rounded up for convenience.

Table 16 *Tanzanian government development revenue: internal and external sources compared, 1967–8 to 1975–6 (Shs. million)*

Source	*1967–8*	*1968–9*	*1969–70*	*1970–1*	*1971–2*	*1972–3*	*1973–4*	*1974–5*	*1975–6*
Internal (loans and grants)	84	123	122	270	385	518	681	1039	1851
(%)	(24)	(27)	(20)	(33)	(43)	(54)	(42)	(50)	(60)
External (loans and grants)	260	338	488	559	519	438	954	1091	1161
(%)	(76)	(73)	(80)	(67)	(57)	(46)	(58)	(50)	(40)
Total	344	461	610	829	904	956	1635	2130	3012

Source: Treasury; figures rounded up for convenience.

for the development budget increased more than twenty times between 1967 and 1976; from Shs.84 million in 1967/8 to Shs.1851 million in 1975/6. During the same period, external aid (loans and grants) increased more than four times; from Shs.260 million in 1967/8 to Shs.1161 million in 1975/6.

The contributions of internal and external loans and grants to the development budget (shown in brackets in Table 16) show clearly that Tanzania's policy of self-reliance has not meant a rejection of foreign aid. During the period under review, the policy meant three things: first, to increase the proportion of the local contribution; second, to increase the development budget through internal and external loans and grants; and third, to diversify the external sources of development finance. We shall return to this last strategy below.

Much of the internal borrowing has been through the banking system, especially from the central bank. Other internal sources include premium bonds sold through branches of the National Bank of Commerce and Internal Revenue Offices; national savings bonds; savings accumulated by various provident funds and life insurance plans, and loans to parastatals and communities offered by such financial institutions as the Tanzania Finance Company, the Industrial Promotion Services Limited, the Diamond Jubilee Trust, Tanzania Investment Bank, Tanzania Rural Development Bank, Tanzania Housing Bank and the National Housing Corporation.[44] The effectiveness of the internal mobilization effort is clear from the fact that the domestic share of the total national debt rose from 28 per cent in mid-1966 to 45 per cent in 1970.[45]

Village-based self-help activities

Another strategy for mobilizing local resources has been to encourage village or community-based self-help activities. This strategy started immediately after independence, and the self-help movement was part and parcel of the co-operative and community development movement. The idea was to encourage the people to: (1) contribute their labour and/or funds to projects initiated either by themselves or by the government; and (2) use locally available resources and skills as far as possible so as to conserve foreign exchange.

The concept of self-help has been defined and interpreted in a number of ways. In the mid 1960s it was incorporated in the vague and less effective concept of 'nation-building', and after the Arusha Declaration it was incorporated in the larger concept of self-reliance. After the Declaration, and particularly after the decentralization of administration in 1972, efforts have been made to incorporate self-help in district and village plans, but recent studies have shown that the idea of 'planned self-help' has not been well understood by the local planners, and response has varied widely from one area to another.[46] There is also some evidence that participation in self-help projects in the rural areas has diminished in the 1970s for reasons beyond the scope of this paper.[47]

There are, however, examples of successful self-help activities, especially in the building of schools, dispensaries and personal houses – things that have a direct benefit to the individual or the community. Self-help has been particularly useful in the field of urban housing. With the growth of urbanization, the National Housing Corporation (NHC) was unable to provide housing whose rent is within the reach of the lower income groups. Thus the government encouraged formation of building co-operatives which, with the financial and technical assistance from the NHC, would build houses for their members. The monthly rent for such dwellings would be within reach of the lower income earners. Admittedly, however, many of such co-operatives have not been as successful as it was hoped, mainly because of financial mismanagement and poor organization.[48]

Another strategy has been to encourage village-based small-scale industries, especially after the launching of the second development plan in 1969. A Small Industries Development Organization (SIDO) was later created to spearhead the growth of cottage industries among rural and urban communities, emphasis being placed on locally available materials and skills. It is expected that this effort will greatly benefit from the movement to collectivize the rural population which will be completed by the end of 1976. Thus, the villagization movement, the small industries development organization and the decentralized administrative structure, together with the Rural Development Bank and the other financial institutions, provide a sufficient organizational infrastructure for mobilizing local resources.

External mobilization of resources

As we noted earlier, foreign aid increased dramatically between 1967/8 and 1974/5. It should be noted, however, that the government has deliberately diversified its sources of aid to avoid becoming a satellite of any one country or any ideological block. The foreign aid strategy has several interesting features.

First, between 1969 and 1976, bilateral agreements with individual Western and socialist states yielded more aid than agreements with multilateral organizations (see Table 17). From 1969/70 to 1975/6 the bilateral sources provided a total of Shs.3062 million as compared with Shs.1207 million from multilateral sources during the same period.

Table 17 *Loans and grants to Tanzania: multilateral and bilateral sources compared, 1969–70 to 1975–6 (Shs. million)*

Source	*1969–70*	*1970–1*	*1971–2*	*1972–3*	*1973–4*	*1974–5*	*1975–6*
Multilateral	43	77	67	138	102	326	453
Bilateral	79	193	318	380	579	577	937
Total	122	270	385	518	681	901	1390

Source: Treasury; figures rounded up for convenience.

Table 18 *Aid to Tanzania from Western and socialist countries compared, 1969–70 to 1975–6 (Shs. million)*

Source	*1969–70*	*1970–1*	*1971–2*	*1972–3*	*1973–4*	*1974–5*	*1975–6*
Socialist	7	3	160	210	203	2	60
Western (including Japan)	71	190	158	170	376	574	864
Total	78	193	318	380	579	576	924

Source: Treasury; figures rounded up for convenience.

Second, in keeping with its non-alignment policy, the Tanzanian government has sought aid from both socialist and Western blocks, its ideology of *Ujamaa* notwithstanding. At the time of independence the West, especially Britain, provided much of the aid and monopolized trade links with Tanzania. Links with socialist countries were established in the mid 1960s with official visits to the Soviet Union, China, and then the Eastern European socialist countries. Although these links have been strengthened after the Arusha Declaration, the West has still managed to retain the upper hand in the provision of aid, technology and technical personnel; in trade links (discounting the Tanzania–Chinese Commodity Agreement relating to the building of the Tanzania–Zambia Railway); in cultural and communication links. Whereas aid from Western (capitalist) countries (including Japan) between 1969/70 and 1975/6 totalled Shs. 2043 million, aid from the socialist world during the same period amounted to Shs. 645 million. The aid from socialist countries was substantial from 1971/2 to 1973/4, owing mainly to the big Chinese loan for the construction of the Tanzania–Zambia Railway. As can be seen from Table 18, aid from the socialist camp dropped drastically as the railway approached completion.[49] This continued reliance on Western aid has naturally invited criticism from a number of Marxist scholars, who have wondered whether Tanzania's brand of socialism and policy of self-reliance can succeed without a conscious move to 'disengage' from the West and their multinational corporations.[50] The debate on this issue is still going on in academic and political circles within Tanzania.

Third, the Tanzanian leadership has preferred aid from the smaller, non-imperialist states to aid from the Western super-powers. This is due partly to the leadership's awareness of the dangers of the country becoming a satellite of a super power, as well as to the fact that the smaller Western states have generally been more sympathetic to Tanzania's development strategy. Thus relations with the Nordic countries (Sweden, Norway, Denmark and Finland) have been strengthened, and aid from these countries has increased tremendously since the Arusha Declaration. The growing importance of the Nordic countries *vis-à-vis* all the other sources of finance can be clearly seen in Table 19. Whereas aid from the Nordic countries between 1973/4 and 1975/6 amounted to Shs. 1110 million, aid from all other countries during that period amounted to Shs. 982 million. Furthermore, much of the Nordic aid was in the form of grants, whereas much of the aid from the other countries was in the form of loans. Thus, out of the total Nordic aid of Shs. 1110 million, Shs. 882 million was in the form of grants and Shs. 228 million in loans; whereas out of the Shs. 982 million from the other countries Shs. 823 million was in the form of loans and

Table 19 *Aid to Tanzania from Nordic countries and all the other countries compared, 1969–70 to 1975–6 (Shs. million)*

Source	*1969–70*	*1970–1*	*1971–2*	*1972–3*	*1973–4*	*1974–5*	*1975–6*
Nordic countries	53	71	75	118	271	332	508
Other countries	26	122	242	262	308	245	429
Total	79	193	317	380	579	577	937

Source: Treasury; figures rounded up for convenience.

Table 20 *Tanzanian government recurrent expenditure, 1967–8 to 1975–6 (Shs. million)*

Sector	*1967–8*	*1968–9*	*1969–70*	*1970–1*	*1971–2*	*1972–3*	*1973–4*	*1974–5*	*1975–6*
Economic services	232	267	307	349	376	440	656	435	590
Social services	291	335	435	502	560	665	881	1045	1136
General administration	346	369	480	533	543	479	944	1261	1157
Other purposes	196	215	305	247	301	372	304	733	745
Total recurrent expenditure	1066	1186	1527	1631	1780	1956	2785	3974	3628
Surplus	65	84	51	52	79	130	238	16	200
Total	1130	1270	1578	1683	1859	2086	3023	3990	3828

Source: Treasury; figures rounded up for convenience.

only Shs. 159 million in grants. There is also a general feeling within the Treasury that there are less strings attached to aid from the smaller Western countries and fewer delays in getting projects started once the agreement has been signed.[51]

Conclusion: some outstanding issues

On the surface, at least, it would appear from our discussion so far that Tanzania has already established a satisfactory political, financial and administration infrastructure for the indigenization of the economy. Unfortunately, we are unable in this paper to examine the actual implementation process, which would have revealed the salient features of the indigenization process as well as the strengths and weaknesses of the Tanzanian approach. However, we shall attempt in this concluding section to give a brief outline of some of the outstanding issues that are still being debated with regard to the Tanzanian strategy.

The growing cost of administration and services

One of the criticisms of the structure of the Tanzanian economy is that the cost of administration and services is too high relative to the expenditure in the more directly productive sectors. For example, during the period 1964–75 government and parastatal investments were as follows: agriculture, 11.5 per cent; industry and mining, 16.9 per cent; social services and general administration, 71.6 per cent. As it can be seen clearly in Table 20, the cost of administration and social services rose rapidly after the Arusha Declaration, multiplying more than three times from 1967/8 to 1975/6. There are several reasons for this rapid rise in social services and administrative costs.

First, as we noted earlier, the government wants to improve the human resources by extending the basic social services to the rural population; hence the great emphasis on education, rural health and water supplies since 1971. Second, the parastatal system has resulted in increased administrative costs, for a number of senior posts have been created. New parastatals and senior posts seem to have been created hurriedly without due consideration of costs or of whether or not their functions could be performed by existing ones. There was also little control over the employment of the middle and lower cadres in these mushrooming parastatals. Third, on the government side, the administrative decentralization of 1972 increased the recurrent expenditure astronomically, having enlarged the regional and district employment opportunities. Thus by 1975, about 80 per cent of the regional recurrent budget was spent on personal emoluments. To cut down these costs, the government reduced the personnel in the civil service by 20 per cent in early 1976 and encouraged the parastatals to do the same. Further, the government undertook to review the regional and district administrative structure with a view to reducing costs. It does not appear, however, that these measures will lead to significant reduction in administrative costs.

It is important to distinguish the large services sector in an underdeveloped economy such as that of Tanzania from the large tertiary sector in a developed country. In the Tanzanian case, the services sector is not based on a strong secondary sector, a fact that makes it essentially parasitic. In a developed economy, on the other hand, the tertiary sector is a child of a strong secondary sector, and therefore forms part of an integrated economy. Issa Shivji is correct in asserting that, in so far as the Tanzanian economy remains externally oriented, the tertiary sector cannot avoid being 'the internal reflection of the economy's external links with international capitalism'.[52] This point is clarified below.

Export and consumption orientation of the economy

Another feature of the Tanzanian economy that is at odds with the country's declared indigenization policy is the continued dependence on the export of primary products, agricultural and mining, and the consumption orientation of the secondary sector.

Ironically, the Arusha Declaration has thus far made no significant changes in the country's export orientation. For example, in 1962 primary products accounted for about 66 per cent of total exports. The figure had been reduced to 59 per cent by 1967 (the year of the Declaration), but it was still 59 per cent five years later (1972).[53] Admittedly, processing industries have increased rapidly since 1967, but this has not changed the basic pre-Arusha structure of the economy. C. Thomas has attributed this to the divergence between domestic resource use and domestic demand, and considers the discrepancy as one of the 'laws' of underdevelopment.[54]

The external orientation of the economy is reinforced by the smallness and consumption orientation of the secondary sector. Here, too, the Arusha Declaration has not made a significant difference. Thus, for example, whereas the secondary sector (including manufacturing, handcrafts, electricity, water and construction) accounted for 14.2 per cent of the total GDP (at current prices) in 1967, it had only risen to 16.1 per cent by 1972. The change over the five-year period is obviously too small to be called radical transformation of an underdeveloped economy. Moreover, about half of the change in this sector was accounted for by construction; but only about half of the amount spent on construction during that period related to the basic economic infrastructure, e.g. construction of roads, bridges, ferries, etc. Similarly, in the manufacturing field, emphasis has been on consumer goods, accounting for 59 per cent of the total GDP in 1970; and out of the total consumer goods in 1970, luxury goods constituted about 30 per cent of the gross value of the output.[55]

Furthermore, although there has been some change in the pattern of imports – in both type and source – the change cannot be called 'revolutionary'. For example, whereas the imports for 1967 consisted of 35 per cent consumer goods, 41 per cent intermediate goods and 24 per cent capital goods (of total value of imports), the corresponding figures for 1971 were 27, 43 and 30 per cent respectively. The fall in consumer goods imports was mainly due to import substitution in such areas as textiles, beverages and tobacco. However, imports of consumer goods (especially food) rose again between 1972 and 1976, owing to the long droughts and famine. For example, the imports of food rocketed from Shs. 183 million in 1971 to Shs. 312 million in 1972.[56]

Three things should be noted here. First, although the government has been successful in reducing imports of cars and other transport equipment (whose value had rocketed dramatically from Shs. 93 million in 1962 to Shs. 371 million in 1972), there has not been a dramatic rise in the capital goods imports. This is due partly to the rising demand and cost of consumer goods (including the high cost of petrol). Second, the import substitution effort has been constrained by the high import content of all import substitution industries and by high costs of production. Third, consequently it has been impossible to 'disengage' from the capitalist bloc, which remains the main source of loans and grants, with all the attendant political strings and repayment problems.

Lack of an industrial and transformational strategy

Tanzania's practice has to date not measured up to the expectations of its revolutionary ideology. This is due to the lack of a well articulated industrial and transformational strategy. It is true, as we have already noted, that there have been attempts since 1969 to set out industrial priorities in both the modern and traditional (rural) sectors; yet it is also true that these attempts have not resulted in an integrated transformational plan.

For example, the predominant tendency among the bureaucrats has been to consider the rural development effort (under the policy of *Ujamaa Vijijini*) simply as a strategy to enable the lagging rural population, as it were, to 'catch up with' the modern urban sectors, rather than as a radical strategy for transforming the society and the economy. This has meant, then, bringing the rural population together to produce much the same primary goods for export to the same traditional markets. With the exception of a few areas, even such an important programme as the small-scale industries has not been geared to the processing of the primary products, although this is one of the main aims of the programme.

Up till now (1976), rural development policy has not clarified the essential link between rural development and industrialization. It is necessary, for example, to have a strong industrial sector which provides the requirements of the agricultural sector. Rural productivity will ultimately depend on it. A well defined industrial strategy, moreover, will enable Tanzania to reduce its present technological dependency on the metropolitan centres.

A well conceived transformational strategy would also provide solutions to the problems of inefficiency, corruption and 'opportunism' – problems that are now acknowledged by the central leadership as a menace to the Tanzanian revolution. The solutions provided so far have been ineffective, largely because the problems have been handled as isolated occurrences rather than being diagnosed in the larger context of the production and distribution system as a whole, locally and internationally. A typical solution for inefficiency or corruption, for example, has been either expulsion of the individuals concerned (if caught) or dismantling the organization concerned and replacing it with a more 'complex' one. The roots of these problems have not been fully examined.

To conclude, therefore, we can say that Tanzania has gone further than most Third World countries in defining a strategy for overall development and indigenization of its economy. That strategy, however, has thus far lacked the kind of dynamism and internal consistency necessary to generate a self-reliant and self-sustaining development. Among the problems that require immediate solution are those relating to efficiency, productivity, corruption and technological dependency. Success or failure of the economy will depend on how soon these problems are solved.

Notes

1 TANU, *The Arusha Declaration and TANU's Policy on Socialism and Self-Reliance* (Dar es Salaam: Government Printer 1967).
2 J. Nyerere, *Freedom and Socialism* (Dar es Salaam: Oxford University Press 1968), p. 264.
3 The relevant subsequent policy papers following the Declaration

include *Education for Self-Reliance* (1967), *Socialism and Rural Development (1967), Mwongozo* (1971) and *Decentralization* (1972).

4 J. Nyerere, *Ujamaa – The Basis of African Socialism* (Dar es Salaam: Government Printer 1962).

5 S. S. Mushi, *Revolution by Evolution* (Dar es Salaam, forthcoming).

6 For fuller details see the Appendix to the *Arusha Declaration.*

7 United Republic of Tanzania, *Tanzania Second Five-Year Plan for Economic and Social Development, Vol. I* (Dar es Salaam: Government Printer 1969), p. 59.

8 ibid.

9 Peter Meyns, 'Some Aspects of Planning and Socialism in Tanzania', in Lionel Cliffe and John Saul (eds.), *Socialism in Tanzania*, vol. II (Dar es Salaam: East African Publishing House, 1973).

10 See pp. 208–18 and 220–31 below.

11 See Bank of Tanzania Act, 1966; Bill no. 21, December 1966 or no. 2, January 1966.

12 ibid.

13 Bank of Tanzania, 'A decade of operation', in *Daily News* (14 June 1976).

14 ibid. See also Exchange Control Ordinance. Chapter 294, and the Subsidiary Legislation and Rules made under it.

15 Bank of Tanzania, 'A decade of operation'.

16 United Republic of Tanzania, Acquisition of Building Act, 1971.

17 TANU, *Mwongozo*, February 1971.

18 Interviews with Treasury Officials, NBC and Bank of Tanzania officials between April and June 1976.

19 See the relevant essays in Cliffe and Saul, *Socialism in Tanzania*, especially those by Seidman and Shiviji. See also Peter Neerso, 'Tanzania's policies on private foreign investment', in Carl Widstrand (ed.), *Multinational Firms in Africa* (Uppsala: Nordiska Afrikainstitutet 1975).

20 Neerso, p. 185.

21 J. Rwevemamu, *Underdevelopment and Industrialization in Tanzania* (Nairobi: Oxford University Press, 1973) p. 85. See also Nathan Rosenberg, 'Neglected Dimensions in the Analysis of Economic Change', *Bulletin of the Oxford University Institute of Economics and Statistics* (February 1964), and 'Technological change in the machine tool industry, 1840–1910', *Journal of Economic History*, vol. 23, no. 4 (December 1963), pp. 217–70; W. P. Strassman, 'Interrelated industries and the rate of technological change', *Review of Economic Studies* (October 1959).

22 The Plan was implemented during the 1976/7 financial year.

23 For a more thorough examination of these issues, see Neerso, p. 186.

24 For a detailed analysis, see Issa Shivji's *Class Struggle in Tanzania* (Dar es Salaam: Tanzania Publishing House 1975), especially chs. 11, 12 and 13.

25 The Co-operative Societies Ordinance was passed on 12 February 1932. In 1933 the Kilimanjaro Native Co-operative Union (KNCU) was registered to handle the marketing of coffee. Other co-operative societies followed suit. See T. R. Sadler, *The Co-operative Movement in Tanganyika* (Dar es Salaam: Government Printer 1961); H. P. Bomani, 'The co-operative way', *Spearhead*, vol. 1, no. 2 (December 1961); J. F. Moffet, *Handbook of Tanganyika*, 2nd ed. (Dar es Salaam: Government Printer 1958), pp. 117–93.

26 United Republic of Tanzania, *Report of the Presidential Special Committee of Enquiry into the Co-operatives and Marketing Boards* (Dar es Salaam: Government printer 1966), p. 5.

27 Hon. J. S. Kasambala, MP, Minister of Commerce and Co-operatives, 'Policy statement to the budget session of the National Assembly', 26 June 1964, p. 13.

28 United Republic of Tanzania, *Report of the Presidential Special Committee of Enquiry into the Co-operatives and Marketing Boards,* p. 5.

29 See particularly pp. 8–13 of the Declaration.

30 J. K. Nyerere, *The Arusha Declaration Teach-in* (Dar es Salaam: Information Services 1967), p. 4.

31 ibid.

32 *The Arusha Declaration*, p. 13.

33 ibid., pp. 8–10.

34 United Republic of Tanzania, *Taarifa ya Uchunguzi wa Hali ya Uchumi, 1968* (Dar es Salaam: Government Printer 1969), p. 92.

35 See H. H. Binhammer, *The Development of a Financial Infrastructure in Tanzania* (Kampala: East African Literature Bureau, 1975), p. 149.

36 See ibid. for details.

37 ibid., pp. 80–1.

38 ibid., p. 81.

39 ibid., p. 82.

40 Interviews with NBC officials, April 1976.

41 Act no. 69 of 1964.

42 Binhammer, pp. 85–6.

43 See also Andrew Coulson, 'The Financial Aspects of Decentralization' (University of Dar es Salaam, 1975, mimeo).
44 For details of these financial institutions see Binhammer, ch. IV, pp. 92–128; and ch. V, pp. 129–46.
45 ibid., p. 152.
46 See particularly undergraduate political sciences dissertations for the 1976/6 academic year, the University of Dar es Salaam.
47 See D. Leonard with G. Hyden, J. Maeda and S. Mushi, 'An analysis of a pre-test sample of development projects implemented under Tanzania's decentralized administrative structure' (Faculty of Arts and Social Science, University of Dar es Salaam 1975, mimeo).
48 The Mwenge Project in Dar es Salaam in an example of a building co-operative that faced problems after a promising beginning.
49 The railway was officially handed over to Tanzanian and Zambian authorities in mid 1976.
50 See articles by I. Shivji, John Saul, T. Szentes and W. Rodney in Cliffe and Saul, *Socialism in Tanzania*, vol. 1. See also Issa G. Shivji, *Class Struggles in Tanzania* (Dar es Salaam: Tanzanian Publishing House, 1975).
51 Interviews with Treasury officials, April–June 1976.
52 Shivji, *Class Struggles in Tanzania*, p. 157.
53 These figures can be found in the *Annual Economic Surveys*, 1963–73.
54 C. Thomas, 'The Transition to Socialism: Issues of Economic Strategy in Tanzanian-type Economies' (University of Dar es Salaam 1972, mimeo).
55 See the *Economic Surveys*, 1968–73.
56 ibid., 1968–75.

References

Rweyemamu, J. F., *Underdevelopment and industrialization in Tanzania*, Nairobi: Oxford University Press 1973

Rweyemamu, J. F., 'The formation of an industrial strategy for Tanzania', *African Review*, vol. 6, no. 3 (1976), pp. 275–288

10 Ethiopia

Befekadu Degefe, *Research Associate, Institute of Development Research, University of Addis Ababa*

This contribution is a result of a study of the indigenization process in the Ethiopian economy. The term 'indigenization' in its generic sense means either transfer of ownership from foreigners to the nationals of the country, or the replacement of foreign employees by the nationals, or both. In this paper it is taken to mean both.

The process of indigenization in the Ethiopian context deviates from the normal gradual transfer of ownership.

1 It was a product of a political shift rather than a deliberate indigenization process within the existing politico-economic framework.
2 The process did not discriminate between foreign and Ethiopian interest - where it was deemed necessary both owners were expropriated.
3 The end result in most of the cases was a transfer of ownership not to the indigenous people, but rather to the state.

As for indigenization with respect to employment, again this was a result of the nationalization rather than a conscious, independent drive.

The indigenization process in Ethiopia may also be unusual in terms of its abruptness. One regime went out of its way to encourage foreign investors to participate in the economic activity of the nation, while the next regime expropriated most of the foreign interests and prohibited their future participation save for limited activities and in conjunction with the state and subject to negotiated terms of participation. Thus came to an end an era of foreigners' influence that had its beginning three decades earlier.

The process of foreign interests' penetration into the country had its real beginning during the Italian occupation of 1935–41, although their trace could be found here and there in the country even earlier. During this period the Italians started building industries and began their exploitation of Ethiopia's natural resources. By the time they left, even though they had not done much in terms of establishing large manufacturing and extractive industries, a beginning had been made towards this end. The Italian influence, and the desire of the then leadership to modernize the country, meant the building and expansion of the manufacturing industry.

However, for an underdeveloped country like Ethiopia where the skill and the means did not exist, the only way such a dream could be fulfilled was through foreign capital and know-how. The stronger the urge, the greater became the need for such foreign assistance, and the more the country was opened up for the participation of non-Ethiopians.

The process of opening up the country to foreign exploitation continued until the popular uprising that began in February 1974 brought the regime to its end. Caught in the storm of rapidly moving events, the old political order proved incapable of dealing with the situation and in September of the same year gave way to a new order under a military government that reversed the former policies.

At the time of the revolution, the economy of the country had come a long way from that inherited from the Italian occupation three decades earlier. There were more roads, more schools, better communication facilities, etc. Nevertheless, the fruits of the economy were not equally shared. The Ethiopian masses grew poorer while the upper class and the foreigners grew richer. The exploitation of the urban proletariat by foreigners and of the rural masses by the landlords was intensified. *Per capita* income was estimated at E$186[1] in 1972, while the per capita income in the agricultural sector was less than E$100. Disease and ignorance were prevalent in the countryside, for modern schools and health centres were confined to the urban centres. The disastrous drought that affected eight of the fourteen provinces took a heavy toll in human lives.

It was against this background that the military regime assumed power. This paper examines the policies of the past regime and presents those of the new government with respect to the activities of the foreigners and Ethiopians within the economic sphere.

The paper is divided into three parts. The first summarizes the investment policy of the past regime and its effect on foreign capital and employment; the second presents the policies of the new government, and the final section looks at the prospects. It concludes by pointing out the awesome responsibility the Ethiopian government and people have assumed in beginning the development of the country.

Economic policy up to February 1974

The official economic policy of the Haile Selassie regime was couched in terms of establishing the material basis that would improve the living conditions of the people. Better education, better nutrition, better health and better communication were among the main ingredients of the policy statements. This required the transformation of an economy based on subsistence agriculture to one based on a dynamic industrial sector. The way to achieve these declared objectives was through a sustained increase in the gross national product.

The transformation of the economic base from agriculture to industry and the increase in the gross national product required the active participation of the masses and the careful management of the available resources. The free enterprise system was regarded as the instrument by and through which the people could participate in the development of the country, and planning was introduced to enhance the proper management of resources. The nation was said to be short of critical development elements such as capital, skilled manpower and technology, and the solution was to invite all three from whatever possible sources.

While this was the general economic policy, its operational aspect was totally different, especially as regards the domestic front. Once every five years since 1957, a plan has been drawn up that would supposedly guide the development of the country in general and the flow of resources in particular. Since each plan was drawn up without really understanding what was to be done, and since no effective institutional authority existed to check its performance, it remained ineffective.

The transformation of subsistence agriculture, which is the backbone of the economy and means of livelihood of more than 80 per cent of the population, required the participation and the encouragement of the rural masses. But this was not forthcoming. The feudal landholding system was a fetter on its development. It was legal for landlords to claim as much as 75 per cent of the tenant's produce; this limited their productive activity. Tenants were not protected against eviction and could be thrown out at the will of the landlord. This must have acted as a barrier to their taking a more active interest on the land, making permanent improvement on it through better soil management, erosion control and other cultural practices. As a result, the soil, and with it the tenants, grew poorer and poorer until the point was reached where the once cereal-exporting country became an importer of grains. The country's general approach to development – the development of the urban areas and the landlords' conspicuous consumption – intensified the degree of rural exploitation.

Exploitation of the rural sector was not limited to the landlords. The state was also a prime exploiter in its need to finance its increasing urban and industrial development. Though the rural population contributed to the financing of the central government, they got nothing in return – schools, health facilities and other modern amenities remained the exclusive right of the urban centres.

The policy of inviting foreign capital, skill and technology was pursued very aggressively and successfully under the direction of the Emperor himself. In a nationwide address on 11 October 1962, Haile Selassie said:

> We have never ceased to encourage foreign capitalists to work either in co-operation with our people or to invest their money on development works on their own. It has for long been part of the tradition of Ethiopia to welcome foreigners and to safeguard their rights and interests during their stay here. In the case of these foreigners who especially have invested capital on development projects in this country, apart from working in co-operation on the part of both our government officials and our people, there has never been a case in Ethiopia's history when the property of a foreigner has been unlawfully confiscated. This is a source of pride for Ethiopia. Ethiopia will at all times welcome foreign investors who may be willing to employ their money for development works either in partnership with Ethiopians or as private entrepreneurs.

Thus the government looked more and more to external sources for the 'development' of the country. The implementation of the Emperor's directives came in the form of investment policies that grew more and more liberal at each amendment.

Ethiopianization of posts was nominally pursued. But as foreigners were encouraged to invest their capital, no questions were asked about their employees, even though laws existed in the books that conditionally limited posts open to foreigners. In response to popular pressure from indigenous employees with respect to Ethiopianizing certain posts, the *Ethiopian Herald* in one editorial, on 21 April 1971, said, 'while Ethiopianization is desirable in principle, we desist from executing it for its own mere sake. One must not force the pace of things. In other words Ethiopianization should be instituted only in those circumstances where it is justified'. By whom such justification was to be made was not mentioned.

In general, a totally outward-looking policy was pursued by the Selassie regime with domestic factors of development playing a secondary role to the imported elements. The result has been the building up of a modern sector totally dependent on the external forces and wholly divorced from the traditional sector.

Economic planning and foreign investment

First five-year plan and foreign investment

The history of the investment policy in Ethiopia must be looked at in conjunction with the overall policy of the past regime. The need to change the static subsistence economy of the postwar period into a dynamic monetized economy required the channelling of all efforts and resources into activities that would have a quick pay-off towards realizing the declared objectives. This obviously required a definition of the objectives, the setting of priorities and the creation of the necessary vehicles for their implementation. Although the government of the day had neither the desire nor the capacity to plan, it nevertheless started putting general intentions on paper and presented this as a plan along with vague ideas as to their implementation.

The first of such declarations was the ten-year industrial development programme of 1945, out of which nothing much was realized; a comprehensive 'guideline' did not come out until 1957, when the first five-year plan was launched. The plan was to run from 1957/8 to 1961/2 and the major objectives were:[2]

1 the development of an infrastructure;
2 raising the level of education with emphasis on technical training;
3 the acceleration of agricultural development;
4 the establishment of industries to process domestically produced raw materials;
5 the creation of economic and financial policies towards mobilizing resources.

The achievement of these objectives required a planned investment of E$673.6 million over the five-year period, distributed among the different sectors as given in Table 21. As a result of this pattern of investment allocation, national income over the plan period was to have increased by 16 per cent, amounting to an annual growth rate of 3.2 per cent.

Owing to the low savings capacity of Ethiopians, foreign capital was to have an important role in the financing of the planned investment. To this end the government started creating the necessary machinery

Table 21 *Planned investment in the main sectors 1957–8 to 1961–2*

	Allocation (E$ million)	*Per cent*
Agriculture	92.1	13.7
Mining, power and manufacture	138.0	20.5
Transport and communications	240.0	35.45
Social services	57.0	8.5
Housing	122.5	18.2
Other	24.0	3.6
Total	E$673.6	100.0

through and by which the foreign investors could be enticed to invest in the country in the early 1950s.

The first such legislation was in the form of a notice (Notice of 1950 for the Encouragement of Foreign Capital Investment) that extended benefits, in the form of an exemption from tax for five years, remittance of earned profits, and duty-free importation of machinery by investors, to foreign investors but not to Ethiopian investors.

The second measure related to the marine industry (Proclamation no. 137 of 1953). Under this proclamation merchant ships registered under Ethiopian law were exempted from payment of all taxes, dues, fees and charges other than:

1 an annual tax of not more than E$1.25 per registered ton;
2 taxes, dues, fees and charges imposed equally on all ships and vessels calling on Ethiopian ports;
3 registration fees, which should not be more than E$2.00 per dead-weight ton.

Owners and crews were all exempted from tax of any kind, and the businesses were also given the right to import fuels, oils, machinery, furniture, utensils and other materials necessary for the maintenance and running of the ships and vessels without restriction and dues.

The same proclamation exempted marine industrial enterprises from all kinds of taxes and duties for a period of five years, provided they invested in the country not less than $500,000. They were further exempted from import duties on their ships and vessels, and on parts and machinery required for the enterprises' development.

The third investment proclamation was that of the Agricultural and Industrial Expansion Proclamation (Proclamation no. 145 of 1954). This exempted investors from all kinds of taxes and duties on imported agricultural and industrial machines that would be used directly in the exploitation and development of agricultural and industrial resources.

The fourth investment legislation was the Income Tax Proclamation (Proclamation no. 173 of 1961), which exempted enterprises engaged in industry, transport and mining activities from income tax:

1 for a period of up to five years if the investment was E$200,000 or more; and
2 for three years if E$500,000 was invested in an extension of an already existing enterprise, provided the extension was operated as a separate technical unit with separate accounts.

Hence, between 1950 and the end of the first five-year plan period in 1961 four different pieces of legislation were enacted to encourage foreign investors. Owing to the unavailability of records on the planned and actual inflow of foreign capital, the effect of these legislations cannot be measured except to say that, as the implementation report of the first five-year plan pointed out, inflow of the foreign capital was not as much as expected, especially towards the beginning of the plan period.

Second five-year plan and foreign investment

In 1963 the government launched the second five-year plan, and the so far scattered investment laws were consolidated under one body of law, the Investment Decrees of 1963.

The second five-year plan was to run over the five-year period of 1963/4 to 1967/8. The main targets of the plan were:[3]

1 to shift the structure of the economy from agriculture to agro-industrial activity;
2 to change the pattern of production by introducing new processes and methods;
3 to increase the productive capacity of the economy with a view to diversifying production, and increasing the rate of growth.

By the end of the plan period GNP was to have risen from E$2166 million in 1962 to E$2718 million, an increase of 26 per cent at an annual growth rate of 4.6 per cent. *Per capita* income was to increase from E$103 in 1962 to E$119 in 1967, at an annual rate of 2.8 per cent.[4]

The achievement of the objectives was planned to be realized with a total expenditure of E$2655 million dollars, of which E$1451 was slated for capital expenditure and the balance to finance the recurrent expenditure.[5]

The planned expenditure was much more than what the country could raise from domestic sources, hence the necessity of inviting foreign capital to realize the goals of the plan. The plan envisaged an inflow of E$639 million from foreign sources to cover 44 per cent of the capital expenditure or 24 per cent of the total planned expenditure.[6]

The investment policy

As pointed out above, among the reasons given to explain the failure of the first plan to achieve its targets was the shortage of inflow of foreign capital, especially during the early stages. To ensure an adequate inflow, the government legislated an investment policy and for the first time created an institution that would implement it.

The 'Decree Providing for the Encouragement of Capital Investment in Ethiopia' in effect consolidated the investment policies enacted up to that period and broadened their scope. This included the Notice of 1950, the Marine Industry Proclamation, the Agricultural and Industrial Expansion Proclamation and the Income Tax Proclamation of 1961. It extended also the benefits to Ethiopian investors.

At the same time, the decree created the 'Investment Committee', composed of the Ministers of Commerce and Industry (chairman), Finance, and Agriculture, the Commissioner of Planning and the Governor of the National Bank of Ethiopia or their designates. The Investment Committee has a secretariat and is located in the Ministry of Commerce and Industry. Although they were the members of the committee, they and especially the secretariat were to work closely with other ministries and autonomous government offices.

Towards the end of the second plan period, the Investment Decree was promulgated as a proclamation approved by Parliament. The incentives were broadened to include agriculture, mining, transport and tourism. The salient incentives granted included the following.

Income tax relief Newly established enterprises in any of the above enumerated activities were granted exemption from payment of income tax, provided the investment was not less than E$200,000. The exemption period was five years starting from the date of operation.

The privilege was also extended in the case of expansion of existing enterprises if the investment in extension was not less than E$200,000 and provided the extension was operated as a separate technical unit with its own set of accounts. In such cases the privilege was extended for a period of three years only.

Import duty relief (1) Agricultural and industrial machines, implements, appliances or parts imported for exclusive use in agricultural and industrial activities were exempted from the payment of all taxes and duties levied on imports; (2) structural and building materials imported for the construction of industrial buildings could be exempted from the payment of import duties and all other taxes.

However, in both cases exemption is possible only on those goods that are not produced domestically.

Export duty relief Manufactured finished goods destined for the external market could be exempted from export duties and transaction taxes on exports, provided that such an exemption was necessary to keep the prices of the goods within a competitive range in the world market.

Remittance of foreign exchange The National Bank of Ethiopia makes available foreign exchange for:

1 remittance of profits of foreign investors to their countries of origin;
2 repatriation of the net proceeds of a foreign investor upon partial or total sale of liquidation of his investment;

3 payment of interest and the repayment of foreign loans contracted by enterprises in accordance with the provisions of the Investment Proclamation;
4 remittance of savings of foreign personnel in enterprises to their countries of origin;
5 the purchase of replacements and spare parts and other materials and goods required in connection with the operation of the enterprises.

Acquisition of immovables Foreign investors were allowed to purchase land for the purpose of establishing industrial enterprises.

Dividends Under the income tax law dividends were not subject to income tax.

Protection Protection was guaranteed to industrial enterprises, upon satisfaction that such protection was necessary. This included the levying of high tariffs as well as the banning of the import of those commodities that might adversely affect domestically produced goods.

Plan assessment and flow of foreign capital

The second five-year plan was hailed as a success by the government. Gross domestic product registered a growth rate of 4.6 per cent as compared with the planned 4.3 per cent per annum. As Table 22 indicates, actual investment exceeded planned investment by more than 10 per cent. Both the total domestic and foreign resources were higher than the planned target.

The third five-year plan and investment policy

The third five-year plan was launched in 1968/9 and was to be completed by 1972/3. However, owing to delays and setbacks, especially during the first and second years of the plan, the plan period was extended by one year and was to last until 1974.

Table 22 *Ethiopia's second five-year plan and actual investment*

Source	*(E$ million)* *Planned*	*Actual*
Domestic	2017.0	2089.4
Foreign, *of which*:		
Public loans	339.5	304.1
Aid	121.8	338.8
Private	177.2	194.2

Table 23 *Financial requirement and methods of financing Ethiopia's third five-year plan*

Financing required	*(E$ million)*
For fixed investment	2960
For external debt servicing and dividends	490
Total	3450
Financing available	
Gross domestic saving	2400
Gross foreign capital inflow	1050
Total	3450

The plan envisaged a total investment of E$3445 million, of which E$550 million was investment in kind and E$3100 million was monetary investment. Of the total monetary investment, E$1435 million or 46 per cent was investment by the private sector and the balance was that of the central government and autonomous agencies. The public sector was to concentrate on the development of the infrastructure, such as health, education, welfare and transport, while the private sector was expected to invest in directly productive activities. Table 23 explains the financial implication of the third five-year plan and how the government planned its financing.[7] The above expenditure was to have resulted in the increase of gross domestic product from the 1967 estimate of E$3600 million to E$4800 million, an increase of 33 per cent over the five-year period. This meant an annual growth rate of about 6 per cent. Assuming a population increase of 2.2 per cent per annum, *per capita* income was to increase from E$151 in 1967 to E$181 in 1973, at an annual growth rate of about 3.7 per cent.[8]

As usual foreign capital was intended to play a significant role in the financing of the investment expenditure. This time it amounted to E$1050 million, or 33 per cent of the projected financial requirements. Of this total E$205 million was to cover interest and dividend payments, E$265 million for amortization, and E$15 million for repatriation of capital and an anticipated increase in foreign reserve. Net foreign capital inflow to the tune of E$565 million was anticipated.

Assessment of the plan and inflow of foreign capital

The third five-year plan failed to achieve its objectives. The plan was slated for completion by 1973 but was later extended to run until 1974. Gross domestic product (GDP) registered an annual growth rate of 4.3

per cent, far below the anticipated 6 per cent. Agricultural GDP grew by 2.2 per cent per annum whereas the plan targer was 2.9 per cent. Non-agricultural GDP did not fare any better, rising by 6.7 per cent as against the targeted 9.8 per cent per annum. Furthermore, the rate of population growth moved up from the anticipated 2.2 per cent to 2.3 per cent, as a result of which *per capita* income increased by 2 per cent against the planned 3.7 per cent.

The financial implication of the plan period has not been worked out in full. At the beginning of 1972, total monetary outlay was estimated at E$1580 million or 44 per cent of the total planned investment. During the four-year period gross foreign capital inflow amounted to E$441 million or 39 per cent of the total expected inflow. It is very unlikely that expenditure during the remainder of the plan period would have covered the balance.

Extent of foreign penetration

With the limitations to the reliability of the available statistics, no definite picture can be made on the extent of foreign investment in all the different sectors of the economy and especially in the agricultural and tertiary sectors. Below, the inflow of private long-term capital and the extent of its holdings in the manufacturing industries are presented. The emphasis on private long-term capital and the manufacturing industries needs explanation. In the Ethiopian context, both private and public bodies are the sources of foreign capital. However, while the latter is limited to loans and/or grants in aid, the former comprises of private investment and loans of which that of investment is by far the largest. The funds that are invested, unlike in many other developing countries, are not in export-oriented industries but are in import-substitution industries, and are therefore concentrated in the manufacturing industries.

Direct private investment

Private foreign capital inflow for the purpose of direct investment amounted to E$122.5 million during the second five-year plan period (1963–7) and E$192.9 million during the third five-year plan period (1968–74). During the second five-year plan period the highest annual inflow amounted to E$30.5 million (1963) and the lowest was E$7.8 million (1967). During 1966, the year in which the investment decree was changed by proclamation when Parliament gave its approval of the regulation that made the decree, the amount of foreign capital inflow was E$27.4 million, while that of the next year saw this amount decrease by close to 75 per cent.

The early years of the third five-year plan period showed a consider-

Table 24 *Inflow of foreign capital for direct private investment in Ethiopia*[9]

Plan period	*Year*	*Amount* (E$ million)	*Total* (E$ million)
	1963	29.4	
	1964	30.5	
Second five-year plan	1965	27.4	
	1966	27.4	
	1967	7.8	122.5
	1968	14.8	
	1969	6.7	
	1970	9.6	
Third five-year plan	1971	14.2	
	1972	22.3	
	1973	65.0	
	1974	60.3	192.9

able decrease over that of the second five-year plan period. The 1968 amount was double that of the 1967 figure; the next two years showed a decline from this figure. Between 1970 and 1973, inflow of foreign capital for the purpose of direct investment was on the increase and reached the all-time high figure of E$65.0 million. This and the amount for 1974, which was E$60.3 million, more than made up for the low level of the first four years (see Table 24).

Share in the domestic equity of the manufacturing industries[10]

Out of the paid-up capital of E$340 million in 273 manufacturing establishments at the end of 1971/2, foreign capital amounted to E$141 million or 41 per cent of the total (see Table 25).

Foreign capital owned 61 per cent of the food industry and 54 per cent of the textiles industries, the two giants in the manufacturing sector. In the lesser establishments the extent of their control amounted to 72 per cent in leather and shoes, 61 per cent in wood and wood products, 68 per cent in metallics and 51 per cent in the iron and steel industries. All in all, foreign capital owned major equity holding in six of the twelve manufacturing industries.

While Table 25 gives the distribution of foreign capital in the 273 industrial establishments surveyed in 1971/2, Table 26 shows the concentration of foreign capital in each sector of the manufacturing industry.

Of the 64 firms in the food sector, foreign capital owned 22 of them (34 per cent) completely, while in other 9 firms they owned more than 50 per

Table 25 *Share of foreign capital in the total capital of 263 Ethiopian manufacturing establishments, 1971–2*

Industry	*Total capital* (E$ million)	*Foreign capital* (E$ million)	*Share* (%)
Food	86.2	53.3	61
Beverages	26.0	5.0	19
Tobacco	4.3	—	—
Textile	81.6	44.4	54
Leather	6.9	5.0	72
Wood	7.0	4.3	61
Paper	11.8	4.1	34
Printing and publishing	6.0	0.8	13
Chemical	68.3	7.1	10
Non-metallic	25.2	6.7	26
Metallic	8.2	5.6	68
Iron and steel	8.6	4.4	51
Total	340.1	140.7	41

Table 26 *Ownership shares in different Ethiopian industries, 1971–2*

Industry	*Total number of industries*	*100% ownership*	*Ownership more than 50% but less than 100%*	*50% ownership*	*Ownership less than 50% but greater than 0*
Food	64	22	9	3	6
Beverages	29	10	—	—	4
Tobacco	2	—	—	—	—
Textile	42	12	9	2	4
Leather and shoes	16	6	3	1	—
Wood	24	12	4	—	2
Paper	6	2	1	—	1
Printing and publishing	16	7	1	—	—
Chemical	25	10	6	1	3
Non-metallic	28	12	4	—	3
Metallic	18	6	4	—	3
Iron and steel	3	2	1	1	1
Total	273	101	42	8	27

cent of the paid-up capital and in another 9 they had 50 per cent or less interest. In all, foreigners had interest in 40 of the 64 food-processing firms surveyed with majority holdings in 31 of them. In the beverages industry, they owned 10 firms completely. In the textile industry, out of 42 industries, 12 are 100 per cent owned and in 9 others they own a major share.

In all of the 273 firms in the 12 manufacturing sectors surveyed, foreign capital owned 101 firms (37 per cent) completely while in another 42 firms (15 per cent) they owned more than 50 per cent of the paid-up capital. Thus in 143 industries (52 per cent) they owned the major part of the paid-up capital.

Table 27 gives the percentage shares of the foreign capital in each industry. Even though the figures given are partial, the available evidence from 273 firms surveyed suggests that foreign capital owned a considerable amount of the manufacturing industries. Two points worth mentioning here are that these 273 industrial establishments represent a major portion of the whole and include the largest firms in each sector. Second, since what is given is paid-up capital, i.e. capital at the time of the firms' establishment, it does not include the capital of the firm as of the reporting date; some of the industries have undergone considerable expansion after their establishment, the investment of which may have been their profit. Such factors would definitely increase

Table 27 *Percentage shares of foreign capital in Ethiopia, 1971–2*

Industry	*100%* (%)	*Less than 100% but greater than* (%)	*50%* (%)	*Less than 50% but greater than* (%)
Food	34	14	5	9
Beverages	35	—	—	14
Tobacco	—	—	—	—
Textiles	29	21	5	10
Leather and shoes	38	19	6	—
Wood	50	17	—	8
Paper	33	17	—	17
Printing and publishing	44	6	—	—
Chemical	40	24	4	13
Non-metallic	43	14	—	11
Metallic	33	22	—	17
Iron and steel	67	3	—	—

the total amount, and probably the percentage share of foreign capital in these industries.

As for nationalities, those with the highest contribution to the paid-up capital were Italians, with E$32.9 million in the 273 industries. This forms 10 per cent of total capital and 23 per cent of the foreign capital. Italy is followed by the United States (E$7.9 million), Greece (E$6.9 million), and Japan (E$6.8 million). Seventeen other nations own a total of E$86.2 million or 25 per cent of the total paid-up capital of the 273 industries surveyed.

Foreign employment

The Selassie government's dependence on foreign capital to finance its capital investment forced it to liberalize its investment policy. This same dependence had a great influence on the policy regarding foreign employment. This was enunciated in the Foreign Nationals Employment Regulation of 1954. According to that regulation, any foreigner working in Ethiopia needed to get a work permit from the Ministry of Labour and Social Affairs. The Ministry would issue a work permit to any foreigner to work in private industrial, commercial, agricultural or other activities in the country if:

1 the proposed employment would contribute essentially to the promotion and/or strengthening of the Ethiopian economy or to some other important aspect of national development;
2 an Ethiopian national with the necessary skills to meet the requirements of the proposed employment was not available;
3 provided that: the employer would train Ethiopian nationals in the skill(s) required in order to replace the foreigner.

Issuance of work permits was automatic with respect to foreign employment in:

1 any private enterprise pursuant to a government agreement;
2 any enterprise controlled and administered by the government directly or indirectly;
3 any international organization;
4 any non-profit public or private organization;
5 an investment project approved by the Investment Committee in accordance with the Investment Proclamation.

By the end of 1970 there were close to 70,000 foreign nationals residing in Ethiopia.[11] Of these, 20,000 were Italians and 22,000 Yemenese. These two nationalities accounted for about 60 per cent of the foreign residents. Though no reliable statistics exist, it is the opinion of some informed people that at least 80 per cent of the above number were engaged in the private sector.

Table 28 *Foreign employees in Ethiopian industries, 1971–2*

Industry	*Number of industries*	*Number of foreign employees*
Food	64	180
Beverages	29	45
Tobacco	2	9
Textiles	42	200
Leather and shoes	16	35
Wood	24	40
Paper	6	12
Printing and publishing	16	31
Chemical	25	64
Non-metallic	28	73
Metallic	18	53
Iron and steel	3	23
Total	273	765

Statistics from the Department of Labour at the Ministry of Labour and Social Affairs show that the Department issued renewed work permits for 315 persons in the private sector in 1970, 2568 in 1971, 1844 in 1974 and 1431 in 1973.

Of the total number of foreigners, upwards of 90 per cent are estimated to have held the three most important management posts, namely as general managers, technical managers and financial managers.

The study conducted by the Ministry of Commerce and Industry in 273 establishments placed the number of foreign employees at 765 persons. The detail is given in Table 28. The records of the Ministry of National Resource Development show that, at the date of nationalization, there were about 271 foreign employees in the industries that come under its jurisdiction. This is a partial figure, as the management of the nationalized industries were distributed under different ministries and other public agencies.[12]

Emoluments

In the Ethiopian economy of the Selassie regime, which purported to develop on the free enterprise system, there was no income policy. Payments in wages and salaries were solely a function of the parties involved. The wages and salaries paid out to foreigners were enormously higher than those paid out to Ethiopian nationals. A recent study by the Ministry of Labour and Social Affairs[13] disclosed that, in 339 public and non-public organizations, 355 foreigners drew salaries above E$18,000

Table 29 *Monthly foreign earnings in Ethiopian public and private establishments, 1974*

	Foreign employees		
Salary range	*Public*	*Private*	*Total*
1500–2249	81	46	127
2250–2299	55	29	84
3000–3749	40	17	57
3750–4499	17	6	23
4500–5249	28	6	34
5250–5999	6	2	8
6000–6749	1	2	3
6750–6999	1	—	1
7000–8499	6	3	9
8500–9999	5	2	7
10,000–12,500	2	—	2
Total	242	113	355

per annum; of these, 191 had a *per capita* income of above E$24,00 per annum and 18 foreign employees (13 in the public sector and 5 in the private) had a salary exceeding E$84,000 per annum each. The highest salaries drawn by Ethiopians in the public and private sectors were E$60,000 and E$48,000 respectively. The details of monthly foreign earnings are given in Table 29. Even though these data were only for 149 public and 97 private enterprises, they give some idea of what foreigners were paid. On the other hand, it is worth pointing out that the total number of foreigners in the 246 public and private enterprises might have been higher than what is indicated above since the information excluded those earnings less than E$1500 per month (E$18,000 per annum).

The study by the Ministry of Commerce and Industry for the 273 industrial establishments gives a detailed report on foreign earnings (see Table 30). The 765 foreign employees forming 1.4 per cent of the total employment claimed 16 per cent of the total wages and salaries paid out by the 273 industrial establishments in 1971/2. The E$11.5 million paid out to them amounts to an annual *per capita* salary of over E$15,000. On the other hand, 53,227 Ethiopian employees, accounting for 98.6 per cent of the total employment, claimed 84 per cent of the wages and salaries bill. The E$58.1 million paid out to the Ethiopians amounts to an annual *per capita* income of E$1291. The *per capita* salary of the foreign employees was about twelve times that of their Ethiopian counterparts.

The salaries given in Table 30 for foreign employees are definitely

Table 30 *Wages and salaries totals and their distribution among foreign and Ethiopian employees, 1971–2*

Industry	*No. of estab-lishments*	*No. of employees*			*Wages and salaries (E$ million)*		
		Total	*Foreign*	*Ethiopians*	*Total*	*Foreign*	*Ethiopians*
Food	64	8901	180	8721	11.5	2.6	8.9
Beverages	29	3016	45	2971	5.0	0.8	4.2
Tobacco	2	590	9	581	1.1	0.1	1.0
Textile	42	23744	200	23574	25.6	3.8	21.8
Leather and shoes	16	2199	35	2164	2.4	0.2	2.2
Wood	24	4238	40	4198	3.4	0.5	2.9
Paper	6	692	12	680	0.9	0.2	0.7
Printing and publishing	16	1600	31	1569	2.8	0.3	2.5
Chemicals	25	2673	64	2609	8.1	0.9	7.2
Non-metallic	28	4097	73	4024	5.0	0.8	4.2
Metallic	18	1531	53	1478	2.3	0.6	1.7
Iron and steel	3	681	23	658	1.5	0.6	0.9
Total	273	53,992	765	53,227	69.6	11.5	58.1

lower than what they actually got, as it gives gross salary only. Additional income in the form of the vehicles, fuel and housing allowances that most of the foreign employees got is not included in these figures.

The basic justification for such high salaries for foreign employees was the shortage of skilled natives. While this was an excuse granted by the government, it was grossly abused. Incidents where a foreigner without any skill was given a post with very high salary were not uncommon, especially in the private sector and especially in activities where foreigners owned the whole establishment. While foreign employment was conditional upon the unavailability of the requisite skill and upon the establishment training Ethiopians for the posts, such guidelines remained paper tigers, especially in the private sector.

Contribution of foreign capital to the nation's development[14]

At this point it seems fair to examine the contribution of foreign capital in the development of the nation. The industrialization policy of the Selassie regime found its first vent in the untapped consumer goods sector, as a result of which most of the industries were of import substitution type. The establishment of these industries decreased the share of imports of consumer goods to total domestic supply (defined as gross value of production plus imports including taxes minus exports) from the level of 73 per cent in 1954 to 30 per cent in 1970, with a noticeable decline in sugar, textiles and leather footwear industries, which decreased from 86, 94 and 55 per cent in 1954 to 5, 32 and 14 per cent in 1970.

However, over the same period imports of raw material and intermediate goods increased in absolute terms from E$18 million in 1954 to E$90.3 million, an increase of more than five-fold.

Even greater was the import of capital goods. In 1970 the import of capital goods amounted to 83 per cent of the total domestic supply. The domestic consumption of these goods increased from E$1.5 million in 1950 to E$330.0 million in 1970.

While the rationale for the import substitution drive is to decrease a country's dependence on imports, the opposite seems to have taken place. Even though the nation's dependence on the imports of consumer goods has been reduced, its dependence on the import of capital goods as well as primary and intermediate inputs has increased.

The efforts made to supply the industries with domestically produced raw materials has not been satisfactory. There are industries that rely exclusively on the imports of inputs, either because the raw materials are not domestically available or because, even when a potential supply exists, the would-be producers are discouraged by the would-be purchaser owing to the threat such a supply poses to one of their hidden sources of income, namely the higher revenue they make through over-invoicing imported inputs and through tariff protection.

On other scales of contribution to the country's development, the industrial sector does not fair any better. A study conducted by Stephen Guisinger[15] concluded that the domestic resources cost of saving or earning a unit of foreign exchange, which is 'a measure of industry's relative efficiency', amounted to negative for ten of the twenty-three industries surveyed. On the social profitability basis fourteen of them were found to be unprofitable.

The studies conducted by UNCTAD and Dr Steven Barac came up with startling conclusions with regard to the contribution of foreign capital (see Table 31). According to these two studies of the manufacturing industries with 1969/70 data, the contribution of foreign companies to the development of the manufacturing industries was negative. Both studies defined 'contribution' as the difference between foreign exchange cost and the value added. Foreign capital's contribution to total value added in the industries surveyed was assumed to be equal to their share in the paid up capital for these industries, which in 1969/70 amounted to 44 per cent. The estimated value added by foreign capital amounted to E$71 million. On the other hand, the cost of foreign companies working in Ethiopia is estimated at a high of E$108 million (UNCTAD) and a low of E$71 million (Barac). Hence, the contribution of foreign capital to the development of the manufacturing industry had been negative, with cost varying between E$5 million according to Barac to E$37 million according to the UNCTAD study.

Among the advantages that foreign capitalists enjoyed in the country was protection against competition with imported commodities (see

Table 31 *Foreign exchange cost of foreign companies working in Ethiopia, 1969–70*

Item	*Estimates*	
	Barac (E$ million)	*UNCTAD* (E$ million)
Management fees and salaries of expatriate personnel	18	20
Value of declared returns on paid up capital	22	22
Overpricing of intermediate imports	16	32
Overpricing of machinery	15	34
Underinvoicing of imports	5	—
Total	76	108

Table 32 *Nominal and effective rates of tariff for selected manufacturing industries in Ethiopia, 1969–70*

Product	*Nominal tariff* (%)	*Effective tariff* (%)
Synthetic textiles	140	522
Cotton yarn	53	502
Galvanized iron sheets	49	435
Cotton cloth	93	388
Shoes	110	230
Ceramic tiles	68	188
Men's suits	83	165
Soaps	42	126
Jute and sisal bags	70	90

Table 32). While the nominal tariff (price of imported commodities after tax as compared with the price of the domestically produced commodity) varied between a low of 42 per cent (for soaps) to a high of 140 per cent (for synthetic textiles), the effective tariff (protection of the process of production rather than the product or protection of domestically value added rather than the final price) varied between a low of 90 per cent (for jute and sisal bags) to a high of 522 per cent (for synthetic textiles).

The overall effort of such a high tariff protection led industries to increase their inefficiency while the increasing domestic demand was balanced with supply not by increased output, but through an increase in prices.

Economic policy since February 1974

The popular revolution that broke out in February 1974 culminated in the ousting of the Haile Selassie regime and the establishment of a new government, the Provisional Military Administrative Council, in September of the same year.

On 20 December 1974 the new government declared that henceforth 'Socialism would be the guiding principle of the nation'. The policy directives state that Ethiopian socialism embraces five fundamental concepts:[16]

1 Ethiopians will live under the umbrella of their own country in peace, brotherhood and unity, without any distinction on the basis of tribe, sex, language and religion, and with complete equality, freedom and social justice.
2 The legitimate interest of the masses will be maintained and past

injustices which led to social inequalities and mass poverty would be reduced.

3 The right of participation in managing their own affairs, which in the past was denied to the people, will be restored and the people will have the right to run their own affairs at the village, district, provincial and regional levels.
4 Respect for labour and the dignity of the toiling masses will be maintained.
5 Above all, the sacred unity of Ethiopia will be upheld.

While the above five points formed the conceptual framework of the policy of Ethiopian socialism, its functional aspect was declared to be 'self-reliance'.

The economic policy of Ethiopian socialism was defined in the same declaration. The policy enunciated that

> those resources that are either crucial for economic development or are of such a character that they provide an indispensable service to the community will have to be brought under government control or ownership. Essential economic activities which are not amenable to centralized public management will, though outside the public sector, be subject to public monitoring to ensure that the public interest is properly served. Activities in the private sector which are not harmful to the interest of society will be left in private hands in so far as they do not impede the objectives of 'Ethiopia Tikdem'.

The declaration further elaborated that 'industrial activities, the exploitation of natural resources, the development of small-scale enterprises will be carried out on the basis of the principle of self-reliance', which is the cornerstone of the 'Ethiopia Tikdem' (Ethiopia First) philosophy.

Foreign capital and know-how 'will be given the opportunity to participate in national development in so far as they promote overall economic development and bring benefit to our society'.

In summary, the economic policy divided control of resources and participation into two parts. As far as control is concerned, (1) resources that are crucial for development; and (2) activities that provide indispensable service to the community would come under government control or ownership, while other resources and activities are left to the private sector but under government supervision.

As for participation, the government identified three parties that could be involved in economic activities. These are:

1 Ethiopian public capital;
2 Ethiopian private capital;
3 foreign capital.

The new economic policy

These declarations were followed by a wave of nationalization, which left the private sector (both Ethiopian and foreign capitalists – especially the latter) in so much disarray and confusion that the government found it necessary to elaborate on its economic policy.

The detailed economic policy came out in the booklet entitled *Declaration of Economic Policy of Socialist Ethiopia* in February 1975. In it the government expounded the justification of the policy it intends to follow (to pull the Ethiopian masses out of their extreme poverty and to end their exploitation), as well delineating areas in which the different owners of capital can participate. It defined areas in which public and private capital can participate as follows.

Activities exclusively reserved for the state

1. Exploitation of precious metals and radio-active materials;
2. large-scale salt mining;
3. basic industries such as iron and steel, ship building, cement;
4. petroleum refining and natural gas;
5. textile industry;
6. leather and leather products manufacturing;
7. large-scale rubber manufacturing and fertilizer industry;
8. drugs and medicines;
9. tobacco;
10. glass and bottle manufacturing;
11. large-scale printing and publishing;
12. electricity, gas and water;
13. railway, air and sea transport;
14. radio, TV, posts and telecommunications.

Areas where the state and foreign capital (public and private) could jointly operate

1. Exploration and exploitation of carbons and hydrocarbons;
2. mining of ferrous and non-ferrous metals;
3. mining of chemical and fertilizer materials;
4. processing, canning and preserving of meat, fruits and vegetables which are mainly export-oriented;
5. paper and pulp industries;
6. manufacturing of plastic and other synthetic materials;
7. large-scale construction works;
8. tourism.

Activities left to the private sector

1 Food processing, canning and marketing;
2 quarrying;
3 dairy;
4 small-scale grain milling and pressing of oil seeds;
5 bakery;
6 small-scale manufacturing of wood and wood products;
7 fabricated metal products;
8 small-scale weaving, knitting, spinning, sewing and tailoring;
9 cottage industries;
10 repairs and maintenance;
11 small-scale construction work;
12 export and import trade;
13 wholesale and retail trade;
14 surface transport other than railways;
15 small-scale inland water transport;
16 entertainment services;
17 other activities including hotels, bars, restaurants, tea shops, groceries;
18 others not elsewhere classified.

A further explanation of the economic policy

In December of the same year the government issued a quasi-investment policy governing the private sector. The proclamation excluded: (1) activities that came into being prior to its enactment; and (2) construction work, surface transport, publishing of newspaper and magazines. It defined the amount of capital (defined as cash, the value of receivables, stocks invested in trade and fixed assets excluding land and buildings) that would be permissible in three activities. These were wholesale trade (E$300,000), retail trade (E$200,000) and industry (E$500,000), and no activity by the private sector was permitted to have more capital than this. It prohibited the pulling together of capital, whether the form of partnership or share company. Licences were to be given to one individual, provided the individual did not have a permanent job or any other source of income.

Indigenization through nationalization

The provisional military government's policy of controlling and/or owning 'resources that are crucial for development . . . [and] activities that provide indispensable service to the community' was implemented in a series of nationalization decrees. The nationalization drive began on 1 January 1975, when financial institutions were nationalized. On 2 February 1975 seventy-two industries and commercial firms were nationalized, and in another twenty-nine industries the government became the majority shareholder. On 4 March 1975 rural land commercial farms were nationalized, and as of 7 August 1975 all urban land and extra houses were nationalized.

Thus, by the stroke of the pen the government assumed the ownership of those activities that form the commanding heights of the economy.

Indigenization of employees

The decrees that nationalized financial institutions, industries and commercial farms were silent with respect to foreign employees. Since owners were relieved of their property, they were replaced by managers who were appointed to their posts the day the establishments were nationalized. With regard to commercial farms, previous owners were told to manage the farms on the state's behalf until the state was ready to take over. As for the other employees, it is conceivable that the decision was left to the new managers of each plant whether to keep them or replace them.

The decision of whether to stay on the job or not was not only that of the government: some of the expatriates left their jobs (and the country) of their own free will, even though their skills were required.

No complete statistics are available on the number of foreign employees in the nationalized industries and none at all as far as commercial farms are concerned.

Indigenizing financial institutions

Indigenization of ownership

On 1 January 1975 the government nationalized banks, financial intermediaries and insurance companies. These included three banks (Addis Ababa Bank, Banco Di Roma (Eth.) and Baco Di Napoli (Eth.), thirteen insurance companies and three financial intermediaries. The overall management responsibility was passed to the National Bank of Ethiopia and the Ministry of Commerce and Industry.

In both Banco Di Roma and Banco Di Napoli, the parent banks in Italy had majority shares while in the Addis Ababa Bank, National and Grindlay's of Britain had a sizable share.[17]

The insurance companies' foreign interest could not at any time be greater than 49 per cent of the paid-up capital (Insurance Proclamation no. 281 of 1971), and the insurance law forbade foreign insurance companies operating in Ethiopia through branches; hence the amount of foreign interest nationalized is at the most 49 per cent of the total paid-up capital.[18]

At the date of nationalization, the insurance companies had an asset estimated over E$33 million, spread in portfolio investments such as land and buildings (24 per cent), debtors (24 per cent) cash and fixed deposits (20 per cent) shareholdings (7 per cent) and government securities (7 per cent).

Employment indigenization

The three nationalized banks were later reorganized to form Addis Bank and their management was completely Ethiopianized. The thirteen insurance companies were also reorganized to form the Ethiopian Insurance Corporation, and their management was taken over by Ethiopians. Since most of the posts in these institutions were already held by Ethiopians, the employment indigenization process affected those foreigners who were owner–managers.

Indigenization in the agricultural sector

Nationalization of rural land

On 4 March 1975 the provisional military government nationalized all rural land in the country. Of the many important points contained in the proclamation, the following may be cited as the basis of the end of one type of relation in production and the beginning of a new one:

1. the conversion of all rural land from private ownership to public ownership;
2. the recognition of any person's right to possess rural land, provided he is willing and ready to work the land himself;
3. the abolition of the relationship between landlords and tenants, including freedom from any indebtedness the tenants may have incurred to their landlords;
4. the prohibition (with some exceptions) of the use of hired labour on private farms.

Land was to be equally divided among residents of a given area up to a maximum holding of ten hectares. The law also provides for the formation of peasants' associations and outlined their responsibilities.[19]

As for the commercial farms, two measures were taken. Some of the commercial farms were given to the peasants' associations of the areas, with the view that either they were to be farmed and managed on a co-operative basis, or, where such farms had been acquired by the eviction of tenants, the land was to be given back to the former tenants. The

Table 33 *State farms under the Ethiopian Ministry of National Resources Development, 1975–6*[20]

Co-operatives	*Location*	*No. of farms consolidated*	*Size of farms (hectares)*
Upper Awash	Awash Valley	6	10,000
Middle Awash	Awash Valley	3	3,040
Gewane	Awash Valley	2	1,980
Tendaho	Awash Valley	3	10,078
Chilalo	Arusi Province	5	26,000
Rift Valley	Shoa Province	8	17,100
South Western	Gemu Gofa, Keffa	8	14,400
Eastern	Harrarghe	3	1,121
Cheffa	Wollo	1	2,050
Chebo-Gebe	Shoa-Kefa Govt Gen.	4	1,705
Total		43	87,474

peasants associations and the Extension and Project Implementation Department (EPID) of the Ministry of Agriculture were to manage and use the farm machines that were expropriated from the former owners.

Other commercial farms were turned into state farms and their management was passed over to a number of government ministries and autonomous agencies, of which the Department of Agriculture of the Ministry of National Resources Development (MNRD) was entrusted with the lion's share. Other managing bodies included EPID, the National Coffee Board, the Addis Ababa Dairy Development Agency, the Livestock and Meat Board and the Chilalo Agricultural Development Unit (CADU).

The Department of Agriculture of the MNRD organized the nationalized farms into co-operatives for ease of management. At present there are ten co-operatives with a total farm size of 87,500 hectares. Table 33 gives the details.

Ownership indigenization in agriculture

The nationalization of rural land and commercial farms indigenized the ownership of both the land and farms. The nationalization decree did not discriminate between Ethiopian interests and foreign interests. What percentage of the nationalized farms belonged to foreigners is not possible to estimate yet. Because possession of land more than ten hectares was made illegal, anyone with more than this limit lost it. Moreover, since all commercial farms – and this meant all farms that were operated by machines (tractor, combines etc.) – were nationalized, and since the agricultural operations in which foreigners had interests were at this level, one can say that indigenization within the agricultural sector was 100 per cent fulfilled.

Employment indigenization

The number of foreign employees in the agricultural sector was not deemed to have been very large. What foreign employment existed was in the very specialized professions of engineering and insect and pest control. In some of the larger commercial farms such as the Tendaho Cotton Plantation there were foreigners in management.

With the nationalization of land, foreign owner–managers of commercial farms were replaced by Ethiopians. As for foreigners with special skills, where these could not be replaced by Ethiopians the government made special efforts to retain them on their posts. While some accepted the government's offer and stayed on the job, others left on their own volition.

Indigenization in the manufacturing industry

On 2 February 1975 the provisional military government announced the nationalization of seventy-two companies previously owned by the private sector. Just like the nationalization of commercial farms, no distinction was made between foreign and Ethiopian interests.

The nationalized companies included thirteen in the food industries, eight in beverages, fourteen in textiles and eight in chemicals (see Table 34). The amount of total paid-up capital in these industries is not

Table 34 *Number of nationalized industries in Ethiopia, by sector, as of 2 February 1975*

Sector	*No.*
Food	13
Beverages	8
Textiles	14
Leather and shoes	9
Printing press	4
Chemical	8
Non-Ferrous	2
Iron and steel	5
Miscellaneous	9
Total	72

Table 35 *Total paid-up capital and foreign capital in some of the industries nationalized in Ethiopia as of February 1975*

Sector	*No. of industries nationalized*	*Total paid-up* (E$ million)	*Foreign capital* (E$ million)	*Foreign as proportion of total* (%)
Food	13	13.5	13.0(11)	66.7
Beverages	8	14.1	6.1(5)	43.3
Textiles	14	58.8	39.4(12)	67.0
Leather and shoes	9	5.8	3.3(6)	56.9
Printing and publishing	4	1.7	0.2(1)	11.8
Chemical	7	8.7	1.7(5)	19.5
Non-metalic	2	12.3	0.2(1)	1.6
Iron and steel	5	11.6	5.6(5)	48.3
Total	62	132.5	69.5	52.5

available. However, some of the industries are included in the survey made by the Ministry of Commerce and Industry in 1971/2. Table 35 gives the total paid-up capital of those industries nationalized on aggregate sectoral base. The figures in brackets give the number of industries for which the size of foreign interest was available.

Out of the seventy-two industries that were nationalized on 2 February 1975, data on total and foreign paid-up capital were available for sixty-two industries. The total paid-up capital of these industries in 1971/2 was E$132.5 million.

Of the E$132.5 million paid capital E$69.7 million, or 53 per cent was foreign-owned, while the remainder belonged to the Ethiopian private owners and the Ethiopian government. Even though the dearth of reliable statistics makes it impossible to get the total amount of foreign interest in the nationalized industries, the figures given in Table 35 could be indicative of the extent of foreign interest taken over by the government. The statement is made on the ground that most of the industrial establishments were established in the country by foreigners at the time when Ethiopian capitalists were not yet established enough to invest substantial capital in the development of industrial establishments.

The February 1975 decree marked the beginning of a nationalization drive. It is known that there were industries that came under government ownership after that date. For example, the Ministry of National Resources Development at the end of 1975 had eighty-four industries under its management, while in February of the same year the figure was seventy-two. Some of these industries the government was forced to take

Table 36 *Distribution of management of the nationalized industries as of 2 February 1975*

Institution	*Number of industries*
Addis Ababa Municipality	1
Ministry of National Resources Development	67
Ministry of Public Health	1
Ethiopian Cement Corporation	1
Ethiopian Electric, Light and Power Authority	2
Total	72

over because they were abandoned by the previous owners who had fled the country.

The management of the nationalized industries was transferred from the owners to the different ministries and autonomous agencies. However, the major responsibility was the Ministry of National Resources Development (MNRD), which took the responsibility to run sixty-seven of the seventy-two nationalized industries.

In twenty-nine other industries the government became the majority shareholder. These included four fuel distributors, eleven food processing industries, two textile industries, six woodwork industries, three chemical industries, two metal industries and one pulp and paper industry. The management of these companies was transferred to the state. Eleven of them were to be managed by the MNRD, eight under the Livestock and Meat Board, six under the Forestry Department of the Ministry of Agriculture, and four under the Assab Oil Refinery.

The rationale as to why these industries were partially and not wholly nationalized was not given by the government. However, a closer examination of the industries in this category can give some clue. The fuel industries are the branches of the multinational oil industry, namely Shell, Mobil, Agip and Total. Since the nationalization of the distribution outlet does not decrease the country's dependence on oil, the government must have thought that their full nationalization might prove detrimental. The food industry includes eight export-oriented meat processing industries whose export outlets are the parent companies located outside the country. Where these industries are not well established to do export business on their own, the total severance of the outlet of their produce built up by, and between, the previous owners and firms outside the country might do more damage to the industries. Other reasons might be technical and managerial problems as well as access to imported input required for the industries.

Table 37 *Corporations under the Ethiopian MNRD as of early 1976*

Corporation	*Number of industries*
Food	21
Beverages	15
Textile	14
Leather and shoes	12
Fiber	3
Iron and steel	6
Building materials	6
Soap and detergent	3
Salt	2
Total	82

Later in the year the Ministry of National Resources Development (MNRD) organized some of the fully nationalized industries into corporations for ease of management. At the moment, the Ministry has nine corporations. These and the number of industries under each corporation is given in Table 37.

As for the partially nationalized industries – those industries in which the government had a majority share – the management was at the plant level.

Employment indigenization

Statistics on the number of posts turned over to Ethiopians are not available. One definite thing one can say with regard to employment indigenization is that the previous owner-managers have been replaced by Ethiopians.

Data available from the Department of Industries of MNRD give the number of foreign employees in the industries they were managing at 271 as of the date of nationalization. Of these, more than 90 per cent held the three top posts in each plant, namely managing director, technical manager and financial manager. By December 1975 this figure had decreased to 96, and 90 per cent of these are now working as technicians under the management and supervision of Ethiopians. The details in terms of the sectoral distribution of foreign employees of these industries whose management is under MNRD is given in Table 38.

Compensation

The January decree that nationalized financial institutions, the February decree nationalizing industries, and the March decree nationalizing commercial farms promised former owners full compensation. To this end a compensation commission has been established.

Table 38 *Foreign employees in industries under Ethiopia's MNRD*

Sector	*As of the nationalization date*	*As of December 1975*
Food	39	11
Beverages	28	11
Chemical	11	3
Leather and shoes	24	11
Fiber works	10	3
Textiles	52	12
Metal works	20	7
Others	87	38
Total	271	96

Nationalization and indigenization

The indigenization process in Ethiopia has taken a course that may be an exception rather than the rule. The military government declared a new economic policy and a new ideological framework, nationalized large industries, financial institutions, land and commercial farms.

The complete reversal of the economic and political policies of the old government by the new government, and the steps that have been taken to make them functional, are said to mark the beginning of an era of self-reliance. Foreigners can no longer invest in the country under their own terms. The military government has taken over their assets. Where dependence on external development factors has been the rule in the past, this is to be replaced by self-reliance in the future.

For the present, the extent of foreign interest has been controlled – if not completely, at least in a major way. Foreign employees have decreased in number. The effect of all this, and what it means in terms of future policies, will be discussed in the next section.

Prospects

The economic policies of the military government, and indeed the revolution that brought about not only a change in government but also the total shift in the basic ideological framework, is barely five years old. The environmental context within these few years has not been stable enough for the new politicio-economic policies to run their natural course. Hence the focus of this section is to examine some possible effects of the policy on major developmental factors such as transfer of technology, foreign investment, growth of entrepreneurial capacity and labour productivity, rather than to evaluate the effects of these policies.

Self-reliance and economic development

The military government has embarked on a policy of self-reliance. It has not only nationalized foreign interests, but has also limited their participation to activities where the country lacks both the technological and the financial capacity to do it on her own. These include the extractive industries, such as the exploration and exploitation of petroleum, ferrous and non-ferrous metals, and some capital-intensive industries. The new policy limits not only their participation, but also the terms of their participation, which is subject to negotiation between the two parties.

The minimization of dependence, which is the goal of self-reliance, lies in accelerated industrialization; and in a country like Ethiopia, where the level of technological development is at a rudimentary level and the financial capacity to import capital goods is low, policies that would enhance the augmentation of these factors must be created.

The development of technology would come through the increase in the adaptive capacity of the people and an improvement of the already existing technological base. The adoptive capacity can be increased through an expansion of technical training, so that the trainees can be capable of absorbing the principles of the freely available technology embodied in the imported capital goods and in related literatures. Once the capacity to absorb the principles is acquired, then these people must be able to translate the ideas into functional equipment and instruments. Admittedly, this process may be slow and difficult, but the capacity to develop one's own technology is the basis for building up an independent nation.

While the adaptive capacity may be important for developing the type of technology useful in the modern sector, the traditional sector will have to depend more on improving the rudimentary techniques available in the rural areas. Already the rural sector has its own method of weaving cloths, smelting metals, producing farm implements and household equipments, making its own type of fertilizers, etc., and rural industrialization must be based on the development of these techniques. Activities based on rural technology are carried out by individuals with occasional help from the family labour whenever this is available. Furthermore, they have remained secondary occupations, practised either to fulfil a felt need or to fill time during slack seasons, since the main preoccupation of the rural residents is usually agriculture; as a result of this the level of such rural technological activities has remained small.

Perhaps all this has to change. Individuals with the same know-how can be brought together on a co-operative basis to produce goods to satisfy the demands of the people in that area. Rather than being taken as a secondary preoccupation, perhaps it should be developed into a primary one and the people involved should be encouraged to up-grade and develop their techniques. The creation of a diffusion mechanism between the urban technology and the rural know-how can prove advantageous.

The import of capital goods from abroad is another method of transferring technology. However, the danger of increasing dependence must be minimized through developing the raw materials used by that particular technology as well as, perhaps, the development of facilities to manufacture the relevant spare parts.

Emphasis must be placed on the development of technology if the country is to grow yet remain independent. Development through the import of capital goods may come at the cost of being less independent, since the more the country depends on imported technology the greater is the level of dependence and the less the degree of self-reliance.

As for capital accumulation, the country will have to look more to within its own borders than to the outside. While room is left for foreign capital to participate in the development of the nation, the greater burden must be carried by the country itself. Furthermore, owing to the policy of limited private indigenous capital's participation in both the kind and extent of activity, capital from this sector would remain small. This, coupled with the nationalization scare, would shift the greater burden of capital accumulation to the state.

The state has to reorient its expenditure pattern from consumption to investment. So far up to 80 per cent of the government's budget has gone to finance ordinary expenditure while the balance has accounted for capital expenditure. And in order to fulfil the extensive capital requirement, less has to be spent on recurrent expenditure and more in investment.

Foreign investment

The policy of nationalization has expropriated some of the foreign interests. Those not nationalized have continued to carry on business.

As for future investment, the government has delineated areas in which foreign investors, both public and private, can participate, subject to negotiated terms of participation. But this participation is with the state. On the other hand, nothing is said about foreigners who want to invest and carry on business by themselves. If this is allowed, then it will be in activities that are reserved for the private sector. Even if this is possible, one does not know whether they are eligible to the benefits extended to investors by the investment proclamation, such as tax exemption for up to five years if the investment is more than E$200,000, or whether this also is an area in which the terms of participation are subject to negotiation. Answers to such questions are not found in new policies, but if the tone of nationalization and the objective behind it (i.e. self-reliance) are to suggest a solution, it is of minimizing foreign participation to the maximum possible and encouraging the development of indigenous entrepreneurs.

Foreign investment and heavy industry

The government has outlined areas in which foreign capital is to participate with the state in the exploitation of natural resources. Such a concession has been made necessary by the low level of the country's technological development and the need to get to that type of technology development that is not freely available. The country wants to take advantage of the capital, know-how and the latest technological developments, which happen to be the private property of big corporations without whose direct participation it is impossible to get. At the same time, dependent as the country will be on technologies developed outside, it wants to minimize the condition of the dependence by negotiating their terms of participation case by case.

Whether such arrangement is acceptable to foreigners that have the capacity to establish the industries in which the state is interested, and what conditions are acceptable to the state for their participation, remain to be seen.

Direction of inflow of foreign capital

So far the source of more than 90 per cent of the foreign capital has been the Western developed countries. Now that Ethiopia has taken an ideological turn that is not acceptable to the capitalist world, and depending upon the conditions that are offered for their participation, this traditional source of capital may cease to play an important role in the nation's developmental activities. Instead, the country may shift to the East for the technical assistance and the capital goods it required for its development.

Indigenous private investment

As pointed out earlier, indigenous private investors have been allowed to participate in some activities subject to certain conditions, including a limit on the amount of capital in each activity, engagement in only one activity, and the prohibition on establishing the business through partnership or any kind of association.

The degree and extent to which the private sector will respond to the government's offer depends upon the level of confidence they entertain; and the government has gone out of its way to inculcate and develop the confidence of existing businessmen and future investors, including issuing assurances against being expropriated. It has gone to the aid of those owners whose interests have been expropriated by labour unions, peasants' associations and urban dwellers' associations and has dealt harshly with the would-be expropriators.

In general, the policy for private sector participation is broadly based and seems to be favourable at least on two counts: (1) the condition that private investors are allowed to invest in only one activity, and in that to only a given extent, limits its monopolistic development; (2) the fact that an investor is limited to one specific activity gives room for other entrepreneurs to join the business community.

Thus, while allowing indigenous private investors to participate in certain activities and at the same time limiting the extent of their participation, in terms of both capital and the area of activity, the government has created the means to stifle the expansion of the developed entrepreneur and to encourage the development of other entrepreneurs whose talent has remained latent. The private business is to remain small in size but to grow large in terms of numbers of participants.

Labour productivity, productivity of investment and income distribution

It is certainly hoped that labour productivity in the industrial sector will increase more than it has so far owing to the change in ownership. Up to now, the industrial labour force has been forced to increase output and decrease cost as much as possible by the owners. Now that the exploitative nature of the previous owners has been replaced by communal ownership in which the proletariat has a stake, it is to be hoped that labour productivity will increase not because of coercion, but because of the conviction that what is produced will help the worker as well as the rest of the society through creating the means for a better standard of living, which will help to move the country closer to the realization of its objective.

The proletariat is in a better position now than it was when working for private profiteers. The government has turned the workers into civil servants and included them among those who get pensions. An employee is not to be fired anymore at the will of the owner. He has been guaranteed tenure, so to speak, on his job. True, the high rate of inflation has eaten into his take-home pay, but the government has promised an adjustment in income soon.

The greatest positive effect of the indigenization and labour productivity as well as investment may be in peasant agriculture. The nationalization decree grants a maximum of ten hectares of land to farmers. Those who were landless and used to live as tenants never had an interest in producing more than they needed for their own survival and were careless about what happened to the soil. The fact that they now possess the land on which they work, and that what they produce belongs to them may change the face of the rural areas through increased agricultural output and better care for the land.

This may bring about another problem. In the past the landlords collected their dues from the tenants in kind, sold this produce in the urban market and spent the money on imported commodities. Now that the landlord is not there and the farmer owns what he produces and sells whenever he feels like doing so, the supply of the agricultural produce and especially food items may be strained. In turn, this may influence the industrial and distribution policy of the government if the 'scissors crisis' is to be avoided.

One way to entice farmers to sell their output is to supply them with the kind of industrial goods they would require, for if the farmer does not have a use for money, he will prefer to hold onto his output. This would require the establishment and expansion of the industries that produce what the farmer would need, and distribute it to the rural areas.

Another aspect of the effect of nationalizing rural land will be felt by the state farms. Since the industries require technical crops to process, and in large quantity (such as cotton for the textiles industries, oil crops for the oil and soap industries etc.), the government will have to be the major supplier in this area. Further pressure for the expansion of the state farms may be owing to a shortage of food items in the urban areas. Here too the government must supply a good portion of the required quantity and so must expand the state farms.

The emphasis on the measurement of the productivity of investment should shift from the amount of private return on invested funds to the decree of social profitability. This has already had consequences on the effort of the government to remedy regional imbalance as between provinces (with Shoa and Eritrea as the most favoured and Bale and Gemu Gofa as the least favoured in terms of hospitals, schools, roads, industrial establishments and other communication means, etc.) and between urban and rural areas.

The previous government saw to it that the urban areas became and remained the centres of development. Resources moved into these areas from the rural sector without the latter getting anything in return. The policy of the present government is to reverse this trend. Measures taken so far, although insignificant in terms of redressing the injustice done to the rural areas, point to the fact that the government intends to carry out this policy. More schools, health centres and roads are being built in the rural areas compared with the urban centres.

Redistribution of political power base has so far been the greatest achievement of the military government, both in the rural areas and the urban centres. The decree nationalizing rural land created peasants' associations to implement the law and as a means to mobilize the rural people and resources to develop the rural area. The nationalization of urban land and extra houses created the urban dwellers' association in each area with similar objectives as that of the peasants' associations. The peasants associations' in the rural areas and the urban dwellers' associations have been granted legal and political power to decide on matters that affect their members as well as their associations. Membership to both of these associations has been limited to those who owned land with a maximum holding of the ten hectares in the rural areas and those who at the most had only one house and never rented it out.

Through these two associations the broad mass of the Ethiopian rural and urban dwellers are expected to exercise political, social, economic and legal powers through their elected executive and judicial committees. Furthermore, all employees in government or private organizations are to devote two hours every week in political education with the objective of raising their level of consciousness in order to enable them to participate in the affairs of the state.

Conclusion

Over the past five years, Ethiopia has undergone a radical transformation. Politically the country has moved from conservative right to a far left. Private ownership of land has been abolished. Industries and financial institutions have been nationalized. Its development policy has shifted from an outward-looking to an inwardly concentrated effort.

Above all, Ethiopians have been given more responsibility in running their own affairs both at the state and private level. The shift in ownership in most of the foreign-owned enterprises has devolved management responsibility on Ethiopians. Both in agriculture and non-agricultural private enterprises, avenues have been opened through, and by which, the people can participate in the efforts of developing the country.

Thus, in the struggle being waged against underdevelopment, the Ethiopian people are to play the major role. The degree to which they triumph against poverty, disease, ignorance and the country's overall backward nature depends upon how well they play their role.

Notes

1 Currencies, unless otherwise stated, are in Ethiopian dollars; currently the exchange rate is US$1.00 = E$2.07, £1 = E£3.64
2 Imperial Ethiopian Government, *Second Five-Year Plan (SFYP)* (Addis Ababa 1962), pp. 39–40.
3 UNCTAD, *Major Issues Arising from the Transfers of Technology. A Case Study of Ethiopia* (Geneva 1974), p. 16 and *SFYP*, *Passim.*
4 *SFYP*, p. 76.
5 *ibid.*, p. 95.
6 *ibid.*, pp. 82 and 95.
7 Imperial Ethiopian Government, *Third Five-Year Plan (TFYP)* (Addid Ababa 1968), p. 59.
8 ibid., p. 42.
9 National Bank of Ethiopia, *Quarterly Bulletin* (n.s.), vol. 1, no. 3 (1975), p. 81.
10 The data in this section are based on the Ministry of Commerce and Industries' *Survey of Manufacturing Industry 1971/72* (Addis Ababa, mimeographed).
11 Central Statistical Office, *Statistical Abstract of Ethiopia* (1975), p. 45 (includes diplomats and employees of international and interregional organizations such as ECA, OAU, UN specialized agencies, representatives of various businesses and other organizations).
12 For details see page 267.
13 Ministry of Labour and Social Affairs, *Draft Report on the Study of Wage and Salary Levels* (April 1975, mimeo), various tables.
14 This part of the paper leans very heavily on the UNCTAD papers: *Major Issues Arising from the Transfer of Technology. A Case Study of Ethiopia* (TD/B/Acll/21) (Geneva June 1974); Steven Barac, *Some Problems of Development in Ethiopian Manufacturing Industry; Market Report* (Commercial Bank of Ethiopia, May–June 1975) and *Import Substitution in Ethiopia – Some Reflections, Market Report* (Commercial Bank of Ethiopia, September–October 1974).
15 Stephen Guisinger, *Tariffs and Trade Policies for the Ethiopian Manufacturing Sector* (August 1972, mimeographed).
16 *Ethiopian Herald* (21 December 1972), pp. 1,3.
17 In both the banks and insurance companies it was impossible to get figures on the extent of foreign interest.

18 See n. 17.
19 For details see the author's paper, *Peasants' Association and Rural Transformation*, presented at the East African Rural Science Co-ordinating Committee, Nazareth, Ethiopia, March 1976.
20 Agricultural Division, NNRD.

11 Southern Africa

Frank Baffoe, *Senior Research Fellow, Institute of Labour Studies, National University of Lesotho*

The countries of Botswana, Lesotho and Swaziland (commonly referred to as the BIS countries) all attained formal political independence from British colonial administration during the second half of the 1960s: Lesotho and Botswana became independent in 1966 while Swaziland achieved her independence in 1968. An an effective means of decolonization, all three countries on attainment of political independence embarked on various development programmes in order to promote economic growth and to achieve economic independence. On the strength of their economic growth, in quantitative terms, the countries expected to improve the living conditions of the growing population.

These countries viewed the objective of economic independence with great and serious concern. They were all deeply dissatisfied with the inherited, unhealthy and suffocating dependence on (and, indeed, virtual integration in) the economy of the Republic of South Africa. Their desire to work for economic independence from the stranglehold of the South African economy is reflected in the various development programmes initiated since independence to achieve a structural break with their colonial legacies of dependence. In a sense this objective implies an attempt not only to eliminate the inherited colonial structures, but also to forestall neocolonial development, which tends to perpetuate the dependence status. In this context, the specific nature of the BLS countries' struggle to liberate their economies from external domination and exploitation requires special attention, but only against the background of socioeconomic alienation.

The BLS countries realized that there were a number of critical components of the political and socioeconomic environment of the southern African situation that not only fostered and perpetuated their dependence status, but also decisively influenced their desired development patterns.

In this respect the main areas of great concern have been the nature of the inherited production structures, which tend to be externally oriented with regard to both inputs and outputs; the dominance of foreign-owned and controlled institutions, especially in the commercial banking system; the dominance of the distribution and services sectors (wholesale, repairs and spare parts, insurance, hire-purchase, etc.) by foreign entrepreneurs, especially those based in the Republic of South Africa; and the unhealthy dependence of their labour force on job opportunities in the economy of the Republic of South Africa. For our purpose, these issues of complexity could be reduced to two fundamental problem areas: the fact that these economies are externally oriented and thus 'conditioned', and the fact that the economies are to a great extent integrated in the economy of the Republic of South Africa.

This study examines the historical–structural aspects of the economies of the BLS countries in the analytical context of their dependent relationship with the Republic of South Africa. The examination of the nature of their dependence status *vis-à-vis* the Republic of South Africa will be followed by an analysis of the specific developmental policy measures and strategies that these countries have pursued as a means of dynamically internalizing the vital forces of socioeconomic change in the sense of 'indigenization'. Here indigenization will be understood as a dynamic strategy of restructuring the institutional and production nature of a colonial economy in a serious effort to realize domestically set and relevant socioeconomic goals. As Professor O. Aboyade (1965) succinctly puts it:

> The starting-point of a decolonisation process is the consolidation of the nation for social cohesion and the elimination of foreign discretionary powers in the economy. Through aggressive indigenization, even at the expense of initial loss in the growth of output, the nationals must acquire full control over the mobilisation, allocation and utilisation of their natural, human, financial and other resources.

In examining the various programmes to indigenize the BLS economies, the study will critically evaluate the programmes and strategies with regard to the degree of goal realization and the associated implications for the future development paths of the economies.

Analytical framework of the study

Before turning to the historical background of the present southern African situation, it is appropriate to make explicit the analytical framework of the study.

The socio-political and economic impact of colonial and imperialist penetration in Africa has been well documented. The uniqueness of the southern African colonial history lies in the specific structures that the settler–cum–colonial administration created and has maintained up to the present. Generally, however, the development path that was initiated by the colonists and imperial powers in the former High Commission Territories (as the present BLS countries used to be designated) at the close of the last century is not different from the common pattern of imperialist expansion and exploitation in Africa.

In the southern African regional setup, the starting point of the process of colonialist exploitation was the forceful subjugation of the traditional African mode of production through the introduction of the capitalist mode of production. The subjugation first took on the form of appropriation, not only of vast stretches of land, but also of the *best* land areas, from the Africans. The domination of the traditional African mode of production was rendered more effective through the appropriation of the economic surpluses generated in the area by the capitalists. In other words, in the specific southern African situation the colonists had a vested interest, at the very initial stage, in preventing the emergence of the capitalist mode of production on any significant scale in the subjugated areas. This was of course in the spirit and logic of capitalist and colonial exploitation. The emergence of a wide-scale capitalist mode of production in those areas could have led to the internalization of the dynamic process of socioeconomic transformation at that early stage.

Basically, the preservation of the pre-capitalist mode of production was an efficacious political means of control over the economic resources and surpluses in the dominated territories for purposes of capital accumulation in the imperialist centre and sub-centre. The ultimate consequence of the process was the creation of the periphery or dependent economy which is beset by a variety of institutional and economic structural rigidities. Besides, the periphery economy is always caught in a dependence-and-dominance relationship to the core (Frank, 1969; Baran, 1962).

For our analytical purpose, the centre–periphery dichotomy helps us to divide the southern African economy into a dynamic, rapidly growing centre (the economy of the Republic of South Africa) and its peripheries (Botswana, Lesotho, Swaziland, Malawi, Mozambique, Angola, Namibia and Rhodesia), which directly and indirectly subsidized the centre.

In essence, the periphery/dependent economies are tributary areas that are drained of their resources, manpower and scarce capital. The historical evolution of this highly unequal capitalist system of centre–periphery relationships in the southern African economy is very crucial to the development of the whole region. The issue is not simply that of barriers to markets and technical know-how and management. Obviously, the process of capitalist imbalance cannot be corrected by the unfettered and automatic working of the market; rather, the initial structural imbalance is reinforced by the working of the market. Thus most attempts by the periphery economies to be self-reliant and independent in their development efforts have been rendered rather difficult and in some cases near impossible.

Another important aspect of the centre and periphery relationships is the chronic exploitation of consumers and labour in the dependent economies. Labour is exploited in the sense that many sectors (especially the mines) in the centre have been able to withdraw a large number of cheap labour from the pre-capitalist, subsistence agricultural sectors of the periphery economies at exceedingly inadequate wages. To perpetuate this situation, policies emanating from the dominant centre have aimed essentially to maintain the archaic production structures in the dominated sectors. This has resulted in the consolidation of the dependence relations as a means of creating and sustaining the flow of surplus labour.

Finally, it must be mentioned that the perennial nature of the dominance and dependence relationships is reflected in the fact that industrial activities in the periphery economies have tended to lack local linkages, because foreign capital and technical and managerial expertise have exercised control over the utilization of surpluses generated in these economies.

In the final analysis, therefore, we are dealing with different sets of conditions coexisting in the southern African economy which interact to accentuate the process of underdevelopment in the dominated sectors. As Theotonio Dos Santos (1973) says of the phenomenon of 'under-development', it is

> far from constituting a state of backwardness prior to capitalism, is rather a consequence and particular form of capitalist development known as dependent capitalism . . . dependence is a *conditioning* situation in which the economies of one group of countries are conditioned by the development and expansion of others. A relationship of interdependence between two or more economies or between such and the world trading system becomes a dependent relationship when some countries can expand through self-impulsion while others, being in dependent position, can only expand as a reflection of the expansion of the dominant countries, which may have positive or negative effects on their immediate development. In either case, the basic situation of dependence causes these countries to be both backward and exploited. . . . Dependence, then, is based upon an international division of labour which allows industrial development to take place in some countries while restricting it in others, whose growth is conditioned by and subjected to the power centres of the world.

This centre–periphery model is crucial to any discussion of indigenization in the BLS countries. It enables us to appreciate the nature and objectives of the indigenization approaches in the BLS countries since their attainment of formal political independence. The typical behaviour patterns of capital that came into these economies during the colonial period were those of the 'dominant' and 'representative' type, and they aimed to foster liberalism and imperialist exploitation. We are here dealing with the behaviour patterns of 'merchant capital' and 'finance capital'. The economies of the High Commission Territories, as with all subjugated and periphery economies, were not destined to feel the pervasive impact of 'industrial capital'. Thus the types of industrial and commercial organizations introduced into these pre-capitalist societies lacked internal growth dynamics. The dominance of finance capital and merchant capital is a critical aspect in a situation of core–periphery relationships.

The next stage of the study examines the historical background data of the present southern African situation with reference to the salient features of the colonial dependent economies and the present socio-economic structures that have persisted beyond formal political independence to necessitate the various approaches of indigenization in the BLS countries. The following section serves as a brief historical review of the origins and rationale of the external relationships that were created during the colonial era and inherited at independence.

The southern African situation: a brief review

The most important single aspect of the southern African regional situation, in historical perspective, has been the unyielding process of polarization of industrial activities since the discovery of precious metals at the end of the nineteenth century. The capitalist exploitation of these minerals initiated the process of polarization, which in turn has fundamentally influenced the internal characteristics and structures of the economies of the BLS countries. Externally, two types of relationships emanated from the process. First, the colonial economies of these countries were drawn into the world capitalist system in a dependent status in relation to Great Britain, including the issue of incorporation with South Africa during the years 1910–60. Second, the economic relationship with South Africa has involved them in membership of the South African Custom Union, the use of South African currency, the employment of a large proportion of their labour force (especially Lesotho, with over 45 per cent of her able-bodied male labour) in South African mines and industries, a significant inter-territorial trade and the considerable investment of South African capital (especially in Swaziland and Botswana) and skills (expecially in Swaziland).

Essentially, the history of colonialism in the former High Commission Territories of Botswana, Lesotho and Swaziland underlines the basic fact that the colonial economy has always been designed primarily for exports and controlled by commercial capital in the 'national' and 'international' metropolis. In the case of the High Commission Territories the commercial capital that controlled their economies was based 'nationally' in South Africa and 'internationally' in the United Kingdom.

The pre-eminence of the export sector in the colonial economy has been historically observed to create deficiencies in internal markets. According to A. G. Frank (1969) the structure of the export mechanism that was imposed and inculcated within the colonial exploitation mechanism generated a process of structural underdevelopment in the colonial economy. In other words, colonial policy in the southern African economy led to the creation of growth poles based on the need to integrate the colonial sectors into the world capitalist system.

As periphery economies, the BLS countries in the southern African economic setting were to supply the growth centres of the South African economy with the ablest of their manpower, to provide markets for the ever-expanding South African economy, and to experience substantial outflows of scarce capital to South Africa. Basically, therefore, the growth points in the South African economy acted as centres for the mobilization of the export of primary products from the peripheries; as distribution centres for imports of manufacturers; as a location for financial and other institutions associated with trade and the mobilization of investible funds in the peripheries; and as a seat of economic power.

The main objectives of colonial policy in the region were to organize and control the socio-political and economic life of the colonial territories. Consequently, the economic linkages that were established served to drain the economies of the BLS countries of their men of working age and investive capital rather than to distribute capital and skills to them. Levels of economic activities and spatial integration were shifted from their economies to that of South Africa. Thus the distortions inherent in the internal characteristics and economic structures of the BLS countries have a common root in the colonial or neocolonial nature of their economic relations, which have both regional and metropolitan aspects.

In essence, these distortions have taken on the forms of:

> control over domestic resource allocation by foreign monopoly capital, instability of income growth, disparity between the growth of domestic and national products, prevalence of growth without development such as leads to a widening process of economic discontent and social alienation, the paradoxical existence of good development potential with poor development performance, absurd internal contradictions between resource availability and resource use,

and the absence of the critical minimum size of public-sector power as a leverage for conscious social mobilization and national development. [Aboyade, 1965]

Furthermore, the economic life of the BLS countries is greatly complicated by being landlocked with the strong South African economy on their borders. Indeed, South Africa, which forms the South African Custom Union with the BLS, is at a more advanced level of economic development than the BLS; besides, it is substantially larger (in terms of GDP and other economic indicators) than all three countries combined. For instance, for the periods 1974/5 and 1975/6 the recorded total imports of the BLS countries were only 4.6 and 5.9 per cent respectively of the South African figures. In simple economic terms, these countries are completely overshadowed by the economy of South Africa, and the exercise of options in relation to indigenization is of great importance.

In summary, at independence the economies of the BLS were characterized by an undesirable dualism, namely the coexistence of a relatively prosperous, advanced modern sector which is largely owned and controlled by foreigners on the one hand, and a poor subsistence sector offering livelihood and employment for the bulk of the people on the other. Generally, foreign-owned enterprises account for most modern economic activities. For instance, foreign-owned commercial agricultural enterprises account for over 90 per cent of production in Swaziland.

The BLS also depend internally on a few foreign-owned and -run enterprises for most of their entire industrial production and all of their commercial agricultural production. The export trade is largely in the hands of foreigners. The distribution system and most of the wholesale and retail trade, particularly in urban areas, are controlled by foreign-owned enterprises. Tourism is almost entirely in the hands of expatriates while the countries heavily rely on the expertise of foreign professional and technical manpower.

Finally, the core–periphery relationship between the BLS and South Africa has had polarizing effects on the economic development of the periphery countries. The greater proportion of their imports originate in, or pass through, South Africa, and a substantial part of their exports go to South Africa. Their tourists generally come from South Africa; and between 45 and 70 per cent of their governments' revenues are derived through the arrangement of the Customs Union, whose bigger and dominant partner is South Africa. This obviously leaves very little room for manoeuvre by these governments in their fiscal and monetary policy.

The BLS are therefore faced with the urgent task of reducing the extreme dependence of their economies on a few factors or a group of foreign institutions or individuals. The task is certainly a formidable one, but unless this is effectively tackled it will be equally formidable to conceive how these countries can attain a greater measure of self-reliance and economic independence.

The nature of incipient indigenization in the BLS countries

Against the background of these structural characteristics that are associated with the BLS economies' dependence status within the southern African economy, the analysis will now focus on the strategic policy measures of these countries in their attempt to achieve economic independence. Undoubtedly, the main objectives of any strategy of indigenization will be reflected in the urgent need to gain (or rather regain) firm and effective control by the nationals over the resources and behaviour of the domestic economy. As Professor O. Aboyade (1965) rightly puts it

> This means not only that the discretionary powers exercised by foreigners in the allocation of domestic resources be eliminated, but also that in a structural sense the umbilical cord of primary export dependence as the main engine of national economic growth should be cut.

All three governments are fully aware of the fact that at independence the inherited structure of laws and institutions severely circumscribed the role of the central authorities in influencing the conduct and process of economic affairs. The first line of action was therefore to create the institutions and instruments necessary for a more effective guidance and control of the economy.

The government of Botswana acknowledges this fact thus:

> Botswana is economically a small country; it is landlocked; and it is virtually surrounded by much larger and more developed countries ruled by minority racialist regimes. At Independence the pattern of investment, the lack of physical and social infrastructure and the orientation of the infrastructure that there was, all emphasized the country's dependence on its neighbours. The lack of manpower, the shortage of other domestic resources and the lack of any major exports other than beef contributed to Botswana's vulnerability. Economic independence therefore became, for economic as well as political reasons, a major objective and one that has to temper the quest for rapid economic growth.

In principle there are two possible approaches open to a colonially created and perpetuated economy that is struggling to liberate itself from the colonial past and the neocolonial status: the capitalist or the socialist approach. The socialist approach will tend to socialize the production and distribution relationships and the associated institutions in order to internalize the forces of socioeconomic transformation. The capitalist approach will, on the other hand, tend to extend the embryonic capitalist production and distribution relationships as a means of achieving a greater integration of the domestic economy as well as a greater integration into the international capitalist system. In general policy terms, these two extreme approaches may be reduced to the common dichotomies of 'inward-looking' and 'outward-looking' strategies.

For our analytical purposes, the choice of approach deserves to be viewed against the background of the general proposition that the real essence of development is the process of mobilizing and effectively utilizing the total domestic resources (natural, human and financial). In the process it is very necessary to create and exploit market opportunities, both externally and internally. The local relevance becomes, however, paramount. The nature of the inherited structural distortions needs clear identification in the first instance. The goals of development and transformation must be deduced from the objective socioeconomic setup. The next step in the decision-making process is to design feasible programmes for eliminating the observed structural distortions as a means of achieving the set goals (cf. O. Aboyade, 1965).

Indigenization as a policy for socioeconomic transformation and economic independence is very new in the toolbox of the BLS. This is again a reflection of the hard fact that economic imperialism as 'a foreign policy that seeks political and economic control over backward areas to guarantee an outlet for idle savings and surplus manufactured goods in exchange for strategic raw materials' (Blaug, 1961) is very pervasive indeed. Our analysis of the historical origins and rationale of the specific relationships that were created and inculcated in the BLS throws some light on the future prospects of indigenization as a means of internalizing the dynamics of socioeconomic transformation in the BLS.

The first and major step towards indigenization in the BLS countries was made with the establishment of development corporations some years after the attainment of formal political independence. A very important element in the indigenization approach of the BLS relates to the creation of new financial institutions designed to mobilize local resources and lessen reliance on South African capital; the National Insurance Corporation is one of these institutions. Another method designed to more efficiently concentrate funds is a 'deferred payment scheme', which provides for repatriation to the Lesotho Bank of 60 per cent of the earnings of migrant workers. The Chamber of

Mines of South Africa previously held these savings with no interest accruing to Lesotho. Under the new scheme these deposits earn interest at a rate of 5 per cent per annum. At the inception of the scheme it was estimated that by the end of 1977 (when all migrant workers were expected to be covered) the fund would have accumulated between R20 and R24 million, which could be partly used for development purposes.

In spite of all these apparent financial gains, it is admitted by the Lesotho government that the degree of dependence on South Africa 'makes Lesotho extremely vulnerable to development over which the Government has no control'. The government seeks, therefore, during the course of the second five-year development plan (1975/6–1980/1) to (1) localize most of the posts held by expatriates through training programmes specifically geared to development needs; (2) further diversify the sources of external sources of assistance; and (3) maximize the mobilization and domestic use of national savings.

In general policy terms, the government of Lesotho attaches great importance to 'direct foreign investment in providing the capital and know-how for the industrial development of Lesotho'. Thus, 'the primary objective of government's industrial policy is to promote such investment', and 'the second objective of industrial policy is to promote the development of indigenous small manufacturing enterprises'.

This eclectic stance towards foreign investment is the common thread in the policies of all the BLS countries. It is in the same spirit in which the Minister of Commerce and Industry, G. Chipe, announced early in 1977 that Botswana was considering various incentives to industry such as guarantees of the rights of ownership and freedom to repatriate profits. In emphasizing the need to attract foreign capital and skills to develop businesses, the minister said: 'it is a key feature of government policy in regard to the development of all manner of industrial activity in Botswana to welcome and encourage the fullest participation of foreign investment, especially foreign private investment'.

Paradoxically, while the BLS seek to diversify both their foreign markets and their sources of foreign private investments, their eclectic attitude towards *deux machina*, foreign investment, has tended to increase the involvement of capital from outside, especially from the Republic of South Africa. Essentially, therefore, the outward-directed development strategies being pursued by the BLS countries have the tendency of replacing a colonial dependence structure by a new dependence structure characterized by a high export of investment funds (as dividends and profits repatriation), a high level of consumption and capital goods imports, and a great dependence on forgien private investment and development assistance.

It is against this background that I submit we must study the unfolding relations between the BLS and the more advanced partners, particularly South Africa.

The next stage of the analysis focuses on the specific programmes followed by the BLS by way of indigenization.

Programmes of inchoate indigenization

Botswana

The Botswana Development Corporation Ltd (BDC) was established in April 1970 as a government-owned company. Unlike many other corporations, the BDC is a limited liability company and not a statutory body. This unique aspect of BDC was determined by Botswana government's declared policy of encouraging private investors (both local and foreign) with a general development strategy of mixed economy. As stated in the Corporation's Article of Association, it is 'to promote and facilitate the economic development of Botswana' and promote commercially viable businesses which 'will contribute to national goals as stated in the National Development Plan'. (These are the nationals goals we discussed earlier.) I submit that the declared broad socio-political goals and the narrow commercial goals can be contradictory within the framework of indigenization.

The Botswana Development Corporation was set up to provide finance to encourage and assist business whenever a viable opportunity could be found – with the exception of mining, where the government is a sole custodian. Since its inception in April 1970 it has made investments in over thirty-one businesses. For instance, it has participated on a wholly owned basis in the establishment and running of the national carrier, Air Botswana, the Botswana Diamond Valuing Company, the first property management company and the first equipment leasing company of Botswana. It has also participated as a minority shareholder in tyre retreading, aircraft servicing, insurance, estate and property valuing as well as charter air service.

The BDC has been requested by the government to take over all its investment in tourism. It is also to be involved in the construction and renting of industrial premises that have long been (and indeed still are) in the hands of South African firms.

Through consultancy and research the Corporation has been able to stimulate considerable local interest in tanning, brewing, soft drink bottling, basic commodity wholesaling, and bicycle assembly projects. Prospects for road-haulage, galvanized-sheet rolling, commercial vehicle assembly, semi-precious stone cutting, etc., are all seriously being investigated by the BDC.

All these diverse activities of the BDC, whose assets are now worth about 9 million pula, testify to the indigenization of ownership and control of major enterprises in the economy. However, the more specialist trades are still dominated by foreign concerns. The greater part of the commercial sector is still handled by foreign-owned enterprises operating mainly in the urban centres.

Another important government agent is the Botswana Enterprises Development Company Ltd (BEDCOL), which was established to encourage the establishment and promotion of small-scale enterprises owned by local entrepreneurs. It is also charged with the responsibility of constructing industrial estates and providing other facilities and services needed by local entrepreneurs. An Industrial Advisory Board has been created under BEDCOL's auspices to combat some of the bureaucratic obstacles to speedy consideration of industrial investment proposals.

Among the government's main agent for industrial, commercial and agricultural promotion is the National Development Bank, which provides medium-term finance at favourable rates of interest to small businesses which are usually locally owned.

Essentially, the government of Botswana is determined to place investment of short-term balances locally. In the absence of a developed money market, however, the greater difficulty is to identify suitable short-term investment opportunities when actually needed. Such short-term balances are channelled to the National Development Bank for seasonal agricultural credit, or to the Botswana Housing Corporation for home ownership loans, or to the Botswana Development Corporation as short-term working capital for its subsidiaries.

The legislative framework for these institutions consists of the Industrial Development Act, the Trading Act, the Trade Amendment Act, and the Liquor Act, which are all concerned with licensing industrial and commercial enterprises in pursuit of national economic independence, rapid economic growth, social justice and sustained production. According to the government of Botswana (1975), the

> development of Mining has formed the core of the Government's policy in promoting the country's economic independence, first through the establishment of a basic physical infrastructure and administrative machinery, and second by the development of new sources of revenue that would enable the country to lessen its dependence on outside financial assistance.

The development in the mining sector seems to have strengthened the government's aspiration of economic independence. The tremendous revenues from mining have both strengthened its financial position and dramatically affected the GDP, which has expanded at the rate of about

20 per cent at constant market prices between 1968 and 1975. Over the same period the relative share of mining and construction of GDP has risen from a meagre 1 per cent to 21 per cent. Ironically, however, the nature of the development in the mining sector has increased the involvement of South African capital in the economy, mainly from the Anglo-American Corporation and De Beers Consolidated Mines. This is certainly contradictory to the majority objective of economic independence. The government is now intent on expanding its participation in the ownership and management decision-making of new mining ventures.

Finally, we must turn our attention to Botswana's attempt to achieve monetary independence from the Rand Monetary Arrangement; these attempts gained formal status in 1969, after about sixty years during which South African currency was sole legal tender in the BLS countries. The Bank of Botswana was established on 1 July 1975, and on 23 August 1976 Botswana acquired a national currency for the first time in its history. The official monetary unit is the *pula*, which is equal to 100 *thebe*. The pula is pegged to the US dollar.

The main objectives of the new monetary system are (1) to make more effective use of domestic financial resources, and (2) to encourage the development of local financial institutions and to influence the expansion and distribution of available credit. For this purpose the reserve and liquidity requirements applicable to financial institutions operating in the country will be adjusted by the Bank of Botswana as the need arises. With the issue of Treasury bills one has the beginning of a local money market. Through its management of the fiduciary issues and in its regulation of credit and interest the Bank of Botswana can now play an active and effective role in the development of the country. The Bank can pursue independent monetary policies necessary for national development needs. As President Khama said in 1974, 'in deciding to create out own central bank and to issue our own currency, we are seeking to achieve a greater measure of influence over our own monetary and financial situation'.

It is to be noted that Botswana's membership of the Southern African Customs Union, which goes back to 1910, is not affected by her withdrawal from the Rand Monetary Arrangement. Her continuation in the Customs Union is a necessity born out of her geographical situation as well as her heavy dependence on external factors which critically determine the value of her foreign exchange earnings.

The construction of the Kazungula–Franciston road link with Zambia was an obvious endeavour to lessen Botswana's dependence on South Africa. The government has also established a local enterprise (Sefolana sa Botswana) to take over the activities of the South Africa

Bechmalt Group. The company's primary purpose is to provide a boost for cattle and maize production in the country. It is the country's sole miller. Its most important activity is its animal feed plant at Lobatse, to make cattle, pig and poultry feed. It also processes industrial agricultural crops; it is involved in marketing and storage of grain, and in general trading in the urban areas (Gaborone, Lobatse, Selebi-Pikwe, Serowe and Franciston).

Like all underdeveloped African countries, one of the major constraints on Botswana's national development relates to the acute shortage of managerial, professional and technical manpower resources. This situation is exacerbated by the lack of relevant and adequate education programmes in the technical, managerial and professional areas, which has necessarily led to heavy dependence on a substantial amount of expatriate skilled labour.

The acuteness of the shortage of skilled manpower was revealed by the Manpower Survey of April/May 1972. It was observed that, of the total wage employment of about 48,000 people, only 25 per cent could be classified as skilled labour. On the other hand, among the whole African skilled labour force there were over 60 per cent of citizens and 17 per cent of non-citizens (mostly from neighbouring African countries) who had no more than primary education.

In view of this precarious situation, and in pursuance of the localization policy, the government of Botswana has declared that educational and training programmes in the country should be adapted 'to ensure that educational resources are used to the best advantage in the pursuit of the national objectives of economic growth, social justice, economic independence and sustained development'. Thus the accelerated educational and training programmes are to provide for the expanding needs for growth and localization. It is envisaged that the many posts now held by expatriates would be localized by 1988.

In the private sector, the government's localization policy embodies an incentive to foreign enterprises to set off 125 per cent of the cost of approved training scheme against tax with regard to citizen-ownership of industrial ventures and replacement of expatriate manpower by locals. The progress made here has been rather slow and unsatisfactory-

Lesotho

As in all colonial countries, the historical evolution of the economy of Lesotho has left as vestiges certain characteristic features. However, among the BLS countries, Lesotho's economic dependence on South Africa is the most precarious. It is economically a small and weak economy ,fully surrounded by the Republic of South Africa. I once described the nature and degree of Lesotho's economic dependence on South Africa thus (Baffoe, 1975):

> the substance of the commercial, financial and economic relationships between the Lesotho economy and the South African economy is one of economic dependence and economic domination. This relationship has been sustained through the specific nature of economic dependence which has its historical explanation and momentum.

Consequently, I postulated.

> no matter how much thought and effort the Government of Lesotho puts into its development planning, the end result will be determined by the nature and degree of the economy's dependence on the Republic of South Africa.

The Lesotho economy is virtually integrated with the economy of South Africa. It is characterized by the dominance of subsistence agriculture, which is in turn based on a land tenure system that in practice inhibits efficient production methods on a large scale; by tourism, which depends largely on the vast South African market; by migration for employment in the mines of South Africa; and by reliance on monetary policies controlled by the South African Reserve Bank. Lesotho's membership in both the Southern African Customs Union and the Rand Monetary Area extremely aggravates her status as a sovereign state within the southern African economy. Thus Lesotho's subordination to, and close integration with, the South African economy are the most crucial factors in both national development policy formulation and implementation.

The first step taken by the nationalist government in the direction of breaking out of the colonial legacies was the establishment of a National Post Office Savings Bank. Until 1966 the Post Office Savings Bank was an integral part of the South African Savings Bank, which actively mobilized funds in Lesotho and channelled them to investments in South Africa. The accumulated balances of the former Post Office Savings Bank formed the basis for the establishment of the Lesotho National Development Bank, commonly known as the Lesotho Bank.

The second five-year development plan has the broad aims of balanced economic growth, social justice, maximum domestic employment and economic independence. The government realizes that economic independence can be achieved only by building the capacity of the people and instutitions to use the nation's resources to maximum advantage.

The Lesotho National Development Corporation (LNDC) is a 100 per cent government-owned statutory body established in 1967 'to initiate, promote and facilitate the development and processing industries, mining and commerce in a manner calculated to raise the level of income and employment in Lesotho'. At independence in 1966 Lesotho was almost entirely without industrial development. In the 1960s the Basutoland Factory Estates Development Company (BAFED) was established, and it initiated the Maseru Industrial Area and other enterprises. The assets of BAFED were transferred to LNDC on the latter's establishment in 1967. The LNDC is to provide the equity capital and long-term loans required by both large and small enterprises mainly in the industrial and tourism sectors. It is empowered to manage businesses for these purposes. Essentially, the Corporation fills in an institutional lacuna which existed in the country's financial environment.

In addition to its financial activities, the LNDC is the principal vehicle of the government's industrial policy; it is responsible for attracting foreign investors and, where it is unable to locate such investors, to take the initiative in establishing and managing suitable enterprises.

As the principal vehicle of the government's industrial policy, the LNDC is, however, primarily concerned with the promotion of foreign investment and larger-scale enterprises. The government's industrial policies are stated as follows:

> Because of the importance of direct foreign investment in providing the capital and know-how for industrial development of Lesotho, the primary objective of government's industrial policy is to promote such investment. . . . The second objective of industrial policy is to promote the development of indigenous small manufacturing enterprises, and the government therefore provides free training and technical assistance to such enterprises. (LNDC, 1976).

Within this broad policy framework, Lesotho offers very generous incentives to industrial enterprises. The 'Pioneer Industries Encouragement Act' of 1969 provides generous tax incentives to 'pioneer industries'. These incentives include a choice between a six-year tax holiday or depreciation allowances of up to 150 per cent of the initial investment during the first year of operation; a citizen training allowance equal to 110 per cent of the approved cost to the manufacturer; and a citizen wage allowance equal to 10 per cent of the wages paid to Sotho employees. The incentives related to the training and employment are within the context of the government's localization policy.

Paradoxically, the acute shortage of suitable Sotho managerial, professional and technical skilled labour has resulted in the country's heavy reliance on overseas aid organizations to finance expatriate staff for a majority of key positions in LNDC industrial ventures. For instance, until the recent appointment of a Sotho, Mr Sam Montsi, as the managing director of the Corporation, out of the total professional staff of nineteen, nine were expatriates – including the important post of the financial controller.

Since its inception the LNDC has assisted in variety of projects with equity investments, loans, buildings and guarantees. LNDC's financial operations from establishment up to 30 June 1976 are given in Table 39. The projects that received assistance from LNDC operate in a large variety of sectors such as food processing enterprises, handicraft manufacturing enterprises, hotels, commercial undertakings, and construction enterprises. Much of its lending has, however, been to the tourism sector. Its largest loan was R800,000 to the Amalgamated Hotels Ltd, which owned the Holiday Inn complex in Maseru.

As of 1976 the LNDC had sixteen subsidiary companies which held 50 per cent of its equity portfolio. There has been an unsatisfactory financial performance of the directly managed LNDC subsidiaries. For instance, for the year ended 31 March 1976 only four of the sixteen subsidiary companies and only five of the twelve associated companies showed profit gains. This poor financial performance has been due mainly to poor and constantly changing management, inadequate management information (and for that matter, lack of an effective information system) and poor marketing programmes and networks.

Generally, the operations of the LNDC as the principal institution for promotion and long-term financing of medium- and large-scale non-agricultural enterprises in Lesotho have tended to exacerbate the country's dependence on external factors, especially foreign capital and expertise. On the other hand, the nature of its outstanding capital investments has contributed very little to the process of indigenizing ownership, control and management. Admittedly, the LNDC has succeeded in diversifying the sources of Lesotho's foreign capital requirements; the country has shifted from her previous reliance on just South African and British capital loans. Essentially, however, the country has replaced one type of external dependence with another type. The economic independence that emerges from such a situation is hard to assess. It is hoped that in the long run the country may succeed in strengthening its bargaining position.

The Basotho Enterprises Development Corporation (BEDCO) was established in 1975 as a limited liability company with the aims of promoting the establishment and development of small-scale Sotho-owned enterprises. In mid-1976 BEDCO became a wholly owned subsidiary of LNDC. Under its Memorandum of Association BEDCO is empowered to provide financial assistance to Sotho entrepreneurs through equity investments, loans and financial guarantees. It also provides factory shells, equipment and technical knowledge to such

Table 39 *Lesotho National Development Corporation loan allocations, 1967–76*

	Total approved		*pf which, subsidiaries*		
	Number	*Amount* (R million)	*Number*	*Amount* (R million)	%
Equity investments	30	0.9	16	0.5	56
Loans	20	1.8	12	0.3	17
Factory buildings	20	1.3	4	0.1	8
Guarantees	11	0.7	5	0.2	29
Total	81	4.7	42	1.1	23

entrepreneurs, and is empowered to promote and develop subsidiaries and to borrow or raise money for its operations.

Thus, BEDCO complements the operations of LNDC by providing financial and other facilities to Sotho-owned small-scale enterprises. This is a step in the right direction in the country's indigenization programmes. On the other hand, the Corporation relies heavily not only on external finance but also on foreign expertise. Out of its professional staff of eleven, five are expatriates. In addition to the managing director, Mr Don Pruden (a Canadian), there are expatriate managers of the business extension and equipment pool units, all financed by Canadian aid. The deputy managing directir is Mr Ben Debatane, who is a Sotho on secondment from the Ministry of Commerce and Industry.

In the light of this dependence on foreign profrssionals, and also in view of the government's localization policy, BEDCO provides a Sotho counterpart to every expatriate with a view to phasing out the latter's assistance by 1981.

The financial environment of Lesotho is characterized by a dominance of foreign institutions. The country is a signatory to the Rand Monetary Agreement. It uses the rand currency as its sole legal tender and is largely dependent on monetary and credit policies set by the South African Reserve Bank. Until the establishment of the Lesotho Bank in 1972 and the promulgation of the Financial Institutions Act of 1973, the two commercial banks, Barclays and Standard, completely controlled the mobilization of domestic resources and their allocation. The operations of these two foreign-based commercial banks led to 'a perverse flow of investive funds'. Instead of mobilizing funds in the core-sector (South Africa) and channelling these funds to the periphery-sector (Lesotho), they rather concentrated on the financing of foreign trade and commercial activities in addition to mobilizing local funds and reinvesting them outside Lesotho. Thus Lesotho was in the very strange position, as an underdeveloped economy, of exporting capital to South Africa through funds mobilized by commercial banks, insurance companies and building societies.

In pursuit of economic independence, the Lesotho Bank was established as a fully government-owned commercial bank in 1972 to mobilize more domestic financial resources and to improve the channelling of credit to local businesses. The Bank was developed out of the old Post Office Savings Bank. It is now the largest of the three commercial banks in the country. The greater proportion of Lesotho Bank's resources are, however, either loaned to public agencies, used to acquire fixed property or, ironically, deposited temporarily with the other commercial banks. In other words, the success of Lesotho Bank in mobilizing more local savings has not been matched by a provision of more credit facilities to local businesses. Instead, by depositing some of its resources with the other commercial banks it is indirectly intensifying the tendency of these banks 'to invest most of their funds abroad because of limited opportunities for short-term investment in Lesotho'. This is certainly contradictory to the major tenet of government policy, 'namely to attempt to maximize the mobilisation of national savings and their productive use within Lesotho'.

Other financial institutions operating in the country include the Lesotho Credit Union Scheme for Agriculture (LECUSA), various small credit unions, and branches of many South African building societies and insurance companies.

The realization of the lack of necessary financial institutions and instruments led the government to enact the Financial Institutions Act of 1973. Under this Act all commercial banks and other financial institutions in Lesotho are subject, since 1 September 1974, to the regulatory provisions of the Act, which *inter alia* stipulate required minimum capital and reserve accounts that each financial institution must maintain. Besides, the Act seeks to regulate the specific lending operations of the banks and provides for mandatory audit and inspection of their annual balance sheets and profit and loss accounts. The Act also specifies that every financial institution should maintain prescribed investments of an amount not exceeding 5 per cent of its current liability in Lesotho.

By and large, the establishment of the Lesotho Bank in 1972 and the increased control as a result of the Financial Institutions Act of 1973 have effected an increase in the level of domestic savings and their employment within Lesotho.

In recent years, the government has taken a number of actions in the monetary and fiscal areas to ameliorate the degree of dependence on

South Africa. As has already been mentioned, a recent addition to the financial landscape is the 'Deferred Payment Scheme', which provides the country with the repatriation of 60 per cent of the earnings of Sotho migrant workers. The latest addition is the newly created National Insurance Corporation, which is expected to mobilize domestic resources for development and was indeed long overdue. It will go a long way to stop the flow of accumulated funds for investment in the Republic of South Africa.

On the communications scene the establishment of a direct telecommunication link with Nairobi in early 1976 has lessened Lesotho's previous dependence on South Africa and increased her unhindered contact with the outside world which is extremely necessary for her development. The government is presently working very hard on the construction of an international airport, which will solve some of the transit problems emanating from Lesotho's heavy dependence on services provided by Jan Smuts Internal Airport.

The manpower problem in Lesotho is very serious; there is an acute shortage of skilled labour and high-level manpower. The consequence of this is that many planned projects in the development programmes are postponed because of a lack of skilled personnel. The seriousness of the problem is demonstrated by the high vacancy rate at the degree entry level (32 per cent in 1975) and the fact that expatriate personnel in the public sector numbered over 300, including volunteers. The majority of these expatriates work in education, agriculture and development planning.

The need for training is very great indeed. In the public sector, for example, high-level training is desperately needed to provide for growth of public service, for localization, upgrading and replacement of retired persons. Most of pre-service training for the public sector is provided by the National University at Roma for professionals and sub-professionals. For training courses not offered at the National University, and for other upgrading courses, the country relies on foreign technical assistance for fellowships and scholarships.

Generally, training for high-level manpower has been primarily for the public sector. The private sector is still small and rudimentary. About 90 per cent of those engaged in the sector have little or no training for their jobs, while just about 1 per cent have professional or sub-professional training.

The major objectives of the second five-year development plan are the expansion of vocational and technical training programmes and the integration of training facilities into a polytechnic institute and national training colleges. The ultimate aim is to localize most of the posts now being held by expatriates. Apart from the National University, the following training institutions are to expand their programmes and student intakes: National Teacher Training College, Lerotholi Technical Institute (polytechnic), Commercial Training Centre, Lesotho Opportunities Industrial Centre and the Lesotho Agricultural College, etc.

In sum, Lesotho is still at the preparatory stage of indigenization. The country is still economically dependent on South Africa. The situation is rather complicated by the fact that the government's proclaimed industrial policy is to rely largely on foreign private investments, which basically will tend to increase rather than decrease the country's external dependence.

Swaziland

The policies and programmes set forth in the second national development plan have been guided by two broad objectives: first, to promote a greater degree of participation of the Swazi people in the development of the economy; and, second, to achieve a greater measure of independent control over the economic affairs of the nation.

As it has been demonstrated, the historical and economic ties between Swaziland and South Africa have perforce strongly influenced all major developments in the former, which is linked up with South Africa by common customs and monetary arrangements. One major unfavourable consequence of this link is the polarization of industry in favour of the South African economy. This has in turn increased the dependence status of Swaziland. This has been succinctly described by the *JASPA Report* (Jobs and Skills Programme for Africa, a programme initiated by the International Labour Organization):

> The second feature of the economy is intimately linked with its dualistic structure which is the all-pervasive dependence of the economy on a few external as well as internal factors. The most obvious and important dependence is with respect to the Republic of South Africa. The core–periphery relationship between South Africa and Swaziland has had polarising effects on developments in the latter. [ILO 1977]

With regard to the internal structural relationships, the same Report continues:

> Internally, the country is dependent on a few foreign-owned and foreign-run establishments for most of its industrial and agricultural production. Export trade is largely in the hands of foreigners and even the distribution system and most of wholesale and retail trade, at least in urban areas, is controlled by foreign-owned enterprises. The expanding tourism sector is almost entirely in the hands of expatriates. Further, the country relies heavily for expertise on foreign professional and technical manpower.

The government's main concern since the attainment of political independence is to break the hegemony of South African in terms of attaining economic independence through its industrialization strategy. For this purpose the government has created some important institutions, both financial and corporate. Such institutions and instruments are deemed necessary for the more effective guidance and control of the economy.

The National Industrial Development Corporation (NIDC) was formed in 1971 'as an autonomous statutory body to promote and assist private investment in industrial, commercial, agricultural and mining enterprises in Swaziland'. Shares in the Corporation are held by the government and by various private shareholders such as the Barclays and Standard Banks. In general policy terms, the 'Corporation's primary emphasis is on the development of Swaziland's industrial sector, and it is directing its efforts particularly towards the establishment of industries which will take the greatest advantage of Swaziland's natural resources and growing supply of labour'.

The main criteria for the promotion and assistance of any private enterprise are that the projects concerned have employment effects and linkage effects, use local raw materials, generate revenue for the government, and contribute to either import substitution or export promotion. The government also expects the NIDC, as its instrument of development strategy, to cover its operating costs and make profits. All surpluses from the Corporation are retained and reinvested.

In pursuit of its indigenization policy the government of Swaziland participates through the NIDC in major enterprises; however, 'without impairing their commercial viabilities'. The government's policy in this respect categorically states: 'The policy seeks to establish a more balanced relationship between foreign and domestic ownership and control of modern enterprises through the creation of mutually advantageous working partnership with foreign capital.' Thus the government's direct participation in certain major enterprises is on the basis of minority shareholding. The NIDC also maintains just 50 per cent interest in the major private wholesale and minority interests in several other commercial and manufacturing enterprises.

Within this general framework of industrial strategy, the incentive system for prospective foreign private investors is very attractive indeed. The incentives include: tax holidays for companies not in mining activities; a low rate of 33.3 per cent on taxable income; no tax on capital gains; a total allowance on capital investment of 130 per cent for manufacturers (consisting of normal depreciation allowances and special investment allowance of 30 per cent of the cost of new or unused machinery, plant and factory buildings); and additional allowances of

100 per cent of capital investments which are claimable over specified periods in respect of certain employees' housing and hotel buildings or improvement to existing hotels.

Obviously, these incentives are tempting to prospective investors (and as a matter of fact, have been very effective in enticing them to invest in Swaziland), but they militate against the objectives of promoting 'a greater measure of independent control over the economic affairs of the nation'. With the influx of foreign private capital into the economy a situation emerges that aggravates the already inherited external dependence of the economy on foreign capital, expertise and technology, which in turn jeopardizes the whole exercise of indigenizing ownership, control and management structures as well as the technological content and the financial source of the economy.

To mitigate this unhealthy development, the Small Enterprise Development Company (SEDCO) was formed to promote enterprises that are mainly owned by Swazis. SEDCO's programme is based on providing factory shells, workshops and technical knowledge to small Swazi entrepreneurs on industrial estates located throughout the country. These estates are owned and administered by SEDCO, which provides assistance by advancing equipment and materials on a rental basis. For this purpose, it operates joint-procurement and joint-marketing services.

SEDCO's enterprises include pottery, handicrafts, garments, leatherwork, light metalwork, woodwork and fall-oil manufacturing. The Company's capital subscription falls under three categories:

1 24 per cent government;
2 24 per cent Swazi Credit and Savings Bank;
3 52 per cent private investors, commercial banks.

The programmes of SEDCO are presently too rudimentary and too low-level effectively to correct some of the indigenization difficulties emanating from the externally oriented large- and medium-scale activities of the National Industrial Development Corporation. The Company, however, can be a necessary and effective instrument 'to promote a greater degree of participation of the Swazi people in the development of the economy' and 'to promote a greater measure of independent control over the economic affairs of the Nation'.

An issue of great concern to the government of Swaziland since independence has been the lack of local financial institutions and instruments, and of legislative framework necessary for the mobilization and channelling of domestic resources for development. Until their local incorporation in early 1974 Barclays and Standard Banks had extremely close links with related banks overseas and especially in South Africa.

This resulted mostly in an outflow of investment funds from the Swazi economy, which naturally influenced the potential level of domestic investment at any one time.

In recent years the government has taken fundamental steps to effect significant changes in the institutional organization of the monetary and financial structure of the Swazi economy in order to increase its power. Essentially, all the steps taken so far are in the line of breaking the hegemony of South Africa and other external influences.

By the Swazi Development and Savings Bank order of 1973, the SDSB was established, among other things to (1) mobilize domestic savings and resources for development purposes, (2) establish or promote agricultural and rural industries, and (3) train Swazi citizens to enable them to play a full role in the economy.

With the local incorporation of Barclays and Standard Banks in 1974, the government acquired a 40 per cent share and also the responsibility to appoint the chairman of the board of directors of these banks.

The Swazi Royal Insurance Corporation was formed in 1974 as a monopoly to take over the services previously offered by various South African insurance companies which invested virtually all their funds in South Africa. The government has a 51 per cent share and the rest is owned by Munich Reinsurance, Swiss Reinsurance, Commercial Union of South Africa, and Eagle and General. The government appoints six of the Corporation's directors with the other partners appointing four. The Corporation has been effective in reducing the drain of Swazi savings into the South African banking system.

The creation of the National Provident Fund in 1975 gave the government an additional financial instrument to direct funds collected for pensions, etc. into investment ventures for development purposes. While increasing the volume of savings available to finance government spending, the National Provident Fund clearly reduces the availability of scarce resources for other purposes, particularly consumption. It is to be noted that some part of such savings have been channeled to South African financial and monetary institutions in the past.

On the monetary and financial scene again, the most ambitious scheme for increasing the local control of financial and monetary flows relates to the creation of the Monetary Authority of Swaziland (MAS) and the issue of a national currency in 1974 under the Financial Institutions Order no. 19 of 1973. The main aims of the MAS are: (1) to obtain compensation for the loss of interest on South African money circulating in Swaziland; (2) to issue money; and (3) to co-ordinate and control the operations of the financial institutions and intermediaries in Swaziland. In respect of compensation and issue of money, MAS deposits one rand with the South African Reserve Bank for every *lilangeni* (the national unit of currency is the *emalangeni*, which consists of 100 *lilangeni*) issued. The reserves with the SARB earn 7¼ per cent interest.

It is to be noted that the tripartite monetary agreement with South Africa and Lesotho in March 1974 severely limits the fiduciary powers of the MAS and thus ensures continued dependence on the South African financial system. This has led to the conclusion that Swaziland has the worst of both worlds: she has the expenses of her own monetary authority, but without the freedom to operate the currency as her domestic circumstances dictate. This is certainly a rather hard indictment. The point is that, through the operations of the Monetary Authority, the government has been able to foster the development of a money and capital market (however embryonic) and, in particular, to increase the use of government debt investments. This, in turn, has enhanced greater efficiency on the flow of resources from surplus to deficit units and hence has reduced the extent to which surplus funds are held idle.

Finally, with regard to manpower and technology, the government of Swaziland has been concerned to pursue a progressive localization of professional, managerial and technical posts at a pace consistent with efficiency. To expedite progress in this field the government has established a Training and Localization Council, whose membership consists of representatives from the public and private sectors. The Council is responsible, in consultation with the private sector, for working out appropriate training and localization schemes for individual sectors of the economy.

However, the general framework for localization and training programmes remains the responsibility of the Department of Establishment and Training which is advised by the Training and Localization Council. The Department is also advised by the Scholarship Selection Board, which is responsible for the selection of suitable candidates for studies in Swaziland and abroad.

The localization policy of the government is clearly set out in the second national development plan as: (1) to achieve complete localization in public and private sectors by the end of 1980; and (2) to set up an administrative structure that enables detailed training and localization programmes for both private and public sectors to be planned and implemented effectively.

In addition to creating the necessary administrative structure, the government has taken effective measures to gain control over the educational and training systems in the country, which to a great extent have been in the hands of religious missions. This step has been taken as a result of the emerging problem of unemployed youth. Thus, the accelerated educational and training programmes call for a proper and effective manpower planning mechanism since in the absence of such a mechanism such programmes would lead to a perverse pattern of development.

As a matter of fact, an indication of a perverse pattern of development is the emerging problem of the drain of skilled and semi-skilled manpower. In its recent report the ILO (1977) Jobs and Skills Programme for Africa (JASPA) Employment Advisory Mission states:

> An examination of the contracts of employees in South Africa, certified by the Labour Office in Mbabane, shows that during the first three months of 1976, a number of skilled and semi-skilled workers were allowed to go to South Africa to work. These include drivers, clerks, carpenters, mechanical fitters, operators of various types of machines, welders, fitters, handymen, builders, quality-control persons, foremen, etc.

Even though this drain has not yet assumed any great dimension, it must be viewed as disturbing. There is an urgent need for an effective manpower planning mechanism to forestall such a development. It is not enough to have accelerated educational and training programmes without matching them to the nation's development activities. The consequence will again be the increase of dependence of the country's middle-level technicians and manual skilled and semi-skilled labour on employment opportunities in the Republic of South Africa. In addition to the loss of such manpower, the country will be subsidizing the South African economy in the form of human capital.

The government has made some progress in the localization of the public sector. With the exception of specialist technical posts, it has made great progress in localizing the civil service. Progress in the private sector has however been very insignificant. Thus, according to the already quoted JASPA Report (ILO 1977),

> despite attempts at localization for the last several years, about 36 per cent of professional and technical, 58 per cent of administrative and managerial, 15 per cent of clerical, and 42 per cent of skilled jobs in the private sector in 1974 were still held by Non-Swazis. In the public sector, too, about 25 per cent of professional, technical and administrative jobs were held by expatriates in 1974.

The slow progress in the localization drive is the result of complex factors. On one hand, there is an acute shortage of qualified and experienced Swazis to occupy the commanding heights of the educational and training systems that should train the required manpower. On the other hand, the needs of the expanding Swazi economy for skilled labour are beyond the capacity of the existing educational and training facilities in the country. In addition, the nature and workings of the country's institutional control mechanisms allow some private enterprises room to frustrate the declared localization objectives and efforts of the government.

One can only repeat the advice given in March 1967 to the Swazi government by Dr Robert Gardner, then executive secretary of UN Economic Commission for Africa on the issue of localization. Dr Gardner (1967) said: 'I would like to plead with the Government and people of Swaziland to make sure that they do not sacrifice the substance of independence for the form or appearance of independence'.

Concluding remarks

It has definitely not been possible, within the compass of this brief study, to examine all of the multi-faceted aspects of the relationships within the southern African economy and the implications of such relationships for the development of the BLS countries. What I have attempted to demonstrate had a very modest aim. It has been shown that in economic terms the BLS are overshadowed by, and dependent on, South Africa to the extent that their exercise of options in connection with labour flows, capital flows, fiscal and monetary policies becomes very crucial.

The study has shown that the structural distortions and the concomitant external orientation, and thus the dependence, of the economies of the BLS are reflections of the heavy hand of colonial exploitation. Colonialism is really pervasive! Paradoxically, the BLS countries seem to rely on both private and public foreign investment as the vital prerequisites for achieving the aspired objective of economic independence, in the definition of R. H. Green (1973),

> as a situation in which national institutions (including private business and interest groups) have the right, capacity and power to take and to implement decisions affecting the national economy and its component units without a *de jure* or *de facto* veto power being held by foreign individuals, enterprises, interest groups or governments.

Admittedly, the BLS have in recent years initiated several institutional changes and innovations which have had profound implications for their external relationships, particularly in respect of their position within the southern African economy. It appears, however, at least on a cursory observation, that there is some desire, unconsciously or consciously, on the part of the BLS countries to become integrated into the world system of unequal exchange.

In this context the basic problem of the BLS countries is that common to all 'conditioned' economies, namely the general issues of development strategy, objectives and policy. Our analysis has underlined the fact that the BLS countries are overtly pursuing a development strategy in which foreign investments have been allocated a critical position. There is the sad indication that these countries are acting upon the false notion of 'a non-political investment'. The fact is, by its nature, 'capital' (commercial, industrial and finance) is nationalistic.

Thus it follows from the nature of foreign investment, which all the BLS countries are actively soliciting, that it leads to 'an increasing concentration of decision-making of the central organisation' (Sanjaya Lall 1976). Besides, foreign investment has its own priorities, and hence enters specific industries to take the advantages of specialization. As Lall says, 'it thrives in oligopolistic industries'. The idea of transcending its frontiers and forming the various operational units into a united nation is the motivating force of capital. All these salient features of foreign investment tend to militate against the development priorities of a dependent economy.

It may be very useful to recall what President Julius K. Nyerere (1968) of Tanzania wrote about a decade ago:

> Ideological differences between countries affect the method, not necessarily the fact, of securing national control. The real ideological choice is between controlling the economy through domestic private enterprise, or doing so through some state or collective mechanism. But . . . it is extremely doubtful whether it is a practical choice for an African nationalist. The progmatist in Africa . . . will find that the choice is between foreign private ownership on the one hand and local collective ownership on the other. . . . A capitalistic economy means a foreign dominated economy. The only way in which national control of the economy can be achieved is through the economic institutions of socialism.

From the days of 'trade as engine of growth' through the strategy of 'export promotion cum import substitution' to the current strategy of 'integrated rural development', the dependent economy has always been made to maintain its dependence status in the games nations play. Nothing has changed radically with the dependent economy's conditioned stance of being a reactor rather than an actor. In all the strategies that have been offered so far, the dependent economy has been put in the strange position of having to rely on foreign capital, technology and expertise as a means of breaking out of dependence.

The structural effects of the embryonic indigenization programmes of the BLS countries have so far done little to transform their dependence position within the southern African economy. The degree of self-reliance achieved is rather offset by new relations of dependence, especially dependence on foreign capital, technology and expertise. There has been some progress made in respect of financial and monetary institutions, particularly in Botswana and Swaziland. Indeed, all BLS countries have gone a long way to mobilize internal resources for development.

In view of the variety of factors that determine the development process, it is of paramount importance to establish an efficient mechanism to control and co-ordinate these factors in order to achieve certain pre-conceived objectives over time. As far as possible, such a control and co-ordinating mechanism must not only encompass all the sectors of the economy, but must also, most importantly, have realistic objectives. Because of the inherent bias of marked forces, and, indeed, in view of the existing unintegrated markets of the BLS countries, there is an urgent need for a dynamic planning machinery that should perform the basic function of controlling and co-ordinating the development process.

In this context the planning machinery should transcend the hotch-potch pre-independence approaches as well as the investment-soliciting catalogue plans of recent years. The basic problem emanating from the policies in the BLS countries is that they have tended to satisfy the needs of the world markets without internalizing the dynamics of socio-economic transformation. The caution is for them 'to make sure that they do not sacrifice the substance of independence for the form or appearance of independence' (Gardner, 1967).

References

Aboyade, O. (1965), 'A note on external trade, capital distortion and planned development' in I. G. Steward and H. W. Ord (eds.), *African Primary Products and International Trade* (Edinburgh: University Press)

Baffoe, F. (1975), 'Lesotho and the Republic of South Africa: an economic relationship of partnership or paternalism?', paper read at UN/IDEP Conference on the Economic, Social and Political Problems of Southern Africa, Dar es Salaam, December 1975

Baffoe, F. (1976), 'Indigenization of finance: problems and prospects of mobilizing and directing domestic surpluses for rural development', in AAPAM Seminar Publication on the Prospects and Problems of the Indigenization of the Private Sector of African Economies, published by the Government of Lesotho, Maseru

Baffoe, F. (1977), *Population, Manpower and Employment in Southern Africa with Special Reference to Botswana, Lesotho and Swaziland*, (Geneva, International Education Materials Exchange (IEME 318)).

Baffoe, F. (forthcoming), 'Realities of landlocked and least developed countries in Africa: the Lesotho experience', Council for the Development of Economic and Social Research in Africa

Baran, P. A. (1962), *The Political Economy of Growth* (New York: Monthly Review Press)

Blaug, M. (1961), 'Economic Imperialism Revisited', *Yale Review*, vol. 50 (March 1961)

Cohen, B. J. (1973), *The Question of Imperialism: The Political Economy of Dominance and Dependence* (New York: Basic Books)

Demas, W. G. (1965), *The Economics of Development in Small Countries* (Montreal: McGill University Press)

Dos Santos, T. (1973), 'The crisis of development theory and the problem of dependence in Latin America', in H. Bernstein (ed.), *Underdevelopment and Development* (Harmondsworth: Penguin)

Fair, T. J. D. *et al.* (1969), *Development in Swaziland – A Regional Analysis* (Johannesburg: Witwatersrand University Press)

Frank, A. G. (1969), *Capitalism and Underdevelopment in Latin America* (New York: Monthly Review Press)

Friedman, J. (1972), 'A general theory of polarized development', in Nils H. Hansen (ed.), *Growth Centres in Regional Economic Development* (New York: Free Press)

Gardner, R. K. A. (1967), 'From colonial grievances to a national challenge, address given at the Seminar on National Objectives at Independence held at Swaziland Agricultural College and University Centre Luyengo, March 1967

Ghai, D. P. (ed.) (1973), *Economic Independence in Africa* (Nairobi/Kampala/Dar es Salaam: East African Literature Bureau)

Green, R. H. (1973), 'Economic independence and economic co-operation', in D. P. Chai (ed.), *Economic Independence in Africa* (Nairobi/Kampala/Dar es Salaam: East African Literature Bureau)

Gurr, Roger (ed.) (1977), *Transnational Corporations and Developing Countries: Proceedings of a Conference Organized by the Lesotho National Development Corporation on behalf of the government of Lesotho* (Maseru)

ILO–JASPA (1977), *Reducing Dependence – A Strategy for Productive Employment and Development in Swaziland*, report to the Government of Swaziland by Jobs and Skills Programme for Africa (JASPA) (Addis Ababa: ILO)

Lall, S. (1976), *Development Countries and Multinational Corporations – Effects on Host Countries' Welfare and the Role of Government Policy*, Commonwealth Economic Paper no. 5, (London: HMSO)

Leistner, G. M. E. and Smit, P. (1969), *Swaziland – Resources and Development*, Communications of the Africa Institute no. 8 (Pretoria)

Maasdorp, G. (1973), *Small Enterprises for Small Countries: The Case of*

Swaziland Southern Africa Technology Development Group, Occasional Paper no. 2

Myrdal, G. (1957), *Economic Theory and Underdevelped Regions* (London: Duckworth)

Nyerere, J. K. (1968), 'Economic Nationalism' *in Uhuru na Ujamaa* (Dar es Salaam: Oxford University Press)

Selwyn, P. (1975), *Industries in the Southern Africa Periphery* (London: Croom Helm in association with the IDS, Sussex)

Singer, H. W. (1970), 'Dualism revisited: a new approach to the problems of dual society in developing countries', *Journal of Development Studies*, vol. 7, no. 1

Smit, P. (1970), *Botswana: Resources and Development* (Pretoria: Africa Institute)

Stahl, C. (1975), 'A commercial strategy in the labour export market with reference to BLS', *Botswana Notes and Records*, vol. 7

UN–IMF (1973), *Survey of African Economies*, vol. 5 (Washington: UN–IMF)

Winai-Strom, G., (1972), 'The influence of MNCs on Lesotho's politics and economics', *African Review*, vol. 5, no. 4 (1972), pp. 473–98

Government publications

Botswana

National Development Plan 1973–78, part 1
National Development Plan 1976–81
BDC, *Business Investment in Botswana – A Brief Guide*, Gaborone 1975
Employment Survey (various issues)

Lesotho

First Five-Year Development Plan 1970/71–1974/75
Second Five Year Development Plan 1975/6–1979/80
LNDC, *Investment Guides* (1976)

Swaziland

Post-Independence Development Plan 1969/70–1973/74
Second Five Year Development Plan 1973/74–1977/78
MAS, *Annual Reports*, 1975/76 and 1976/77
NIDC, *General Policies and Forms of Investment Assistance* (n.d.)

12 Senegal

1 The development of the Senegalese business bourgeoisie

Samir Amin, *Director, African Institute for Economic Development and Planning, Dakar*

The purpose of this contribution is to outline the stages of the constitution and development of the Senegalese business bourgeoisie. This is a bourgeoisie whose history can be followed over a particularly long period for tropical Africa – more than a century, which is exceptional for that continent. This history, moreover, shows us that the French colonial authorities did not always adopt the same attitude towards the new local bourgeoisie that were engendered by the colony's integration into the world capitalist market.

Up to the beginning of this century, the public authorities and colonial trading firms promoted the development of Senegalese traders who, before the Mourid religious brotherhood, had introduced and developed groundnut growing in the rural areas of their country. From 1900 on, the colonial authority proceeded to eliminate this initial peripheral bourgeoisie for the direct benefit of the colonial firms or of new subordinate agents of these firms, Lebanese and *petits blancs*. Since 1955, and above all since Senegal's independence, there has been a very pronounced revival of a local business world: we shall briefly describe the stages of its growth before tackling the problem of the lessons to be learned from this history – primarily the characteristics and prospects of a Third World bourgeoisie, the emergence and development of which are superimposed on to the integration of its country in the international market: in other words, a peripheral bourgeoisie.[1]

The rise of the Senegalese bourgeoisie (1820–1900)

Senegal has a very old history of colonization. The French settlements in Saint Louis and Gorée date back to the first half of the seventeenth century. Until 1816 the trading posts lived mainly on the slave trade, and very secondarily on that of gum. These trades had been monopolies of the various companies of Senegal and of India from 1664 to 1763, and then, after a short period of British occupation from 1763 to 1770, had become 'free', direct royal administration having been established in 1770.

After the restoration of the French monarchy, with freedom of trade, a local commercial capitalism developed side by side with the installation of Frenchmen from Bordeaux. It was between 1815 and 1860 that the great families of Saint Louis and Gorée, whose ancestors were often soldiers or commercial agents of the former companies, asserted themselves. This was the high period of the development of the gum trade, which in turn led to the constitution of a first generation of Saint Louisien contractors who settled in the Senegal River ports (Dagana, Podor, Matam, Bakel, Medine) or operated with canoes. Apart from gum, Saint Louis exported gold, which the *signare*[2] women of the city – during the Restoration and the July Monarchy – fetched from the Bambouk.[3] But a fall in the price of gold following the discovery of the deposits of America, Australia and South Africa began in 1870.

The conquest of the hinterland of Senegal took place about thirty years before that of the continent as a whole. The Senegalese bourgeoisie of Saint Louis played a major role in the development of this first colonial territory. It provided the swarms of contractors in the first French trading posts of the coast down to Gabon, and gave Senegal the first generation of groundnut dealers.

As early as the Faidherbe period (1854–61, 1863–5), we have to distinguish between the traders and dealers settled in Saint Louis and Gorée and the contractors of the trading posts of the Fleuve region and the coast. They were still nearly all Senegalese, some of mixed blood, originating from Saint Louis and Gorée. The large-scale trade was in the hands of nine firms. They exported gum and imported all kinds of goods; they supplied the retailers of the town, the contractors and the trading posts. Some of the firms were from Bordeaux or were linked with these first by alliance or partnership. But others – with the same names – gradually loosened their links with the metropolitan country. Coming after this first group were about twenty smaller traders, retailers and import–export merchants. There was also in Saint Louis a bourgeoisie of prominent *métis* families which did some trading; in different generations they were found sometimes in liberal professions, sometimes as traders or politicians. There were the same type of families in Gorée and later in Rufisque and in the Sine. The main branches of the great *métis* families of Saint Louis never left Saint Louis, where they ran trading posts on the Senegal River and on the coast, and later in the hinterland. The Saint Louis contractors were mostly black Senegalese or descendants of secondary branches of the *métis* families.

At the beginning of the second half of the century, there were, apart from Saint Louis and Gorée, about 250 contractors: 150 in the Senegal River region, about 60 on the Petite Côte and in the river ports of the South, and about 50 in trading posts outside present-day Senegal. They were all from Saint Louis and Gorée: two-thirds were black and one-third *métis*, all of the latter having lost their ties with France. Some of these gum contractors on the Senegal River were already major dealers. This type of trade was to continue and extend its scope between 1870 and 1900. Around 1870 there were nearly 200 major Senegalese traders, including about 100 in the Fleuve gum trade.

The building of the railway from Saint Louis to Dakar and the conquest of the Cayor very early on opened up the hinterland for groundnuts: the average annual output rose from 21,000 metric tons between 1870 and 1874 to 86,000 tons at the end of the century (1910–14). The new trade – at least until 1900 – was the almost exclusive preserve of Senegalese settled along the railway and in the Cape Verde. The conquest of the hinterland of Saloum and Casamance was followed by new settlements of Saint Louisiens. But in those regions Senegalese trading was still secondary; the great expansion of groundnut growing there was to come later. The conquest of the Western Sudan made Médine and Keyes the centres of large-scale trade, both of the gum trade and of transit trade to Bamako and beyond.

Around 1900 there were nearly 850 licensed traders in Senegal: over 100 in the regions served by the Dakar–Saint Louis railway, about 150 in Dakar and Rufisque, more than 200 in the Thies region, more than 150 on the Petite Côte, in the Sine, the Saloum and Lower Casamance. Of these at least 500 were Senegalese: more than 100 in Saint Louis and on the Senegal River, about 60 in the Cayor, about 100 in Cape Verde, nearly 200 in the regions of Thiers, Kaolack and Sine.

This first generation of Senegalese traders was made up of men who varied greatly in culture and education. There were many French-oriented *métis* who were relatively well educated. But there were also men with a more traditional background, having received a good Koranic culture with the Mauritanian *marabouts* in whose care it was customary to place the boys of the great families since the islamization of the Fleuve, Cayor and Djolof regions. But even these had concurrently received a sound French education. The two groups were distinct: they only married within their group because of religion. The Senegalese in the Fleuve region traded in gum, and those in the Cayor, in groundnuts. But they did not import or export: it was Bordeaux firms that supplied them and that exported the commodities. They had relatively large material resources: although only the large Bordeaux firms had river cargo boats, the contractors had fleets of decked canoes.

For the groundnut trade, they hired the services of caravan carriers who transported the groundnuts on donkeys and camels up to the trading point on the railway line. However, a few Senegalese did some direct importing. In the Guinea trading posts the Senegalese traded in palm kernels. On the Senegal River they also traded in millet for the supply of Saint Louis. In Médine, as well as the gum trade, they supplied the traditional Malinke-Dioula traders, who then took over and went as far as Mopti, Kankan, Kong and beyond. The Dioula constituted – as they still do today – a very different world, which remained traditional. They brought gold from Siguiri and Bambouk, and cloth from Mopti, taking back imported goods. But they did not supply Senegal with kola which, at that time and up to around 1920, came by sea from Sierra Leone. The Akou of Sierra Leone, who carried on that trade, were indeed supplanted by the Lebanese before the Malinké-Dioula took it over. The volume of business of course varied, but was sometimes quite considerable. It was Senegalese traders who were the first vehicles of development of the groundnut economy, being relayed later by the Mourids.

The decline of Senegalese trade (1900–55)

Until about 1900, the policy of the colonial administration had been favourable to Senegalese trade. Faidherbe had only limited military resources, and the conquest of the African hinterland was not yet finished. On the political plane, protectorates over the African kingdoms were still the only formula envisaged. The French colonial empire was not yet completely constituted, and was confined to the West Indies, Algeria and the establishments of Senegal and the Far East; and a policy of partial assimilation and a settlement type of colonization seemed feasible. In that context, the Saint Louisiens and Goréens, rather like the West Indians, provided the assimilated cadres for the future colonization of the hinterland. So Faidherbe wished to promote the constitution of an assimilated merchant bourgeoisie; he envisaged a policy of racial intermingling and had forbidden the Europeans to go themselves to trade in the Fleuve region.

But around 1900 things began to change; the 'colonial party' was constituted; the French firms went to establish themselves directly in the conquered territories which were under direct administration; the protectorate treaties were denounced one after another; the Senegalese bourgeoisie was systematically destroyed, and the dream of assimilation went up in smoke. Senegal was no longer to be privileged, like the West Indies; it was to be treated like the other African colonies.

Thus, as from 1900 the trading bourgeoisie underwent a series of assaults, which reduced it by the eve of the Second World War to a very subordinate role. First came the gum crash at the beginning of the century; and then, even before 1914, the establishment of trading posts of the big colonial firms – from Bordeaux and Marseilles – in the hinterland of the country; next, from 1920, came the avalanche of *petits blancs* and Lebanese; and lastly came the Depression of the 1930s. Hence, when Senegalese private enterprise revived, first timidly during the war and in the ten years after it, and then more forcefully after 1958, it did not start from zero. The consequence was a much more intense development than elsewhere in French-specking tropical Africa.

At the end of the century, Senegalese commerce had suffered a first blow. The revolt of the Mahdi in Sudan had suddenly deprived Europe of Kordofan gum. From 1885 onwards, the price of Senegalese gum rose, from 1 franc to 2, and then to 3.50 francs a kilo. This was the great period of prosperity: increasing numbers of Senegalese contractors were established; they built houses in Saint Louis and became accustomed to a comfortable life-style. But in 1898, with the re-conquest of the Sudan by Kitchener's Anglo-Egyptian armies, Kordofan gum reappeared. The prices collapsed, and a large number of contractors were unable to adjust to the crisis. It was at that time – around 1900 – that a number of Bordelais and *métis* turned to groundnuts, often moving to the Cayor, or even going to the new regions of the Saloum. In any case the gum trade, as Paul Holle had predicted, no longer sufficed for Saint Louis, whose population had greatly increased, to make a living.

Having barely recovered from the gum crash, the Senegalese contractors had, after 1900, to face the direct competition of the French trading posts. The output of groundnuts was already sufficient to enable the trade to sustain European trading posts in the hinterland. Pacification was complete; the hour of the 'colonial party' had come.

The contest between the French trading posts and the Senegalese traders was very acute from 1900 to 1920. The veterans of the time still remember that the decision to liquidate Senegalese commerce was a political one; for suddenly the import firms decided to sell in all their depots at the same price, whatever their geographical location, thus establishing a price equalization – and they decided to supply the Senegalese contractors at the same prices. The latter, having no direct access to importing, were then systematically placed in a position of inferiority. They tried to defend themselves by seeking to establish direct relations with suppliers in France or elsewhere, particularly in Great Britain. They failed, partly because of lack of financial resources (bank credit was refused them), but also because the administration and the colonial firms took advantage of their authority to hamper them in these attempts. Some of them managed to subsist for about twenty years, but they finally lost their independence around 1925. They were then offered the opportunity of serving as employees in the colonial trading firms. Many did so; but, aware that the future of Senegalese trade was henceforth blocked, they encouraged their sons to enter the civil service. It is from that period that the civil service began to attract young Senegalese men. This is evidence not of a lack of capacity for risk-taking among the Senegalese, as is often claimed on the basis of superficial observation, but simply of an awareness that economic responsibility was henceforth going to be assumed more and more directly and completely by foreigners.

Around 1920, the number of independent licensed traders greatly diminished, following the establishment of the depots of the large companies. There were no longer more than about 450, including nearly 200 in Dakar and Rufisque, nearly 100 in Saint Louis and the Fleuve region, about 80 in the old groundnut zone of the Cayor and the Diambour and the same number in the new region of Saloum and Baol. But there were now only about 100 Senegalese among them, of which half were in Dakar and Saint Louis. And there were already about thirty Lebanese settled in Dakar and Kaolack.

The inflow of Lebanese speeded up after the First World War, facilitated by the French Mandate in the Levant. From fewer than 100 in 1900, including families, and 500 in 1914, there were more than 2000 of then in 1930 and nearly 4000 on the eve of the Second World War. A new hierarchical structure began to be organized between the Lebanese and the big colonial companies.

How did the triumph of the Lebanese over their Senegalese predecessors come about? First, because the Lebanese cost less to the colonial companies. The Senegalese trader was already relatively well off; he had a family to provide for; so he could not accept being reduced by the colonial firms to a subordinate role, or to live on a slender margin. The Lebanese, who had come without his family – it was only after the Second World War that the structure of this population changed – accepted all the situations, at least at the start, Second, the colonial firms decided to support them against a Senegalese bourgeoisie, perhaps because it was felt that the latter might have some political aspirations. It has often been said that the African contractors did not allow any credit to the peasants, as the Lebanese were able to do; that the African contractors merely bartered, that they did not know how to 'handle money', whereas the Lebanese had developed an economy based on money. This is to forget that one is comparing two different periods: it is a fact that before 1914 the peasant, even if he grew groundnuts, was as yet ignorant of money – he wanted goods immediately; after 1920, he began to get accustomed to money, the type of trading evolved, and credit – alas! – became possible. During the same period there was an influx of *petits blancs* from poor French *départments*, particularly Ariege, after demobilization. The 'millet-eaters' were as numerous as the Lebanese; and the administration and the colonial companies helped them to obtain positions so far held by Senegalese.

The 1930 Depression finally eliminated the positions of the last Senegalese traders, who were the first victims to be sacrificed by the system. There are many examples of ruin and bankruptcy at this time. Indeed, the crisis of the 1930s was very difficult: the groundnut exports fell in 1932 to 135,000 tons. Yet the groundnut marketing apparatus had been set up with quite different prospects: in the 1920s, continuing their advance prior to 1914, the colonial firms had settled in the smallest sales points, and this gave rise to the expansion of the road network and the use of lorries. At the beginning of the Depression, the French firms tried to survive by competing with their own customers, the Lebanese retailers. They subsequently abandoned this strategy and withdrew to the main centres, leaving the Lebanese, whose costs were much lower, to manage the minor depots. The necessary reduction of trade margins made an economist of the time, Pierre Barris, already envisage the need to rationalize the groundnut trade, which could no longer be profitable.[4] The Senegalese contractors, the first victims of the rationalization process, were at that time reduced to the subordinate role of groundnut collectors on behalf of the Lebanese and the colonial firms; as the first middlemen, they were in direct contact with the peasantry. Many of them were then reduced to an inferior social status, becoming 'village nobilities' who were to be found thirty years later in the co-operatives of independent Senegal, mainly as weighers or accountants. The luckier ones were again employed by the colonial firms when the latter replaced European personnel in order to reduce the management costs of their depots.

The destitution of the Senegalese traders after 1930, the mediocrity of their social status, income and responsibility – which continued until independence – were to make people forget the previous existence of a large-scale Senegalese trade. In fact, after the war there was no recovery of Senegalese trade until 1958. Between 1945 and 1953 the number of Lebanese doubled, rising from 4000 to 8000. It was they and the *petits blancs*, who had got rich during the war, who were the only ones to benefit from the period of shortage of the first postwar years. This was the time when the most substantial of them freed themselves from the tutelage of the colonial firms and obtained access to direct importation. When they become rich, the Lebanese abandoned certain operations such as the kola trade, which they had grabbed from the Akou after 1914, importing the product henceforth from Ivory Coast. It was the

Malinké traders from the hinterland who took over this heritage during and after the war. After the long stagnation of the period between the wars, the groundnut economy started to expand again: the output, which between 1920 and 1940 had been an annual average of 430,000 tons, rose towards the end of colonization, during 1955–9, to an annual average of 680,000 tons. But all the efforts at 'Senegalization' of economic responsibilities attempted in this period failed, and the Senegalese were still driven inexorably towards the civil service and real estate speculation.

All the difficulties they encountered made the Senegalese lose all business acumen. After the First World War the people of Saint Louis encouraged their children to enter the civil service and politics. In this connection the *métis* frequently benefited from their cultural lead. A new type of business man emerged – indeed, more of a public and political figure than a business man; more of a 'business dealer' than a trader. Since ordinary commercial business was no longer lucrative, being reserved for Europeans and Lebanese, these men became successively commercial agents, traders on own account, or politicians, depending on circumstances. Conditions like this are not conducive to the consolidation of wealth, or to habits of stability. The Senegalese traders of this period were looking for the 'miraculous big deal' rather than for regular business; under the pressure of the terms under which they had to operate, they did not invest in their business, did not build permanent-material shops, and lost the habit of managing business matters properly.

Revival and vicissitudes of Senegalese commerce (1955–70)

During the last two decades there has been a revival of Senegalese commerce unequalled in the other countries of tropical Africa that emerged from French colonization. Until then, the colonial trade had occupied the stage almost exclusively. Owning import offices, wholesale stores and networks of retail depots, these companies operated the classic colonial trade system, the monopoly of which it shared with the Lebanese. The creation in 1960 of the Office Commercialization des Arachides (Groundnut Marketing Board) and the concurrent setting up of co-operatives put paid to this traditional formula of colonial commerce. In the prevailing atmosphere of the time, new formulas of association between the colonial companies and the Senegalese private traders were proposed: this was a failure, marked by the disappearance of the 'mixed' enterprises, SOSECOD and then AFRIDEX. Actually, the reviving Senegalese trade did not regard these forms of association as desirable: the best of these traders considered themselves capable of filling by themselves the vacuum that was going to be created by the closing of these old-time depots.

This recent rebirth of national commerce is reflected in the success of the Compagnie Sénégalaise du Sud-Est, a private Senegalese firm whose turnover rose considerably in these years, which had a network of forty-eight stores and access to direct importing and rediscount facilities. The Chaine Africaine d'Importation et de Distribution (CHAIDIS), the Consortium Africain and the commercial activities of certain great *marabouts*, particularly Mourids, were successes evidencing the same phenomenon.

Between these new 'greats' of commerce and the former colonial trade there was often a bitter struggle. While the gradual nationalization of the groundnut trade put an end in 1967 to the activities of the 'stocking agencies' (private traders, usually Senegalese, who acted as middlemen between the rural producers and the marketing board and of whom about ten did a very large volume of trade), on the other hand the government distribution of rice quotas greatly helped not only the major Senegalese firms but also about fifteen large traders and about fifty of the most important of those who had grouped together in 'co-operatives' in the hinterland. Rice, together with a few other major mass consumption products, is the basis on which, during the last few years, the wealth of the new 'commercial district' in Dakar has been built up, where there are now about fifty major Senegalese traders, as well as the wealth of the large-scale general trade of the hinterland (about sixty important individual or associated traders).

Added to this revival of large-scale general Senegalese commerce, now detached from the groundnut trade, there has been in the last few years a rapid expansion of specialized trades. The association in 1964 of about twenty large traders in kola nuts, established under the same name (SIDICO) in Ivory Coast – which produces the nuts – and in Senegal – the principal consumer – is a good example of Africanization of a sector controlled before the war by the Lebanese. Equally spectacular has been the break-through of a dozen wholesale butchers, mostly of Mauritanian origin, who now have the virtual monopoly for supplying the country's slaughterhouses, have organized their collecting network and have eliminated the foreigners, even in such delicate sectors as export, ship victualling, and the supplying of major stores and public bodies. Less spectacular, but no less significant, is the recent break-through of the Dakar wholesale fishmongers, some of whom are now important business men, and that of new traders in fruit and vegetables, who are forward-linked to a world of market gardeners; they are capitalists who, in the Cape Verde region, have grouped nearly 500 'large market gardeners' in a syndicate.

Road transport – largely Africanized since the postwar period – has not experienced a similar development during the last decade. On the contrary, the excessive equipment that characterizes it has considerably reduced the margins on which the operators live, and this in turn has entailed – after the failure of attempts to form co-operatives – a recent movement of concentration to the advantage of the most powerful leaders of about twenty 'groups'. The same difficult situation is a feature of the building sector, although its Africanization is very recent: only about ten firms can survive the devastating competition between a far too large number of entrepreneurs. But here there has not so far been any trace of a serious attempt at concentration.

Private Senegalese capitalism is practically confirmed to these sectors of commerce, transport and building. In the industrial field, only groundnut shelling has given rise to an Africanization movement, and that very recently. The private Senegalese enterprises now process a third of the harvest. In the other sectors of industry, the positions of private Senegalese capital are far more modest. About the only exceptions are a medium-sized printing house and a few small ones, some establishments making metal goods and a lemonade-making enterprise. If we add a cluster of modern service firms (engineering, insurance broking, transit and handling, some hotels and tourist enterprises, chemist shops and private clinics), we will have practically encompassed all the national private capital.

During the last few years, Senegalese business men have become increasingly aware of their group interests. Despite various vicissitudes, these interests are now organized in employers' associations.

The lesson of history

The history of the Senegalese business world is by no means lacking in interest: dating back over more than a century, which is very exceptional in tropical Africa, in one of the countries whose economy was among the earliest and most profoundly integrated into the international market, it enables us to analyse more closely the obstacles that foreign capitalism, which dominates through this international market, sets before the development of a national capitalism, and the non-autonomous but peripheral nature of the latter.

The Senegalese world of commerce had already proved its vulnerability in the past. After having experienced almost half a century of brilliant development it had been totally liquidated by colonization. Its contemporary renewal remains marked by this extreme vulnerability which is reflected in frequent bankruptcies. The lack of credit facilities forces the businessmen to plough back their profits systematically and to immobilize them to the extreme limit, and so places Senegalese enterprise at the mercy of the slightest, even temporary, difficulty, for lack of an autonomous national banking support. On the other hand, the few sectors that did not need to have recourse to the banks – such as the wholesale butchers – were able to develop more rapidly. Here we can detect phenomena of primitive accumulation in the context of an expanding domestic market, which are very different from those of secondary accumulation, grafted onto the international market and which remains limited by the domination of foreign capital. The feeling that this domination is the main obstacle is shared by everyone, and the demand is formulated quite clearly – the hope that a national private bank can help to overcome the most obvious types of dependence is continuously repeated in the 'statements of grievances' of the African business world. There is no other explanation for the ambition to 'import': being forward-linked to dominant foreign capital, national capital feels a very immediate 'need' to have direct access to external relations without going through the old colonial mercantile capital. But this hope, which is everyone's dream, actually means that one's development is conceived within the context of the international market. Hence it is largely an illusory dream, because even if this access to importing may possibly free one from the traditional mercantile colonial capital, it cannot free one from the domination of the large-scale capital of the developed metropolitan centres.

Furthermore, the explosion of the last decade should give us food for thought about its real and deep-seated causes. It was possible only because dominant foreign capital withdrew from certain sectors. Yet it often withdrew only from sectors that had lost their erswhile profitability. This withdrawal was carried out either to the advantage of the state (as regards the groundnut trade – the deterioration of the terms of trade having reduced the margins, only the state could make up for the absence of private capital and 'socialize the losses') or, secondarily, to the advantage of private national capital: this is the case of road transport, of building construction, and (for example in the Congo and Gabon) of forestry. The inequality of the contending forces here reduces the share of national capital, thus ensuring for dominant capital a better profitability in the sectors it retains. It is probable that the appeal for state support, characteristics of a weak bourgeoisie, stems largely from this situation.

Thus the opportunities for accumulation within the reach of the Senegalese bourgeoisie are extremely limited. That is why this bourgeoisie is almost solely commercial. Access to large-scale modern industry is still practically closed to it, even though some of the strongest commercial enterprises are contemplating some small- and medium-scale industrial projects. Their means of accumulation are limited precisely because this is a peripheral bourgeoisie, grafted on to the international market, and because the mechanisms of that market operated in the direction of the centralization of peripheral capital towards the centre. Added to this are the specific conditions of tropical Africa: absence of great landowners like those who, in the Arab East, Asia and Latin America, have provided relatively large amounts of capital by exploiting the rural masses. However, it is not impossible that certain great *marabouts*, Mourids particularly, may in Senegal turn into big modern landowners and thus derive from farming large incomes which they might invest elsewhere. There are some obvious signs of an evolution in this direction.

The means of accumulation also depend, nevertheless, on government policy. The history of Senegal reminds us that in the colonial period the policy of the mother country towards the colonial bourgeoisie was not always the same, just as it reminds us that the decision to liquidate this Senegalese bourgeoisie, which had been the principal agent for establishing the new colonial trade economy in the rural areas and a fundamental political ally, had itself been a largely political decision. Today the government's policy can certainly accelerate or hinder the development of this bourgeoisie.

But to what extent? The study of the Senegalese case continually reminds us that the international market sets very narrow limits to the overall development of the country. It is not therefore a question of an autonomous bourgeoisie around which a self-reliant national capitalism is being organized; but of a peripheral bourgeoisie, just as the economy itself remains entirely peripheral, i.e. continually shaped according to the needs of the international market; oriented in its structures by the domination of the developed capitalist centres; reduced to the function of a changing complement whose 'prosperity' or stagnation never ultimately depends on itself.

If there is no real development other than self-reliant and self-sustained, there is no possible development without breaking out of the straitjacket of the international market; apart from the illusion that sometimes takes shape during periods of 'prosperity' – when the shaping of a dependent structure, which is of interest to the centre at one stage in its development, makes possible a rapid growth, but without development. This co-called development, by an increasingly close integration into the international market, constitutes the continually reappearing hydra. It is accompanied by the necessary theory of development of the bourgeoisie, as a 'necessary stage', in defiance of the most important lesson in history; i.e. that the bourgeoisie that is developing in the periphery on the basis of the unequal international division of labour is incapable of acquiring the mastery of the process of accumulation.

2 The economic situation pre- and post-independence, and the concept of indigenization[5]

Hassatou Diallo, *Programme Assistant, PNUD, Dakar*

On the eve of independence in 1960, Senegal was in an exceptional situation. The existence of an educated élite with administrative experience, the expansion of the groundnut economy and the establishment of a chain of light industries had given the country a distinct economic profile among the countries of Francophone Black Africa.

In order to establish its sovereignty on a more solid basis, the state began to move from the sectoral programming inherited from the colonial area towards an integrated development planning strategy. The first two four-year development plans (1964–8) pledged the government towards:

1 taking stock of its resources and defining the economic and social potentialities of each of the sectors;
2 respecting in each of its interventions a just balance between the 'productive' and the 'social' sectors;
3 directing its actions as much as possible towards reducing the marked regional disparities.

During the period of the third four-year plan (1969–73), a series of structural reforms were undertaken, including: the nationalization of the trading sector as well as certain foreign-owned strategic services; state investment in other dominant enterprises; educational reform and administrative reform; and a decentralization in decision-making that emphasized the participation of local communities. From 1969, a long-term development strategy was also initiated, with the objective of tripling its *per capita* income. In this strategy, Senegal intends to aim wholly at promoting its domestic market, mostly African, by reducing the foreign dependence of the economy without at the same time leading the country to autarchy.

Indigenization policy after independence

Immediately after independence, several measures were taken by the government to promote the integration of Senegalese businessmen into various sectors of the economy.

First, there was the establishment of village co-operatives with production and marketing functions. These co-operatives, which cover very diverse activities – agriculture, animal husbandry, fishing, forestry, and handicrafts – developed very quickly. In 1961 there were 810 co-operatives covering 100,000 rural producers, while in 1976 there were 2000 co-operative or semi-co-operative bodies, covering 600,000 rural producers. This co-operative system made it possible to transform the major farming structure of the peasants and to start restructuring the intermediary trade. At present, the co-operatives have a monopoly on the marketing of the major crops, namely groundnuts and cotton. Furthermore, co-operative actions have been strengthened by Decree no. 64–46 of 17 June 1964, which states that 'one cannot exercise ownership right on the soil but only usage right'. Previously, 95 per cent of the national territory was claimed by 15 per cent of the entire population. At present, the management and supervision of lands in each region is entrusted to rural councils.

A nationalization policy is, however, being pursued with some caution in Senegal, partly because of a shortage of trained Senegalese administrators. Joint-stock participation was originally favoured by the government, for it was believed that this method offered influence in the operations of the company as well as promoting the practical training of a Senegalese management cadre. No doubt the state has often succeeded in imposing its control on the private sector in the strategic sectors of the economy by this method, but in a number of cases public participation accounts for only small cash inflows to support enterprises in difficulty or to assist the launching of investment projects whose profitability conditions were not totally ensured. The set-backs suffered in this field have led the government over the years to give preference to supporting private investment instead of joint investment. The very significant reduction in credit distribution to joint enterprises between 1964 and 1972 reflects this change in government options (see Table 40).

It was in this context that the new investment code (Decree 72–73 of 12 June 1972) was promulgated in 1972. Its main purpose was to attract sizeable amounts of foreign capital, but special measures were taken for the establishment and extension of small- and medium-scale enterprises

Table 40 *Distribution of medium-term credit in Senegal from government sources*

			(%)		
	1964	*1966*	*1968*	*1970*	*1972*
Credits to joint enterprises	61.3	67.6	60.5	56.2	33.3
Credits to private enterprises	38.3	32.4	39.5	43.8	74.7
Total	100	100	100	100	100

for national entrepreneurs without adequate financial means. These special measures constitute the subject of Decree 72–46 of 12 June 1972, dealing with incentives for the establishment and expansion of small- and medium-scale Senegalese enterprises, in which tax exemption benefits and customs and fiscal privileges are linked with the implementation of a small investment programme, 5 million CFA francs for industrial activities and 3 million for agricultural activities. The state also gives support for technical and industrial research so as progressively to reduce technological dependence, which is a hindrance to development. These measures strengthen the action initiated in 1970 by the Société Nationale d'Etudes et de Promotion Industrielle (SONEPI), whose main objectives are to provide national entrepreneurs in the trading and industrial field with management assistance and guarantees for the banking institutions. Although the investment code aims principally at attracting foreign capital, in selecting projects priority is given to labour-intensive industries. This leads industrialists to make a reassessment of the technologies in order to select those that are most adapted to the needs of Senegal.

The expansion of economic activity activated by government investment saw a corresponding rise in participation by Senegalese manpower at management (and other) levels. In the industrial sector the number of African staff rose from 12,277 in 1962 to 26,503 in 1974, while the number of expatriates (non-African) employees remained practically stable, rising from 1151 in 1962 to only 1267 in 1974. Table 41 demonstrates the extent of Africanization in various sectors.

There were 1708 cadres and Senegalese experts in 1974 as against 467 in 1962, exceeding the number of expatriate cadres, which went up from 883 in 1962 to 1148 in 1974. Out of the 59,194 African workers (including African non-nationals) counted in 1974 in the modern sector,

Table 41 *Composition of Senegalese workforce in selected sectors, 1974*

Sector	*Total no. of employees (including non-nationals*	*No. of Senegalese employed*	*Percentage of total workforce*
Industry	27,769	25,972	93
Building and public works	6,634	6,889	95
Commerce	10,905	9,769	89
Services	16,896	15,808	93
Total	62,204	57,858	93

there were 4907 of them who occupied highly skilled jobs and 54,287 who occupied jobs demanding little or no skill. The highest concentration of skilled jobs are in commerce and the services, whereas industry and building have a higher proportion of less skilled jobs.

Salaries paid to African industrial workers (including social services) went up from 3.37 billion CFA francs in 1962 to 13.14 billion CFA francs in 1974. Nominal wage has therefore nearly doubled for the African industrial workers, whose number went up during this period from 12,000 to 26,000.

State investment participation

State participation by investment in 135 joint stock companies, 4 public establishments and 4 regional development companies points to a significant localization of capital in Senegal. The companies include the two largest enterprises in the country, ONCAD in the commercial sector and C.S. phosphates de Taiba in the mining sector, which together in 1974 realized 72 per cent of the turnover of the public and semi-public sector. In the same year twenty-four joint stock companies (those exceeding a turnover of over 1 billion CFA francs) realized 23 per cent of the turnover of the modern sector, 17.5 per cent of the sectoral share of the GDP, and one-third of the sectoral value-added. These companies engaged 16,407 persons (including 15,898 Senegalese), who account for more than one-quarter of staff employment in this sector.

The state's direct participation has amounted to 21,133 million CFA francs out of the total capital of 45,097 million CFA francs of these 135 joint-stock companies, which is 46 per cent direct participation. To get the exact amount of state participation, the 1970 million CFA franc investment held through public establishments must be added to the first amount. State investment therefore amounted to 23,103 million CFA francs. To that must be added the annual subsidies that the state must give in order to meet the operating deficits of certain companies. These stood at 1.7 billion CFA francs in the 1973/4 financial year and rose to the order of 12 billion CFA francs in the 1975/6 financial year.

The state also participates indirectly in the decisions of the board of directors of companies in which the following institutions have financial interests: Union Senegalaise de Banques (USB), la Banque Nationale de Developpement du Senegal (BNDS), la Société Financière Sénégalaise pour le Developpement de l'Industrie et du Tourisme (SOFISEDIT), la Banque Internationale pour le Commerce et l'Industrie du Senegal (BICIS), la Banque Centrale des Etats de l'Afrique de l'Ouest (BCEAO). It is in this way that the state indirectly controls 12 million CFA francs invested in companies by BNDS and USB, 46 million CFA francs by

Table 42 *Senegalese state participation in joint stock companies, 1972*

Sector	*No. of enterprises*	*Capital of companies*	*Amount of state direct participation*	%	*Participants – public establishment*	%	*Total state participation direct and indirect*	%
Agriculture	6	3878	2127	54	851	21	2978	76
Mining	5	6087	2991	49	0	0	2991	49
Food industry	8	1202	78	6	180	14	258	21
Processing industry	16	4749	570	12	50	0.1	620	13
Banks, financial institutions, insurance	8	7639	3971	51	75	0.1	4046	52
Infrastructure and transport	16	12,574	6680	53	80	0.06	6760	53
Real estate	11	1320	1029	77	13	0.09	1042	78
Tourism	12	4639	2474	53	0	0	2474	53
Miscellaneous	6	1732	438	34	681	39	1119	64
Telecommunication, information, leisure and publicity	11	1277	775	60	40	31	815	63
Total	99	45,097	21,133	46	1970	13	23,103	51

BICIS, and 36 million CFA francs by SOFISEDIT (see Table 42).

The state has a substantial stake (see Table 42) in all sectors except industry. So far the industrial production sector has been characterized by foreign domination of share-holdings and management.

Financing indigenization

Senegalese capitalism, like all emerging capitalisms, needs state protection. Senegalese businessmen solicit this assistance, conscious of the fact that Senegalese capital is very weak. This is why it is being demanded that laws be enacted to reserve exclusively for nationals some areas of trade, in particular the wholesale trade. Prospective Senegalese merchants and industrialists have also urged easier access to credit facilities. It was with this in view that the government had initially established in 1966 the Comité des Investissements Industriels, making it possible to centralize feasibility studies and to co-ordinate decision-taking and the direction and control of projects.

The second step was marked by the establishment and development of assistance and support institutions in the industrial and trade sectors.

The Société Nationale d'Etudes et de Promotion Industrielle (SONEPI), a state corporation, was established on 1 January 1969 as the effective instrument of Senegal's industrial development policy. It is responsible for evaluating projects in the plan, for inviting investors and for generally promoting national small-scale industry. One of the most important functions is to make funds available on a participation and guarantee basis. It is allowed to purchase shares amounting to 5 per cent of the value of a Senegalese enterprise and is able to provide guarantees for loans amounting to a further 5 per cent.

The Société National de Garantie et d'Assistance au Commerce (SONAGA) was established in 1971 in response to a national requirement for a credit-issuing institution benefiting Senegalese traders. SONAGA is a joint-stock company with state majority participation, to which are linked BCEAO, local banks and chambers of commerce. Its main objective is somewhat similar to that of the guarantee fund of SONEPI – to give grants, as well as technical assistance, not only to small- and medium-scale trading enterprises but also to the small- and medium-scale industrial enterprises and to various craft enterprises.

Despite these support institutions, the level of credit available to private Senegalese entrepreneurs remained small in 1972, as Table 43 demonstrates. This situation was improved by funds made available under the 1972 investment code and by special central bank support for SONEPI and SONAGA in 1973. Since 1977 substantial funds at low interest rates have become available from the government to finance

Table 43 *Credit utilization in Senegal, 1972 (CFA francs '000)*

Type of credit	*Senegalese public sector*	*Private enterprises belonging to Africans*	*Private enterprises belonging to Lebanese and Syrians*	*Foreign enterprises or subsidiary companies*	*Total*
Short-term credit	17,677	2647	1461	21,119	42,904
(%)	41	6	3	49	100
Medium-term credit	1400	784	99	2200	4483
(%)	31	17	2	49	100
Long-term credit	2167	155	1	3232	7555
(%)	28	2	—	70	100
Total	21,244	3586	1561	28,551	54,942
(%)	39	6	3	52	100

new enterprises and to buy out foreign concerns. This support seems necessary. A 1974 survey indicates that only 5 to 10 per cent of the entire industrial and commercial sector is in private Senegalese hands.

Notes

1 See S. Amin, *Le Monde des Affaires Senegalais* (Paris: Edition de Minuit 1969), which deals with current problems of Senegalese private capitalism.

2 Name for women of the Saint Louis aristocracy. See George E. Brooks Jnr, 'The *signores* of Saint Louis and Gorée: women entrepreneurs in eighteenth-century Senegal', in Nancy J. Hafkin and Edna G. Bay (eds.), *Women in Africa* (Stanford University Press 1976).

3 Traditional name in upper Senegal.

4 In two studies: 'Une Solution technique au probleme de l'arachide', in *Rapports de l'Union coloniale française a l'Exposition coloniale internationale de Paris en 1931* (Paris 1932), p. 523; and 'Le redressement économique du Sénégal', cited by Y. Mersadier in 'La Crise de l'arachide sénégalaise du début des années trente', *Bulletin de l'IFAN*, no. 3–4 (1966).

5 A recent survey of Senegalese development is Rita Cruise O'Brien (ed.), *The Political Economy of Underdevelopment: Dependence in Senegal* (Beverly Hills and London: Sage 1979).

Part Three

Practical problems

13 Foreign direct investment and African political economy

Reginal Herbold Green, *Professorial Fellow, Institute of Development Studies, University of Sussex*

The nature, level and role of private foreign investment

Direct private foreign ownership of fixed assets and/or firms has not been a uniform feature of the development of the capitalist world economy over the past five centuries, either in Africa or elsewhere. Equally, foreign private investment has not always been incompatible with economic development, nor is it always associated with radical inequality between the state of the investor and that of the investment location.

These facts are not merely of antiquarian or intellectual interest: they raise questions of very immediate practical concern as to whether, when and how foreign investment and national economic objectives can be compatible in Africa, and whether over the next twenty years direct foreign private investment will remain the dominant form of external capitalist penetration or will be replaced by new forms requiring new responses. A brief review of the changing historic roles of private investment in the incorporation of Africa into the world economic order is therefore a useful prelude to a more detailed look at present empirical data.

In the pre-colonial period[1] of European penetration, up to the later nineteenth century, foreign private investment in Africa was generally small, both absolutely and relative to economic involvement. Production in Africa was almost totally by Africans, although its nature was often radically altered by external influence; the European dominance was in external commerce. this is not to argue that the trade was unimportant to Africa, or to certain European firms and, on occasion, to key aspects of European accumulation, expansion and state building. Nor is it to imply that capital was too small to achieve commercial objectives. However, the mercantile nature of the penetration required investment in circulating capital, in the sense of stocks of goods, ships and expenses of expeditions, rather than of directly productive fixed investments in Africa. The resultant fixed investments were rather in mines, plantations and slaves in the Americas.

The colonial phase of integrating Africa into the Eurocentric would order in the late nineteenth century and first decades of the twentieth century was characterized by several sub-patterns of economic structure and private investment.[2] The most important of these were (1) African smallholder production, (2) mineral extraction, and (3) plantations based on European productive enterprises of significant size, and European settlers operating smaller units of production. Most territories were dominated by one pattern but rarely to the total exclusion of the other two.

In each structure a major supportive role was played by public sector investment, particularly in railroads and port facilities. There was little fixed private investment in trade – a few warehouses, commercial premises and minimal processing units. The private sector investment in Africa remained predominantly in shipping, in working capital and in manufacturing for local European demand. The plantations and mines, however, provide examples where large investments in fixed capital assets were necessary to ensure production. The settler pattern included, especially after its first few decades, some similar corporate investment, but more usually a fairly large number of small fixed investments in farms and smaller businesses.

Post-colonial economic planning in the independent African states increased the role of public sector fixed investment financed from abroad. The petty foreign capitalist's (settler or semi-permanent resident, European or Asian) role has been steadily eroded in favour of the transnational corporation (TNCs) (in manufacturing and specialized commerce), the public sector, and the emergent African medium-scale private capitalist strata. What remains on the direct private fixed asset side are large corporate units, which now include more manufacturing and specialized commerce while still continuing to operate mines and plantations. However, increasingly the TNCs and other foreign firms are moving to joint ventures, management or technical contracts and selling arrangements, thereby reducing commitment in fixed assets physically located in Africa, but maintaining control via 'leasing' of knowledge and captial.

The situation is by no means static or simple. Certainly, new foreign private fixed investment is flowing into some African territories and sectors. Some large enterprises, for example the Katanga mining complex, were always dominated by management groups with a tenuous formal stake in the actual producing units.[13] Equally, the more rapid retreats, as in Libya, Algeria and Tanzania, have been a result of heavy African state pressure, not of a TNC decision that fixed asset ownership in Africa had become less critical with ownership of relevant knowledge, technology and related assets.

However, the trends are clear and the pace of change is much more likely to accelerate than to be reversed. Risk minimization and capital shortages alike are causing foreign investors to prefer joint ventures at the African fixed-asset, holding-unit level, with tied fees and sales more critical and African-located enterprise profits less so. Just as direct colonial rule begins to appear to have been a rather short-lived form of external penetration and domination, both preceded and followed by more indirect and locally mediated domination, so the phase of dominance of direct foreign private investment begins to show a similar pattern. The prospect, it should be made clear, is not so much for an end to foreign economic penetration or TNC dominance as an alteration in forms and instruments.

This historical review does not reduce the past and present importance of direct private investment so much as place it in perspective. Foreign public sector investment by colonial governments, or subsequently via loans and aid, has usually been larger. Trade on an unequal basis has for many territories and most products been at least as critical a means of territorial surplus extraction to the benefit of nationals of metropolitan economies as has foreign investment. Both in the private (patents, royalties, management, consultancy and technical fees) and the public (technical assistance) sectors, the ownership of knowledge may be in the process of becoming at least as crucial a factor in continued penetration and dominance (and, from the other side of the 'exchange', as crucial a source of power and profit) as fixed-asset ownership.

Thus any current survey runs the risk of being 'historical', and, in a different sense, 'out of date'. This is so only to a minor extent, because its empirical data are a few years old; that alone is rarely enough to alter basic relationships except in cases in which the change can be demonstrated even without detailed figures. More fundamentally, there is a danger of treating the relationships and trends of the recent past as those of the future, and therefore of being continually one step behind events. For academic historians that matters little, albeit it explains why most of them avoid serious analysis of the recent past. For an applied social scientist concerned with presenting and interpreting reality and with providing a framework for informed action to change the situation; and for a policy-maker concerned with knowing and meeting the present and future strategy and tactics of those with whom he negotiates, confronts or does business, being somewhat 'out of date' is an ever-present and ever-serious risk.[14]

Patterns of foreign private investment

The total foreign private investment from Development Association Committee (DAC) member countries in independent African states and Zimbabwe was of the order of US$7500 million in 1967 and US$9400 million in 1972 (see Table 44).[15] The 1976 level, on a comparable basis, is probably of the order of $11,500–$12,000 million. Other foreign private investment, except that of South Africa in immediate surrounding territories (perhaps $500 million), is not significant, so that the figures are relatively complete as an indicator of the magnitude of direct investment by medium and large foreign firms.

The data are not, however, very accurate or even consistent estimates of 'values'. First they do not in practice include all small-scale, and often resident, foreign investment, especially in the states that were formerly Portuguese colonies and in the case of British subjects of Asian and Greek ancestry in East Africa. This omission is in some ways helpful – the technical, economic and political nature of that type of foreign investment (and the implications and requirements for Africanization of ownership and control) are normally significantly different from those of the investments of large foreign firms.

Table 44 *Level of private foreign direct investments (from DAC member countries) in Africa, 1967–72 (US$ million)*

	Stock end 1967	*Percentage of total*	*Stock end 1972*	*Percentage of total*	*Growth 1967–72 (%)*
Botswana[1]	3	0.0	35[2]	0.4	1300[2]
Gambia	2	0.0	5	0.1	117
Ghana	260	4.0	360	3.8	38
Kenya	172	2.6	235	2.5	37
Lesotho[1]	0.5	0.0	2	0.0	300
Malawi	30	0.5	55	0.6	83
Nigeria	1109	16.8	2100	22.3	89
Sierra Leone	68	1.0	75	0.8	-10
Sudan	37	0.6	35[2]	0.4	5
Swaziland[1]	29	0.4	35	0.4	21
Tanzania	60	0.9	65[3]	0.7	8
Uganda	48	0.7	30[3]	0.3	-38
Zambia	421	6.4	300	3.2	-29
Former British colonies	2239	34.0	3332	35.5	49
Algeria	703	10.7	250[3]	2.7	-64

Table 44 *(continued)*

	Stock end 1967	*Percentage of total*	*Stock end 1972*	*Percentage of total*	*Growth 1967–72 (%)*
Morocco	179	2.7	250	2.7	39
Tunisia	135	2.0	200	2.1	48
Cameroon	150	2.3	210	2.2	40
CAR	37	0.6	50	0.5	37
Chad	18	0.3	20	0.2	12
Congo PR	90	1.4	100	1.0	11
Dahomey (Benin)	18	0.3	25	0.3	40
Gabon	265	4.0	375	4.0	41
Guinea	93	1.4	175	1.9	88
Ivory Coast	202	3.1	340	3.6	69
Madagascar	72	1.1	95	1.0	31
Mali	7	0.1	8	0.1	23
Mauretania	101	1.5	150	1.6	48
Niger	23	0.4	35	0.4	50
Senegal	154	2.3	210	2.2	37
Togo	42	0.6	65	0.7	53
Upper Volta	16	0.2	18	0.2	11
Burundi	14	0.2	18	0.2	27
Rwanda	15	0.2	17	0.2	12
Zaire	481	7.3	620	6.6	20
Former French and Belgian colonies	2815	42.7	3231	34.4	15
Angola[4]	193	2.9	290[3]	3.1	50
Guinea-Bissau[4]	—	—	—	—	—
Mozambique	102	1.6	125[3]	1.3	22
Ethiopia	50	0.8	70[3]	0.7	39
Liberia	300	4.5	360	3.8	20
Libya	578	8.8	1560[3]	16.6	170
Somalia	13	0.2	15	0.2	19
UAR	58	0.9	100[2]	1.1	72
Other independent Africa	1294	19.7	2520	26.8	95
Zimbabwe[1]	237	3.6	315	3.4	33
Total[5]	8586	100.0	9398	100.0	42.7

1 Total significantly affected by non-inclusion South African investment.
2 Post-1972 sharp increase foreign-private investment stock.
3 Post-1972 sharp reduction foreign-private investment stock.
4 Portuguese corporate investment included; settler- and 'provincial'-firm Portuguese investment not covered.
5 South Africa and Namibia excluded.

Table 45 *Foreign investment–gross national product ratios*

	Foreign private investment as % of GNP		*Foreigned-owned enterprise turnover 1967*	
	1967	*1971*	*Value* (US$ million)	*% of GNP*
Botswana	4	10	6	8
Gambia	10	6	4	20
Ghana	15	15	520	30
Kenya	15	11	344	30
Lesotho	1	2	1	2
Malawi	14	9	60	28
Nigeria	21	22	2218	42
Sierra Leone	18	13	136	36
Sudan	2	2	74	4
Swaziland	39	44	58	78
Tanzania	7	4	120	14
Uganda	7	4	96	14
Zambia	36	19	842	72
Former British colonies	17	15	4477	34
Algeria	23	4	1406	46
Morocco	7	6	358	14
Tunisia	14	10	270	28
Cameroon	19	17	300	38
CAR	19	19	74	38
Chad	7	6	36	14
Congo PR	72	33	180	144
Dahomey	10	8	36	20
Gabon	147	103	530	294
Guinea	30	39	186	60
Ivory Coast	19	17	404	38
Madagascar	10	9	144	20
Mali	2	2	14	4
Mauretania	65	73	202	130
Niger	8	6	46	16
Senegal	19	20	308	38
Togo	21	21	84	42
Upper Volta	6	5	32	12
Burundi	10	8	28	20
Rwanda	16	7	30	32
Zaire	36	32	962	72
Former French and Belgian colonies	21	14	5630	42

Table 45 *(continued)*

	Foreign private investment as % of GNP		*Foreign-owned enterprise turnover 1967*	
	1967	*1971*	*Value* (US$ million)	*% of GNP*
Angola	—	13	386	(35–40)
Guinea-Bissau	—	—	—	—
Mozambique	—	5	204	(17–20)
Ethiopia	3	3	100	6
Liberia	125	100	600	250
Libya	37	48	1156	72
Somalia	10	7	26	20
UAR	1	1	116	2
Other independent Africa	11	13	2588	22
Zimbabwe	22	18	237	44

Second, the figures tend to represent the amount that the foreign firm records its African investment in its country of origin. There is no consistency at all in such recording. Every possibility, from a nominal, decades-old, initial investment in a firm that has grown from retained earnings to a gross over-valuation with a view to selling the investment back to the African state or its nationals, can be found. On balance, under-valuation is the more common, and this is exacerbated when comparing investment stocks with current price investment flows or output because the recorded 'values' are rarely systematically adjusted for inflation.[6]

Compared with national product, foreign private investment ranges from under 5 per cent to over 100 per cent with an average of about 15 per cent (see Table 45). Compared with total capital stock – including tree crops, land improvement, cattle and other investment categories very imperfectly covered in statistics – this suggests a foreign private ownership share of perhaps 6 per cent. However, excluding infrastructure, housing and capital associated with very small-scale activity, the ratio is about 40 per cent of modern, medium- and large-scale directly productive activity. That is, about two-fifths – and in many states much more – of the capital in manufacturing, mining, large-scale forestry, fishing, agriculture, finance, modern construction and large-scale commerce is foreign private-owned (see Table 46). The very low levels are sometimes associated with a relatively structurally developed and relatively nationalist or socialist state pursuing state capitalist development (e.g. Algeria, Egypt) – sometimes with an attempt to achieve a

Table 46 *Sectoral distribution of direct foreign private investment, 1967*

	Primary			*Secondary*		*Tertiary*					
	Agriculture and forestry (%)	*Petroleum production* (%)	*Other mining/ smelting* (%)	*Manufacturing* (%)	*Public utilities* (%)	*Transport* (%)	*Petroleum distribution* (%)	*Other commerce* (%)	*Banking* (%)	*Tourism* (%)	*Other* (%)
Botswana	—	—	20.0	40.0	—	—	20.0	—	20.0	—	—
Gambia	—	—	—	56.5	—	—	13.0	21.7	8.7	—	—
Ghana	0.6	—	30.9	34.2	—	—	9.2	20.9	3.8	—	0.4
Kenya	21.4	—	—	39.9	—	0.6	5.8	16.9	4.9	4.4	6.2
Lesotho	—	—	—	—	—	—	60.0	—	40.0	—	—
Malawi	39.3	—	—	9.0	—	—	13.3	10.0	6.7	—	21.7
Nigeria	0.5	65.5	1.4	16.1	—	—	1.8	9.9	2.4	—	2.4
Sierra Leone	—	—	85.6	8.5	—	—	5.1	8.7	1.5	—	0.6
Sudan	—	—	1.4	68.7	—	5.5	8.2	9.5	6.8	—	—
Swaziland	—	—	37.9	51.7	—	—	6.9	—	3.5	—	—
Tanzania	34.4	—	(1)	52.0	—	—	9.9	—	—	—	3.6
Uganda	8.3	—	18.8	38.5	—	—	16.7	3.1	12.5	—	2.1
Zambia	1.8	—	82.4	7.8	—	0.2	1.9	3.3	0.7	1.0	0.9
Former British colonies	4.0	31.0	26.0	17.3	—	0.2	3.9	9.5	2.7	0.5	2.3
Algeria	—	90.9[2]	—	8.1	—	—	—	0.4	0.1	—	—
Morocco	—	0.6	21.8	39.0	—	2.8	10.0	6.3	5.0	0.6	4.5
Tunisia	—	20.0[2]	5.9	47.3	—	3.7	7.8	3.7	3.0	10.0	3.0
Cameroon	24.6	—	12.0	46.4	1.7	—	8.7	4.4	2.3	5.7	—
CAR	34.4	—	5.5	35.3	11.2	—	8.2	2.7	2.7	—	—
Chad	15.7	—	—	67.4	—	—	11.2	2.8	2.8	—	—
Congo PR	54.2	1.1	22.2	9.8	—	—	6.1	3.7	3.0	—	—
Dahomey	13.4	—	—	36.9	—	—	27.9	14.0	7.8	—	—
Gabon	6.1	46.6	34.7	4.0	3.9	—	0.9	3.0	0.8	—	—

Guinea	—	—	88.3	8.6	—	—	1.0	2.2	—	—	—
Ivory Coast	34.5	—	6.0	38.6	8.2	—	4.7	5.5	2.5	—	—
Madagascar	13.3	—	6.9	40.4	7.6	5.5	13.8	5.5	6.9	—	—
Mali	—	—	—	30.8	—	—	38.5	15.4	15.4	—	—
Mauretania	5.4	—	92.4	0.4	0.6	—	0.7	0.1	0.1	—	—
Niger	12.9	—	23.8	35.9	10.3	—	8.6	6.4	—	—	—
Senegal	31.1	—	18.5	36.1	4.6	—	3.6	3.9	—	—	0.7
Togo	2.6	—	68.6	5.4	—	—	10.6	9.4	—	—	—
Upper Volta	18.8	—	—	26.5	13.6	—	24.7	12.4	—	—	—
Burundi	7.0	—	3.5	57.8	7.0	—	10.6	7.0	—	—	—
Rwanda	—	—	26.3	47.4	6.6	—	6.6	6.6	—	—	—
Zaire	14.6	—	13.1	41.1	2.1	15.6	1.7	7.3	2.5	—	—
Former French and Belgian colonies	12.2	29.4	15.4	22.9	2.4	3.3	5.2	4.1	2.1	1.1	0.5
Angola	1.6	11.4	18.9	9.8	—	54.8	1.6	1.0	1.0	—	—
Guinea-Bissau	...	...	...	...	...	...	...	...	...	...	...
Mozambique	5.9	6.9	11.7	44.0	2.9	9.4	5.9	9.4	3.9	—	—
Ethiopia	6.0	—	—	—	—	43.7	9.9	2.6	2.0	—	—
Liberia	19.5	—	62.0	6.3	—	—	1.0	9.5	1.7	—	—
Libya	—	77.7	—	15.0	—	0.7	1.4	1.9	1.0	—	2.3
Somalia	—	—	15.9	52.4	—	19.8	11.9	—	—	—	—
UAR	—	60.3	—	12.1	—	—	17.2	5.2	—	5.2	—
Other independent Africa	5.5	39.6	18.2	15.5	—	9.5	2.8	4.3	1.4	0.2	1.0
Zimbabwe	3.7	—	10.7	57.5	—	1.0	7.2	4.7	2.1	—	13.1
Total[2]	7.5	30.8	19.4	23.2	1.0	3.8	3.9	6.0	2.1	0.7	1.7
Sectoral totals	Primary: 57.7			Secondary: 24.2		Tertiary: 18.1					

[1]Listed as 0 in OECD data because diamond joint venture with De Beers group is formally Bahamian and practically South African. Of the order of total foreign private investment of $10 million or 16%.
[2]Includes pipelines from fields to export terminals.

transition to socialism in a much weaker economy (e.g. Ethiopia, Tanzania); but also in some cases with economies so weak and underdeveloped that private foreign investors have seen little chance to reap surpluses (as in Mali and Lesotho). Very high levels are usually associated with economies centred on petroleum, mineral and forestry export enclaves; examples are Liberia, Gabon, and pre-nationalization Algeria and Libya.

Relating foreign enterprise turnover to national product yields higher ratios with a somewhat different distribution; the commercial, construction and import substitution manufacturing sectors, with high turnover and low value added relative to sales, account for much of the variation. Because data on company turnover and on total transactions are very poor in most cases, and because the sales of a high turnover to value added sector (e.g. wholesaling) are not readily comparable in meaning to those of high value added to turnover (e.g. mining), there are grave problems in analysing these data.[7]

Further, it needs to be recognized that overall foreign private capital to GNP ratios at any one time or over time, for one economy or between economies, must be interpreted with care. For example, in the late 1940s and 1950s the major West African colonial trading houses carried out a systematic redeployment of activity away from produce buying, retail trading and general import–export and wholesale activity. These areas were both subject to African competition (lowering profitability) and sensitive to nationalist action (raising risk). The new areas of concentration included department stores, pre-export processing of raw materials, specialized commerce and import substitution manufacturing. In these fields, not only were surplus margins wider, but nationalist actions tended to increase them – either generally, by venting new markets, or directly, by offering specific incentives. Such redeployment normally increased effective penetration of the territorial economy by the world economic system and foreign firms, but it also tended to lower the ratio of foreign enterprise turnover to GNP.[8]

Sectorally, investment was dominated by primary production units in agriculture, forestry, petroleum production and mining. The 57.7 per cent of total foreign private investment in these sectors in 1967, combined with their new total export orientation, underlines very clearly the role that African territories and people still play in the international economic system: a role of hewers of wood and drawers of water, or – less dramatically – of producing raw materials favoured by African climates or found in African soils for use in the metropolitan industrial centres. That role does not necessarily require direct foreign investment in production. In the case of smallholder crops, marketing and finance dominance over African petty producers by foreign firms domestically, and the nature of international commodity markets globally, allowed continued surplus extraction even when domestic marketing has been taken over by the state. In forestry, mining and petroleum production the high cost and technical complexity of the units resulted in near 100 per cent ownership until a decade ago. Even today ownership is still more often predominantly foreign than domestic, and the domestic firms are often managed and dominated by foreign private minority (or technical) partners.[9]

Investment in manufacturing had risen to just under a quarter of total foreign private investment in 1967 and by 1976 it was around 30 per cent. Unlike the primary sector, investment in manufacturing is rarely export-oriented, and the exceptions – notably in Kenya – relate to exports to other African territories or to first-stage raw material processing, which might more accurately be sectorally combined with export agriculture.

Manufacturing investment is, however, export-linked in a broader sense. Its main markets are the recipients of income from export-oriented primary production, including the independent African states and their employees. It is import-oriented because the salaries of foreign personnel plus operating inputs and capital goods from abroad bulk very large relative to domestic purchase and value added. Even in an industry such as cement, where the basic raw material is local, expatriate salaries, fuel, packaging, head office charges and costs related to plant and equipment added up to a true 70 per cent of import component in the ex-factory price of Tanzanian cement in the early 1970s.[10]

In the case of manufacturing, investment has usually been either to avoid loss of a market to a competitor, to gain a market, or incidental to a machinery sale. The first two reasons are closely linked to national fiscal regimes and the third to national investment policies. As opposed to the Latin American experience, where initial import substitution manufacturing was largely domestic and was dominated by foreign firms only two to three decades later, African manufacturing grew up on a 'branch plant' basis.

Tertiary sector investment is less than a fifth of the total. However, this is a sector in which the figures representing external equity can be deceptive. Further, the degree of foreign penetration varies widely from one line of activity to another. Transport (like public utilities), with a few exceptions, is not a major area of foreign private investment. Even the colonial states were obliged to carry the bulk of transport investment, either to achieve administrative and military control or to stimulate private sector growth in primary production. The exceptions, such as Ethiopia, Somalia and the Central African Republic, are exceedingly poor states with both limited state resources for infrastructure development and very small total private investment.

Petroleum distribution is predominantly foreign and represents about two-fifths of the private foreign investment that is in commerce. Other commercial investment is increasingly concentrated on specialized import–export, wholesale and service activities. Heavy earth-moving equipment is the second largest remaining private import sub-sector in Tanzania, while the largest is the private sector of the petroleum business. In these sectors investment data are misleading; the key assets are inventories and receivables largely financed either by local banks or by foreign suppliers. Therefore, in many states (e.g. Senegal) a very modest equity investment (about $15 million) is consistent with domination of import–export and central wholesaling business.

This is even truer of banking, in which the 1967 equity investment of about $175 million in fact meant the domination of African banking in all but a handful of states. The investment allowed the collection and allocation of very much larger domestic deposits. Given the exceedingly traditional operating principles of most foreign banks in Africa, it also led to concentration on short-term loans backed by inventories (i.e. commerce), longer-term loans secured by mortgages (i.e. real estate), and foreign firm borrowing backed by head office guarantees. The share of loans to African enterprises (usually public sector or African public/foreign private joint ventures) has grown, however, over the past decade, and the loan criteria have become less rigid. In many territories banking in Africa in 1976 was still significantly foreign in ownership and control, and often fifty years out of date in operating guidelines, even in locally owned banks.

Tourism was still a minor area for foreign investment in 1967. It has since grown markedly in countries such as Tunisia and Kenya, and is another sector in which foreign equity investment is a deceptive measure. Foreign dominance centres on ownership of foreign-based promotion and transport firms and management, or on other contractual controls, rather than on full direct ownership of hotels and other physical assets in African countries. Typically, even the hotels whose equity is wholly or largely foreign-owned have secured the bulk of their finance from domestic loans, often at subsidized interest rates, as in Morocco and Tunisia.

National data vary widely in total foreign private investment ratio to GNP and sectoral makeup. In 1972 the largest single total was £2000 million in Nigeria, 22 per cent of the independent Africa (and Zimbabwe) total and over 60 per cent of that for former British colonies. Of the Nigerian total almost two-thirds was in petroleum production. Similarly, of the $1560 million investment in Libya at that date, over three-fifths was in petroleum production. The $620 million in Zaire and $395 million in Gabon showed differing sectoral patterns. In Zaire, manufacturing (about 40 per cent) was followed by plantation agriculture, forestry and mining ($27\frac{1}{2}$ per cent), while in Gabon petroleum production and other mining (largely iron ore) activities accounted for over 80 per cent of foreign private investment. Investment in Gambia was only $5 million and in Mali, $8 million. The low Gambian figure flows from the lack of evidently profitable investment opportunities in a very small economy, and the latter from the handicap of a landlocked economy without either mineral production or major export-oriented agricultural sectors. The states that have carried out major nationalizations were not necessarily at the bottom of the list in 1971, partly because, in the cases of Algeria, Zambia and Tanzania, the nationalizations were still in progress while those of Libya, Ethiopia and Madagascar had yet to begin, and partly because nationalization has often been followed by new joint ventures (e.g. in Zambia and Tanzania) or even new export enclaves with predominantly foreign private ownership, as in Guinea.

Foreign private investment exceeded GNP in two African countries – Gabon and Liberia – in 1971. In both cases a mineral or forestry enclave (petroleum and mining in Gabon and rubber and forestry in Liberia) dominates the economy and is in turn dominated by transnational corporation subsidiaries. The lowest ratios are a mixture of very poor economies which investors perceived as offering little chance of amassing surpluses, e.g. Mali, Ethiopia, Sudan, Lesotho and those states that had nationalized a large share of private enterprise, e.g. Tanzania, Algeria and Egypt.

The pattern of foreign investment sources is still predominantly a colonial heritage, even in respect of post-independence investment. In every ex-British colony (with the possible exception of Tanzania by 1976) the largest single source is that of British investors and in a majority it exceeds 50 per cent. Among former French colonies only Guinea, with its US bauxite enclave, has another national investment source surpassing that of France. Similarly, the dominant holders of foreign investment in Zaire, Rwanda and Burundi are Belgian and in Somalia, Italian. Because of the underdeveloped nature of Portugal, the pattern in Mozambique and Angola was different, with British private investment exceeding Portugese in the late 1960s.

In a majority of African states the second largest body of foreign private investments are American. This is particularly true of former British and French colonies, although by independence it probably held true in Angola as well. This represents a change during the 1960s. Prior to that date British investment tended to hold second place in French colonies and Dutch or French held second place in British colonies.

Changes in overall and country investment patterns during the mid-

1960s and 1970s have been significant but somewhat difficult to interpret in any simple fashion. Foreign private investment has declined as a share of total world private investment. From 1967 to 1971 its share fell from about 6.3 per cent to just over 5.5 per cent.[11] The decline was most notable for the United Kingdom and France and least so for the United States and Japan, whose investment penetration of African basically began in the 1960s. The reasons for this decline are at least sixfold:

1 the continual dominance of primary production for export in Africa combined with the slower growth of this sector in the world economy;
2 a trend toward TNC retreat from some branches of primary production and commerce because basic production unit surpluses were low and adequate control of supplies and prices could be maintained at the international trade level;
3 the relatively slow growth of markets for import substitution manufacturing and the perception by TNCs of Africa as a poor place for export-oriented manufacturing satellite units;
4 diversification of Third World investment away from Africa by the ex-colonial powers, partly offset by diversification to Africa by the USA and Japan;
5 conscious policies of economic nationalism in a number of African states and systematic strategies of transition to state capitalism or socialism in a more limited number;
6 the beginning of a new TNC strategy concentrating more on selling knowledge (including management, commercial services, hard and soft technology) to national market-oriented Third World units and less on outright ownership of subsidiaries.

The changes in particular countries are even sharper. Major increases have almost all been associated with opening up of new mineral or petroleum-producing units as in Botswana, Nigeria and Guinea. Major declines – Uganda, Zambia and Algeria over 1967–72 and Libya, Ethiopia, Tanzania and Madagascar since that date – have been linked to national strategies for achieving a socialist or at least non-capitalist development path. In Egypt at a rather earlier period an overall economic nationalist strategy radically reduced the total of foreign private investment. Once implemented, the Egyptian policy became state capitalism *faute de mieux* and encompassed much of the domestic private sector as well. The 1973 shift towards a larger domestic private sector role was paralleled by a rise in foreign private investment.

Illustrative country situations

Even a brief sketch of the features and trends of foreign private investment in Africa in the recent past leads to a number of analytical and policy implications. Perhaps the most general of these is the need to examine concrete situations in detail and to contrast them before making conclusions. For example, the independent government in Angola perceived that in 1976 OPEC had made it possible for any significant petroleum producer to capture most of the surplus from crude oil; that the surplus from the Cabinda fields was urgently required to pay for basic services and to launch a transition towards a socialist, nationally oriented economy; and that in the short run nobody other than a major oil company could operate the fields. Thus, its decision to secure the return of Gulf Oil as operator and not to nationalize at once is an arguably correct one in terms of inward-looking, socialist-oriented development, even though foreign private investment in general has a minor place in such strategies under most circumstances.

The varied nature and scope of foreign private investment in Africa also counsels against simple generalizations. In the case of Kenya, Mauritius, Egypt and Tunisia there is evidence for TNC interest in setting up export-oriented manufacturing units based on cheap labour and, to a lesser extent, on local raw materials. This is not, at least not yet, true in respect of most other African states. Equally, the degree of control exercised over foreign firms and the extent to which foreign private investment is sought varies widely – Tanzania[12] has relatively high control and low incentives, while Mauritius has the opposite.

Recognition of the real situation of particular cases is especially relevant to avoiding fixed asset and equity ownership fetishism. For some lines of activity, notably banking and commerce, fixed assets are of distinctly secondary importance. Size and dominance are secured by using more of other people's money than by enlarging equity. Similarly, a TNC with oligopolistic control over technology, markets, management and sources of supply can dominate and extract surplus from an operating enterprise even if it has a minority or no equity stake.[3] An increasing number of TNCs are acting on their realization of that fact; usually under state pressure, true, but also as a deliberate tactical withdrawal and redeployment strategy. There is, therefore, no reason to argue that the declining ratios (measured in 1967, 1972 and 1976) of foreign private investment to GNP and total capital stock in independent Africa necessarily mean a parallel relative decline in foreign control or ability to extract surpluses.

The question of appropriate strategy is another area that is almost impossible to deal with at continental level beyond a few generalizations. Whatever their ideology or political base, African decision-makers wish to enlarge the absolute surplus under their state's control and to increase their leverage over major economic decisions in, or directly affecting, the territorial economies of their states. However, generalizations that apply to the Ivory Coast and Tanzania, Kenya and Algeria, Mozambique and Mauritius, Botswana and Nigeria are too sweeping to give much guidance as to how any set of national decision-makers should, in terms of their own perceptions of goals and constraints, pursue them.

Foreign private investment is sought to enhance economic growth and create a larger flow of economic surplus, parts of which can be earned by citizens, tapped by the state and/or induced to remain in further investment expansion. Taken as a source of finance, it is rather expensive on both surplus share and foreign exchange counts; large firms expect a 25–33 per cent return in cash flow on new investment in Third World countries,[4] and – especially after they have built up a significant territorial unit – usually tend to direct most of it to their home base. Even if domestic savings and taxation cannot be enhanced, or their realization in specific uses is limited by foreign balance constraints,[5] foreign borrowing from official bodies or the Eurodollar market is normally a much less costly way to secure funds.

Therefore, the ultimate justification – from an African point of view – of the presence of foreign private firms is not that they bring capital but that they transfer technology and capitalists, i.e. operational and institutional knowledge allowing the effective utilization of financial and physical resources. Hence the increasing appeal of the joint venture or management contract combined with domestic or foreign loan capital for African decision-makers. The triangular ventures combining European technology, domestic equity and Arab petrodollars are perhaps among the clearest examples of this trend.

This approach is not unacceptable to many TNCs, especially if majority subsidiary ownership is simply not an option open to them in that state. Indeed, it is one they have used extensively in their dealings with European socialist states. When including sales of capital equipment and operating inputs as well as technology, and linking exported output into the TNCs' global marketing system, such a pattern can economize on TNC capital requirements and yield a higher rate of return on those employed as well as giving fewer hostages to fortune in the form of fixed assets in African states. Certainly it may give less and less direct control over economic decisions in the host country, and the future profit flow is probably more subject to erosion in the face of a diligent national surplus share maximization strategy. However, at the same time the perceived African state–foreign investor area of common concern (whether correctly seen or misperceived) is likely to be larger, and relations more amicable and less prone to sudden unexpected changes.[16]

No African decision-makers perceive themselves as able to develop their economies without foreign knowledge inputs. In the directly productive sectors these are often available only from foreign firms. Manpower institution and applied technology development are long-term strategies. In the short and medium run the options are either uncritical wooing of almost any foreign firm on its own terms or selective negotiation for specific key inputs to secure them on the best of terms the African state can get and on terms that, at the least, increase nationally controlled and retained surplus flows and national economic decision-making power and capacity.[17] Of these the latter option appears more desirable irrespective of whether a transition to socialism, to state capitalism, or to a nationally owned and controlled private capitalism is sought by national decision-makers.

Equally, whether an inward-directed national economy with a state monopoly of external economic relations or a full integration into the TNC system as a regional sub-centre ('relay point') is sought, so long as any foreign private involvement is seen as useful it is likely to pay to bargain carefully on the division of costs and gains.[18]

Effective bargaining must begin with a clear perception of specific goals, how they can be furthered by particular foreign involvement, what price is worth paying and how the foreign firm is likely to evaluate different forms of involvement and divisions of gains. To do this requires rather more precise specification of objectives, greater attention to collecting and analysing data and more care in evaluating in detail why and to what degree any individual potential foreign partner is interested, than typifies most African states' present approaches.[19] It also requires more self-confidence based on knowledge that African states do have some bargaining power and a willingness to see negotiations 'fail' if 'success' would mean paying more than the foreign involvement was worth.[20]

One integral element in this type of negotiation is the quest for 'unpackaging'. At the simplest this can mean separating sources of knowledge in whole or in part from sources of finance. Equally, it can mean separation of specific fiscal or other incentives from a *carte blanche* to the foreign investor to write his own fiscal, labour and other economic legislative rules. However, there are more complex levels. Specific technical and external marketing contracts represent unpackaging compared with general management contracts; hiring a nationally determined package of consultants, designers, constructors, capital goods suppliers and individual managers can – even if many elements in that package are foreign – increase national control and surplus share in contrast to a package deal with a TNC, which is then responsible for all subsequent formulation and implementation.[21]

The use of the principle of negotiated selection to increase African surplus share and control necessarily implies that foreign elements should be additive to and complementary with African elements, not substitutes for them. It further implies that arrangements that promote the development of African inputs are worth a higher initial cost than those that do not. These simple considerations are the heart of the case for negotiated unpackaging.

Strategy and policy implications

Foreign private investment data on Africa can be said both to illuminate some characteristics of African economies and to suggest areas for further analysis leading to improved strategy and policy formulation. They demonstrate that in most African countries a high proportion of large-scale economic activity is owned by foreign enterprises but that some states have sharply reduced this share. Further, they indicate that, at least to date, export-oriented primary production plus import substitution manufacturing, commerce and banking sectors linked to, or dependent on, incomes from primary exports dominate foreign private investment in Africa. Africa's role in the TNC global economic sub-system is predominantly that of raw material supplier. As a result, foreign private investment in Africa is not growing very rapidly; it is not providing a real dynamic force towards the growth of territorial output.

The analytical implications of this picture include issues such as the relationship between formal ownership and control and the question of whether foreign knowledge or foreign capital is the key to enhanced production and, even if both are needed, whether they need, or even should both come from, the same foreign firms. The answers depend on the variable operating in any country at any point in time; detailed answers require detailed micro-analysis.

In respect of strategy and policy, the same need arises for specific analysis related to specific cases. However, generalizations are possible. Almost all African decision-makers see a need for foreign knowledge inputs and relations with foreign private firms, even if they largely reject foreign private equity investment. Equally, almost all seek to increase their and/or their states' control over economic decision-making and share in surplus generated territorially. Therefore, a bargained and selective – not an open-door – approach to foreign private firm involvement is needed. Because the use of the maximum number of African or African-organized inputs (whether of finance, manpower or knowledge) will tend to increase the degree of African control and the African share of surplus, unpackaging of foreign firm proposals to limit their inputs to those genuinely unobtainable from other sources is a critical element in negotiation.[22]

No continental survey within the limits of an article can do more than identify what its author sees as the crucial relationships, patterns and issues. In this regard two cautions are in order. Any such presentation may err in its choice of critical relationships and will require adjustment in balance and detail to apply to any specific analytical problem in a particular place, at a particular time, within a particular context and for a particular purpose. Furthermore, the acceptance of the empirical facts and of the analysis does not necessarily answer policy questions. On the one hand, a junior partnership with TNCs may be seen by some decision-makers as path in the way of their group's interests;[23] and on the other, objective necessity may cause decision-makers to adopt 'second-best' tactics in respect of foreign direct investment.[24]

Notes

1 See W. Rodney, *How Europe Underdeveloped Africa* (Dar es Salaam: Tanzania Publishing House 1972), and R. H. Green, 'The integration of Africa into the world capitalist system', African Studies Association (USA), 1975 Conference Papers Series.
2 See Green, 'Integration of Africa', and S. Amin, 'Underdevelopment and dependence in Black Africa', *Journal of Modern African Studies*, vol. 10, no. 4 (1972).
3 Société Generale dominated Union Minière but it did so as a manager with a small minority stake. Its control rested on backing by the Belgian state, which was the largest single shareholder.
4 Very long-term 'pure' models of basic forces do not readily yield answers to 'what is to be done' at the level of one state. Cruder empirical projections in effect take the patterns and trends of the recent past as given and almost always miss precisely those recent shifts that give room for (or give rise to a necessity for) state intervention and bargaining power.
5 The data used are from OECD (DAC) sources compiled by M. Hveem, in 'The extent and type of direct foreign investment in Africa', in C. Widstrand, *Multi-National firms in Africa* (Uppsala: Scandinavian Institute of African Studies 1975). The Development Assistance Committee (DAC) of the Organization for Economic Co-operation and Development (OECD) consists of the 17 richest Western industrialized nations: Australia, Austria, Belgium, Canada, Denmark, Finland, France, West Germany, Italy, Japan,

the Netherlands, New Zealand, Norway, Sweden, Switzerland, the United Kingdom and the United States.

6 The point here is not as to appropriate firm accounting but that historic stock values compared with present flow values understate the importance of the stocks.

7 Logically, sector-by-sector turnover and value added data for foreign firms should be analysed. However, such data are not available – indeed, the OECD data used are relatively arbitrary in respect of turnover.

8 See B. Beckman, *Organising the Farmers: Cocoa Politics and National Development in Ghana* (Uppsala: Scandinavian Institute of African Studies, 1976).

9 Despite a variety of indigenization measures, Nigerian control over oil, large-scale manufacturing, banking and specialized commerce remains very low. Nigerian finance and personnel are increasingly integrated into institutional patterns dominated by foreign (usually TNC)-knowledge suppliers, who may or may not have a significant investment stake.

10 Data derived from a study by P. Masette-Kuuya, now published in J. Rweyemamu (ed.), *Industrialization and Income Distribution in Africa* (Dakar: CODRESIA 1980).

11 For a fuller discussion see Hveem, 'Extent and type. . .'.

12 Cf. P. Neerso, 'Tanzania's Policies on Private Foreign Investment' in Widstrand, *Multi-National Firms in Africa.*

13 As the Société General case cited above suggests, this is not a totally new development. Similarly, the nature of firm–marketing board interaction in West Africa was influenced partly by firm ability to guide and use boards in such a way as to reduce firm investment requirements without any parallel fall in surplus generating capacity (Cf. Beckman, *Organising the farmers*).

14 In the presence of exchange controls, unequal tax rates and state reaction to high profits, less of this total will appear as open profit on the African subsidiary's books. Similarly, a planned selective divestment of some activities creates an incentive to arrange surplus extraction from them on a transfer price and knowledge sale basis; e.g., a traditional trading company planning to specialize in import/export, wholesaling, departmental stores may well raise wholesale and reduce retail margins to maximize retained surplus generating capacity.

15 Because the direct and indirect import component of fixed investment in Africa outside small- and medium-scale agriculture and construction is rarely less than two-thirds to three-quarters, it is not possible to realize domestic saving if foreign exchange is not

available to supply the needed inputs. If the requisite foreign exchange cannot be earned it must be borrowed to sustain realized local savings. Thus over 1973–5 a real loss of 10 per cent of GDP from terms of trade shifts in Tanzania was paralleled by a 10 per cent fall in domestic savings. Investment fell only slightly but could be realized only when matched by increased foreign borrowing because of the worsened external balance on current account. An attempt to maintain domestic savings in this context would *ex post* simply have reduced GDP unless the goods not consumed could have been exported.

16 There is a parallel danger to the African state or firm that it will underestimate the degree of effective foreign control and surplus acquisition and overestimate the degree of common interest and equitability of the new form of interaction.

17 If the starting point is one of very low levels of productive forces, the initial results will include higher direct private foreign investment absolutely and relatively both to GDP and total capital stock. If – as is likely in such a case – the initial foreign interest is in raw material production for export, at least some more general indices of external dependence will rise. Mauritania and Botswana illustrated this phase over 1960–70 and 1965–75. What is critical to attaining a more self-reliant development in such cases is the subsequent use of the nationally controlled surplus share and the measures taken to increase it. There is a real danger of being trapped into using more and more of the nationally controlled surplus to support the expansion of the enclave, thereby moving away from internal economic integration, balance and control.

18 For example, Tanzania and Kenya both bargained with foreign firms and both achieved substantial modifications of initial proposals. In some cases, indeed, Kenya appears to bargain better at the particular enterprise level. What is different are the basic perceptions of foreign firms' role in development and therefore the types of negotiations and the critical issues in them.

19 The need for identifying the goals of the African side clearly and operationally is not uniquely related to transition to socialism. It is just as relevant to a strategy seeking African state capitalism with or without semi-permanent integration into the TNC world order. For example, 40 per cent (or even 60 per cent) citizenization of foreign-controlled companies' equity in the form of dispersed holdings by individuals while the foreign firm retains the dominant single shareholding and management control does not help genuinely African enterprises or transfer control over foreign ones. By building up a formation of citizen rentiers with a vested interest

in continued dividends, it probably inhibits local control and local enterprises. However, it does share TNC surpluses derived from the African territory with a segment of the citizen élite. Whether such shareholding spin-offs are useful, therefore, depends on the actual state decision-maker's goals in respect of control, local entrepreneurs and surplus sharing.

20 True, some such cases of expensive 'success' result from corruption. However, it is equally true that, for any given level of corruption, the better informed and more confident the African negotiators, the more nearly they will come to achieving their priority targets. Admittedly, that might simply mean a larger bribe, but such a criticism is of the goals of the African negotiators, not of the ability of better negotiating to yield shifts of gains from the TNC to some African beneficiary.

21 The operative word is 'can'. Unpackaging is a necessary condition for securing overall control but not a sufficient one. If badly handled it may increase costs and reduce national surplus generation with little real gain as to control.

22 Cf. Green in Widstrand, *Multi-national Firms in Africa*, for a fuller outline of strategic and tactical approaches.

23 Cf. F. Stewart in U. Damachi, *Development Paths in Africa and China* (Macmillan 1976), and C. Leys, *Underdevelopment in Kenya* (London: Heinemann 1975).

24 This applies in both directions – selective use by decision-makers basically negatively oriented to foreign investment, and selective limitations by decision-makers basically favourably oriented to it.

14 Administrative and managerial implications

S. I. Edokpayi, *Chief, Public Administration Management and Manpower Division, ECA Secretariat**

Indigenization of commerce, industry and other economic activities is basic to any national economic policy for the attainment of self-reliant, self-sustaining economic growth and transformation. Its ultimate goal is national economic independence in the context of regional and world economic co-operation and interdependence. As a national policy it aims at transferring the control and direction of economic powers from foreign to indigenous hands, both public and private. This policy is much broader and more complex than the issue of localization or Africanization of the public or parastatal services: it is directed at ownership, control, direction and effective management.

Such a policy is neither new to economic history nor peculiar to developing African countries. It was extensively and intensively practised in sixteenth- and seventeenth-century Europe, notably by England, Holland, France and Spain. The English mercantile laws, for example, were designed to strengthen English naval supremacy, conserve foreign exchange, monopolize the trade of the colonies, reserve essential raw materials for English industries, and ultimately ensure the potency of the English nation and economy.[1] To this end England needed capable lawyers, economists and administrators to formulate, implement, review and plan the mercantile laws and related institutions, including colonial administrations, to ensure that the laws and regulations achieved what they were designed to do. Her administrative and managerial capability was therefore as important as her naval strength in integrating colonial economies with her domestic economy.

By the middle of the twentieth century, administrative and managerial capability had become as important to the nascent economies of the then colonial African territories as it had been to the English economy of the mercantilist era. However, there was one major difference. The economies of today have become more complex in their structure and technical requirements; the master–servant relationship, which facilitated the authority, directives, connivance or duplicity of

*The views expressed in this article are the author's and do not necessarily reflect those of the ECA or of the UN.

colonial administrators in the implementation of regulations dominating colonial economies, had virtually ceased to exist by the 1960s; the old vanguard of expatriate businessmen and their descendants have strengthened their economic hold through world-wide networks of finance, commerce, shipping, patents and technology to exercise real control over the economies of developing African countries. Consequently, the generation of indigenous administrators and business managers who succeeded their colonial predecessors needed greater wit and intellectual capacity to be able to contend with the numerous devices the representatives of transnationals had resorted to in order to maintain their dominance of local economies.

Such a capable and efficient administrative and managerial resource is vital to the success and effectiveness of indigenization policy and programmes. Accordingly, this chapter will attempt to do the following:

1 briefly outline the forms and stages of indigenization experiences in various African countries;
2 with that background, to relate administrative and management issues and functions to their operation; that is, to attempt to identify and analyse the operational scale of administrative and managerial involvement in taking action required by policy measures and decisions;
3 to draw up lessons learnt from the experiences of a number of African countries where the administration of indigenization policies and programmes were fairly advanced; and to envisage a need for continuing indigenization efforts requiring planned administrative action as a basis for successful and effective policy.

The gradual development of indigenization policies and programmes

The characteristics of indigenization policies, strategies and programmes in each African country, and their evolution over time, to a great extent reflect the degree of erstwhile colonial economic domination, the existence and resilience of indigenous entrepreneurs, and the level and complexity of local economic transformation. The existence of political will and the determination of national leaders to make political independence a reality by striving for economic self-determination and local control over national economic activities and natural resources are equally important. Consequently, the operation of these forces has influenced the national approach to, and the form and scale of, indigenization policies and programmes pursued, especially as between the differences in the approach to the issue by English- and French-speaking African states. It is therefore difficult to generalize and to attempt any classification of forms and stages of evolution that is not open to debate. This notwithstanding, it is still possible to identify some common characteristics and trends, as well as major differences, in the indigenization policies and measures pursued by several African countries, at least since they attained political independence. A particular measure might have operated at two different stages but at varying degrees of intensity. Some countries might have first tried a strategy of special assistance to indigenous entrepreneurs and subsequently switched to one of protection; for some other countries protection might have preceded special assistance programmes; and for still others both measures might have been offered concurrently but each operated with varying degree of intensity and impact.[2]

A clear national policy declaration with goal-oriented programme measures to indigenize the national economy is a very recent affair in African countries. For most countries such a policy is still in formation or is being tried only piecemeal rather than in an integrated and comprehensive manner.[3] However, even before political independence various actions and legislative measures, albeit very limited, had been taken under 'enlightened' colonial administration to safeguard the economic interests of colonial peoples in Africa. The so-called enlightened administration did not start taking action to safeguard indigenous economic interests until the economic depression of the early 1930s compelled indigenous traders to agitate for protection. As a result, colonial administrations adopted a series of institutional arrangements during the 1940s and 1950s to restrict expatriate businessmen's intrusion into colonial economic activities, to protect indigenous enterprises, and to provide specific assistance enabling indigenous entrepreneurs to survive and compete with expatriate business firms. However, the effort of colonial governments at this stage 'was concentrated on the setting up of cooperatives more for the marketing of agricultural produce than for the promotion of commerce generally or industry'.[4] The measures were designed to transfer the domestic and overseas trade in export commodities from expatriate control to indigenous hands.

Further measures included the launching of the Colonial Development Schemes in 1946 and the establishment of Development and Loans Boards in territories under British administration. The credits and marketing facilities were aimed at strengthening the competitive position of African businessmen and traders, both individually and collectively. In addition, the industrial estates and related technical services were meant to introduce African entrepreneurs for the first time into manufacturing undertakings.

In the French-speaking and Portuguese-speaking colonial Africa, the time for such a change of attitude and policy of protection for indigenous entrepreneurship had not yet come; metropolitan citizens in 'overseas territories' had free entry and freedom of enterprise in the colonial territories.

By the first half of the 1960s most African states had become independent and had changed from colonial development planning to planning for independent nations. Their first preoccupation was to Africanize the decision-making and key executive positions in their public services and parastatal enterprises. Through their development plans, economic policies and development strategies were being oriented towards *promoting, expanding and strengthening indigenous participative entrepreneurship.* The objective was not just to ensure an indigenous competitive position, but also to increase participation in commercial, industrial and other economic activities, including plantation agriculture. In pursuance of this objective, the operations of various colonial credit and development institutions were reviewed and streamlined in order to make them generate greater facilities for indigenous entrepreneurs. More funds were made available; technical extension services were expanded; and new industrial development centres were established.

Two other measures designed to increase indigenous participation in economic activities were aimed at improving African management capability: the first was the use of immigration regulations and expatriate quotas; the second was the establishment of management development institutions and programmes for the training of African management cadres. With Africanization making a good headway in the *public* services of the relatively more advanced developing African states by the second half of the 1960s, increasing attention was being drawn to the need to Africanize top management in the *private* sector as well. At independence, large expatriate firms in their own interest, even if for 'window dressing' and appearing to be complying with government policy, had begun to Africanize lower-management positions in their enterprises.

As national development plans were being reviewed and reformulated, increasing attention came to be placed on restructuring the entire national economy, ending its colonial domination and increasing indigenous involvement beyond mere participation to effective control. Many African states have pursued this objective with varying degrees of determination and with varying degrees of impact. In general, they have sought to increase government participation, first by converting quasi-government economic services departments such as the railway and road transport, coal mining, electricity generation and air transport, which were established by colonial administrations, into business-oriented public enterprises; and second by establishing new development corporations to provide pioneering ventures in fields where private enterprise was reluctant to invest. Programmes of financial and technical assistance for indigenous entrepreneurs were also being expanded in several new directions.

The early 1970s saw increasing regional and international sanctions for the indigenization objectives. Besides the ECA resolution adopting the Africa strategy for development in the 1970s and the OAU declaration adopting a charter of economic independence in May 1973, the declaration in December 1973 of the Cairo Conference of African Ministers of Industries relating to 'Principles and Guidelines for Cooperation and Development in the Industrialization of Africa' specifically called upon African governments, *inter alia* 'to take action to establish policies, programmes, services and institutions to foster the development of African entrepreneurship and the formulation of policies and implementation of programmes that would result in the earliest replacement of expatriates engaged in conceiving programming and operating industrial projects and enterprises in their countries'.[5]

Initially the main interest was concentrated in utilities and strategic industries, but by the 1970s the interest has grown into staking a share in what, in Nigeria, has been styled the 'commanding heights of the national economy'. To do this, several African governments have gone into partnership ventures with foreign governments and private investors, and have embarked upon negotiated nationalization of some strategic businesses. As a result many African governments have assumed control of important sectors in the economies. In the Ivory Coast, for example, state capitalism has been pursued through the operations of over thirty state-owned corporations producing goods and services as well as technical studies. In Uganda parastatal businesses and organizations increased from fourteen in 1972 to sixty-two in 1976. By means of nationalization and other measures Egypt, Algeria, Tanzania and Ethiopia also substantially increased public participation in economic activities. In this way indigenization was being pursued through making both indigenous entrepreneurs and the state increase their participation, ownership, control and management of national economic activities.

The indigenization measures initiated in a number of African countries since the early 1970s can thus be seen to constitute the first major step in a series of action programmes designed to push towards the achievement of economic independence, that is, *effective domestic control of the national economy*. The ultimate goal is economic independence within the context of regional and world economic co-operation and interdependence. The goal seeks to exercise full sovereignty over natural resources, and in particular the ownership, control and management of economic activities at all levels. While this policy objective will continue to be pursued vigorously over the next two decades and beyond, action is already being taken by some countries to effect full control in specific economic sectors.

Attempts to achieve domestic control of particular economic sectors have taken different forms in various African countries.[6] Besides negotiated nationalization of mines and the oil industries in some countries, there have also been revolutionary nationalization of banks, industries, houses, etc., with or without compensation, in countries such as Egypt, Tanzania, Uganda, Algeria, Mozambique and Ethiopia. Political and ideological factors have contributed to the suddeness and arbitrariness in the steps taken. Other measures that have been tried to bring about increased domestic control of the national economy have included public majority equity shareholding in partnership ventures; provision by legislation of minimal equity shareholding by nationals as in the Nigeria Enterprises Promotion Decree; outright buying out of foreign investors in certain lines of business; and the establishment of enabling institutions (credit and investment facilities, stock or capital market arrangements, educational and training institutions) facilitating the rapid growth of indigenous entrepreneurship.

Administrative and managerial action in the indigenization process

The preceding section has provided a fair background to the gradual evolution and development of what in a number of African states can today be described as clear policies and programmes that will gradually and ultimately lead to effective control and management of the national economy. Variations in forms and approaches as well as in programme measures have been noted. In the present section I shall attempt to analyse some of the administrative actions and experiences necessitated by the form and scale of indigenization decisions and measures and the managerial implications of government direct involvement in production and services. As much as possible, attention will also be paid to new challenges, constraints and performance results under given circumstances.

Laissez-faire policy

Initially, colonial administrations were not expected to do anything to ensure the growth of indigenous entrepreneurship; rather, they were motivated by a desire to promote the immediate and future interests of metropolitan economies. Regulations were simple, and were designed to perpetuate the control exercised by traders and businessmen from metropolitan countries. Where there was potential local challenge prohibitive orders were instituted against local industrial entrepreneurship.[7] Although it might be claimed that British colonial administrations successfully resisted expatriate demands for agricultural plantation ventures in West Africa and gave way to pressure in East and Central Africa, it was not so much any real interest in protecting peasant agriculture as such, but rather the force of the indigenous land tenure laws and ecological factors in West Africa that made it impossible for large tracts of land to be expropriated from the native beyond what was required for 'demonstration plantations'. By contrast, there were less fundamental constraints in the French- and Portuguese-speaking colonies against the expropriation of large tracts of land for plantation agriculture since expatriate investors were operating in overseas territories of the same state where the same laws prevailed.

In this period, therefore, there was a very limited amount of regulations governing entrepreneurial ventures outside commerce. What commercial regulations operated were simple; consequently, the administrators of that era needed no special skills other than their basic preparation for colonial administration to interpret and apply the regulations and report on their implementation in their domains.

The marketing co-operatives and marketing boards that were established by colonial administrators were meant to do no more than provide the advantages of bulk transactions in selling produce to expatriate shippers and to relieve the white traders of the risk of trading in the bushland where producers marketed their produce through a chain of middlemen-buyers. It was simply the organization of trade channels, and the system had no linkages with production in agriculture, industry or even transportation.

Actual control of trade was in the hands of the chambers of commerce, whose membership during this phase was exclusively European. For instance, in Nigeria, where prominent African traders had participated in the establishment of the Lagos Chamber of Commerce in the 1890s, their membership had been dispensed with, and it was not until the mid 1920s that African members were again accommodated.[8] The European-dominated chambers of commerce safeguarded their members' interests through their overseas and shipping ties and local associations with European managed banks and insurance houses. African traders were individual venturers, but their rival European merchants were corporate bodies and amalgams of strong firms. In the light of these developments there were no serious local threats to economic welfare, and colonial administrators therefore saw in their interventions in administering trade regulations a mere extension of their normal task of maintaining law and order.

The decade of colonial development

From 1946 through the early 1960s African states experienced the establishment and administration of development corporations, development plans and specific regulations to protect and assist the survival and growth of indigenous entrepreneurship under the leadership of colonial administrations. For the first time colonial administrators were learning to conceive, formulate and implement development programmes in consultation with the native rulers. Their tasks were specific. They were now required to design, implement and review specific measures and programmes to promote indigenous entrepreneurship.

The new responsibilities required new administrative units concerned with development matters and a new cadre of staff knowledgeable in social, economic and financial matters. This was the time the development officers cadre was being added to colonial establishments. Some commercial and accounting officers were needed to guide the operations of the marketing boards, co-operatives and loans boards which were to develop indigenous collective bargaining strength in trade. New technical officers were also required to provide extension services specifically for indigenous entrepreneurs. Information services on trade opportunities had to be developed to help indigenous traders. Some research and market studies had to be undertaken. The training and grading of these cadres of technical and professional officers added new dimensions to colonial personnel administration.

In the legal department extra work was involved in the formulation and review of legal instruments for the establishment of various development institutions specially designed to help African entrepreneurs hold their own. The task also involved the review of colonial regulations, which had to be amended to remove restrictions on indigenous enterprises or to ensure their exclusive advantage. These developments were more common in the English-speaking colonies than in other areas.

Thus the colonial development decades involved new administrative and management functions for colonial administrators. It resulted in the strengthening of staff resources with persons having developmental and financial management skills, the creation of new administrative units, and the development of new attitudes, even though somewhat paternalistic, in colonial administrators.

These colonial administrators were learning for the first time that it was their duty to prepare colonial peoples not only for political independence but also for economic self-reliance, and their overall performance in promoting indigenous entrepreneurship can be regarded as fairly creditable. They set up and guided the operations and management of the various development corporations and institutions with diligence and care. With limited data and a poor background knowledge of the social situation, they attempted to formulate development plans, the implementation of which they pursued with real dedication. These plans were usually under-fulfilled by wide margins, not for lack of funds but largely owing to inadequate executive capacity. The loan funds were underutilized because African producers who really needed the assistance were not covered by the credit facilities. The marketing boards succeeded in their task of bulk marketing and thereby accumulated large reserves, a greater part of which was later used to finance general development infrastructures.

Colonial administrators were very keen to see each administration finance its way, that is, achieve financial self-reliance and build up reserves, as good evidence of wise administration. Thus preoccupation with revenue-earning agricultural occupations led to a concentration on agricultural services for cash-crops and to the virtual neglect of food crops and agro-based industries.

The simple agricultural economy of the time had very little to test the integrity and managerial capability of colonial administrators. They were free from the political, tribal and family pressures that later bothered the integrity of their African successors. Even when they were obliged to change sides and help African entrepreneurs, the latter were still unorganized business groups and therefore less articulate and less able to create insurmountable problems in the administration of incentive schemes. They did not experience the pressure of party politics or of ministers who wanted their orders executed irrespective of whether they were legal or not. Thus colonial administrators charged with fostering the growth of indigenous entrepreneurship did not have the thorns, temptations and pitfalls that later events in the indigenization processes developed for succeeding administrators of independent African countries.

After independence

In the post-independence years a combination of public and private business ventures – a sort of mixed economy – was emerging. This was the type of economy that was acquiring more complex industrial and technological elements, which African administrators and managers had to promote. Tradition, political ideology and revolutionary developments exercised varying degrees of influence on the relative extent of indigenous private and public dominance in the evolving mixed economy. Whatever the form and relative degree of public/

private share in ownership, control and management of the resulting enterprises, administrative and managerial implications became more extensive and intensive. In this involvement some new and more complex responsibilities have emerged, while developmental functions aimed at protecting indigenous enterprises as in the interwar years continued to be operative, albeit on a more extensive scale. In the analysis that follows consideration will be given only to particular *new* elements and responsibilities in administrative and managerial implications of indigenization measures in selected African countries.

Promoting the growth of indigenous private enterprises

In African countries that have opted for mixed economies, both the public and the private sectors have been used as agencies for bringing about economic transformation as well as for the realization of the long-term objective of economic self-reliance. Here indigenization has been pursued on a planned basis since the attainment of political independence. In national development plans concrete measures have been adopted to foster the growth and strengthening of indigenous entrepreneurship – not only in such traditional areas as trade, agriculture and transportation, but also in the newer fields of industry and technical services. These measures have been backed by a clearer articulation of government policies for fostering either indigenous private enterprise or state enterprise or both. From time to time, especially in the preparation of new national development plans, performances have been reviewed and appropriate adjustments made in policies, strategies and promotional programmes. Particular attention has been given to government extension services in agriculture, small-scale industries, co-operatives and commerce. In all these activities senior civil servants were involved in the planning, implementation, control and review of policies and programmes.

French-speaking African states, in particular OCAM member states, have attempted to harmonize their approaches to the indigenization of their economies. The issues and objectives involved were discussed in the OCAM-sponsored symposia held in Abidjan in April 1969 and in Bangui in November 1970. The main principle of indigenization was adopted by the Yaounde Summit Conference of January 1970. Essentially, the principle placed emphasis on self-help, support from the public sector, co-operation among African businessmen, training of specialists to administer enterprise promotion centres, and training of managerial personnel. The immediate goal was to prepare African entrepreneurs to play a greater role in the development of small- and medium-scale enterprises. Unlike the Ivory Coast, they have underplayed the role of foreign private enterprise in providing logistic and financial support to the development of African enterprises.[9]

In Kenya and Zambia trade and transport licensing and work permits were among important instruments used to foster indigenous enterprises after independence. The Kenyan Immigration Act of 1967 required employers to obtain work permits for the employment of non-nationals in certain specific skilled employment. Similarly, the Trade Licensing Act of 1967 was aimed at transferring ownership of largely Asian-dominated medium- and small-sized businesses to African hands and at promoting the growth of African businesses.[10] By its provision non-citizens were excluded from trading in rural areas and the periphery of urban centres as well as from handling goods reserved for African entrepreneurs. The work permit was managed by the Kenyanization of Personnel Bureau. Tanzania and Ethiopia also operated a work permit system. Ghana, Nigeria and several other African countries have operated expatriate quotas for specific job areas. In Zambia the economic reform measures that were initiated in 1968 and further broadened in August 1969 and November 1970 were aimed at creating an economy that was locally controlled and geared to meet Zambian needs. Under these measures certain lines of trade were reserved for Zambians only.

Work permits, expatriate quotas, trade and road licensing systems affected expatriate businessmen who stopped at nothing to exercise pressures on senior officers concerned with administering these regulations and controls. Pressures brought to bear on these officials by political personalities, tribal and family groups and by wealthy traders have frequently led to corruption in administrative practices. In Kenya the transport licensing act also generated pressures and corruption. As in trade, pressure of mass communication from below was matched by pressure of non-African citizens and large-scale foreign operators at the top. The results were scandals about Africans who hired or sold licences to non-Africans or those who kept within the law but hired their vehicles to non-Africans.[11]

According to Karuga, although the Kenyanization of Personnel Bureau was supposed to detect such malpractices, the agency was understaffed and lacked the powers to enforce strict adherence to the letter and spirit of the Immigration Act of 1967. Cases of violations that were settled by the Immigration Department were not always satisfactory, and occasionally charges of corruption in the administration of work permits erupted in Parliament.[12] In Nigeria the immigration quota system would have been an effective instrument for increasing indigenous participation in management control and decision-making, but the manner of its administration reduced its effect because of corrupt practices.[13] These unfortunate experiences were not peculiar to the countries cited; other African countries have had their experiences of corrupt practices affecting the effectiveness and integrity of senior officials who administered programmes and policy measures designed to promote the growth of indigenous entrepreneurship.

Administrators had two sets of measures designed to promote indigenization: one set dealt with controls such as immigration regulations and the licensing systems aimed at preventing or controlling the entry of expatriates into business lines that were considered within the entrepreneurial capacity of indigenous investors; the other set comprised financial incentives, technical advice and the facilitation of developmental institutions designed to foster the growth and entrepreneurial capability of African investors. Both sets of measures were liable to administrative malpractices. The first set affected expatriate firms more directly, and some of them were not unknown to have used devious devices, including corrupt practices, to beat indigenization regulations.

Besides, the machinery meant to exercise the control measures was not always adequately funded and staffed. Thus, when expatriate quotas were fixed for a particular firm and an obligatory training of local staff agreed with the granting authorities (which could be the Manpower Ministry as in Tanzania), staff was not always available to follow up on compliance with the schedule of training and Africanization. It was then easy for the firm concerned to argue a good case for renewing the quota after the initial period because the administering officials did not possess the inside knowledge. If the officials proved too uncompromising the affected business manager would settle matters with the officials' administrative and/or political bosses.

With regard to the incentive schemes aimed at the growth of indigenous entrepreneurship, most of the administrative malpractices were connected with managerial omissions, lack of a sense of dedication, tribalism and inadequacy in material and human resources for the effective discharge of services. Classical cases of malpractices in the administration of loans and related incentive schemes, for example, have been exposed in many national commissions of inquiry such as the Coker Commission in the former Western Region of Nigeria. In relation to the needs of the people to be assisted, the field service and the administrative points of contacts were for budgetary reasons restricted so that services and incentive schemes could hardly reach those who needed them most. It should further be pointed out that the administrators were, by pre-service and in-service training, not always prepared to render objective selfless services.

Nigeria is one of the few African states that have developed an elaborate scheme of indigenization. The Nigerian Enterprises Promotion Decree no. 4 of 1972, together with the later tightening up of its provisions by Decree no. 3 of 1977, was designed to assist Nigerians to increase their stake in the Nigerian economy in terms of ownership, control and management at all levels and in all sectors of economic activities. In spite of the years of experience in planning for the growth of indigenous enterprise, the operation of the decree has revealed discrepancies and loopholes that expatriate businessmen did not hesitate to abuse in order to reduce the impact of the decree. The government White Paper on the implementation of the decree clearly admitted a number of administrative and legislative weaknesses in its provisions. According to the White Paper on the Report of the Indigenization Exercise, only one-third of the affected enterprises complied with the provisions by the countdown on 30 June 1975, and even among these, the primary objectives of ownership and control were largely thwarted by diffusion or by fronting.[14]

In an attempts to plug the leakages in the indigenization scheme and strengthen the effectiveness of the enforcement machinery, Nigeria found it necessary under the 1977 Decree to appoint a full-time executive chairman and secretariat for the Enterprises Promotion Board and to reorganize the board itself. A number of the board members then came from outside the public services. The chairman became fully responsible for the day-to-day management of the affairs of the board, while the secretary to the board headed the board's secretariat and became responsible to the chairman. Under the 1977 Decree the board has been empowered 'to advance and promote enterprises in which citizens of Nigeria shall participate fully and play a dominant role. The Board will also advise the Federal Commissioner for Industries on clearly defined policy guidelines for the promotion of Nigerian enterprises and on measures that would assist in ensuring the assumption of control of the Nigerian economy by Nigerians in the shortest possible time.'[15] The board has been given powers to seal off the premises of defaulting enterprises and to prosecute their proprietors.[16] Thus, under the second phase of the indigenization scheme the Nigerian government became determined to make its policy and programmes effective and to advance indigenization to a reasonable and desirable level.

It took the Nigerian government some five years fully to appreciate that indigenization policy measures must be well planned and that full-time, adequately staffed administrative and promotional machineries were needed. Not all potential investors and entrepreneurs always had all the information they needed in order to take advantage of the indigenization measures. Apart from the constraint of ignorance, sheer physical distances from state and federal capitals, inefficient postal and telecommunications facilities and the unco-operative attitudes of middle-level officials who were often unwilling to render service to the public without some private consideration also affected the effectiveness of incentive schemes. A large country such as Nigeria would have needed a network of incentive and information dissemination points in order to bring promotional services reasonably within easy reach of indigenous entrepreneurs.

The point brought forth by the Nigerian experience is that, where senior public servants had direct personal interest in the opportunity offered by indigenization measures and had themselves become major or petty capitalists while still in the public service, it was difficult to maintain that level of integrity characteristic of pre-independence administrations. It also further demonstrated that effectiveness in the implementation of indigenization measures depended not only on the integrity of officials but also on the adequacy of administrative arrangements, including the staffing and funding of the services responsible for the execution of policies and programmes.

Educational and training institutions, in particular management development programmes, have been established to help indigenous businessmen build up their manpower resources. It was not always lack of capital that handicapped the efforts of African private enterprise; more attention could have been paid to the development of executive and entrepreneurial capability simultaneously with the initiation of the various loan schemes of the post-independence years. Technology and business know-how were real constraints in the growth of African enterprises. These factors were hardly appreciated by the administrators of the 1960s. In Kenya, for example, it was proving difficult by 1970 to find capable Africans to replace Asian business concerns that government wanted to Africanize. In 1971 the Minister of Commerce and Industry had to confess that in Nairobi and Mombasa 262 shops had been given quit notices but only 63 Africans had applied to take over from the Asians.[17] This was not just due to lack of funds, as credit institutions were anxious to lend. The sheer shortage of Africans with managerial and entrepreneurial capability seriously affected response to the indigenization measures. The constraint was particularly severe with regard to industrial ventures requiring a good mix of modern technology.

The Ivory Coast has achieved spectacular economic growth since independence by using foreign investment to develop cash-crops, an infrastructure and industries. In this effort the government has paid only lip-service to the development of indigenous entrepreneurial and managerial potentials, notwithstanding the outstanding growth in formal education enrolment. Between 1966 and 1975 the concerted effort to Africanize and Ivoirianize resulted in limited changes in the proportion of non-Africans in the total labour force. 'Government plans for "Ivoirianization" of the private sector do not appear to be serious, as the administration does not want to coerce the foreign businessmen upon whom it relies.'[18] His Excellency, the President, had a dialogue with his ministers and top government officials in November 1969 on the status of Ivoirianization. 'In the discussion which followed, many attacks were made by officials against each other concerning the slow rate of Ivoirianization and the nepotism, general behaviour, and management of public services. Ethnic conflicts were brought out, particularly claims that the Baoule were manopolizing many key positions.'[19] If the Ivory Coast did not do much to build up its indigenous entrepreneurial capability it was because it had full confidence in its strategy of reliance on foreign investment, which was convincingly showing outstanding results.

In a number of African countries management practices by expatriate-controlled firms have made indigenization a difficult task to accomplish. That was the business group that considered itself most adversely affected by the indigenization schemes. Consequently, expatriate firms have not hesitated to indulge in malpractices so long it was in their interest to do so and they could get away with it. They have, at least through the influence of their home-based parent companies, used political and commercial pressures to decry indigenization measures and have given wide publicity to the inherent risk of driving away foreign capital. A classical case was Uganda since 1972. With the wholesale nationalization and expulsion of British and Asian businessmen in 1972, political and commercial pressures built up to castigate the country – foreign aid in the form of grants, loans and personnel dried up overnight; Uganda was denied the normal commercial credits in overseas transactions and was made to pay six months in advance for all import orders placed abroad while receiving late payments for her export sales. It did not always receive the full consignment of goods paid for, as shipments were sometimes short of orders to allow for inflationary effect in the interim.[20]

There were other sinister practices by those who managed foreign enterprises. Bribery in cash and kind was offered to highly placed officials and politicians in order to circumvent the regulations designed to promote indigenization. Excess expatriate quota and work permits were received or extended at a price. Sometimes the temptations offered to civil servants administering the regulations were too attractive to be missed. They have used business tactics and other unscrupulous devices to beat the provisions of various indigenization control measures. When pressed to Africanize their management they have done so by 'window-dressing', that is, recruiting Africans who met their particular requirements, training them and appointing them as 'managers' – officers with big offices, big titles, fat salaries and fringe benefits, but who really never participated fully in the management of the enterprises in which they were employed. Quantitatively, the number of African managers was growing in the 1960s, but they were concentrated in the functional areas of administration, legal services, public relations and personnel management. Even when they were placed in the right fields, their positions were subordinate and their expatriate superiors made sure that the grooming period was unduly protracted, with opportunities for participation in responsible decision-making in the interim very rare.[21] For direct appointment, several years of practical managerial or technical experience was demanded, and in most cases hardly any African could meet such a requirement.[22]

When governments became determined to see to it that their citizens participated in the ownership and control of businesses and adopted regulations for total or partial takeover from expatriates, various devices were used to negate the effort. Some expatriates found it necessary, as in Kenya, to become citizens and so continue their business interest. In Nigeria a number of expatriate firms that were obliged to sell their concerns sold to African 'proprietors' who lacked experience in the line of business. These they used as 'fronts' while they continued to retain the real management control of the enterprise by serving in the backroom office as 'technical consultants' to the new proprietors. Still others, particularly the big companies, used pressures to get extended dates for compliance with the law. Some foreign investors sold out and hurriedly repatriated their proceeds rather than reinvest in new businesses. Some firms deliberately handpicked eminent citizens and loyal employees, got them to 'purchase' sizeable shares with loans they helped them secure and which were repayable from dividends earned on shares, and later got them membership of boards of directors, where they remained ever-grateful for the opportunity to share in the fortunes of the enterprises rather than in real management. These and other devious and calculated management malpractices that served to slow down the pace of indigenization have been exposed in a number of official enquiries and related White Papers in Nigeria and other African countries.[23] These were some of the experiences that administrators who formulated the various indigenization measures never anticipated, and to which they had to react as resourcefully as circumstances permitted them.

State participation: public enterprises

State participation in economic ventures beyond the range of utilities, infrastructure and strategic industries was often designed to ensure domestic ownership, control and management of 'the commanding heights of national economy'. Thus, state and indigenous private entrepreneurships have had the joint task of bringing about economic independence. Up to a point, foreign private enterprise could assist in this effort. In the Ivory Coast state enterprise was being pursued in strong partnership with foreign private investors; in Egypt, socialist Ethiopia and Tanzania foreign private investors were meant to play only a limited role. To African countries in general indigenization was an issue not of the relative role of public and indigenous private sectors, but rather of the effectiveness of their combined efforts in ultimately eliminating foreign domination and control of national economies.

Government participation in economic ventures since independence has taken two main approaches: planned intervention and revolutionary intervention. Different economic and political justifications have been advanced for the various approaches. Socialism, capitalism, mixed economies and even sheer tradition have each provided a base for action. Government participation has been claimed to have been made on behalf of the people it represents and leads. In Nigeria justification for state participation was clearly indicated in the second national development plan as follows: 'It is vital, therefore, for Government to acquire and control on behalf of the Nigerian Society, the greater proportion of the productive assets of the country. . . . In order to ensure that the economic destiny of Nigerians is determined by Nigerians themselves, the Government will seek to widen and intensify its positive participation in industrial development.'[24]

Planned public participation in economic activities has taken many forms. New statutory corporations have been established in fields where the government felt action was necessary but where indigenous entrepreneurship was lacking or private enterprise was reluctant to venture.[25] Ghana's venture into the shipping business was partly so motivated and partly designed to assist indigenous shippers to reduce the monopolistic hold of the West African Conference Lines. In another direction public corporations have been specially established to give development leadership to neglected areas such as the river basins and deltas in Nigeria. Where foreign control affected strategic sectors such as oil refinery, petroleum oil distribution, cement manufacture and commercial banking, the government had sought control through partnership equity shareholding with its position moving from minority to majority shareholding. In some cases it has been outright nationalization and takeover, involving protracted negotiations on compensation. In other cases, where experience after a brief period of public ownership proved nationalization to be the wrong choice, denationalization was undertaken for a given line of business, as in Zaire and Egypt.

Action leading to such state participation has usually been planned over time; care was generally taken to ensure smooth operation and government investments were judiciously made. In some cases action was anticipated in national development plans and financial provisions were thereby ensured. Such planned action has enabled public servants involved in their implementation to anticipate bottlenecks, prepare for action, set up special units to execute required action, monitor implementation and even train staff in advance.

An example of well planned state intervention to bring about rapid economic growth is the Ivory Coast. Its strategy was a combination of a free enterprise system adequately backed by foreign investment and state enterprises. It has established well over thirty state-owned corporations to engage in economic activities. These corporations were managed by leading members of government, often deputies of the National Assembly. Their activities were co-ordinated by the ministries of planning and economic affairs which controlled a large development planning machinery, including the Bureau National des Etudes Techniques du Developpement. Cabinet-level committees and individual ministries were involved in carrying out major development projects. In fact, there has been intensive active public involvement in the management of development efforts and this has produced spectacular economic growth since independence.[26]

However, according to Samir Amin, the Ivory Coast has experienced spectacular economic 'growth without development' in the sense that *per capita* growth of economic indicators has not been accompanied by indigenous participation in the growth process.[27] The point being made is not whether private indigenous enterprise, the permanent basis for the country's economic self-reliance, has not participated as it ought to have done, but that civil servants have played a major role in bringing about accelerated economic growth. For the present it was not government policy to specially nurture the growth of indigenous entrepreneurship as Nigeria, Kenya or Ghana would have wished to do or are doing. Rather, senior civil servants in the Ivory Coast were being made to play a major management role in making government policy work, although their self-interest as members of the élite class prevented them from appreciating the fact that the long-term path to economic self-reliance lay in the growth of indigenous entrepreneurship rather than continued exploitation by foreign investors.

The other category of public intervention has been the result of a revolutionary act of nationalization, socialism or public control. Public takeovers of abandoned private enterprises after the wars of liberation, as witnessed when Zaire, Algeria, Angola and Mozambique attained political independence, belong to this group, as do the revolutionary waves of nationalization in Uganda in 1970 and in 1972, and the nationalization of urban and rural lands, extra houses, important industries and departmental stores in socialist Ethiopia in 1974. Egypt also had a wave of nationalization, in the years following the Suez Crisis. These state takeovers came as bombshells to their original owners, who lost their investments with or without compensation, and as a new challenge to the civil servants who were redeployed to manage the seized enterprises.

The administrative and managerial functions and the challenges that were involved in the foregoing planned and revolutionary public participation in risky business ventures were definitely different from the functions that senior civil servants were called upon to discharge in the sphere of protecting, assisting and promoting indigenous private enterprises. They were required not only to plan, control and review performances by public enterprises, but also to actually control or oversee the management of an increasing number of public undertakings which were required to show profits. This was more than the post-independence task of administering the process of socioeconomic change and development; they were in fact being required to act and behave in some cases as businessmen, yet remain in work habits and integrity as civil servants. Reconciling these conflicting interests and work motivation were some of the new challenges administrators have had to cope with in recent years.

A number of problems were experienced. First, regarding the revolutionary nationalization of private enterprise, as in Uganda in 1972–4, the situation initially was totally chaotic and confused. With the exodus of experienced managers and the resultant harsh international climate generated by the Western industrialized world and by India, it was extremely difficult to manage the acquired enterprises. Working records were scarce; suppliers' credits were unavailable; suppliers' and buyers' customs were cut off; contracts were dishonoured; and there was general disorder in business relations. That was the situation that the few available experienced administrators were asked to manage. They did their best in the circumstances. It was not surprising that many factories had to fold up, and to this day many still suffer from lack of spare parts, inadequate stock and instability in managerial staff.[28]

In such revolutionary takeovers of private enterprises, administrators were called upon to exercise unusual swiftness of action; to operate without appropriate machinery, staff and funds; without basic information and data; and without a previous plan of operation. An administrative bureaucrat would suddenly find himself redeployed by decision of government to become a business executive or 'general manager' of a major corporation or manufacturing enterprise because his capability in the civil service as an administrator had been commendable. The unlucky official would have had no opportunity to reorient his attitude and acquire the relevant tools of his new trade from a local or overseas management institute. In response to official instruction, he would move to the new post, to a grand executive office with equally grand problems. He would learn after a brief meeting with his management personnel that the enterprise was virtually grounded or that half of its production capacity was out of use because of lack of machine spare parts, lack of foreign exchange allocation and lack of middle and higher-level technical personnel, since these technical posts were until 1972 monopolized by Asian and British technicians. Thus the administrator now turned business manager would find himself faced with a series of crises, and on the job he learnt and managed from crisis to crisis.

Having settled down and begun to acquire practical skills in management, he would further find that his troubles were not over. Political and party pressures influenced decisions on the location of distribution points; even the appointment of secretaries and messengers, of selling and buying agents, etc., were matters in which outside pressures affected his good judgement. At the meetings of the board of directors the influence of the chairman was predominant. Furthermore, instructions from 'His Excellency' overrode all else. The general manager would have done barely a year on the job when another radio announcement would tell of the establishment of a new public enterprise and the 'trusted official' would again be redeployed to take charge of yet another new public enterprise.[29]

A less chaotic but difficult situation prevailed in Ethiopia following the nationalization of the major departmental stores and a few other enterprises. Certain essential supplies dried up as angry former owners made sure that foreign suppliers withdrew their customs and credits. The new set of 'managers' – former civil servants – were really new to the business world, and had to learn the hard way and slowly. It took some time to negotiate new sources of supply from China and other socialist countries. A more serious problem that the new management had to contend with was the attitude of workers to the new situation and the need to motivate workers to maintain production. If the enterprise was now a government business, it was felt that it was no longer necessary to work all that hard. There was also the problem of the disinterested worker, and of those who felt that, as land had gone to the tiller, so the urban enterprises ought to go to the worker! The ideological revolution that engineered class conflicts as socialism permeated production, services and political orientation resulted in casualties of 'anti-revolutionary elements' which substantially deprived the economy of the more experienced managers, administrators and intellectuals.

State participation in business ventures, including partnership arrangements with local or foreign partners, involves public servants' participation in management planning and control. As a minority or majority equity shareholder, the government nominated top civil servants and politicians to the relevant boards of directors; where the government was the sole owner or majority partner, it provided the chairmen for the various boards of directors. Invariably, the permanent secretaries of the supervising or parent ministries often served as chairmen of these boards. Their deputies and sometimes less senior officers also have attended board meetings of enterprises in which the government had an interest. These men were usually already overworked, and as members of the administrative class were liable to transfer to other services every few years. A permanent secretary that had a large ministry to manage and two or three corporations to chair had to be a superman to survive the physical strain let alone do a good business of managing a profit-making enterprise. If he gave too much attention to the corporations his ministry's other duties would suffer; rather, he would opt to let the technical managers run the enterprises.

In performing these unusually very demanding jobs, civil servants have not had the opportunity to be retrained in modern management techniques and in business management in particular. The result is that most of the vital business decisions of public enterprises are left to technical partners who might be minority equity shareholders. In effect, government majority share ownership has not always resulted in effective control of the business. In Nigeria Professor Nwankwo has denounced the position taken by the government in not wanting to take a real part in management. According to him, effective management control could not be secured by merely owning without controlling and by leaving management (usually expatriate) to do as it pleased, as has been the case with some of the indigenous institutions.[30]

Some problem areas in the management of public enterprises

As already indicated, there were more administrative and management functions in indigenization involving nationalization and public enterprises than in policies and programmes for promoting the growth of private indigenous enterprises. With respect to public enterprise, some attention will now be paid to specific issues and problem areas, namely, planning; administrative or regulatory controls; interest groups; decision-making; leadership styles; and joint ventures.

Administrators in the public sector have had direct responsibility in the planning of public enterprises, from conception through establishment, operation and expansion. They were involved more with financial and personnel planning and less with production, stock and materials planning and management. Planning responsibility for pre-feasibility studies, project selection and financing would tend to be more intense in parastatal organizations providing social services and public utilities, such as tourist-promoting hotels in Uganda. By contrast, civil servants generally left detailed operational and production planning to technical managers in public enterprises that were expected to operate with a profit motive. In both cases, administrators in the supervising or parent ministries had a duty to determine, elaborate and interpret national priorities and development objectives in the sectors served by public enterprises they helped to establish or that came under their jurisdiction.

Administrative or regulatory controls over the operations of public enterprises were necessary to safeguard the interest of the government as the sole or majority equity shareholder in a given enterprise. These controls were both direct and indirect, and in their operation senior administrators were involved.[31] Direct controls were exercised through the board of directors. The government was represented or appointed a chairman to the board. The man for the job was either a politician, a scholar, a permanent secretary or a senior official. Participation in board meetings helped to determine how the general policy of the enterprise should take shape, the general guidelines for running its business and the targets to be reached with given resources. Strong government representation, both quantitative and qualitative, influenced the enterprise more than any weak presence. Through the official representatives the government issued directives to board members on national priorities and development strategies which the enterprise must take into consideration in its investment decisions.

Indirect controls on public enterprises involved substantial and at times excessive administrative intervention. The Ministry of Finance exercised controls through investment programmes, import–export regulations and foreign exchange controls. These controls affected investment decisions, production and expansion planning and loan-raising power. Major decisions on borrowings, price fixing and appointment of senior management personnel frequently required prior clearance with, and ministerial approval of, the responsible or parent ministries. Thus many vital decisions affecting finance, investment policy, pricing, top-level appointment, etc., which affected the operation of public enterprises were frequently made outside the enterprise in government ministries.[32]

In addition to the general monitoring of the operation of public enterprises under their supervision, parent ministries demanded and received annual reports which reviewed all aspects of the operation and performance records of each parastatal enterprise. The auditors' reports also provided fuller insight into the financial management of the enterprise. Administrators needed these reviews to brief their political bosses via performance reports on each public enterprise before Parliament, to which the enterprises were ultimately accountable.

Specific managerial problems were involved in operating the board system in the management of a public enterprise. Various interest groups were often represented at the directors' board – workers, trade unions, government, private indigenous and private foreign investors. It was not always that the conflicting interests of the groups were sufficiently harmonized to be able to define clear objectives and goals for technical managers to strive to attain.[33] Such pressure groups sometimes influenced vital decisions relating to appointment, pricing and investment policies. Operating within such pressure groups really put civil servants representing the government interest to the greatest test of loyalty and integrity; yet they have to strive to maintain to the best of their ability the public interest.

Conflicting interests in the case of joint ventures could prove very challenging to, or even expose, official representatives at the board. The socioeconomic development objectives that public enterprises were expected to serve could conflict with the insistence of the private partners on profit and long-term returns. A situation might develop whereby government representation, for lack of technical background, might become the 'silent' partner, thus allowing the foreign partners to have things their own way. Senior administrators had to work hard to prevent this from happening.

The type of service rendered and the development objectives set for each public enterprise to a large extent influenced the administrative and management styles to be adopted by the parent ministries. As already stated, functions differed between organizations that were of a business and profit-making nature, those for the development of infrastructure such as transport and communications corporations, and those providing utilities and social services.[34] Management and leadership styles in the case of direct business enterprises would tend to be close to the practice and experience of the private sector with minimal administrative interference from the civil service.

Lessons to be learned

The analyses in the preceding sections have shown that public administrations in African countries have had increasing responsibility for the formulation, planning and implementation of policies and programmes to bring about the ultimately effective indigenization of African economies. This task is by no means fully accomplished; for some countries considerable gains have been made; for others realistic beginnings are yet to be made; and for all, the task will continue more extensively and intensively in the coming two or more decades.

The transformation of African economies from the present dependent status to one of self-sustaining growth and economic self-reliance will continue to be a major development task. The strategies for bringing this about will vary according to national and political circumstances. State enterprise backed by strong foreign investments may continue for some countries; others may opt for dominant state control through public enterprise and nationalization, or through socialism; yet other groups may choose the middle way of strong public sector operating side by side with very strong private indigenous sector, relying on their combined effort to effect a real command on national economic activities. In all these combinations of strategies, civil servants will become increasingly involved in administrative and managerial functions of planning, implementing and managing public enterprises, and equally vigorously involved in designing and executing policies, programmes and incentive schemes and services for stimulating the growth of indigenous private enterprise.

In the light of the continuing nature of the task, it would be necessary to view the administration and management of indigenization processes on a long-term and systematically planned basis. This planning action must be an integral part of overall national development planning operations. An appropriate permanent machinery would need to be established, located at an authoritative level and adequately staffed to initiate, monitor and co-ordinate government action aimed at increasing indigenization of the national economy. No longer could African countries afford the unplanned, unco-ordinated and often short-sighted indigenization action of the past. It is not enough to talk about it and shout policy goals at political meetings; sustained concrete action is needed. The goal is economic independence, and African states need to work for this with sustained determination. Public servants must appreciate this need and be totally committed to it.

Political constraints have been an important factor determining the effectiveness of public enterprises as well as the fruitfulness of various schemes designed to promote indigenous private enterprise. Equally, social group pressures have served as contributory factors affecting the integrity and decision-making powers of senior administrators and managers in charge of indigenization measures and the management of public enterprises. Ways must therefore be found to reduce the influence of socio-political pressures, both in the operation of public enterprises and in the administrative practices of civil servants, so that indigenization can be pursued as a national effort, without sectional and personal interests.

Africa's strategy options and indigenization choices, and the means for the attainment of desired goals, need to be re-examined over time. It is necessary to consider the immediate and long-term effectiveness of whatever options are chosen in the light of what serves the country's best interest.

Externally oriented development strategies have in the past made African governments pay merely lip-service to stimulating and assisting the growth of indigenous private enterprises. Shortages of capital and of technical and managerial personnel as well as a lack of investment opportunities and entrepreneurial capabilities will need to be faced more squarely in the future. National prosperity has to be seen to lie in the potentials and growth of indigenous enterprises, which must be nurtured and sustained by deliberate government policies and assistance programmes. The effectiveness of incentive schemes and their administrative efficiency will need to be reviewed and reoriented away from attracting external capital towards mobilizing internal resources and promoting indigenous entrepreneurship.

Experience points to the need for a judicious control in the management of public enterprises. It may be necessary to consider the extent to which effective public control and ownership could be judiciously separated from operational management, especially with regard to parastatal enterprises involved in direct business ventures. These enterprises need a reasonable degree of managerial flexibility and financial autonomy to be able to relate their operations to similar ventures in the private sector. Too much official interference in pricing, appointments, investment decisions and loan policy has caused considerable delays and has affected the competence and operations of public enterprises.

The human element can make or break the effectiveness of administrative action in the indigenization process. Civil servants were not originally trained to be business managers. The change from the administration of law and order to the administration of development activities, a change of only recent origin, has yet to influence substantially the professional and attitudinal dispositions of administrators. Consequently, African countries need rapidly to build up adequate resources of administrators and managers who are properly oriented to the development task.

Greater attention should be paid to the motivation, remuneration and training of administrators charged with responsibility for implementing the indigenization programmes. Training is needed in development attitudes, and re-training in modern business management techniques is particularly essential for senior administrators who are redeployed to manage public enterprises. Above all, a greater effort is called for in the development of both general and functional management skills at all levels, in an attempt to enhance indigenous participation in the real management of enterprises. It is not enough to own enterprises and have majority equity shareholding without effective control of both the overall management and day-to-day technical operation of indigenized businesses. To achieve effective domestic control of 'the commanding heights of the national economy', African states must count on their own human and material resources. Past experiences in the operation of indigenization schemes offer the best training grounds for officers who have to plan and administer new measures to advance indigenization objectives. Countries could learn from one another through attachment training in other African countries and through other ways of exchanging experiences.

Leadership is crucial. On the part of the government there is need for firmness, objectivity, clarity of purpose and resourcefulness in the means and measures for achieving the goals of indigenization. Equally, indigenous entrepreneurs need to accept the challenge and to be prepared to play the self-reliant role expected of a dynamic private sector.

A final word on cost. Indigenization policy is an expensive proposition. It is a cost that must be borne for long-term benefits. Adequate financial resources must be provided, as the indigenization of technologically complex enterprises, for example, is more expensive than that of small- and medium-scale ventures. Funds are required for direct investment by government and for lending to enable private indigenous investors to take over from foreign owners. Resources are also necessary to establish and manage the various institutional and administrative arrangements that facilitate the implementation of indigenization measures, such as investment and credit institutions, stock exchange, extension services, training institutions, consultancy services and other enabling facilities. The central machinery that plans, co-ordinates and oversees the implementation of the indigenization measures must be adequately staffed and provided with resources for effective operation. All these are bound to demand more resources as the indigenization process advances.

Notes

1 I. J. Ebong, 'The policy of indigenization and its implications for national growth', *Proceedings of the Tenth Annual Conference of the Nigerian Institute of Management* (Lagos: National Institute of Management, 1972), p. 9.
2 For a detailed account of the historical evolution of policies and measures designed to foster the early phase of indigenization, or more appropriately indigenous participation, see Ayo Ogunsheye, 'Experience and problems of indigenous enterprises', *Proceedings of the Tenth Annual Conference of NIM*, pp. 12–16.
3 For the Zambian experience in this regard see J. H. Chileshe, 'The indigenization of African economies: case study on the Zambia' (mimeo), p. 64.
4 Ogunsheye, p. 13.
5 Adebayo Adedeji, Presidential Address at the Fourteenth Inter-African Public Administration and Management Seminar, 27 October–3 November 1975, Maseru Lesotho, Seminar Proceedings (Maseru, 1975), p. 15.
6 'Approaches to indigenization', *Proceedings of the Fourteenth Inter-African Public Administration and Management Seminar*, pp. 25–7.
7 Kenyan examples are the Coffee Plantations Registration Ordinance of 1918, which prevented Africans from growing coffee; the Marketing of Native Produce Ordinance of 1935, limiting marketing to Europeans and Asians. See C. Ake, 'The Indigenization of African Economies – A Perspective on Political Constraints', *Proceedings of the Fourteenth Inter-African Public Administration and Management Seminar*, p. 83.
8 Ogunsheye, p. 13.
9 'Indigenization of business enterprises: lessons from developing countries', ECA paper presented to the First National Conference on Management Development Ibadan (Nigeria), 7–9 March 1974 (unpublished).
10 James G. Karuga, 'Africanization and management development in Kenya', Centre for International Studies, Massachusetts Institute of Technology, July 1974, pp. 28–9 (unpublished).
11 Colin Leys, *Underdevelopment in Kenya* (Berkeley: University of California Press 1974), pp. 153ff.
12 Karuga, p. 29.
13 Dr S. U. Ugoh, 'Some Problems of Industrialization: Indigenization Businesses in Nigeria', May 1972, (mimeo).
14 G. O. Nwankwo, 'Nigeria in Search of a Just and Egalitarian Society', University of Lagos, March 1977 (mimeo), p. 9. A com-

prehensive review of the scheme is contained in 'Problems and Prospects of Indigenisation', in *Management in Nigeria*, (Nigerian Institute of Management 1976).

15 *Nigerian Chronicle*, 20 January 1977.

16 G.P.O. Chikelu, 'Aims and Objectives of the Indigenization Scheme', in *Management in Nigeria*, pp. 21–5.

17 *East African Standard*, 14 August 1971.

18 Michael A. Cohen, *Urban Policy and Political Conflict in Africa – A Study of the Ivory Coast*, (Chicago: University Press 1974), p. 157.

19 ibid, p. 125.

20 ECA Mission to Uganda, May 1976.

21 S. G. Odia, 'The Role of Management Training in the Indigenization of the Private Sector', *Proceedings of the Fourteenth Inter-African Public Administration and Management Seminar* pp. 130–3.

22 This can be verified in the advertisement pages of most African newspapers, especially where the requirement is for middle and higher management.

23 Ademola Banjo, 'The Principal Problems of Indigenization', in *Management in Nigeria*, pp. 29–35.

24 *Second National Development Plan, 1970–1974* (Lagos: Government Printer), p. 289.

25 Iddi Simba, 'Public enterprise – the African experience', CAFRAD document TMP/76–II no. 24, pp. 4–6.

26 Cohen, pp. 24–5, 29.

27 ibid, p. 25.

28 Official briefing to ECA mission, May 1976.

29 The narrative here presented is based on but not peculiar to Uganda. Similar events have happened in a number of African countries that have taken revolutionary measures to effect public control. The brief description given here summarized the official briefing the author participated in during the ECA Mission to Uganda in May 1976.

30 Nwankwo, 'Nigeria in search of a just and egalitarian society', p. 10.

31 'The management of public enterprises', CAFRAD document, TMP/76–II, pp. 4–8; Simba, 'Public enterprise: the African experience', pp. 7–8.

32 Marshall Hall, 'Some management problems in public enterprises', CAFRAD document, TMP/76–II, no. 25, p. 2.

33 'Planning in public enterprises', CAFRAD document, TMP/76–II, no. 9.

34 Simba, 'Public enterprise: the African experience', pp. 2–3, 6; 'The management of public enterprises', pp. 2–3.

Part Four

Conclusion

15 Prospects and limitations of indigenization

Adebayo Adedeji

The case studies in Chapters 3–12 reveal an uneven progress in achieving the various national objectives of indigenization. Few African nations, however, have reversed their policies of economic self-determination: most have gone on to build on their achievements and to learn from their failures. Unfortunately, little attempt has been made to co-ordinate efforts between countries; it is not uncommon for one African nation to be seen applying policy measures without taking into account the pitfalls and weaknesses revealed by the experiences of those who have already adopted the same measures.

Africa's strategy for development and indigenization

Recently African states, both individually and collectively, have been involved in serious self-examination of their conditions and their role. They have been asking such basic questions as whether Africa was destined to be poor and underdeveloped given the vast natural resources of the region; whether Africa is destined by design or fate always to play a dependent role in international economic relations, and whether, through collective self-reliance and co-operation, the prevailing order in international relations could not be redesigned in a manner that would enable Africa to participate on a more equitable basis.

This new African consciousness has been articulated at various forums. The debates under the aegis of the North–South Dialogue, the Thirty-Second Ordinary Session of the Council of Ministers of the Organization of African Unity (Nairobi, 23 February–4 March 1979), the OAU/ECA Symposium on the Future Development Prospects of Africa Towards the Year 2000 (Monrovia, 12 to 16 February 1979), the ECA/UNEP Seminar on Alternative Patterns of Development and Life Styles for the African Region (Addis Ababa, from 5–9 March 1979), the ECA Conference of Ministers' Fourteenth Session (Rabat, March 1979) and the OAU Council of Ministers' meeting and the Ordinary Session of the Heads of State and Government (Monrovia, July 1979) offered ample opportunities for African states to review their economic situation and to reassert their determination to end economic dependence and economic exploitation through a sustained effort in co-operation and collective self-reliance. This reaffirmation is but a further articulation of the African Declaration on Co-operation, Development and Economic Independence, adopted by the heads of state and government of the Organization of African Unity at their Tenth Ordinary Session in Addis Ababa on 25 May 1973.[1]

These various forums have striven to give a new dimension to the indigenization of African economies in their regional context. The various resolutions adopted have provided basic principles and guidelines for the further articulation and justification of policy measures for the attainment of national self-reliance and economic co-operation on a sustained basis. National self-reliance is essential to the attainment of collective self-reliance at the regional level, while the pursuit of the latter is bound to accelerate the achievement of the former.

African states fully realize the fragile nature of the present structure of their economies and the risk of their over-dependence on the economies of the industrialized states. This realization has in recent years been brought into sharper focus by the disappointing results of many attempts at the international level to restructure existing international economic relations and usher in a new world order in which the developing countries would have increased opportunities to improve their positions *vis-à-vis* those of the industrialized countries. Examples of these attempts include the North–South dialogue; the deliberate refusal of the technologically advanced economies to transfer technology to the developing countries unless on their own terms; the reluctance of the industrialized countries to relocate industries in developing countries, largely because of domestic opposition from investment and employment interest groups; the failure of international monetary arrangements to restore confidence and stability in those currencies that have been used as foreign exchange reserves; and difficulties over commodity agreements.

What the series of failures have amply demonstrated to African countries is that, as a group, and as the least developed region in the world, co-operation with the prosperous industrialized countries based on trade and aid is not going to help them become prosperous by maintaining traditional economic patterns and dependent relationships, particularly under the classical international division of labour whereby African states remain suppliers of basic raw materials and importers of capital, technology, technical know-how and manufactured products.

It is not that African states do not appreciate the advantages of international economic relations and co-operation: they fully appreciate the benefits. However, in terms of their long-term interests and goals of achieving an economic independence that will make political independence meaningful and effective, they have to strive to put the ownership, control and management of their national economies in their own hands and in the hands of their own citizens. This is the situation in the developed economies, and African states are only demanding the right to control their own development and to determine their own life-styles.

What the resolutions at Rabat and Monrovia have done is to give collective political and moral endorsement to the indigenization objectives and measures that many African states have initiated in the past. Commitment to the 'Strategy for African Development in the 1980s' requires that, in initiating overall integrated national development planning, sufficient measures should be built into national development plans to ensure a sustained application of the principle of co-operation and collective slef-reliance. Translating self-reliance into action requires the indigenization of action at the policy and programme formulation stages, and at implementation and management stages. Such self-reliance can be meaningful if planned on a sustained basis.

For a number of key sectors the Rabat resolution on the 'Strategy for African Development and Plan of Action' stipulated specific guideline principles, policy objectives and action to be taken at national and multinational levels for the attainment of self-reliance and economic independence. Some of these sectors are considered below simply to illustrate future directions in indigenization policy measures.

With regard to natural resources, the strategy aims at substantially strengthening national and multinational capabilities in all aspects of natural resource exploitation and use. This includes capabilities for the collection and dissemination of basic information and data on natural resources, for the management and conservation of these resources, for their planned exploitation and utilization, for the development of policies and institutional infrastructure, and for negotiating skills. These capabilities are necessary to enable African states to exercise effective sovereignty and control over their natural resources for the benefit of their national and local economies. Developing self-reliance by means of creating the required institutional infrastructures and technical competences, if well directed, is expected to lead to an ending of exploitative arrangements and of foreign control of Africa's natural resources.

It is not enough for African states to negotiate and achieve technological transfers from the developed economies to their own economies. Such technology has to be adapted to the African situation and further developed to cope with solving additional developmental problems besides those problems for which imported technology was originally envisaged. This is the process of 'localizing' or indigenizing technology in Africa. To this end, the Rabat resolution and Plan of Action has, *inter alia*, called for the development and strengthening of indigenous agents with a capability to import, develop, apply and adapt technology. The prescribed measures include technology-oriented teaching of science and applied research, the development of African technical entrepreneurs, and the establishment of institutional arrangements facilitating local control on the importation, application, adaptation and diffusion of technology in the development process.

Human resources in the form of technical know-how and managerial skills constitute a further area where the effort to indigenize has frequently come to grief. There have been cases of private enterprises that have been nationalized and were later de-nationalized and returned to private operation, primarily because of lack of managerial and technical manpower to operate the enterprises concerned profitably. Priority should be given to manpower training in such areas as project design, planning, implementation and management.

In according high priority to industrial development, emphasis was given to the need to ensure the necessary linkages so as to increase the multiplier effect of industrialization on other development sectors at the country level. This is to be achieved through a planned systematic industrial development in preference to a sectoral approach. Here again, the guideline for action advocated the promotion of indigenous entrepreneurship, the up-grading and commercialization of indigenous technologies, the regulation, control and adaptation of imported industrial technologies, and the development of industrial manpower and of technological and industrial institutional infrastructures. These are essential ingredients for the development of self-reliant capabilities for industrial development and for ensuring an indigenized industrial growth.

From the foregoing illustrations it would appear that African states have now articulated principles and policy guidelines for the attainment of self-sustaining and self-reliant economic development in a manner that will ensure the full control and management of African economies by Africans and for the benefit of Africans. The guidelines for future action are pretty clear. What is still needed are the foresight, courage and total commitment by political leaders and top executives; the full consciousness of the implications of development through co-operation and self-reliance by leaders in the private and parastatal sectors; and their acceptance of the challenge as an opportunity to demonstrate that they are capable of the trust placed in them. When all these conditions and expectations have been met on a sustained basis, the prospects for realizing indigenization objectives, notwithstanding the earlier setbacks and failures, will be good. Success, of course, breeds success. The more successful African states become with their indigenization measures, the more faith they will have in their goals and strategy; equally, the more faith they have in their capabilities, the better the prospects will be for indigenizing the African economies in the decades that lie ahead.

Economic integration and indigenization

These prospects would be further enhanced if African states could agree on a strategy of co-operation and collective self-reliance. At the core of this strategy is the need for planned, integrated development at both national and regional levels. Today African economies suffer from several disabilities, the principal one being the lack of integration between sectors and sub-sectors and the failure to take advantage of complementarities of resource endowment and markets. Such integration ensures that developments in agriculture, industry, mining and other production sectors are mutually reinforcing and that the various services, transportation, manpower and institutional infrastructures are being developed to support growth in these production sectors, whose primary concern is the satisfaction of domestic demands rather than the traditional preoccupation with foreign exchange earnings through the export of basic raw materials.

Economic integration at regional levels aims to achieve mutual advantages similar to those desired at the national level. Its primary objectives are: (1) to take advantage of complementarities of markets and resource endowment; (2) to develop mutually beneficial linkages between regional poles of development, complementary markets and pools of labour and technology resources; (3) to foster intra-African trade and reduce the present over-dependence on trade and other economic links with the industrialized countries; and (4) to develop greater economic strength for the African region as a whole through the increased economic capacity of individual African states.

Commitments to economic co-operation and integration have been declared since 1963 in several African forums, and pertinent resolutions have been adopted by the legislative bodies of the Economic Commission for Africa and of the Organization of African Unity, all advocating African economic integration. While the resolutions on commitments to economic integration are specific, clear and numerous, however, implementation has been very modest. A number of multinational and sub-regional economic co-operation arrangements have been made, but only a few of the established intergovernmental organizations have worked very well; a number are moribund, while the one-time great hope in regional co-operation, the East African

Community, was disbanded owing to lack of political goodwill. All these belonged to the first generation of experiments in economic co-operation. In recent years African countries have learned from past experiences and are making fresh attempts at co-operation and economic integration. This fresh venture has been led by the formation of the Economic Community of West African States, which seems to be working well. And the countries of eastern and southern Africa have in the last two years began working earnestly to create a Preferential Trade Area which will ultimately lead to a wider economic community covering seventeen or eighteen countries.

One of the other measures being advocated is African joint ventures in industrial operations. This will not only take advantage of the complementarities of natural resource endowments and manpower and financial resources, but will also pool these resources as well as their markets to enable economies of scale to be maximized. Another objective is for such African multinationals one day to become a countervailing force to the transnational corporations.

The real constraint to the realization of African multinational enterprises is the lack of political goodwill. Total commitment to the cause of African economic integration is still more of an ideal than a practice; too often individual African leaders regard economic co-operation as a threat to their political sovereignty. Admittedly, it would not be desirable to substitute exploitation by the industrialized countries by exploitation by the few African countries that are developing strong national economies. This is not likely to be the case, since the type of economic integration arrangements that African states are currently working out (as in the Economic Community of West African States) provides for sacrifices on the part of the better-off members and compensation grants to the weaker ones while the location of joint ventures takes cognizance of the resource endowments and employment needs of the less developed states.

The limiting factors

It is clear that our hope for a successful achievement of indigenization lies in the persuance of an alternative pattern of development based on the principles of self-sustained growth and national collective self-reliance and a reasonable degree of honesty and integrity among those who man the affairs of state at all levels. But important as they are, these principles alone will not be enough. There are many other important factors that bear heavily on Africa's ability to indigenize, and the absence or prevalence of them will determine the limits of the possibilities of indigenization. We shall discuss, albeit briefly, five of these factors: (1) the dynamism of the economy; (2) the availability of investment resources; (3) the availability of technical and managerial manpower; (4) the extent of the involvement of the mass of the people in the indigenization process and the equitable sharing of the proceeds of indigenization; and (5) the rediscovery of Africa's self-confidence in the ability to accomplish and achieve.

How successful can the indigenization policy be in a country whose economy is stagnant? How much can a country overburdened by external debt attempt to indigenize its economy? A country that is overly dependent on external trade and on a vulnerably narrow spectrum of primary export commodities, and where there is a sharp bifurcation between the traditional and the modern sectors of the economy with a circumscribed and fractured industrial base, cannot truly be indigenized. Africa must therefore see indigenization not merely as the taking over of ongoing expatriate concerns, but as a challenge to transform its present colonial economy to an authentically self-reliant African economy with an internally generated and self-sustaining process of development.

Past experiences indicate that those who have profited from a state of virtual economic dependence do not give up their vantage positions without resistance and clandestine sabotage. In so far as private benefits are to be gained by bypassing indigenization regulations, individuals – both indigenes and foreigners – are always ready to undermine the provisions of the established regulations in order to feather their own nests.

There is a growing cynicism among foreign businessmen and corporations operating in Africa in particular and in the developed world in general, about the use of corrupt practices to subvert and sabotage national policies and promote their own corporate interests. This is how a columnist of the London *Daily Telegraph* recently described the overseas operations of a major multinational:

> the more degraded the political and social system [of Africa and Asia] is, the easier it will be to extract the precious oil and minerals, since trade nowadays follows not the flag, but the bribe. According to this view it does not matter a damn – the word is well chosen – who governs Africa or Asia. The more corrupt the regime, the better Britain's interest will be served. That is the new *Realpolitik* disguised under the petty mask of racial equality.[2]

It is amazing the extent to which some of the enterprises affected by the indigenization policy have used these tactics.

And as is to be expected, they have found ready collaboration among the nationals. In this connection an excerpt from the Report of the African Association for Public Administration and Management's

(AAPAM) Fourteenth Inter-African Public Administration and Management Seminar is rather illustrative.

> To ensure continued operation in host countries some of the [multinational] corporations have allied themselves with heads of Government or have placed relatives of politicians or top officials in senior positions in the organisations in an effort to maintain their especial interest. Even though not directly involved in politics, the corporations have on occasions been involved in such activities as the financing of candidates for election.[3]

Leadership and dedication are vital to any policy of indigenization if such a policy is to succeed. This requires the leadership of the country and its executive machinery and agencies not only to have faith in national self-reliance, but also at all times to be prepared and fully committed to work towards the goal of achieving effective and meaningful self-reliance. In implementing indigenization measures there are testing occasions when those who are changed with implementing policies must demonstrate unalloyed loyalty to the national cause of indigenization and remain incorruptible.

The second limiting factor is lack of capital resources. Capital is required to finance the buying of existing foreign enterprises and, above all, to create new productive activities in order to achieve the transformation of the economy. Although Africa with its underdeveloped economy is by definition characterized by capital shortage, this shortage is aggravated by considerable wastage of those resources that already exist. The major leaks in the resource flow system appear to be in the following areas: (1) transferred technology; (2) international shipping; (3) international air transport; (4) foreign business consultancy; (5) international telecommunications and postal services; (6) banking and insurance services; (7) international marketing services; (8) importation of spare parts, components and accessories; (9) the exploration, evaluation, extraction, processing and export of minerals, forest and fishery resources; (10) building materials; (11) the building and construction industry; (12) tourism; and (13) purchasing and supplies. Because of these leakages, the impact of the foreign capital that goes into Africa is considerably reduced. In fact, what we now witness is a recycling of resources between developing African countries and the industrialized countries, with little net result on development and economic growth processes.

The lack of indigenous technical, managerial and entrepreneurial manpower is the third major factor inhibiting the development of a truly indigenous African economy. Here three points are worth making. First, unless there is a bold and imaginative effort nationally as well as co-operatively at sub-regional and regional levels, this will become a permanent characteristic of the African economy and a permanent brake on its development in general and its indigenization in particular. Second, there is an astonishing number of refugees from Africa. Today, twenty years after political independence, these refugees number over 4 million, and only a small fraction is a result of the struggle for self-determination in southern Africa. Over 90 per cent of Africa's refugees were uprooted from their native lands in independent Africa; and among them are to be found a large number of scientists, technologists, managers and entrepreneurs who, seeking refuge from intolerance at home or discouraged by uncongenial conditions of work at home, choose to remain abroad. To meet the manpower gap thus created, the African governments have to depend on expatriate technical assistance personnel, either from the United Nations and its agencies, or from bilateral donor institutions, or from the transnational corporations. Yet African governments proclaim loudly and clearly their determination to indigenize their countries' economies! The third point worth making is that every African country needs a sound national strategy for management education, training and development which will not only provide the required skills but will also inculcate in the trainees positive attitudes to service, as distinct from the present negative or at best indifferent attitudes of many public servants, and an achievement motivation – the will and determination to succeed and to excel in whatever one is doing.

This leads us to the limitations imposed by lack of popular participation in the indigenization process. The acquisition, by sale of public shares, of expatriate enterprises is open to only those few people who have the income, the information and the opportunity. This indigenization as it is now practised has led to the emergence of a new capitalist class and has exacerbated the skewed income distribution in many developing African countries.

According to preliminary estimates developed by the International Labour Organization,[4] it is estimated that out of a total labour force of about 140 million in 1975, about 63 million were either unemployed or underemployed. Thus about 48 per cent of developing Africa's labour force was unemployed in 1975. The economic crises that have been persistent in most African countries during the second half of the 1970s – the energy crisis, food crisis, droughts, – have aggravated the unemployment problem and consequently the skewed income distribution. It is estimated that 69 per cent of Africa's population are seriously poor. The proportion of destitute persons is as high as 39 per cent of the total population. To say that all these cannot participate in the indigenization process is, unfortunately, to say the obvious. For how can there be a genuinely indigenized African economy where *ab initio* some three-quarters of the population are excluded from participating in meaningful economic activities?

Although reliable data on income distribution in Africa are hard to come by, the preliminary data available to the Economic Commission for Africa[5] show that, whereas 5 per cent of the population of nineteen countries[6] on which the data are available had 24.3 per cent of total income in 1975, the poorest 40 per cent had only 13.6 per cent. The richest 20 per cent of the population owned 54.7 per cent of total income, while the remaining 80 per cent owned only 45.3 per cent.

It will be illuminating to give corresponding figures for some of the countries covered by our case studies in Chapters 3–12. In Egypt, Kenya, Senegal, Uganda and Zambia, the richest 5 per cent of the population had a share of 20, 30, 36, 20 and 22 per cent respectively of the total national income while the poorest 40 per cent of the population in these countries received 13, 10, 10, 17.5 and 14.5 per cent respectively. In these countries, 80 per cent of the population received respectively 54, 32, 36, 53 and 43 per cent of total income. While many factors are no doubt responsible for this growing inequality in income distribution, it cannot be denied that the way the indigenization programme has been implemented in these countries has accentuated the situation. Thus, until development strategies pursued in Africa put the individual at the very centre of the development effort and galvanize the latent energies of all the people, the indigenization policy will, like many other socio-economic policies of many an African country since independence, be a mere symbolic gesture, an exercise in futility.

This leads us to our last inhibiting factor in terms of achieving meaningful and worthwhile indigenization of the African economy – the rediscovery of self-confidence by the average citizen, his belief in his own ability, and the recognition by society of such abilities and encouragement to develop them for individual and societal purposes. Many African governments, despite rhetoric to the contrary, have failed fully to comprehend the enormous power of this factor. As I said elsewhere,

> the countries which have broken the barrier of dependence in history are today those which have in one way or another wakened to the realization that there are many things within their abilities to do, if only they want, with sufficient conviction and intensity, to do them. . . . There is simply no way in which we can significantly contribute to the shape of a new national and international economic order than through our own will, talents and resources. It is from this point of view . . . that we ought to examine more systematically the meaning of the now frequently used expression 'the political will'. The recovery of self-confidence may be achieved partly through an appreciation of the record of ancient achievements and partly through successful achievements in chosen theatres of action today.[7]

In view of the crucial importance of the next twenty years – the 1980s and 1990s – to Africa's economic wellbeing, are we prepared to accept the challenge? This is the question to which every African government must provide an answer – and do so urgently – for time is not on our side.

Indigenization and global economic interdependence

We shall conclude this chapter and the volume by making one or two points on the consistency between the African (and, indeed, Third World) search for economic self-reliance and the need for growing interdependence among all the countries of the world. First, it is important to repeat what has been said and written many times before, that the quest for self-reliant development by African governments is not a search for economic autarchy. An analysis of the events of the past four years shows an ever-increasing consciousness of the interdependence of the nations of the world and an ever-escalating evolution of the concept of international co-responsibility. But what *is* urgently needed is the translation of the concept of inter-dependence and international co-responsibility from a rather abstract idea to one of practical necessity based on the principles of equality, justice, and equity. In other words, there is need to strive to make North–South relations in general reflect an equitable interdependence. Since at present much of what goes on in the name of international co-operation and interdependence is heavily loaded in favour of the North,

> there will have to be a deliberate 'tilt' toward developing nations. Such a tilting would require: (a) removal of those aspects of international economic relations which act as restraints on the development of the South; and (b) willingness on the part of the North to make the 'interdependence' concept not a mere cover for protecting its own interests, but rather a means to bring about a genuine complementarity of Northern and Southern interests.[18]

As far as Africa is concerned, such interdependence will be facilitated by the successful implementation of the strategy of self-reliant development, which we have spoken so much about in this volume and particularly in this chapter, and of which the indigenization of the economy as defined in the preceding pages is a major component. The question then is, will the Western market economies, with which over 90 per cent of Africa's economic relations exist (albeit at present on a dependent basis), rise to the challenge and co-operate fully with Africa in accelerating self-reliant development through indigenization? Will the governments of the centrally planned economies do the same?

Notes

1 'Strategy for the African Region in the International Development Strategy for the Third United Nations Development Decade', ECA Resolution 332(XIV).
2 Culled from an article by Peregrine Worsthorne in the *Daily Telegraph*, 10 September 1979.
3 AAPAM, *The Prospects and Problems of the Indigenization of the Private Sector of African Economies* (Maseru, Lesotho, 1976), p. 22.
4 *Employment, Growth and Basic Needs – A One-World Problem* (Geneva: ILO 1976), p. 18.
5 *Survey of Economic and Social Conditions in Africa 1978–79* (Addis Ababa: ECA 1980).
6 The countries are Benin, Chad, Egypt, Gabon, Ivory Coast, Kenya, Libya, Madagascar, Malawi, Morocco, Niger, Senegal, Sierra Leone, Zimbabwe, Tanzania, Tunisia, Uganda and Zambia.
7 Adebayo Adedeji, *The Economic Commission for Africa, Its Origin, Development, Problems and Prospects*, text of the statement delivered at the opening of the Fourteenth Session of the Commission (Rabat, Morocco, March 1979), p. 36.
8 Samuel L. Parmar, 'Self-reliant development in an "interdependent world', in Guy F. Erb and Valeriana Kallab (eds.), *Beyond Dependency – The Developing World Speaks Out* (Washington, DC: Overseas Development Council 1975), p. 17.

Further reading

Adelman, I. (ed.), *Economic Growth and Resources*, London: Macmillan 1979

Bailey, Richard, *Africa's Industrial Future*, Blandford, Dorset: Davison 1976

Browne, Robert S., and Girvan, N., *Africanization of Personnel in the Mining Industry of Selected African Nations*, New York: Black Economic Research Centre 1974

Damachi, U. G., and Diejomaoh, V. P. (eds.), *Human Resources and African Development*, New York: Praeger 1978

Economic Commission for Africa, *The Indigenisation of African Economies*, Addis Ababa 1978

Faundez, J., and Picciotto, S. (eds.), *The Nationalisation of Multinationals in Peripheral Economies*, London: Macmillan 1978

Frank, André Gunder, *Dependent Accumulation and Underdevelopment*, London: Macmillan 1978

Hahlo, H. R., Smith, J. G., and Wright, R. W. (eds.), *Nationalism and the Multinational Enterprise: Legal, Economic and Managerial Aspects*, Leiden: A. W. Sijthoff, 1973

Lall, Sanaya, 'Transnationals, domestic enterprises, and industrial structure in host LDCS', *Oxford Economic Papers*, vol. 30, no. 2 (July 1978), pp. 217–48

Lecomber, Richard, *The Economics of Natural Resources*, London: Macmillan 1979

Legum, C., *et al.*, *Africa in the 1980s: a Continent in Crisis*, New York: McGraw-Hill 1979

Mazrui, Ali, *The African Condition: 1979 Reith Memorial Lectures*, London: Heinemann 1979.

McKern, R. B., *Multinational Enterprise and Natural Resources*, Sydney: McGraw-Hill 1976

Nyilas, Jozsef, *Theory and Practice or Development in the Third World*, Leyden: A. W. Sijthoff 1977

Raja, M. S., *Sovereignty over Natural Resources*, Atlantic Highlands, NJ: Humanities Press 1978

Robinson, Richard D., *National Control of Foreign Business Entry: A Survey of Fifteen Countries*, New York: Praeger, 1976

Rood, Leslie L., 'Foreign investment in African development', *Journal of African Studies*, vol. 5, no. 1 (Spring 1978), pp. 18–33

Rood, Leslie L., 'The impact on nationalisation', *Journal of Modern African Studies*, vol. 15, no. 3 (September 1977), pp. 489–94

Said, A. A., and Simmons, L. R. (eds.), *The New Sovereigns: Multinational Corporations as World Powers*, Englewood Cliffs, NJ: Prentice-Hall 1975
Smith, David Nathan and Wells, L. T., *Negotiating Third World Mineral Agreements: Promises as Prologue*, Cambridge, Mass.: Ballinger 1975
UNIDO, *Industry 2000*, Vienna 1979
Widstrand, C. (ed.), *Multinational Firms in Africa*, Uppsala: Scandinavian Institute of African Studies 1975

Index

Numbers in italics refer to tables.

For Product Safety Concerns and Information please contact our EU representative GPSR@taylorandfrancis.com
Taylor & Francis Verlag GmbH, Kaufingerstraße 24, 80331 München, Germany

www.ingramcontent.com/pod-product-compliance
Ingram Content Group UK Ltd.
Pitfield, Milton Keynes, MK11 3LW, UK
UKHW021501240926
475702UK00035B/32
* 9 7 8 1 0 3 2 5 8 7 5 6 1 *